CINDY'S SUPPER CLUB

seville oranges

pasillas

CINDY'S SUPPER CLUB

tomato

MEALS FROM AROUND THE WORLD
TO SHARE WITH FAMILY AND FRIENDS

by Cindy Pawlcyn

habanero chili

garlic

PHOTOGRAPHY BY ALEX FARNUM

Anderson, S.C.
AND

cilantro

TEN SPEED PRESS
BERKELEY

CONTENTS

Cindy's Supper Club is part travelogue of places I have been and part inspiration from places I want to visit. It is a culinary journey acted out at Cindy's Backstreet Kitchen, my restaurant in the heart of the Napa Valley. The club was started by my friend Marianne Agnew, who is also the graphic designer for the restaurant. We were talking about how nice it would be if people could come after work and dinner would be ready. Marianne put together a great design  of a copper saucepot that looks like a classic 1930s-era French poster, and so we were serving elaborate four-course dinners with wine for, I think, sixty bucks a head.

The debut dinner was held in August 2003, and I prepared my mom's home cooking. At first, we sent out mailers announcing the upcoming menus, and then we did an in-house calendar. In the beginning, we scheduled one Supper Club each month. Some months the dinner sold out and others it didn't. For example, Zen Den, a Japanese menu, was popular. But the Supper Club that coincided with Halloween in 2007 was just the opposite. For inspiration, we drew from *The Taste of Black* by Björn Lindberg and Jonas Borssén, a book about food and the color black. Although the dishes were tasty, it was just too weird for folks. I think only four people, besides the staff, tried the whole menu.

Over time, we realized that four courses were too much for a lot of people to eat midweek. I wanted the Supper Club to be more popular, so in addition to the set menu, we started offering all of the items à la carte. This change proved successful, but I was still getting comments like, "Oh I have a meeting on Wednesday night and can't be here." So we started serving the club menu two nights a week, which has worked well. It keeps both the front-of-the-house staff and the kitchen staff "on their toes," because each week they are dealing with brand-new dishes, ingredients, and cooking techniques.

I've been traveling all my life. My first trips, seated in the backseat of the family car, were summer vacations to see America: Yellowstone, Jackson Hole, all ten thousand lakes of Minnesota (my dad loved to fish), Williamsburg, and Wall Street. We got around. Since the age of sixteen, I have been going to Europe on a regular basis. In the 1980s, I went to China, Hong Kong, and Japan, and later I added South America and Africa to my ever-expanding "hood."

Wherever I have gone, I have always been happiest in a grocery store, farmers' market, or food emporium. In the 1960s, my mother and sister had to drag me out of the food halls of Harrods after four hours. My cookbook collection also reflects my interest in the global table. I started out with both volumes of *Mastering the Art of French Cooking* by Julia Child and the *Gourmet* magazine series books, then I moved on to the Time-Life series *Foods of the World* and Time-Life's *The Good Cook*. I collect cookbooks from all kinds of sources, but one of my favorite places to shop is Kitchen Arts & Letters in Manhattan, which carries thousands of books, both contemporary and out of print, domestic and foreign, on food and drink. The first time I visited the store I spent three hours going through every section, and it is still one of the things I like to do best when I am in New York. In 2008, Celia Sack opened Omnivore Books in San Francisco, which, like my New York haunt, is devoted to volumes on food and drink. Of course, it is much easier for me to visit Omnivore and therefore more dangerous to my bank account. But it is far better than many other addictions.

Many of the dishes served at the Supper Club have come from these two sources: travel and books. Some of them have been huge hits, some not. The recipes that follow are the hits; there are my favorites plus what our customers picked as the most popular and their personal favorites. Thai, Mexican, and Italian menus are always popular, but Hungarian, Ethiopian, and Korean usually require a nudge to get people to try them. When you are deciding what to cook, don't pass up the cuisines that are new to you. Cook and serve something you have never prepared before. The timid can always sit down to Girl Scout cookies and tea.

Because we serve the Supper Club menus year-round, the seasons typically play a big role in what we decide to cook: spring in Paris, winter in Hungary, summer in Brazil, fall in Japan. But other times I will have just gotten back from a trip or just found a new book on an area that we haven't cooked from at all and I'll decide to do a menu that is not just driven by the season. You need to be equally flexible. The recipes that follow have all been tested by home cooks who do not have the experience or the skills of a restaurant chef. If you are nervous, start out small and make just one dish from a menu. Or, try seasonings from a cuisine that is new to you with something that is familiar, like chicken.

One last bit of advice: once you decide which recipe you are going to make, before you take even a spoon out of a drawer, sit down and read the recipe from beginning to end. I have watched professional cooks, recipe testers, and home cooks falter, miss tricks, and get frustrated because they skipped this very important step.

You are now ready to begin retracing my travels around the tables of the world. As Julia Child always said, bon appétit, and because this is a journey of sorts, bon voyage.

CINDY PAWLCYN, 2012

THE AMERICAS

HAWAII

The first time I went to Hawaii was with my family when I was just four years old. After more than fifty years, I don't recall much except that my brother, Butch, buried my shave ice in the sand on Waikiki beach. I also remember that the grasses in the hula skirts that my sister and I paraded around in all summer smelled warm and toasty and just like Hawaii. Coconut palms and sandy beaches are a big part of the draw for a kid from Minnesota, and although we were there in the summer, it was still paradise.

Long after that first trip, I began exploring Hawaiian cuisine, which reflects a complex mix of influences, including the kitchens of its native population, Japan, China, the Philippines, Korea, Portugal, and the mainland. The best tip I can give you when preparing this truly fusion table is to cook with the aloha spirit—with care and respect—and your dishes will taste like the food of the islands.

AHI POKE
WITH CRISPY WONTON TRIANGLES

Poke, diced raw fish mixed with a highly seasoned dressing, is a popular appetizer in the islands. I like to serve it with the Japanese Wakame and Cucumber Salad on page 234 or with the bright green agar agar and seaweed salad you find in sushi bars all over Hawaii. Sometimes I use small butter or iceberg lettuce cups in place of the fried wonton wrappers.

In fish markets, the term *sushi grade* often appears on fish that is deemed safe to eat raw, and although it can mean quality, it carries no legal weight and thus no assurance of quality. The color and firmness of fish can be good clues to excellence, but you can also be easily fooled. For example, carbon monoxide–treated tuna will keep its desirable red color long after it would have faded if untreated. In other words, the fish can be spoiled and still look bright red. The only way to ensure you are getting high-quality fish is to buy from a reputable shop where the fishmonger is able to tell you when, where, and how the fish was caught. | SERVES 6 TO 8

14 TO 16 OUNCES SUSHI-GRADE AHI [YELLOWFIN] TUNA FILLET

¼ CUP SOY SAUCE

2 TABLESPOONS MIRIN

½ CUP FINELY MINCED SWEET ONION, PREFERABLY MAUI

½ CLOVE GARLIC, FINELY MINCED

1 TEASPOON TOASTED SESAME OIL

1 TEASPOON SRIRACHA OR OTHER HOT-PEPPER SAUCE

¾ TEASPOON HAWAIIAN OR OTHER SEA SALT

PEANUT OR VEGETABLE OIL, FOR DEEP-FRYING

1 [12-OUNCE] PACKAGE SESAME OR PLAIN WONTON WRAPPERS, CUT IN HALF ON THE DIAGONAL

2 GREEN ONIONS, WHITE AND LIGHT GREEN PARTS ONLY, MINCED

½ CUP MACADAMIA NUTS, LIGHTLY TOASTED [SEE PAGE 23] AND CHOPPED

Make sure your tuna is very cold and your knife is very sharp. Trim away any tough sinew and membrane, then finely dice the fish. Be careful not to mash it. Work quickly and do only a portion of the fish at a time, keeping the rest chilled in the refrigerator. Reserve the diced tuna in a covered bowl in the refrigerator until serving.

In a small bowl, stir together the soy sauce, mirin, sweet onion, garlic, sesame oil, hot sauce, and salt and mix well. Cover and refrigerate until serving.

Pour the oil to a depth of 1 to 1½ inches into a deep, heavy sauté pan and heat to 360°F on a deep-frying thermometer. Line a large tray or platter with paper towels. Working in small batches so as not to crowd the pan, add the wonton wrappers and fry for about 2½ to 3 minutes, until golden brown. Using a wire skimmer, transfer to the towel-lined tray to drain. Always make sure the oil has returned to 360°F before adding a new batch of wrappers.

Just before serving, add the soy mixture to the tuna and mix gently but thoroughly, and then transfer to a serving platter or individual plates. Shape into an attractive mound and arrange the wonton chips, green onions, and macadamia nuts around for people to compose their own bites.

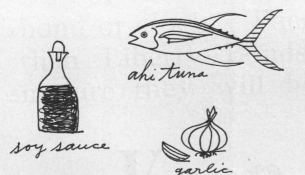

ahi tuna

soy sauce

garlic

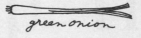

green onion

PORK KATSU

WITH JOHN'S TONKATSU SAUCE, STEAMED RICE, AND MACARONI SALAD

My husband, John Watanabe, spent time in Japan with his sister, Barbara, testing as many *tonkatsu* (fried breaded pork cutlet) shops as possible. He also took many trips to Maui with his son, Cole, to test the *tonkatsu* there. This sauce is a product of all of his research, and I would highly recommend making a double batch for sauce lovers. It will keep in a tightly capped container in the fridge for several weeks. It is also tasty on rice, chicken, fish fillets, or chicken livers.

This combination of pork katsu, steamed rice, and macaroni salad is a typical Hawaiian plate lunch. Where did the plate lunch originate? According to Arnold Hiura, author of *Kau Kau Cuisine and Culture of the Hawaiian Islands*, the now-classic trio of main course, rice, and macaroni salad was probably the creation of Moyo Iwamoto, a widowed woman with six children to support. According to Hiura, after operating a food pushcart for a few years, Iwamoto saved enough money in the mid-1920s to lease "a small space on Channel Street," where she served hungry workers paper plates piled high with rice, a vegetable, and a main that could be anything from pig's feet to beef stew. This pork katsu is reminiscent of the panfried veal cutlets my mom served when I was a kid, and the sauce even includes ketchup, which was always on the table with the veal cutlets.

Traditional accompaniments are steamed regular or sticky (glutinous) rice—we serve brown rice at home and white rice at Cindy's Backstreet Kitchen—and macaroni salad, and I like to add a great vegetable. This is definitely not a diet dish, but it is one of the all-time best-sellers at the Supper Club, sometimes even served on the traditional paper plate.

If pork cutlets between ¹/₈ and ¹/₄ inch thick are available, use them. At the restaurant, we have also used our 10-ounce pork chops and then pounded them, which makes for a nice presentation. You can make the dish fancier by using pork loin in place of the pork butt. Or, you can opt for boneless, skinless chicken breasts instead of pork. For more thoughts on deep-frying, see page 276. If you cannot find baby turnips with their greens attached, substitute an equal amount of bok choy for the greens. | SERVES 6 TO 8

TONKATSU SAUCE

¹/₂ TEASPOON DRY MUSTARD POWDER MIXED
    WITH 1 TABLESPOON BOILING WATER
¹/₄ CUP ORGANIC KETCHUP
1 TABLESPOON SAKE
4 TEASPOONS SOY SAUCE
4 TEASPOONS RICE VINEGAR
4 TEASPOONS WORCESTERSHIRE SAUCE
3 TO 4 TEASPOONS SUGAR
1 THUMBNAIL-SIZE PIECE FRESH GINGER,
    PEELED AND MINCED
1 CLOVE GARLIC, MINCED

sake

ginger

To make the sauce, in a bowl, whisk together all of the ingredients until well blended. Cover and refrigerate until needed.

To prepare the vegetable, cut off the green tops, chop, and set aside. Trim away the root from each turnip. If the turnips are very small, leave them whole. Or, cut into halves or quarters, depending on size. Wash and chop the tender greens. Bring a large pot of salted water to a boil. Have ready an ice bath. Add the turnips to the boiling water and

CONTINUED

Pork Katsu, *continued*

PINCH OF GROUND CINNAMON

PINCH OF WHITE PEPPER OR FRESHLY
    GROUND BLACK PEPPER

PINCH OF GROUND ALLSPICE

turnip

VEGETABLE

2 POUNDS BABY TURNIPS WITH GREENS ATTACHED

2 TABLESPOONS OLIVE OIL

1/2 YELLOW ONION, THINLY SLICED

SEA SALT AND FRESHLY GROUND BLACK PEPPER

PORK KATSU

3 TO 3¹/4 POUNDS BONELESS PORK BUTT

1 TEASPOON SEA SALT

1/2 TEASPOON FRESHLY GROUND BLACK PEPPER

1/2 TEASPOON GARLIC POWDER
    [JUST DON'T SUBSTITUTE GARLIC SALT]

1/2 TO ²/3 CUP ALL-PURPOSE FLOUR

2 LARGE EGGS

1 TO 2 TEASPOONS WATER

3 CUPS PANKO [JAPANESE BREAD CRUMBS]
    OR CRUSHED SODA CRACKERS

CANOLA OIL, FOR PANFRYING

1 MEDIUM-SIZE NAPA OR GREEN CABBAGE, SHREDDED

6 TO 16 LEMON WEDGES

MACARONI SALAD [PAGE 15]

STEAMED RICE [PAGE 15]

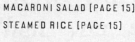
black pepper

cabbage

eggs

lemon

cook for about 2 minutes, until just tender. Scoop them out with a sieve or a wire-mesh skimmer and plunge them into the ice bath to stop the cooking.

In a large sauté pan, heat the olive oil over medium-high heat. Add the onion and turnips and cook, stirring occasionally, for about 3 to 5 minutes, until lightly caramelized (see page 14). Remove from the heat, add the greens to the pan, and let sit while you cook the pork cutlets. You will finish the turnips just before serving.

To prepare the pork, preheat the oven to warm. Trim the pork of any sinew and cut into six to eight 1¹/2- to 2-inch-thick slices. Pound each slice until it is an even ¹/3 inch thick. Season the pork slices with the salt, pepper, and garlic powder and let them sit while you set up your breading station.

Line up 3 wide, shallow bowls or deep plates. Spread enough flour in the first bowl to coat the pork. Break the eggs into the second bowl, add the water, and whisk until blended. Spread the bread crumbs in the third bowl. (This is the order in which you will dredge the pork to get it ready for frying.) Place 1 or 2 baking sheets next to the line of bowls. They will hold the breaded pork slices. (If necessary, you can stack the breaded slices, slipping parchment or waxed paper between the layers.) Line a couple more baking sheets or a couple of big heatproof plates with paper towels and put them in the warm oven.

Now, keeping one hand for the dry dip and one hand for the wet, coat each piece of pork on both sides first with the flour, shaking off the excess; then with the egg, letting the excess drip off; and finally with the bread crumbs. Press the bread crumbs in place— using your "dry" hand, remember—to ensure the surfaces are well coated and gently shake off the excess. Lay the nicely coated pieces of pork on the baking sheet(s) as you go. This step can be done ahead; refrigerate the breaded pork until ready to cook.

CONTINUED

Pork Katsu, *continued*

Pour the canola oil to a depth of $^1/_2$ inch (at the most) into a sauté pan and heat to 370°F on a deep-frying thermometer. When the oil is ready, add as many of the cutlets, one at a time, as will fit without crowding. They need to have plenty of room around them to sizzle and brown. Cook, turning once, for 1 to 2 minutes on each side, depending on the thickness of the cutlets, until golden brown. When the cutlets are ready, using tongs, transfer them to a warmed towel-lined baking sheet and return the sheet to the oven. Repeat until all of the cutlets are cooked, always making sure the oil has returned to 370°F before adding a new batch.

When the final batch of cutlets goes into the pan, return the pan with the vegetables to medium-high heat and cook until heated through and the greens are wilted to your liking.

To serve, arrange shredded cabbage on one half of each plate, top the cabbage with the cutlets, and place 1 or 2 lemon wedges next to the cutlets. On the other side of the each plate put a scoop of salad, a scoop of rice, and a scoop of vegetables. Serve the sauce on the side.

TIPS AND TRICKS
CARAMELIZING ONIONS

CARAMELIZING IS A COOKING PROCESS BY WHICH THE SURFACE AREA OF THE ONION IS NICELY DARKENED ANYWHERE FROM A RICH AMBER TO A DEEP MAHOGANY BROWN AND THE INSIDES ARE COOKED TO A LUSCIOUS SWEETNESS. IN GENERAL, THE SMALLER THE CUT, THE EASIER IT WILL BURN INSTEAD OF CARAMELIZE; THE LARGER THE CUT, THE LONGER THE CARAMELIZING PROCESS WILL TAKE.

START OFF WITH ENOUGH OIL IN YOUR PAN TO COAT ALL OF THE ONIONS NICELY. HEAT OVER MEDIUM-HIGH HEAT TO BEGIN. ADD THE ONIONS AND COOK, STIRRING OCCASIONALLY, UNTIL THE ONIONS PASS THROUGH THE TRANSLUCENT STAGE TO THE GOLDEN STAGE. REDUCE THE HEAT SO AS NOT TO BURN THE ONIONS AND CONTINUE TO COOK AND STIR UNTIL THE ONIONS HAVE REACHED A NICE, RICH BROWN. AS THE ONIONS TURN DARKER, STIR MORE FREQUENTLY TO PREVENT BURNING. THE AMOUNT OF TIME THIS WILL TAKE DEPENDS ON THE AMOUNT OF ONION YOU ARE COOKING, THE SIZE OF THE PAN YOU'RE COOKING IN, AND YOUR BURNER'S HEAT. IT'S NOT UNREASONABLE TO BUDGET 30 MINUTES FOR CARAMELIZING. THE SLOWER YOU GO, THE SWEETER THE FINISHED PRODUCT. BEWARE THAT TOWARD THE END THE ONION CAN GO FROM CARAMELIZED TO BURNED SEEMINGLY IN A FLASH, SO WATCH OUT.

MACARONI SALAD

I make this salad with the traditional elbow macaroni, but it's just as tasty with other shapes of good-quality pasta. My nephew Nicolas ate a ton of it during the testing process. I love the pepperiness of watercress and arugula, so when one of my Hawaiian cookbooks had a recipe for macaroni salad that included watercress, I jumped on it and added arugula here. It lessens the mayonnaise and lightens the dish. I use Best Foods mayonnaise (Hellmann's east of the Rockies). A lesser brand will yield a lesser salad. | SERVES 6 TO 8

1/2 SMALL YELLOW ONION
1 POUND DRIED MACARONI OF CHOICE,
    COOKED AL DENTE AND CHILLED
1 1/2 CUPS MAYONNAISE
1 CUP CHOPPED WATERCRESS
1 CUP CHOPPED ARUGULA
1 CUP SHREDDED, PEELED CARROT
1 CUP FINELY CHOPPED CELERY HEART AND LEAVES
1/2 TEASPOON SEA SALT
1/4 TEASPOON FRESHLY GROUND BLACK PEPPER

Finely grate the onion over a large bowl, capturing the onion flesh along with all of the juice. Add the macaroni, mayonnaise, watercress, arugula, carrot, celery, salt, and pepper and mix well. Cover and refrigerate until well chilled, and then serve chilled.

STEAMED RICE

My husband John likes to soak the raw grains of rice for 30 minutes to 1 hour before cooking. I just rinse and go. If your rice is from a new crop, it won't need as much water as I have listed here. | SERVES 6 TO 8

2 CUPS SHORT-GRAIN WHITE OR BROWN RICE
4 CUPS WATER
1 TEASPOON SEA SALT

Put the rice in a good-size bowl, add water to cover, swish the rice around with your hand, and drain. Repeat the rinsing and draining until the water runs clear.

If using a rice cooker, combine the rinsed rice, water, and salt and cook according to the manufacturer's directions. If using a saucepan on the stove top, combine the ingredients in the pan, cover, and bring to a boil over high heat. Decrease the heat to low, and cook for 20 minutes for white rice or 35 to 40 minutes for brown rice. The rice should be cooked perfectly. If your burners are like mine and you can never adjust the heat low enough, use a heat diffuser (see page 187).

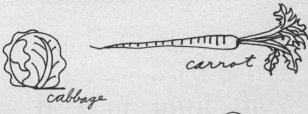
carrot

cabbage

yellow onion

celery

arugula

MACADAMIA AND COCONUT TART

You'll want to use a fluted tart pan with a removable bottom for this recipe. It makes it easy to remove the tart from the pan by just pushing up on the bottom so the rim falls away. I always loosen the tart from the rim with a knife while it is still warm, and let it finish cooling on the bottom of the pan on a wire rack. Light corn syrup is traditionally used in this recipe, but you may want to use rice syrup or maple syrup if you don't like corn syrup. A scoop of coconut sorbet or vanilla ice cream or a dollop of whipped cream is delicious with this tart. | SERVES 8 TO 10; MAKES ONE 9- OR 10-INCH TART

TART SHELL

1¼ CUPS ALL-PURPOSE FLOUR
1 TABLESPOON SUGAR
¼ TEASPOON SALT
½ CUP PLUS 2 TABLESPOONS COLD UNSALTED BUTTER, CUT INTO SMALL PIECES
½ TEASPOON PURE VANILLA EXTRACT
1½ TO 2 TABLESPOONS ICE WATER

FILLING

1 CUP MACADAMIA NUTS
4 TABLESPOONS UNSALTED BUTTER, MELTED
¾ CUP FIRMLY PACKED LIGHT OR DARK BROWN SUGAR
3 EGGS, WHISKED
1 TEASPOON PURE VANILLA EXTRACT
½ TEASPOON SALT
1 CUP LIGHT CORN SYRUP
¾ CUP UNSWEETENED SHREDDED DRIED COCONUT

To make the tart shell, in a large bowl, stir together the flour, sugar, and salt. Scatter the butter over the top and, using a pastry blender or a pair of knives, cut in the butter until pea-size pieces form. Add the vanilla and then add the water, a little a time, and stir and toss with a fork just until the dough comes together in a rough mass. (Add the water slowly as you may not need it all.)

Transfer the dough to a large piece of plastic wrap, shape it into a disk about 1 inch thick, and wrap in the plastic wrap. Refrigerate for 30 minutes.

Butter the bottom and sides of a 9- or 10-inch tart pan with a removable bottom. On a lightly floured work surface, roll out the dough into a 12-inch round. Roll the dough around the pin, position the pin over the prepared pan, and then unroll the dough, centering it over the pan. Gently press the dough snuggly into the bottom and sides of the pan. Take care not to stretch the dough, as it will shrink during baking. Roll the pin over the top of the pan to trim away any dough that extends beyond the rim. Line the tart shell with a piece of aluminum foil and fill with pie weights or dried beans. Chill in the freezer for 30 minutes.

Preheat the oven to 350°F. To toast the nuts for the filling, spread them on a baking sheet and place in the oven for 8 to 10 minutes, until they are fragrant and have taken on color. Pour onto a plate, let cool, and chop into pieces. Leave the oven set at 350°F.

Place the tart shell in the oven and bake for 15 minutes. Remove the weights and foil, return the shell to the oven, and bake for 10 to 15 minutes longer, until just golden brown. Let cool on a rack.

To assemble the filling, in a bowl, combine the toasted nuts, butter, brown sugar, eggs, vanilla, salt, corn syrup, and coconut and mix well. Pour the filling into the cooled prebaked shell. Depending on the size of your tart shell, you may have excess filling. Be sure to include all of the macadamia nuts and coconut.

Bake for 40 minutes, until the surface is a rich golden brown. Let cool on a wire rack for about 10 to 15 minutes, then slip away the rim of the pan and let cool completely on the rack. Aloha!

MEXICO

I moved to the Napa Valley in 1979 and was fortunate to start working with people who had come from all over Mexico. My first experience with Mexican food had been in Minneapolis, circa 1963, when my brother's then-wife invited me for lunch and together we made bastardized *chilaquiles* from canned tortillas, Velveeta cheese, and "mild" jar sauce. I've come a long way!

The Yucatán region has always held great interest for me. I like the Mayan history and architecture, the hot habanero chile and flavorful black beans, the white-sand beaches and warm Caribbean waters. I think I bought my first Diana Kennedy book in 1970. Since then, my collection of Mexican cookbooks and recipes from staff and friends has grown tremendously.

When I travel to Mexico, I always visit as many food markets as possible and you should, too. If you like Mexican hot chocolate as much as I do, look in the market for a *molino* (mill) that grinds chocolate and ask the staff to grind a kilogram of chocolate and flavor it to your taste. I always request the traditional Mexican additions of cinnamon and almonds but only half the usual amount of sugar. Look for freshly made mole pastes, too. They make great gifts.

I can never say no to this kind of food, so this menu is quite large. I have often just served the egg dish for Sunday brunch, the tacos and the fish make a great Cinco de Mayo menu, and the lamb and the salad are a good weeknight supper if you marinate the meat in advance and then quickly grill it when you get home from work. The tiramisu is best when made a day in advance, and then finished with the whipped cream just before serving.

HUEVOS MOTULEÑOS
(Eggs in the Style of Motul)

This dish, which originated in the small Yucatecan town of Motul, not far from Mérida, is perfect for Sunday brunch or Sunday-night supper. If you are pressed for time, feel free to use canned beans rather than freshly cooked, either black or pinto. When I traveled to Oaxaca, I visited local cheese makers and became spoiled by their delicious handcrafted cheeses. As a result, for this recipe I often use a locally made ricotta instead of a processed Mexican cheese from the supermarket.

If you don't want to use your favorite cast-iron pan to char the tomatoes for the sauce, you can roast them on a griddle or on a rimmed baking sheet (the sides ensure you won't lose any of the delicious juices) under the broiler. Don't peel them before you puree them in the blender. The tiny bits of blackened skin add taste and texture to the final sauce. I also like to fry or bake my tortillas until they are a little crispy, though not as crunchy as for tostadas. This step is not traditional, but I like the texture it contributes to the finished dish. | SERVES 6

TOMATO SAUCE

3 TOMATOES, CORED AND HALVED THROUGH THE EQUATOR

2 TABLESPOONS MILD VEGETABLE OIL

1 HABANERO OR 2 SERRANO CHILES, STEMMED, SEEDED
    IF DESIRED, AND FINELY CHOPPED

1/2 YELLOW ONION, FINELY CHOPPED

SEA SALT AND FRESHLY GROUND BLACK PEPPER

3 CUPS POT BEANS [PAGE 22]

6 TABLESPOONS FRESH RICOTTA CHEESE

3 TABLESPOONS SOUR CREAM OR MEXICAN CREMA

1/2 CUP FRESH CILANTRO LEAVES

6 [6-INCH] CORN TORTILLAS

UNSALTED BUTTER OR MILD VEGETABLE OIL, FOR FRYING EGGS

6 ORGANIC EGGS

SEA SALT AND FRESHLY GROUND BLACK PEPPER

To make the sauce, heat a heavy skillet over medium-high heat. Place the tomato halves, cut side down, in the dry pan and cook for about 6 to 8 minutes, until charred. Turn the tomato halves, scraping up as many of the charred bits from the pan bottom as possible, and char the second side the same way, flattening the tomatoes slightly with a spatula so that the rounded sides touch the pan bottom. Transfer the tomatoes to a blender and process to a puree.

Pour the oil into the same skillet and heat over medium-high heat. When the oil is hot, add the pureed tomatoes and fry for a minute or two, scraping up all the flavorful bits stuck to the pan bottom. Remove from the heat, stir in the chile and onion, and season with salt and pepper.

When you are ready to serve, heat the beans and have the ricotta, sour cream, and cilantro ready. Heat a skillet over high heat. Add the tortillas, one at a time, and fry, turning once, for 1 1/2 to 2 minutes on each side, until slightly crispy. (Or, arrange the tortillas on a baking sheet and put in a preheated 350°F oven for about 10 minutes, until slightly crispy.) At the same time, melt some butter in a skillet; when it is foaming a lot, crack the eggs into the pan, sprinkle with salt and pepper, and fry to your liking.

To serve, put a tortilla on each plate and spoon the beans over. Set an egg on the beans, and cover with the sauce. Top each with an equal amount of the cheese, drizzle with the sour cream, and garnish with the cilantro. Serve immediately.

TIPS AND TRICKS

HOW TO FRY A PERFECT EGG

HEAT A LITTLE BUTTER OR OIL IN A SKILLET OVER LOW HEAT. CRACK THE EGG INTO THE PAN, SPRINKLE WITH SALT AND PEPPER, AND COVER. COOK FOR 1 1/2 MINUTES, UNTIL THE WHITE IS SET AND THE YOLK IS STILL RUNNY—THE WAY I LIKE EGGS. FOR A MORE FIRMLY SET YOLK, RE-COVER AND COOK TO YOUR LIKING.

COCHINITA PIBIL TACOS

WITH GREEN RICE, BEANS, AND XNI-PEC AND CHIPOTLE SALSAS

Cochinita pibil is the famed slow-roasted pork of the Yucatán, which is traditionally made by wrapping a suckling pig (*cochinita*) in banana leaves and burying (*pibil*) it in a fire pit. Here, I have served the pork as a main course with traditional rice and beans as accompaniment, but these small tacos also make wonderful hors d'oeuvres for twelve to sixteen partygoers (you can skip the sides in that case). You may have leftovers, which make great hash, omelet filling, quesadilla filling, or a hearty lunch salad.

I like to use small corn tortillas, 2 to 3 inches in diameter, to make two-bite-size party treats. If you cannot find them ready-made, you can cut down larger tortillas. Some folks warm the tortillas by putting them in a steamer basket lined with a kitchen towel and steaming them for 3 to 6 minutes, and then serve them wrapped in the towel in a covered basket. I just flip them back and forth over the flame of a gas burner flame until they are warm and tender.

I have cooked the meat in a covered casserole in the oven, but it would also be delicious done in a slow cooker, roasted in a covered grill, or cooked over an open fire. Any leftovers would make a great hash or Mexican-style salad.

Achiote paste is made from annatto seeds and other spices. It can be found in Mexican markets and well-stocked supermarkets, as can the Mexican oregano. Although you can use another type of oregano, Mexican oregano makes a big difference here. Look for fresh or frozen banana leaves in Asian or Latin markets. | SERVES 6 STARVING PEOPLE

MARINADE

6 TO 8 CLOVES GARLIC

1 1/2 TEASPOONS SALT

3 TABLESPOONS CIDER VINEGAR

GRATED ZEST AND JUICE OF 1 LIME

1/2 (3 1/2-OUNCE) PACKAGE ACHIOTE PASTE

3 TABLESPOONS DRIED MEXICAN OREGANO

1 TEASPOON CUMIN SEEDS, TOASTED IN A DRY PAN
   UNTIL FRAGRANT AND GROUND (PAGE 23)

1 TEASPOON GROUND ALLSPICE

2 TEASPOONS BLACK PEPPERCORNS,
   COARSELY CRACKED

3 POUNDS BONELESS PORK BUTT,
   CUT INTO 3 EQUAL PIECES

allspice

banana leaf

To make the marinade, make a garlic paste with the garlic cloves and salt (see page 26). Transfer the paste to a bowl, add the vinegar, lime zest and juice, achiote paste, oregano, cumin, allspice, and pepper, and mix well. Place the pork in a nonreactive dish, pour in the marinade, turn the pork to coat all sides, and then cover the dish. Or, put the pork in a resealable plastic bag, pour in the marinade, force out the air and seal the bag, and then turn the bag to coat all sides of the pork. Refrigerate the pork for 2 hours or up to 24 hours.

To cook the pork, preheat the oven to 250°F to 300°F, depending on how long you want the meat to be in the oven (the lower the heat the longer the cooking, of course).

CONTINUED

Cochinita Pibil Tacos, *continued*

PICKLED RED ONION

1 RED ONION, THINLY SLICED

JUICE OF 2 LIMES (ABOUT 2 TABLESPOONS),
    OR 2 TABLESPOONS CIDER VINEGAR

1 OR 2 PINCHES OF SEA SALT

1 OR 2 PINCHES OF DRIED MEXICAN OREGANO

2 TO 3 BANANA LEAVES, THAWED IF FROZEN

1 CUP WATER OR BEER, OR MORE IF NEEDED

1 PACKAGE (2- TO 3-INCH) CORN TORTILLAS, OR 6-INCH
    TORTILLAS CUT SMALLER

1 TO 1½ CUPS CRUMBLED QUESO FRESCO
    OR FRESH RICOTTA OR FETA CHEESE, FOR GARNISH

1 BUNCH FRESH CILANTRO LEAVES, FOR GARNISH

2 LIMES, CUT INTO WEDGES, FOR GARNISH

ARROZ VERDE (PAGE 26)

REFRIED BEANS (PAGE 23)

XNI-PEC SALSA (PAGE 27)

CHIPOTLE SALSA (PAGE 27)

While the oven is heating, prepare the pickled onion. In a glass or ceramic bowl, combine the onion, lime juice, salt, and oregano with water to cover, mix well, and then squeeze everything together a few times. This will help the onion and lime juice blend. Let the onion stand at room temperature for at least 30 minutes or up to 12 hours.

Warm the banana leaves to make them pliable by quickly running them back and forth over the flame on your stove top for a few seconds (this is the best way) or by placing them in the oven for 1 to 2 minutes, checking them after 1 minute. Line a large baking dish with the leaves, allowing the excess to overhang the sides. Pile the meat in the center of the leaves and pour any marinade in the bowl or bag over the top. Bring the leaves up around the meat to cover loosely, and then carefully pour the water around the outside of the leaves into the dish.

Cover the dish, place in the oven, and cook for 3 to 4 hours, depending on the oven temperature. Check the dish occasionally and add more water

if it has evaporated. The pork is ready when it is moist and meltingly tender. Remove the dish from the oven, unwrap the meat, let it cool until it can be handled, and then, using a pair of forks, pull the meat apart into rough shreds. Keep the meat warm.

To serve, warm the tortillas by steaming them or holding them over a flame on the stove top (see headnote). Pile some of the shredded pork on each tortilla, sprinkle with a little cheese, and top with some cilantro and a few slices of pickled onion. Serve right away with the lime wedges, rice, beans, and salsas on the side. Be sure to have lots of napkins on hand.

BEANS TWO WAYS

Whether you'll be making saucy beans or refried beans, you need to start by making a batch of pot beans. For the best results, cook the pot beans a day advance, as their taste and texture will improve overnight. The starches in the beans sour easily, so always get your pot of beans on a rack to cool the moment they have finished cooking and then refrigerate them as soon as possible, unless you'll be using them right away. I buy black-and-white-mottled Vaquero beans, an heirloom cousin of the anasazi bean, from Rancho Gordo, a company based in the Napa Valley, but cooks in Yucatán typically use black beans. | SHOWN PAGE 25 | MAKES 3 CUPS SAUCY BEANS AND 3 CUPS REFRIED BEANS

POT BEANS

1 POUND DRIED VAQUERO OR BLACK BEANS

1 YELLOW OR RED ONION, THICKLY SLICED

1 EPAZOTE SPRIG (OPTIONAL)

10 CUPS WATER

SALT

Refried Beans

3 CUPS POT BEANS, MASHED UNTIL SMOOTH
   WITH A POTATO MASHER
1/3 CUP PUMPKIN SEEDS, TOASTED [SEE BELOW]
   AND GROUND
1/2 HOJA SANTA LEAF, FINELY SHREDDED
   [SEE PAGE 26; ABOUT 1/4 CUP, OPTIONAL]
1 1/2 TO 2 CUPS BEAN LIQUOR
2 TABLESPOONS CANOLA OIL
SEA SALT AND FRESHLY GROUND BLACK PEPPER

Saucy Beans

1 CLOVE GARLIC, MINCED
1/2 RED ONION, THINLY SLICED
1 SERRANO CHILE, STEMMED, SEEDED IF DESIRED,
   AND MINCED
2 PINCHES OF DRIED MEXICAN OREGANO
3 CUPS POT BEANS
1 1/2 CUPS BEAN LIQUOR, OR MORE IF NEEDED

To cook the pot beans, pick over the beans for any stones, grit, or misshapen beans, then rinse the beans well. In a large pot, combine the beans, onion, epazote, and water and bring to a boil over high heat. Decrease the heat to a gentle simmer and cook covered, skimming off any foam that rises to the surface, for 1 to 2 hours, until tender. Check often toward the end of cooking and add more water if needed. When the beans have finished cooking, you want to have at least 3 1/2 cups of the bean liquor for making the refried beans and the saucy beans. Place the bean pot on a wire rack and uncover. Stir them occasionally so they release their heat quickly. When cool and tender, taste and season with salt.

Drain the beans, reserving the beans and their liquor. You should have about 6 cups beans and about 3 1/2 cups liquor. If you won't be using them right away, refrigerate them in a covered container as soon as they are cool. Refrigerate the bean liquor in a separate covered container.

To make refried beans, in a bowl, stir together the mashed beans, pumpkin seeds, and *hoja santa*. Add 1 1/2 cups of the bean liquor and stir well, adding more liquor as needed to achieve a smooth, almost saucelike consistency. In a sauté pan, heat the oil over high heat. Carefully add the bean mixture (when it hits the hot oil, it will splatter) and shake the pan to rotate and thoroughly heat the puree through. Season with salt and pepper and serve.

To make saucy beans, in a saucepan, combine the garlic, onion, chile, oregano, beans, and bean liquor and stir to mix. Place over medium-high heat and bring just to a boil. Decrease the heat to a simmer and cook for about 15 minutes, until all of the flavors have developed and melded nicely. Add more bean liquor if the pan seems to be getting too dry. Serve right away.

TIPS AND TRICKS
Toasting Nuts, Seeds, and Spices

TOASTING WHOLE SEEDS AND SPICES RELEASES THEIR ESSENTIAL OILS AND ADDS MORE FRAGRANCE TO THE FINISHED DISH. TO TOAST ON THE STOVE TOP, PLACE WHOLE SEEDS OR SPICES IN A DRY SAUTÉ PAN AND COOK, TOSSING OR STIRRING FREQUENTLY, OVER MEDIUM-HIGH HEAT UNTIL VERY AROMATIC AND A SHADE DARKER. ALWAYS TOAST EACH TYPE SEPARATELY, AS THEIR TOASTING TIME WILL VARY.

TO TOAST IN THE OVEN, PREHEAT THE OVEN TO 350°F. SPREAD THE NUTS OUT IN A SINGLE LAYER ON A DRY BAKING SHEET. COOK UNTIL GOLDEN, GENERALLY ABOUT 5 TO 10 MINUTES.

CONTINUED

mexican oregano

CHIPOTLE SALSA

ARROZ VERDE

XNI-PEC SALSA

COCHINITA PIBIL TACOS

QUESO FRESCO

FISH WITH TOMATO,
HABANERO, AND CITRUS

NOPALES

HUEVOS MOTULEÑOS

POT BEANS

Cochinita Pibil Tacos, *continued*

ARROZ VERDE
(GREEN RICE)

I think this dish looks better when it is made with white rice rather than brown, but you can use the latter. If you do, you will need to increase the cooking time and the amount of stock. Most brown rice, if it has been soaked in cold water for 30 minutes before cooking, takes about 20 minutes longer to cook than white rice, and you will need to increase the stock by 1/2 cup. If using a rice cooker, follow the manufacturer's directions.

Fresh poblano chiles (usually labeled pasilla chiles in California) are almost always available where I live. If you cannot find them, jalapeños will also work. *Hoja santa*, literally "sacred leaf," is a tropical large-leaved aromatic herb. Also known as *yerba santa*, it can be found in Mexican and Central American groceries. It grows like a weed in Texas, New Mexico, and California; keep your eye out for it if you live in those areas. | SHOWN PAGE 24 | SERVES 6

2 CUPS LONG-GRAIN WHITE RICE
   [SUCH AS BASMATI OR JASMINE]
1 CLOVE GARLIC, MINCED
2 TEASPOONS SEA SALT
4 CUPS CHICKEN STOCK [PAGE 59] OR STORE-BOUGHT
   REDUCED-SODIUM BROTH
3 OR 4 POBLANO [PASILLA] CHILES, OR 6 TO 8 JALAPEÑO
   CHILES, ROASTED [SEE PAGE 29], PEELED, SEEDED,
   AND CHOPPED
2 OR 3 ROMAINE LETTUCE LEAVES, OR
   1 OR 2 HOJA SANTA LEAVES, CHOPPED

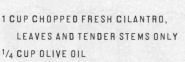
cilantro

1 CUP CHOPPED FRESH CILANTRO,
   LEAVES AND TENDER STEMS ONLY
1/4 CUP OLIVE OIL
1/2 TO 3/4 TEASPOON FRESHLY GROUND BLACK PEPPER

Put the rice in a good-size bowl, add water to cover, swish the rice around with your hand, and drain. Repeat the rinsing and draining until the water runs clear.

If using a rice cooker, combine the rinsed rice, garlic, salt, and stock and cook according to the manufacturer's directions. If using a saucepan on the stove top, combine the ingredients in the pan, cover, and bring to a boil over high heat. Decrease the heat to the lowest setting and cook for 20 minutes. If your burners are like mine and you can never adjust the heat low enough, use a heat diffuser (see page 187). While the rice is cooking, in a bowl, stir together the chiles, lettuce, cilantro, olive oil, and pepper to taste.

When the rice has finished cooking, fold in the chile mixture, mixing thoroughly. Re-cover and let steam for at least 10 minutes before serving.

TIPS AND TRICKS
HOW TO MAKE GARLIC PASTE
CUT OFF THE ROOT ENDS OF THE GARLIC CLOVES. PLACE THE CLOVES ON A CUTTING BOARD AND, ONE AT A TIME, SMASH THEM WITH THE SIDE OF A KNIFE. REMOVE THE SKINS, GATHER THE CLOVES INTO A PILE, AND SPRINKLE THEM WITH SALT. NOW, PLACE THE TIP OF YOUR KNIFE ON THE BOARD TO THE SIDE OF THE PILE OF CLOVES [THIS WILL BE YOUR PIVOT POINT] AND, HOLDING THE BLADE AT A SHALLOW ANGLE TO THE BOARD, DRAG IT ACROSS THE GARLIC, MAKING TINY CHOPPING MOTIONS AS YOU MAKE YOUR WAY ACROSS THE PILE. YOU SHOULD BE SMEARING AND SMASHING AT THE SAME TIME SO THAT GARLIC ENDS UP SPREAD ACROSS THE BOARD. PILE UP THE CLOVES AGAIN AND REPEAT THE DRAGGING AND CHOPPING MOTION, THEN CONTINUE TO REPEAT IT UNTIL YOU HAVE A PULPY PASTE. IF THIS TECHNIQUE IS NEW TO YOU, WORK IN SMALL BATCHES TO MAKE IT EASIER.

garlic

XNI-PEC SALSA

This traditional Mayan salsa is based on fiery habanero chiles, which in some Caribbean markets are mistakenly labeled Scotch bonnet, a close relative. Some cooks, including me, toast the chiles over an open flame to char the skin a bit before using them.

I can sometimes find Seville oranges, also known as bitter oranges, in the market in the winter, and their juice is great in this salsa. Otherwise, a mixture of equal parts lemon, lime, and grapefruit juice can be used. This salsa is best used within a day of making. | MAKES ABOUT 1 CUP

1 SMALL WHITE ONION, MINCED
1 LARGE RIPE TOMATO, PEELED (PAGE 181) AND MINCED
2 HABANERO CHILES, STEMMED, SEEDS AND
    RIBS REMOVED, AND MINCED (OR USE THE SEEDS
    AND RIBS IF YOU LIKE A LOT OF HEAT)
1/3 TO 1/2 CUP FRESHLY SQUEEZED SEVILLE ORANGE
    JUICE OR EQUAL PARTS FRESHLY SQUEEZED LEMON,
    LIME, AND GRAPEFRUIT JUICE
SEA SALT

In a bowl, stir together the onion, tomato, and chiles. Add 1/3 cup citrus juice if the tomato is particularly juicy, or 1/2 cup juice if it isn't. Season with salt, cover, and refrigerate until serving. It will keep for 1 day.

habanero chile

seville orange

CHIPOTLE SALSA

Here is one of my all-time favorite salsas. I make it with canned chipotles if I'm in a hurry and dried if I'm not. If using dried, be sure to toast them, which intensifies their flavor and makes them easier to seed if you want to temper the heat of the salsa. | SHOWN PAGE 24 | MAKES ABOUT 2 1/2 CUPS

6 TO 8 CHIPOTLE CHILES, STEMMED
1 POUND TOMATILLOS, PAPERY HUSKS
    REMOVED AND WELL RINSED
1 SMALL SWEET WHITE ONION, MINCED
1/4 CUP OLIVE OIL
1 CLOVE GARLIC, MINCED
1/2 TO 1 TEASPOON DRIED MEXICAN OREGANO
SEA SALT

chipotle chile

Preheat a griddle, *comal* (round, ceramic Mexican griddle), or skillet over medium heat. Arrange the chiles on the hot surface and toast, turning as needed, for 1 to 2 minutes, just until softened. Watch closely as they burn easily, which will make the salsa bitter. If you want the salsa to be only moderately spicy, let the chiles cool until they can be handled and remove the seeds. You can also toast the chiles in a preheated 350°F oven for 3 to 5 minutes, until they begin to puff and are tender.

In a saucepan, combine the chiles, tomatillos, onion, and water just to cover and bring to a boil over high heat. Decrease the heat to a simmer and cook for about 5 minutes, until the tomatillos are soft and begin to burst. Remove from the heat and let cool slightly.

Working in small batches, add the chile mixture to a blender and process until a smooth puree forms. Transfer the puree to a bowl and let cool. Add the oil, garlic, and oregano and mix well. Season with salt. Cover and refrigerate until serving. It will keep for up to 2 days.

FISH WITH TOMATO, HABANERO, AND CITRUS

I use a whole red snapper here, but you can make this same dish with Alaskan halibut fillets or cod steaks. Red snappers have a huge head, so you need a 5-pound fish to serve six people. If you are using fish steaks or fillets, plan on 8 ounces of bone-in steak or 6 ounces of fillet per person. I like to cook bone-in, skin-on fish because the flavor is better and richer and the fish is less likely to overcook. If you opt for skinned fillets, you will need to reduce the cooking time. A good rule is 10 minutes per inch measured at the thickest point of the fillet. Finally, should you opt for fish steaks or fillets over a whole fish, try to buy one big piece of fish and bake it whole for the nicest presentation. | SHOWN PAGE 25 | SERVES 6

1 WHOLE RED SNAPPER, ABOUT 5 POUNDS, CLEANED

SEA SALT AND FRESHLY GROUND BLACK PEPPER

3 LARGE OR 4 SMALL LIMES, HALVED

¼ CUP CANOLA OR OLIVE OIL

1 WHITE ONION, MINCED

2 HABANERO CHILES, SEEDED, IF DESIRED, AND MINCED

2 CLOVES GARLIC, THINLY SLICED

1 TABLESPOON ACHIOTE PASTE, GRATED, OR 1½ TEASPOONS
 ANNATTO SEEDS, CRUSHED

½ CUP FRESHLY SQUEEZED SEVILLE ORANGE JUICE
 [SEE HEADNOTE, PAGE 27] OR EQUAL PARTS FRESHLY
 SQUEEZED LEMON, LIME, AND GRAPEFRUIT JUICE

2 RED BELL PEPPERS, ROASTED [SEE PAGE 29], PEELED,
 SEEDED, AND DICED

½ CUP PIMENTO-STUFFED GREEN OLIVES OR OTHER PITTED
 PLAIN GREEN OLIVES, SLICED

ARROZ VERDE [PAGE 26]

2 OR 3 HARD-BOILED EGGS, CHOPPED

2 TO 3 TABLESPOONS CHOPPED FRESH CILANTRO,
 LEAVES AND TENDER STEMS ONLY

XNI-PEC SALSA [PAGE 27]

CORN TORTILLAS, WARMED

TIPS AND TRICKS
KEEPING THE FISH MOIST

IN MEXICO, COOKS SMEAR A LAYER OF MAYONNAISE ON THE FISH BEFORE PUTTING ALL THE GOODIES ON IT, AND YOU CAN, TOO. THIS WILL HELP KEEP THE FISH MOIST THROUGHOUT THE BAKING. BAKE IT IN A *CAZUELA* [SEE PAGE 142], IF YOU HAVE ONE.

Preheat the oven to 375°F. Place the fish in a shallow baking dish. Season on both sides with salt and pepper, and then squeeze the lime juice on both sides. (If you are using skin-on filleted fish, place the fish skin side down.)

In a large sauté pan, heat the oil over medium-high heat. Add the onion and cook, stirring occasionally, for 5 minutes, until softened. Add the chiles and garlic and continue to cook, stirring occasionally, for 6 to 10 minutes longer, until the onion is tender, reducing the heat if necessary to avoid browning the garlic. Add the achiote paste and cook, stirring, until the paste has dissolved. Stir in the orange juice, bell peppers, and olives, bring to a boil, and remove from the heat.

Pour the contents of the sauté pan over the fish, pop the fish into the oven, and bake for about 20 minutes (about 10 minutes if using fillets). To check for doneness, with the tip of a sharp knife, cut into the meatiest part of the fish. It should appear opaque (not translucent) and the meat should flake easily.

Serve the fish directly from the baking dish, surrounded by bowls holding the rice, chopped eggs, cilantro, and salsa and a stack of warm tortillas.

lime

red snapper

jalapeño chiles

bell pepper

TIPS AND TRICKS
ROASTING FRESH PEPPERS AND CHILES

PEPPERS AND CHILES CAN BE ROASTED A NUMBER OF DIFFERENT WAYS. I PREFER TO ROAST THEM DIRECTLY OVER AN OPEN FLAME, EITHER OVER A GAS BURNER OR A GRILL FIRE. TO DO THIS, PLACE THE CHILES DIRECTLY OVER THE FLAME AND ROTATE THEM AS THEY BLISTER AND TURN BLACK. WHEN NICELY BLACKENED, TRANSFER THE CHILES TO A PLASTIC BAG TO SWEAT FOR 5 TO 10 MINUTES. THIS WILL LOOSEN THE SKINS SO YOU CAN PEEL THEM OFF. IT'S A GOOD IDEA TO WEAR GLOVES WHEN PEELING HOT CHILE PEPPERS. YOU COULD ALSO PEEL THEM USING THE BAG AS A BARRIER. YOU CAN RINSE MINIMALLY UNDER CLEAR WATER TO REMOVE STUBBORN SKIN BITS, BUT A LITTLE CHARRED SKIN ACTUALLY ADDS GOOD FLAVOR. IF YOU ARE WORKING WITH SMALLER CHILES, USE A GRILL BASKET TO KEEP THEM FROM FALLING INTO THE FIRE.

OR, YOU COULD BROIL THEM IN THE OVEN. TO DO THIS, PREHEAT THE OVEN TO BROIL. SPREAD THE CHILES OUT IN A SINGLE LAYER (ALLOWING SPACE BETWEEN EACH OR THEY WILL JUST STEAM) AND BROIL UNTIL THEIR SKINS BLISTER AND BLACKEN ON THE TOP, 3 TO 5 MINUTES. TURN THEM OVER AND REPEAT ON THE OTHER SIDE. TRANSFER THEM TO A PLASTIC BAG AND, WELL, YOU KNOW THE REST. (A BOWL WITH A PLATE SET ON TOP WORKS WELL FOR "STEAMING" THE ROASTED CHILES—AND SAVES A BAG!)

árbol chiles

cactus pads

NOPAL SALAD

You can find nopales (cactus pads) already cleaned in most Latin markets. If you are working with nopales that still have their spines, don a pair of thick gloves and use a sharp paring knife to cut out the spines, trim the outside edge, and cut off the tough part at the base. | SHOWN PAGE 25 | SERVES 6

2 CUPS CLEANED AND DICED NOPALES
2 TOMATOES, PEELED (SEE PAGE 181) AND DICED
2 POBLANO (PASILLA) CHILES, ROASTED
  (SEE ABOVE), PEELED, SEEDED, AND DICED
1/4 CUP MINCED YELLOW ONION
3 TABLESPOONS OLIVE OIL
4 TEASPOONS RED WINE VINEGAR

Bring a saucepan filled with salted water to a boil. Add the nopales and boil for 5 to 6 minutes, until tender. Drain well, let cool, transfer to a bowl, cover, and refrigerate until well chilled.

In a bowl, combine the chilled nopales, tomatoes, chiles, onion, olive oil, and vinegar and mix well. Cover and refrigerate until well chilled before serving.

pasillas

OLIVE OIL

tomato

BARBACOA-INSPIRED RACK OF LAMB

WITH CREAMED CORN AND ZUCCHINI

In Mexico, the term *barbacoa* refers to the slow roasting—or barbecuing—of seasoned meat, typically a whole goat or lamb, in a pit. Because digging a pit is not easy for most home cooks, I've taken the marinade flavors and used them on a rack of lamb or lamb chops to create an easy, elegant grilled main course with tons of flavor. (Although nontraditional, the same marinade would be good on chicken breasts or pork chops.) For the Supper Club, we serve the lamb with corn and zucchini, lime wedges, and warm tortillas, but it also good with Nopal Salad (page 29), Arroz Verde (page 26), sliced radishes, pickled jalapeños, crumbled *queso fresco*, and the xni-pec and chipotle salsas (page 27).

The marinade calls for three different kinds of chiles—chipotle morita, New Mexico, and guajillo. If you have trouble finding them in your local markets, you can order them from Penzeys Spices. I like to use the small, moist, reddish, smoke-dried chipotle morita chile, which, like the chipotle, is a type of dried jalapeño, because it has great flavor. If you cannot find dried moritas, look for them canned and skip the toasting and soaking steps. | SERVES 6

MARINADE

10 CHIPOTLE MORITAS, STEMMED

11 NEW MEXICO CHILES, STEMMED

4 GUAJILLO CHILES, STEMMED

6 CLOVES GARLIC, MINCED

1 TABLESPOON BLACK PEPPERCORNS, COARSELY SMASHED

4 WHOLE CLOVES, SMASHED

1 TEASPOON CUMIN SEEDS, TOASTED IN A DRY PAN UNTIL
    FRAGRANT AND THEN GROUND [SEE PAGE 23]

¼ CUP APPLE CIDER VINEGAR OR PINEAPPLE VINEGAR

2 TO 3 TABLESPOONS OLIVE OR CANOLA OIL

2 LAMB RACKS OR 12 [2-INCH-THICK] DOUBLE-BONE LAMB
    RIB CHOPS, FRENCHED [SEE PAGE 31]

SEA SALT AND FRESHLY GROUND BLACK PEPPER

1 SMALL YELLOW ONION, MINCED AND MIXED WITH
    1 TABLESPOON DRIED MEXICAN OREGANO, FOR GARNISH

CREAMED CORN AND ZUCCHINI [OPPOSITE]

cloves

yellow onion

To make the marinade, preheat a griddle, *comal* (round, ceramic Mexican griddle), or skillet over medium heat. Meanwhile, put a kettle of water on to boil.

Working in batches, arrange the chiles on the hot surface and toast, turning as needed, for 1 to 2 minutes, just until softened. Watch closely as they burn easily, which will make the marinade bitter. If you want the marinade to be only moderately spicy, let the chiles cool until they can be handled and remove the seeds. Put all of the chiles in a wide heatproof bowl. Pour in boiling water to cover generously, and top the chiles with a heatproof plate to keep them submerged. Let the chiles soak for 30 minutes.

Drain the chiles, reserving the soaking water. Transfer the chiles to a blender, add about one-third to one-half of the soaking water, and process until a thick paste forms, adding more water as needed to achieve the correct consistency. Transfer the paste to a bowl, add the garlic, peppercorns, cloves, cumin, vinegar, and oil and mix well.

Place the meat in a shallow, nonreactive dish, season with salt and pepper, and rub liberally with the marinade. Be sure to cover all of the surfaces well. Cover and refrigerate for at least 3 hours or up to 24 hours. Remove from the refrigerator about 30 minutes before grilling.

Prepare a medium-hot charcoal and/or wood fire in a grill. Place the racks or chops on the grill rack directly over the fire and grill, turning once, until the meat is nicely caramelized on the outside and rare to medium-rare in the center. Depending on the heat of your fire, this should take about 4 minutes per side.

Let the racks rest for about 5 minutes before cutting into chops. Arrange the chops on a warmed platter or individual plates and garnish with the onion-oregano mixture. Pass the corn and zucchini at the table.

TIPS AND TRICKS

RACK TALK

EACH LAMB HAS TWO RACKS, AND EACH RACK HAS EIGHT BONES. THAT'S FOUR (TWO-BONE) CHOPS PER SIDE. A RESTAURANT PORTION WOULD BE A PAIR OF TWO-BONE CHOPS. IF YOU WILL BE SERVING THE FISH COURSE THAT GOES WITH THIS MENU AND FINISHING WITH THE TIRAMISU OR OTHER RICH DESSERT, YOU COULD CUT THE RACKS INTO ONE-BONE CHOPS AND SERVE TWO SMALL CHOPS PER PERSON, DEPENDING ON APPETITES. YOU WILL HAVE FOUR CHOPS OR TWO DOUBLE CHOPS LEFT OVER; IF I'M PLANNING FOR LEFTOVERS, I PREFER TO KEEP THE DOUBLE CHOPS, AS THAT CUT STAYS MOISTER ON THE GRILL. IF YOU DON'T WANT TO TRY TO COOK A WHOLE RACK AND CUT IT YOURSELF, YOU CAN BUY RIB (FROM THE RACK) OR LOIN CHOPS.

CREAMED CORN AND ZUCCHINI

To me, this combination just hollers out summer. The two textures together are fantastic. I use this side dish a lot in the summer. It's also great with grilled salmon, baked ham, and steaks. | SERVES 6

2 ZUCCHINI, TRIMMED AND DICED
SEA SALT AND FRESHLY GROUND BLACK PEPPER
3 EARS CORN, HUSKS AND SILK REMOVED
2 TABLESPOONS UNSALTED BUTTER
   OR VEGETABLE OIL
1/2 SMALL TO MEDIUM RED ONION, MINCED
2 SMALL OR 1 MEDIUM CLOVE GARLIC, MINCED
1/2 CUP MEXICAN CREMA OR HEAVY CREAM
2 TO 3 TEASPOONS DRIED MEXICAN OREGANO;
   1/2 HOJA SANTA LEAF, SHREDDED;
   OR 1 TO 2 TEASPOONS DRIED HOJA SANTA

Spread out the diced zucchini in a dish and sprinkle liberally with salt. Let sit for 20 minutes, then wrap the zucchini in a kitchen towel and squeeze to remove the excess moisture.

Meanwhile, standing an ear of corn stem end down, and using a sharp knife, cut straight down between the cob and the kernels to remove the kernels, rotating the corn after each cut. Repeat with the remaining 2 ears.

In a saucepan, melt the butter over low heat. Add the onion and garlic and cook, stirring occasionally, for about 3 minutes, until tender. Add the zucchini and cook, continuing to stir, for 5 minutes, until coated with butter. Stir in the *crema* and cook for 3 minutes. Add the corn and two-thirds of the oregano, stir well, and continue to cook, stirring occasionally, for 1 to 2 minutes, until the corn is heated through and just tender. Season to taste with salt and pepper and then taste and adjust the seasoning with more oregano if needed. Serve immediately.

YUCATÁN-INSPIRED TIRAMISU

This recipe has a few steps, but they can all be done a day in advance of serving. In fact, some people prefer the flavor and texture of tiramisu made a day ahead. Both the syrup and the initial preparation of the sabayon are done in a double boiler, so I use the same pan of simmering water and switch from one bowl to the other. Select bowls that are not so large that the ingredients are above the rim of the pan or they will scorch.

Be sure to use up all of the syrup when dipping the ladyfingers, or they will turn out dry. A quick two-second dunk is just about right. The dipped ladyfingers should be moist and a little soft but not soggy. Once you have started dipping, stir the syrup every now and again. It thickens easily because of the addition of the chocolate and stirring keeps it fluid.

You will need only a small amount of the whipped egg white to coat the cup of nuts used here. But because the oven is on and the egg white is on hand, consider making a big batch and giving the extra nuts away as gifts or storing them in the freezer. They will keep for up to 2 weeks, tightly covered. One whipped egg white will coat about 5 cups of nuts. | SERVES 8 GENEROUSLY

Syrup

1½ CUPS STRONG BREWED ESPRESSO

2 (3.1- OR 3.3-OUNCE) DISKS MEXICAN CHOCOLATE,
   COARSELY CHOPPED

2 OUNCES UNSWEETENED CHOCOLATE,
   COARSELY CHOPPED

¼ CUP KAHLÚA

¼ CUP DARK RUM

espresso

Sabayon

1 CUP HEAVY CREAM

5 TABLESPOONS GRANULATED SUGAR

4 EGG YOLKS (RESERVE WHITES FOR MAKING
   THE CANDIED ALMONDS)

⅓ CUP KAHLÚA

1½ (3.1- OR 3.3-OUNCE) DISKS MEXICAN CHOCOLATE,
   COARSELY CHOPPED

1 OUNCE UNSWEETENED CHOCOLATE,
   COARSELY CHOPPED

8 OUNCES MASCARPONE CHEESE

1 (17½-OUNCE) PACKAGE LADYFINGERS
   (60 BISCUITS)

sugar

Put a copper or stainless-steel bowl and a whisk in the freezer for whipping the cream for the sabayon. Select a saucepan to use as the bottom of the double boiler, fill it about one-third full with water, and set the pan aside.

To make the syrup, select a bowl that will fit above the water in the saucepan. (The water should not touch the bottom of the pan.) Add the espresso, both chocolates, the Kahlúa, and the rum to the bowl and set aside.

To whip the cream for the sabayon, pour the cream into the chilled bowl, sprinkle in 2 table-spoons of the sugar, and whip with the whisk for about 3 minutes, until thick. Cover and refrigerate until needed.

Bring the water in the saucepan to a boil over high heat, then reduce the heat to a simmer. Place the bowl holding the syrup ingredients over the simmering water and heat gently, whisking often, until the chocolate is melted and everything is well mixed. Remove from the pan and reserve for dipping the ladyfingers.

CONTINUED

Yucatán-Inspired Tiramisu, *continued*

Candied Almond Slivers

EGG WHITE FROM THE SABAYON
1 CUP SLIVERED BLANCHED ALMONDS
1/2 TEASPOON GROUND CINNAMON
1/4 CUP GRANULATED SUGAR, PREFERABLY SUPERFINE

1 CUP HEAVY CREAM
3 TABLESPOONS CONFECTIONERS' SUGAR
SHAVED DARK CHOCOLATE OR UNSWEETENED
   COCOA POWDER, FOR GARNISH

To make the sabayon, combine the egg yolks and the remaining 3 tablespoons sugar in a large bowl and whisk until creamy. In a separate bowl that will fit over the simmering water, combine the Kahlúa and both chocolates. Place this bowl above the simmering water and heat gently, whisking often, until the chocolate is just melted and well mixed with the Kahlúa but not boiling hot. Reserve.

Using a rubber spatula, slowly fold the chocolate mixture into the egg yolk mixture, blending just until combined. (Do not add it too quickly or you may cook the egg.) Next, fold in the mascarpone just until combined, and then the reserved whipped cream.

To assemble the tiramisu, have ready a 9 by 13-inch baking dish. Place the ladyfingers, syrup, and sabayon alongside the dish. Give the syrup a good stir and then start dunking the ladyfingers into it and arranging them, side by side, on the bottom of the dish. You will need 20 ladyfingers to cover the bottom. I like to make sure they soak up a lot of the delicious syrup, so I drizzle a spoonful or two over the layer when I have finished arranging it. Now, gently spread one-third of the sabayon on top of the layer of ladyfingers. Don't worry if it looks like a lot. The sabayon layers are meant to be thick. Repeat the ladyfinger and sabayon layers twice,

drizzling each ladyfinger layer with a little more syrup before you add the sabayon layer. You should have no syrup left when the final layer of sabayon is spread on top. Cover and chill for at least 3 hours or up to 24 hours.

To prepare the almonds, preheat the oven to 350°F. Line a baking sheet with a silicone baking mat or with parchment paper, then oil the parchment paper with vegetable oil. In a small bowl, beat about 1 tablespoon of the egg white until frothy. Put the nuts in a second small bowl and add just enough of the beaten egg white to coat them lightly so the cinnamon and sugar will stick to them. Sprinkle on the cinnamon and sugar and mix well.

Spread the nuts out on the prepared baking sheet. Bake for 6 to 8 minutes, just until golden. Let cool completely on the pan, then break apart any nuts that have stuck together. Store in an airtight container at room temperature until serving.

About 30 minutes before serving, place a copper or stainless-steel bowl and a whisk in the freezer for whipping the cream. When you are ready to serve, pour the cream into the chilled bowl, sprinkle with the confectioners' sugar, and whip until thick. Using an offset or standard spatula, gently spread the whipped cream over the top layer of sabayon, distributing it evenly. Sprinkle the top evenly with the shaved chocolate and finish with the candied almonds. Cut into squares to serve. Alternatively, cut the tiramisu into squares and garnish each serving with a dollop of whipped cream, chocolate, and nuts.

BRAZIL

Daniele Meilhan, a French friend of mine, tested the recipes for this chapter while playing bossa nova music "really loud." As far as I'm concerned, if the recipes made her do that they must be good, and I have accomplished my mission. Viviane Adriao, another friend, loaded me up with palm oil and *farofa* (toasted manioc flour) from Brazil so I would have the correct ingredients to make everything taste authentic.

Brazil has fun and friendly people and varied landscapes, from snow white beaches to rugged highlands to tropical rain forests and vast wetlands near Iguaçu Falls. Where else can you see a toucan—the original Froot Loops bird—and a flock of parrots all in one hour? Well, maybe in Peru and Uruguay, but Brazil does have the bossa nova. I ate *feijoada*, a rich stew of beans and of ears, tails, sausages, and other odds and ends of the pig, in Rio and enjoyed all of the lovely parts, but then I'm a parts eater from way back. The version in this menu is tamer.

HEARTS OF PALM, ARUGULA, AND BUTTER LETTUCE SALAD

This salad is light and refreshing and also very flavorful. The basil is traditionally chopped and added to the dressing, but I skip that step because it causes the basil to darken. I prefer to mix the basil leaves in with the greens so they stay bright in flavor and appearance. If you can find fresh hearts of palm, simmer them in salted water with a little lemon juice until fork-tender, about 10 minutes, then drain and chill before using. | SERVES 6 TO 8

VINAIGRETTE
1 CLOVE GARLIC, MINCED
1½ TABLESPOONS RED WINE VINEGAR
2 PINCHES OF SEA SALT
PINCH OF FRESHLY GROUND BLACK PEPPER
5 TABLESPOONS EXTRA VIRGIN OLIVE OIL

1 (14-OUNCE) CAN ORGANIC HEARTS OF PALM, DRAINED, CHILLED, AND CUT INTO ¼- TO ⅓-INCH-THICK SLICES
1 HEAD BUTTER LETTUCE, LEAVES SEPARATED AND BIG LEAVES EACH TORN INTO 2 OR 3 PIECES, DEPENDING ON SIZE
2 BUNCHES ARUGULA (PREFERABLY WILD) OR WATERCRESS, TOUGH STEMS REMOVED
LEAVES FROM 1 SMALL BUNCH BASIL (ABOUT 1 CUP), SMALL LEAVES LEFT WHOLE, LARGE ONES TORN

To make the vinaigrette, in a small bowl, whisk together the garlic, vinegar, salt, and pepper until the salt dissolves. Gradually whisk in the olive oil in a slow, steady stream and continue to whisk until well emulsified.

In a large bowl, combine the hearts of palm, lettuce, arugula, and basil. Drizzle with about three-fourths of the vinaigrette and toss to mix, adding more vinaigrette if needed to coat lightly and evenly. You my not need all of the vinaigrette. Divide among individual plates, making sure each diner gets a good mixture of all of the ingredients. Serve at once.

black pepper

olive oil

basil

butter lettuce

arugula

garlic

FEIJOADA

WITH FAROFA, KALE, ORANGE SALAD,
AND CHILE-LIME SAUCE

This is the national dish of Brazil. We served it the first time with all of the parts—ears, smoked tongue, trotters, and so forth—and both fresh and cured pork. It was a massive platter of food and people loved it. I have restrained myself here, offering a simpler grocery-store version, except for the addition of blood sausage, one of my favorite foods. After reading one recipe that included blood sausage, I knew that I had to add it. If you cannot find it or you don't like it, leave it out. Some cooks insist on all pork; others add *carne seca* (beef jerky) to the mix. I could find only teriyaki jerky and Cajun jerky in the stores where I live, and I didn't want to introduce those flavors here. At the restaurant, we make our own *carne seca*, so it is easy for us to include it for the Supper Club meal. Portuguese linguiça, a garlicky smoked pork sausage, is a good addition because Portugal's many years of colonial rule left their mark on the Brazilian table. Most Brazilian cooks use small, shiny black turtle beans. I have used a number of different types of black beans, most recently Ayocote Negro from Napa-based Rancho Gordo.

Feijoada is the perfect dish to feed a crowd. You can prepare it all in one big cooking day or you can do it over a few days. However you cook the dish, be sure to go easy on the salt, as a lot of the ingredients are fairly salty. I like to use my Le Creuset colorful enameled cookware for the final cooking; you might want to use something festive as well.

When I ate *feijoada* in Brazil, it was on a Saturday afternoon and everyone in the restaurant was also eating it. The meal was long, slow, and wonderful. The stew was accompanied with *farofa*, a brightly flavored chile-lime sauce, a refreshing orange salad, rice, and sautéed shredded kale. Diners sprinkled the *farofa* over their own serving of meats and beans and then helped themselves to the side dishes. It was quite a feast—Brazil's answer to France's cassoulet. | SHOWN PAGE 40 | SERVES 6 TO 8

BEANS

2 CUPS SMALL DRIED BLACK BEANS, RINSED AND
    PICKED OVER FOR DEBRIS

10 CUPS WATER

7 OUNCES SALT PORK, CUT INTO LARGE DICE

2 SLABS ST. LOUIS-STYLE PORK SPARERIBS,
    ABOUT 2 1/2 POUNDS TOTAL, MEMBRANE
    REMOVED FROM BONE SIDE

SEA SALT AND FRESHLY GROUND
    BLACK PEPPER

3 TO 4 TABLESPOONS OLIVE OIL

2 SMALL YELLOW ONIONS, DICED

1 CELERY STALK, DICED

3 OR 4 CLOVES GARLIC, MINCED

BOUQUET GARNI OF 2 BAY LEAVES, 8 TO 10 FLAT-LEAF
    PARSLEY SPRIGS, AND 8 TO 10 THYME SPRIGS,
    TIED TOGETHER IN A CHEESECLOTH BUNDLE

2 DRIED CHILES, STEMMED AND LEFT WHOLE
    (I USE PERUVIAN LIMO ROJO)

1/3 CUP SHERRY (SUCH AS PEDRO XIMÉNEZ OR AMONTILLADO)

6 CUPS CHICKEN STOCK (PAGE 59) OR BEEF STOCK

1 HAM HOCK (ABOUT 1 1/2 POUNDS)

7 OUNCES LINGUIÇA, CUT INTO
    3-INCH CHUNKS

6 OUNCES BLOOD SAUSAGE,
    CUT ON THE DIAGONAL INTO
    2-INCH-THICK SLICES (OPTIONAL)

celery

To cook the beans, in a large pot, combine the beans and water, cover, and bring to a boil over medium-high heat. Decrease the heat to a simmer and cook for 2 to 3 hours, until just tender.

Meanwhile, in a saucepan, combine the salt pork with cold water to cover and bring to a full rolling boil over high heat. Drain and repeat the process twice, starting with cold fresh water each time. Drain well.

When the beans are just tender, add the blanched salt pork and continue to cook for 20 to 30 minutes, until the beans are very tender. Remove from the heat and drain the beans in a large sieve, capturing the cooking liquid in a bowl. Transfer the beans to a bowl. Let the beans and liquid cool.

In a blender or food processor, combine 1 cup of the cooled beans and 1 1/2 cups of the cooking liquid and process until smooth. Stir the puree back into the beans. Cover and refrigerate the beans and the remaining liquid separately. (The beans may be cooked up to 2 days in advance. Refrigerate them promptly as they can "go off" quickly.)

Season the spareribs on both sides with salt and pepper. Select a braising pan large enough to hold the ribs and the ham hock and heat over medium-high heat. Add 2 tablespoons of the oil, and when the oil is hot, add the ribs and sear, turning once, until nicely browned on both sides. Transfer the ribs to a plate to drain and reserve.

Return the pan to medium-high heat and add the onions, celery, and garlic and cook, stirring occasionally, for 10 to 15 minutes, until the onions are lightly caramelized and tender (see page 14 for more on caramelizing onions). Add the herb bundle and chiles and cook for 1 minute more. Pour in the sherry and cook, stirring, until it has evaporated. Add the stock and the ham hock and then return the ribs to the pan. Cover, bring to a boil, decrease the heat to a very low simmer, and cook for 1 1/2 hours, until the ribs and the hock are tender when pierced with a fork. As the meats cook, uncover the pan every now and again and skim off any foam that rises to the surface.

Remove and toss the herb bundle. Remove the ribs and ham and set aside on a cutting board to cool until they can be handled. Cut the ribs into 2- or 3-bone portions. Trim away the rind from the hock and pull the meat off of the bone in nice big chunks. (You want big chunks so the meat won't fall apart during the final stewing.) Reserve the meats.

Using a large spoon, skim off and discard the fat from the surface of the stock and set the stock aside until needed. (The meats may be cooked up to 2 days in advance and the meats and stock refrigerated separately. The fat will solidify on top of the stock, making it easy to lift it off just before using the stock.)

To prepare for serving, in a skillet, heat the remaining 1 to 2 tablespoons oil. Add the linguica and blood sausage pieces and sear, turning as needed, until browned on all sides. Remember to brown the blood sausage on the cut sides. Keep warm until needed.

To finish, in a big pot, combine the beans, ribs, ham, and linguica (but not the blood sausage; it would dissolve during stewing if put in with the other ingredients at this point). Add just enough of the bean liquid and the stock to make a saucy casserole. Bring almost to a boil and immediately decrease the heat to a very quiet simmer. Cook slowly for 1 to 1 1/2 hours to meld all of the flavors. Add more liquid if the pan starts getting too dry. (Any leftover stock will make an excellent black bean soup.) A couple of minutes before the dish is done, gently tuck in the reserved blood sausage and bring back just to a boil (do not cook too long or the blood sausage will fall apart).

Spoon the beans and meats onto a large, deep platter, or serve directly from the pan it was cooked in. Serve the *farofa*, kale, orange salad, and chile-lime sauce on the side.

CONTINUED

CHILE-LIME SAUCE

KALE FOR FEIJOADA

FAROFA

FEIJOADA

ORANGE SALAD

Feijoada, *continued*

FAROFA

This calls for flour (sometimes labeled "meal") made from the manioc tree, as is tapioca. It is sprinkled over the top of a finished *feijoada* and adds great texture and taste. Look for *farinha de mandioca* (manioc flour) in a Brazilian, Latin American, or specialty food store or online. In the past, when I haven't been able to find the *farinha*, I have finely ground bread crumbs and toasted them in butter, or I have finely ground tapioca pearls in a coffee grinder and toasted them. It works, but it's not the same. My mom used to make a cracker-and-butter crumb mix for cauliflower, and making this reminded me of it! | SHOWN PAGE 40 | SERVES 6 TO 8 [OR FEWER BRAZILIANS]

3 TABLESPOONS PALM [DENDÊ] OIL OR UNSALTED BUTTER
1/4 RED OR WHITE ONION, MINCED
1/2 CUP FARINHA DE MANDIOCA

In a cast-iron or other heavy pan, heat the oil over medium heat. Add the onion and cook, stirring, for a few minutes, until tender. Add the flour and continue stirring over medium heat or medium-low heat (depending on your confidence and time) for 8 to 10 minutes, until the flour is a nice golden brown.

Transfer to a shallow bowl and let cool before serving. It may be made up to 3 hours in advance and stored in an airtight container at room temperature.

red onion

KALE FOR FEIJOADA

Kale is one of the greens we are told is good for us—lots of flavonoids and fiber—and this is a great way to eat it—simple, quick, and tasty. It keeps its beautiful color, too.
| SHOWN PAGE 40 | SERVES 6 TO 8

2 BUNCHES GREEN OR DINOSAUR/BLACK KALE, TOUGH
    STEMS REMOVED
1/4 CUP PALM [DENDÊ] OIL OR OLIVE OIL
1 RED ONION, HALVED THROUGH THE STEM END AND
    THINLY SLICED INTO CRESCENTS
4 CLOVES GARLIC, MINCED [OPTIONAL]
PINCH OF SEA SALT

Pile the kale leaves in stacks that are manageable to hold flat. Using a chef's knife, cut crosswise into very fine strips or ribbons. (After de-ribbing the bunches, I pile the leaves, roll them up like a cigar, then cut crosswise to create ribbons.)

In a large sauté pan, heat the oil over medium-high heat. Add the onion and sauté for several minutes, until tender and just beginning to caramelize (see page 14 for more on caramelizing onions). Add the garlic and sauté for 1 to 2 minutes longer, until the garlic is fragrant. Add the kale and cook, tossing and stirring to ensure even cooking, for 6 to 8 minutes, until wilted and just tender. If it seems dry you can sprinkle with a bit of water. Season with the salt and serve.

kale

Mint

CHILE-LIME SAUCE

In Brazil, this sauce would be made with fresh or preserved malagueta chiles. I have found these bright and delicious peppers on my travels and have stocked my pantry with them. But because not everyone has had the chance to bring some home, I have come up with this inauthentic but tasty variation. When I make this with malaguetas, I use 6 to 8 peppers, but I like my sauce fiery! If you have sauce left over or you decide to make extra, it is a delicious way to brighten up chicken soup or grilled fish or lamb chops.

| SHOWN PAGE 40 | MAKES ABOUT 3/4 CUP

1 CLOVE GARLIC, THINLY SLICED
1 SERRANO CHILE, STEMMED
    AND THINLY SLICED CROSSWISE
1/2 TO 1 TEASPOON SEA SALT
GRATED ZEST OF 1 LIME
JUICE OF 3 LIMES
1 SHALLOT, MINCED
1 POBLANO [PASILLA] CHILE, STEMMED AND MINCED
1 TABLESPOON EXTRA VIRGIN OLIVE OIL [OPTIONAL]

poblano chile

In a mortar, combine the garlic, serrano chile, 1/2 teaspoon salt, and the lime zest and grind to a paste with a pestle. Or, combine the ingredients in a blender and process to a paste. Transfer the paste to a small bowl and whisk in the lime juice, shallot, pasilla chile, and olive oil. Taste and adjust the seasoning with more salt if needed. Alternatively, finely mince the garlic and serrano chile, transfer to a small bowl, and whisk in the remaining ingredients.

Cover and refrigerate until serving. It will keep for up to 2 days.

lime

ORANGE SALAD

An antidote to the winter doldrums, this easy-to-make orange salad brightens up the table and gives your palate a reprieve from the rich beans and meats of the *feijoada*.

| SHOWN PAGE 41 | SERVES 6 TO 8

6 ORANGES
6 THIN RED ONION SLICES, SEPARATED INTO RINGS
6 TO 8 FRESH MINT LEAVES, FINELY SHREDDED
SEA SALT AND FRESHLY GROUND BLACK PEPPER
JUICE OF 1 LIME OR LEMON
EXTRA VIRGIN OLIVE OIL, FOR DRIZZLING [OPTIONAL]

Working with 1 orange at a time, cut a slice off of the top and bottom just to reveal the flesh. Stand the orange upright on a cutting board and slice off the peel, pith, and membrane in wide strips, working from the top to the bottom and following the contour of the fruit. Cut the orange crosswise into 1/3-inch-thick slices. Repeat with the remaining oranges.

Arrange the orange slices on an attractive platter. Scatter the onion rings and mint over the top, season with salt and pepper, and drizzle with the lime juice and olive oil.

CAIPIRINHA
Two ways

This is one of Brazil's most popular cocktails and perfect for sipping before you dig into *feijoada*, the national dish. These two recipes are from my favorite mixologist, Jennifer Ingellis, who has come up with many variations on the caipirinha over the years. The first recipe is a traditional version; the second one is Jennifer's inspired riff on the classic. The ginger honey used in the nontraditional cocktail will keep in the refrigerator for up to 2 weeks, so you may want to make extra for future batches of cocktails. | EACH RECIPE SERVES 1

TRADITIONAL CAIPIRINHA

3 LIME WEDGES
1 ROUNDED TEASPOON SUPERFINE SUGAR
ICE CUBES
2 OUNCES LEBLON CACHAÇA

In a mixing glass, combine the lime wedges and sugar and muddle (crush) the ingredients together. If you don't have a muddler (a baseball bat–shaped wooden pestle), the handle of a wooden spoon is a good substitute. Add some ice and the cachaça, cover the glass with a shaker, and shake for 5 to 10 seconds. Pour into a double rocks glass and serve.

MANDARIN CAIPIRINHA

GINGER HONEY
1/2 CUP WATER
1/2 CUP HONEY
1 1/2 TEASPOONS PEELED AND MINCED FRESH GINGER

1/2 MANDARIN ORANGE (CUT THROUGH THE STEM END), QUARTERED LENGTHWISE
2 LIME WEDGES, HALVED LENGTHWISE
1 ROUNDED TEASPOON SUPERFINE SUGAR
ICE CUBES
2 OUNCES LEBLON CACHAÇA
DRIZZLE OF GINGER HONEY

To make the ginger honey, in a saucepan, combine the water and honey and place over medium heat. Bring to just under a boil, remove from the heat, and stir in the ginger. Let stand until cool. Strain through a fine-mesh sieve into a jar, cover, and refrigerate until needed. You should have about 1 cup.

In a mixing glass, combine 3 of the orange wedges, the lime wedges, and the sugar and muddle (crush) the ingredients together. If you don't have a muddler (a baseball bat–shaped wooden pestle), the handle of a wooden spoon is a good substitute. Add some ice, the cachaça, and the ginger honey, cover the glass with a shaker, and shake for 5 to 10 seconds. Pour into a double rocks glass, garnish with the remaining orange wedge, and serve.

VELVET CUSTARD

For this recipe, use classic custard cups—the same kind your grandmother used for custard. You can instead use a single large baking dish, but you will need to increase the baking time to about 1 hour and check on the custard often as it nears the end of baking to make sure you don't overcook it. This recipe yields a particularly silky custard, hence the name. It is what you crave in the wintertime when you are not feeling up to snuff—a luscious comfort food. Plus, it goes together in a flash and is ready to emerge from the oven in no time. This recipe doubles easily, and the extra custards are great the next day. | SERVES 6 TO 8

1/2 CUP SUGAR

2 TABLESPOONS WATER

1 (14-OUNCE) CAN SWEETENED CONDENSED MILK

1 CAN WHOLE MILK, MEASURED IN THE EMPTY
    CONDENSED-MILK CAN

4 EGGS, WHISKED

1/2 TEASPOON PURE VANILLA EXTRACT

Preheat the oven to 325°F.

Place a small bowl of water and a pastry brush next to the stove. In a small, heavy saucepan, combine the sugar and water over medium to medium-high heat (depending on your bravery) and cook, swirling (not stirring) the pan gently, until the sugar is completely melted and the syrupy liquid is a rich caramel color. This should take about 5 minutes. If sugar crystals start to collect on the sides of the pan, wash them down with the brush dipped in cold water, being careful not to introduce more water into the caramel. Divide the syrup evenly among six to eight 1/2-cup custard cups. Immediately swirl each cup to coat the bottom evenly. The caramel will harden within a minute or so. (If you ended up with some crystallization in the syrup, pour the syrup through a fine-mesh sieve into the cups.)

In a bowl, whisk together the condensed milk, whole milk, eggs, and vanilla until well blended. Divide the milk mixture evenly among the cups, pouring it into the cups through a fine-mesh sieve.

Place the cups, not touching, in a baking dish. Pull out the oven rack, place the baking dish on the rack, and pour hot water into the baking dish to reach at least two-thirds of the way up the sides of the cups. Be careful not to splash any water into the cups. Carefully push in the oven rack and bake for 40 minutes, or until done. To test for doneness, gently shake a cup; the custard should not wobble.

Carefully remove the baking dish from the oven, and remove the custard cups from the dish. Let the custards cool, then cover and refrigerate for at least 2 hours. until well chilled, or up to 2 to 3 days (but they disappear more quickly in my house).

To serve, run a small, sharp paring knife around the inside of a cup to loosen the custard. Invert a dessert plate over the top, flip the plate and the cup together, and gently lift off the cup. You may need to tap the bottom of the cup a couple of times to release the custard. Repeat with the remaining custards and serve.

PERU

Peru is a heady mix of different landscapes and varied cultures that I find endlessly fascinating. I have stayed in a sophisticated hotel in Lima and eaten from fine china, slept in a tent hut in the jungle and consumed only quinoa and sweet potatoes, and dined on roasted guinea pig during the Festival of the Sun at Cuzco. The population is an equally varied mix of Amerindian, mestizo, European, Asian, and African, all of them contributing to the national table.

For centuries, Peruvian farmers have cultivated squash, corn, chiles, potatoes, and other crops on elaborately terraced hillsides. Cooking skills range from the highly refined cuisine of the cities to the rustic fare of the mountains. At Cuzco, I saw hot rocks piled atop roasting potatoes. Each family arranged their rocks differently, so that when they returned for supper, they would know which pile concealed their potatoes. They would then eat the roasted tubers with a hot green sauce made from *huacatay* (an aromatic green herb), chiles, and peanuts and with cheese reminiscent of Munster.

All of the recipes in this menu, with the exception of the dessert, call for ají amarillo, a hot yellow chile frequently used in Peruvian cooking. If you cannot find amarillo chiles, you can use a jarred Peruvian chile paste instead. Near where I live, I am able to buy three different chile pastes, amarillo, panca, and limo. They are also available by mail order. These pastes are handy to have on hand because they have lots of uses and keep well in the refrigerator—a wonderful shortcut to putting Peruvian flavors on your table.

MUSHROOM CEVICHE

Peru is famous for its ceviche and *escabeche*, which are "cooked" salads or relishes. In the case of ceviche, the acid in lime or lemon juice cooks the food, and in *escabeche*, vinegar and heat do the cooking. In Peru, both preparations are often served with steamed or roasted sweet potatoes and roasted Inca corn, a variety of corn with kernels that are two to four times the size of regular corn kernels. Inka Crops is a popular brand of roasted giant kernels. Roasted Inca corn is similar to corn nuts, a favorite snack food of American teenagers (and some grown-ups), so I have included original-style (salted) corn nuts as a substitute if you cannot find the real thing.

Most people are familiar with seafood or duck ceviche, so I have decided to make a less commonly known vegetable ceviche. The most difficult part of this dish is waiting for the mushrooms to marinate. A tasty olive oil is critical here, so go for the best you can afford. Do not be tempted to substitute shiitake mushrooms for the white mushrooms here. Raw shiitakes are known to cause an allergic reaction in some people, resulting in swelling and prickly rashes.

Serving this ceviche with the sweet potatoes and corn alongside the Artichoke and Fennel Escabeche on page 48 is a great start to a Peruvian supper. | SERVES 6 TO 8

1 POUND WHITE BUTTON MUSHROOMS

¼ CUP EXTRA VIRGIN OLIVE OIL

1 CUP FRESHLY SQUEEZED LEMON JUICE, OR ½ CUP EACH
    FRESHLY SQUEEZED LIME JUICE AND ORANGE JUICE

½ TEASPOON SEA SALT

2 CLOVES GARLIC, POUNDED INTO A PASTE (SEE PAGE 26)

½-INCH PIECE FRESH GINGER, PEELED AND GRATED

2 JALAPEÑO CHILES OR 1 SERRANO OR AMARILLO CHILE,
    STEMMED, SEEDED IF DESIRED, AND MINCED

5 GREEN ONIONS, WHITE AND LIGHT GREEN PARTS ONLY,
    THICKLY SLICED

2 TABLESPOONS MINCED FRESH DILL, CHIVES, OR TARRAGON

1 ORANGE AND 1 YELLOW SWEET POTATO, OR 2 ORANGE OR
    2 YELLOW SWEET POTATOES (OPTIONALLY PEELED), BAKED
    UNTIL TENDER AND COOLED

1 (4-OUNCE) PACKAGE ROASTED INCA CORN OR
    ORIGINAL CORN NUTS

SWEET OR HOT RED PEPPER, CUT INTO JULIENNE STRIPS,
    FOR GARNISH

Trim the stems of the mushrooms and then, for variety, leave some of the mushrooms whole, cut some in half, and quarter others. Place in a bowl, drizzle with the olive oil, and toss to coat.

In a small bowl, whisk together the lemon juice, salt, garlic, ginger, and chiles. Add to the mushrooms, toss well, and marinate at room temperature for 30 minutes.

To serve, add the green onions and dill to the mushrooms and toss to mix evenly. If serving on a single large plate or shallow bowl, thinly slice the sweet potatoes and arrange the slices, overlapping them slightly, around the outside edge of the plate or bowl. Pile the mushrooms in the center of the plate or bowl, sprinkle them with the corn, and garnish with the red pepper. If serving in individual bowls, cut the sweet potatoes into small spears. Divide the mushrooms evenly among the bowls, sprinkle the corn on top, garnish with the red pepper, and arrange 2 or 3 sweet potato spears on the side of each bowl.

corn nuts

mushrooms

ARTICHOKE AND
FENNEL ESCABECHE

Here is a vegetarian appetizer that is hearty enough to stand alone, accompanied with grilled or toasted bread, or be part of a larger spread. It is reminiscent of the vegetable *á la grecque* preparations in the Mediterranean and is a wonderful spring or summertime dish.

Although you can use small artichokes here, I prefer to use the large globe artichokes, as you get more heart for the work! The timing works nicely if you put the artichokes on to simmer and then turn to prepare the remaining ingredients. If you cannot find dried amarillo chiles, you can substitute amarillo chile paste or add an extra jalapeño or serrano chile. If in season, feel free to add a handful of fava beans, tender green beans, or English peas at the very end to brighten things up.

| SERVES 6 TO 8

JUICE OF 1 TO 2 LEMONS

4 CUPS WATER

1 1/2 TEASPOONS SEA SALT

4 GLOBE ARTICHOKES

1/2 CUP OLIVE OIL

3 OR 4 FENNEL BULBS, STALKS AND FRONDS REMOVED,
    TOUGH OUTER LAYER DISCARDED, AND EACH BULB CUT
    LENGTHWISE INTO 6 WEDGES

2 YELLOW ONIONS, SLICED 1/4 INCH THICK AND SLICES
    SEPARATED INTO RINGS

2 OR 3 CARROTS, PEELED AND SLICED INTO THICK ROUNDS

3 OR 4 CLOVES GARLIC, EACH SLICED LENGTHWISE
    INTO 3 PIECES

1 DRIED AMARILLO CHILE, TOASTED [SEE PAGE 49]
    AND JULIENNED OR SHREDDED, OR ABOUT
    1 TABLESPOON JARRED AMARILLO OR OTHER PERUVIAN
    CHILE PASTE [OPTIONAL]

1 SERRANO CHILE, STEMMED, SEEDED IF DESIRED,
    AND SLICED INTO RINGS

1 JALAPEÑO CHILE, STEMMED, SEEDED IF DESIRED,
    AND SLICED INTO JULIENNE STRIPS

1 BAY LEAF

12 OR SO BLACK PEPPERCORNS

1/4 NUTMEG, GRATED

1/2 CUP WHITE WINE VINEGAR

1/2 CUP DRY WHITE WINE

6 TO 8 OREGANO SPRIGS, 2 TO 3 INCHES LONG

CHOPPED FRESH FLAT-LEAF PARSLEY LEAVES, RINSED
    AND SQUEEZED DRY [SEE PAGE 83], FOR GARNISH

In a saucepan, combine the lemon juice, water, and salt. To pare each artichoke down to its edible light-colored heart, trim off the end of the stem. Then snap off all of the leaves by holding the artichoke upright in one hand and snapping each leaf back against your thumb so that the base of the leaf stays with the artichoke. Using a paring knife, trim off any dark bits that are left on the base of the heart and lightly peel the stem. Cut the heart

amarillo chile

fennel

serrano chile

olive oil

artichoke

jalapeño chile

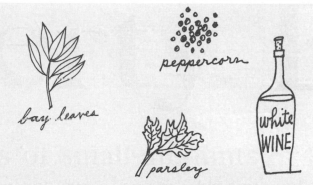

bay leaves

peppercorn

parsley

white WINE

lengthwise into quarters, then carve the choke out of each quarter and toss the quarters into the pan.

When all of the artichoke quarters are in the pan, cover with a heatproof plate that just fits inside the rim of the pan and bring a boil over high heat. Decrease the heat to a simmer and cook for about 10 minutes, until barely fork-tender. (You are only trying to give the artichokes a head start in cooking, not cook them fully.)

While the artichokes are simmering, in a large sauté pan, heat the olive oil over medium-high heat. When the oil is hot, add the fennel, onions, carrots, garlic, and all of the chiles and stir to coat with the oil. Add the bay leaf, peppercorns, and nutmeg and cook, stirring, for a few minutes. Add the vinegar, wine, and oregano and bring to a boil. Decrease the heat to a slow simmer.

When the artichokes are ready, scoop them out of the pan with a slotted spoon or wire skimmer and add them to the sauté pan. Cover and cook for about 10 minutes, until all of the vegetables are tender and the flavors have melded nicely.

Remove and discard the oregano sprigs. Serve warm or chilled, sprinkled with the parsley.

TIPS AND TRICKS
TOASTING DRIED CHILES

TOASTING A DRIED CHILE INTENSIFIES ITS FLAVOR AND MAKES IT MORE MALLEABLE AND EASIER TO WORK WITH. IF YOU ARE GOING TO SEED YOUR CHILES (TO REDUCE THE SPICINESS), IT'S EASIER TO DO SO BEFORE TOASTING THEM, AS RIGHT AFTER TOASTING THEY WILL BE TOO HOT TO HANDLE. THERE ARE A NUMBER OF WAYS TO TOAST CHILES.

TO TOAST CHILES IN THE OVEN, PREHEAT THE OVEN TO 350°F. STEM THE CHILES AND PLACE THEM ON A DRY BAKING SHEET. PLACE IN THE OVEN FOR $2^{1}/_{2}$ TO $3^{1}/_{2}$ MINUTES, UNTIL THEY JUST START TO BECOME AROMATIC. TO TOAST CHILES IN A SAUTÉ PAN, HEAT OVER MEDIUM-HIGH HEAT, SHAKING THE PAN FREQUENTLY, FOR A MINUTE OR TWO, UNTIL AROMATIC. YOU COULD ALSO TOAST THEM INDIVIDUALLY BY HOLDING THEM WITH TONGS OVER A DIRECT FLAME AND ROTATING THEM AS THEY TOAST (SORT OF LIKE TOASTING MARSHMALLOWS). THEY GO REALLY FAST FROM NOT-QUITE-READY, TO PERFECT, TO OVER-TOASTED, SO DON'T GET DISTRACTED WHILE DOING THIS.

ACUADITO OF RABBIT
(Spicy Garlic Stew)

On my visit to Peru, guinea pig, which is indigenous to the Andes, was the most common form of protein on the dinner table. I have used rabbit here, but you may also use chicken or turkey, and orzo or rice could be used in place of the quinoa.

Traditionally, the whole rabbit would be poached in the broth and then broken down into pieces and finished in the stew. For ease, I have started with two rabbits already cut up. Ask your butcher to cut up the rabbits and make sure he or she saves all of the odd parts—kidneys, heart, bony pieces—so they can be put to good use in the stock. Once you have the rabbits home, the first step is to make a great stock and then to use some of it to cook the quinoa and finish the rabbit. I like the dish served as a stew, but if you prefer it as soup, you can add more stock. Either way, I would recommend making it a day ahead, as it is one of those dishes that tastes better the next day. | SERVES 6 TO 8

2 WELL-RAISED RABBITS, 3 TO 4 POUNDS EACH, CUT INTO
    FRONT LEGS, BACK LEGS, AND BONELESS LOIN PIECES,
    WITH KIDNEYS, HEART, AND BONY PIECES RESERVED

STOCK
KIDNEYS, HEART, AND BONY PIECES FROM RABBIT
8 CUPS CHICKEN STOCK [PAGE 59] OR STORE-BOUGHT
    REDUCED-SODIUM BROTH
1 POUND YELLOW ONIONS, UNPEELED, ROOTS TRIMMED
    OFF AND ONIONS CUT INTO CHUNKS
2 CARROTS, PEELED AND SLICED
4 OR 5 CELERY STALKS OR THE CELERY HEART, CHOPPED
1 LEEK, WHITE AND GREEN PARTS, CHOPPED
2 HEADS GARLIC, HALVED CROSSWISE
2 DRIED AMARILLO CHILES, TOASTED [SEE PAGE 49] AND
    SPLIT LENGTHWISE, OR 1½ TO 2 TABLESPOONS JARRED
    AMARILLO OR OTHER PERUVIAN CHILE PASTE
2 JALAPEÑO CHILES, SPLIT LENGTHWISE
1 TABLESPOON ANNATTO SEEDS OR ACHIOTE PASTE
16 OR SO JUNIPER BERRIES
20 OR SO BLACK PEPPERCORNS
6 TARRAGON OR CILANTRO SPRIGS
8 FLAT-LEAF PARSLEY SPRIGS

Reserve the rabbit pieces in the refrigerator. To make the stock, in a large pot, combine the rabbit parts, stock, onions, carrots, celery, leek, garlic, chiles, annatto seeds, juniper berries, peppercorns, tarragon, and parsley. If there is not enough liquid to cover everything, add up to 4 cups water. Bring to a boil over medium-high heat, then decrease the heat to a simmer and cook, uncovered, for 1 hour, until the liquid is reduced to 7 to 8 cups. Remove from the heat, strain through a fine-mesh sieve, and reserve until needed. (The stock may be made a day in advance, covered, and refrigerated.)

CONTINUED

amarillo chile

jalapeño chiles

celery

juniper berries

yellow onion

Aguadito of Rabbit, *continued*

STEW

¼ TO ⅓ CUP OLIVE OR VEGETABLE OIL

SEA SALT AND FRESHLY GROUND BLACK PEPPER

1 YELLOW ONION, MINCED

2 CLOVES GARLIC, FINELY MINCED

2 RED BELL PEPPERS, SEEDED AND FINELY DICED

1 TEASPOON OR SO CAYENNE PEPPER

1 TABLESPOON SPANISH SMOKED SWEET PAPRIKA

SEA SALT

2 LARGE SWEET POTATOES, PREFERABLY YELLOW FLESHED,
    PEELED AND SLICED OR CUT INTO LARGE DICE

4 CUPS WATER

2 CUPS QUINOA, PREFERABLY RED

½ CUP SHELLED ENGLISH PEAS, SHELLED FAVA BEANS,
    OR CHOPPED GREEN BEANS, BOILED UNTIL CRISP-TENDER

3 TO 4 TABLESPOONS CHOPPED FRESH CILANTRO,
    OR FLAT-LEAF PARSLEY, RINSED AND SQUEEZED DRY
    (SEE PAGE 83), FOR GARNISH

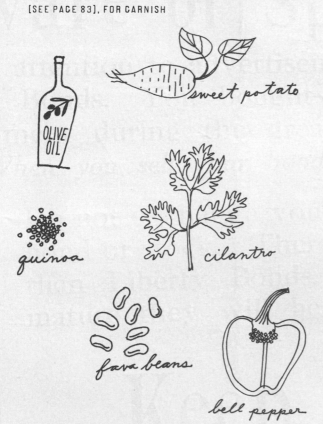

olive oil

sweet potato

quinoa

cilantro

fava beans

bell pepper

To make the stew, in a large, heavy pot, heat ¼ cup of the oil over medium-high heat. Generously season the rabbit pieces on both sides with salt and pepper. Working in batches if necessary to avoid crowding, place the rabbit pieces in the hot oil and sear, turning them as needed, until they are lightly browned on both sides. Transfer the pieces to a plate.

Add the onion, garlic, bell peppers, cayenne, paprika, and 1½ teaspoons salt to the fat remaining in the pot and sauté over medium heat, stirring, for about 10 minutes, until tender. Return the rabbit pieces to the pot, add half of the stock, and increase the heat to high. Bring to a boil, adjust the heat to maintain a gentle simmer, and cook for about 15 minutes. Add the sweet potatoes and continue to cook for about 15 minutes, until the rabbit and sweet potatoes are tender.

Meanwhile, in a saucepan, bring the water to a boil. While the water is heating, rinse the quinoa twice, swishing it well in a bowl of water and pouring off the water. When the water is boiling, sprinkle in some salt and then add the quinoa. Decrease the heat to a simmer, cover, and cook for 10 to 15 minutes, until all of the water is absorbed and the grains are tender.

About 5 minutes before the stew is ready, stir in the peas and cilantro. Then add as much of the remaining stock as desired to achieve the consistency you want, less for a stew or more for a soup. Taste and adjust the seasoning with salt.

To serve, divide the quinoa among deep individual bowls and arrange the rabbit pieces on top. Ladle the stock and vegetables around and over the rabbit pieces and serve right away.

ORANGE AND CINNAMON RICE PUDDING

WITH POACHED PRUNES

My research convinces me that all of the countries that were colonized by Spain now serve a rice pudding. This recipe is inspired by five different Peruvian rice pudding recipes I found. The originals were all too sweet and/or too rich or included an element that didn't appeal to me. One of them, for example, included stirring port-soaked golden raisins into the pudding, which turned it an unappetizing purple gray. I decided to use diced prunes (or dried plums, in modern parlance), which I poach, put on the bottom of Pyrex custard cups, and then top with the pudding. The Pyrex-cup presentation is casual, but you can easily dress up the pudding with fancier glasses. Some folks prefer a pudding that is slightly less sweet and use only three-fourths of the can of sweetened condensed milk. Use a vegetable peeler to cut the strip of orange zest. | SERVES 9

POACHED PRUNES

9 PRUNES, PITTED AND DICED

1/2 CUP PORT

2 TABLESPOONS SUGAR

1 STRIP ORANGE ZEST, ABOUT 4 INCHES LONG

1 CUP SHORT-GRAIN WHITE RICE, RINSED IN COLD WATER
    UNTIL THE WATER RUNS CLEAR

3 CUPS WATER

2 CINNAMON STICKS

2 WHOLE CLOVES

1/2 TEASPOON SEA SALT

1 (12-OUNCE) CAN EVAPORATED MILK

1 (14-OUNCE) CAN SWEETENED CONDENSED MILK

1/2 TEASPOON PURE VANILLA EXTRACT

WHIPPED CREAM, MASCARPONE CHEESE,
    OR CRÈME FRAÎCHE, FOR GARNISH (OPTIONAL)

To poach the prunes, in a small saucepan, combine the prunes, port, and sugar and stir to mix. Bring to a boil over high heat, decrease the heat to a simmer, and cook for 10 to 15 minutes, until nice and plump. Remove from the heat and set aside.

To remove the bitterness from the orange zest, bring a small saucepan filled with water to a boil, add the zest strip, blanch for 1 minute, and drain. Repeat twice, starting with fresh cold water each time. Finely dice the blanched zest.

In a heavy saucepan, combine the diced zest, rice, water, cinnamon, cloves, and salt. Cover, bring just to a boil over high heat, and then immediately decrease the heat to a quiet simmer. Put the pan on a heat diffuser (see page 187) if your burner is too high even on the lowest setting. Cook for 30 minutes, until the rice has absorbed the water.

Remove the pan from the heat and remove and discard the cloves and cinnamon sticks. Stir in the evaporated milk off the heat and then return the pan to high heat and beat until the milk is absorbed. Add the sweetened condensed milk the same way, stirring it in off the heat and then beating it in over high heat until absorbed. Remove from the heat and stir in the vanilla.

Divide the poached prunes and any remaining juices evenly among nine 1/2-cup custard cups and pour the hot rice pudding over the top. If you don't want a skin to form on top of the pudding, immediately place plastic wrap directly onto the surface. Let cool at least slightly before serving. The pudding may be eaten warm or chilled, with or without whipped cream.

sugar

orange zest

cinnamon

EUROPE

AUSTRIA

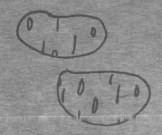

Austria is my paternal grandmother's homeland and a place I still hope to visit. I didn't get as many Austrian foods as I would have liked when I was a child, though I didn't realize what I was missing until I was much older. My mother described her mother-in-law as not being very helpful with recipes (or anything), and she had passed away long before I was around to pester her for information. I wonder whether mom's breaded veal cutlets come from grandma—I'm sure the ketchup she served them with didn't.

Mozart, Strauss, Schubert, and Haydn hailed from Austria, too, strong evidence that it is a country capable of great refinement and beauty. And I have found that people who love music tend to love food, as well. The national cuisine has incorporated many of the culinary traditions of its former partners in the Austro-Hungarian Empire, along with Germany and Italy, and the court cuisine of the empire was heavily influenced by the French table. My dad only talked about his mother's peasant foods, about her dumplings, noodles, and polenta (which he called mush), all of which I like. But Vienna, I know, offers much more, and I have promised myself that I will dine there one day.

LIPTAUER CHEESE

I have been making this delicious cheese spread for a long time. It is nice to put out when guests arrive and it is good picnic fare, too. I like to serve it with rye crackers, dense rye bread, or a baguette (which is so nontraditional!). Here, I garnish the cheese with chives, but capers, minced cornichons, fish roe (caviar), or anchovies are also tasty options. And any leftover cheese is great in omelets, on scrambled eggs, or in chicken or turkey sandwiches.

Using the best-quality cottage cheese available makes this spread light-years better. I purchase mine from Cowgirl Creamery in Petaluma, which is near where I live. If possible, seek out a creamy, rich, locally made product. If you want a little heat, you can add hot paprika, but be careful not to overwhelm the subtle cottage cheese flavor. | MAKES 2 1/2 CUPS

8 OUNCES SMALL-CURD COTTAGE CHEESE
1/2 CUP UNSALTED BUTTER, AT ROOM TEMPERATURE
1/2 SMALL RED ONION, MINCED (ABOUT 3 TABLESPOONS)
1 TO 2 TEASPOONS SWEET PAPRIKA
1/2 TEASPOON CARAWAY SEEDS, CRUSHED
1/4 TO 1/2 TEASPOON SEA SALT
CHOPPED FRESH CHIVES, FOR GARNISH

In a food processor, combine the cottage cheese, butter, onion, 1 teaspoon of the paprika, and the caraway and process until smooth. Taste and season with the salt and with more paprika, if you like. Transfer to a bowl, garnish with the chives, and serve. Or, cover and refrigerate for up to 2 days before serving. Bring to room temperature before serving.

unsalted butter

red onion

caraway seeds

sea salt

cottage cheese

chives

CHICKEN NOODLE SOUP

My paternal grandmother, Stephanie Pawlsyn (she and my grandfather spelled the family name differently), was gone long before I was born. But I have always been interested in Austrian and Polish foods, which I attribute to that genetic connection. Although I grew up eating Campbell's chicken noodle soup, this recipe yields what I have long envisioned as true chicken noodle soup. In my grandmother's day, it would have been made with a stewing hen and cooked until the chicken was falling apart.

In this soup, big chunks of vegetables and chicken meat and hearty noodles float in a flavorful stock. I use an antique Austrian wedding band that my husband found for me as guide for cutting the noodles, which gives them a wonderful authentic quality. If you want the finished soup to have a clear broth, cook the noodles separately in boiling water, divide them among the bowls, and ladle the soup over them.

Homemade noodles make this soup special, but if you are pressed for time, you can use store-bought egg vermicelli. Another critical ingredient is the double-strength broth that comes from poaching the chicken in chicken stock. I find it necessary to do this even with the best-quality chickens to ensure enough flavor in the finished soup.

If you prefer to serve the soup as a main course, rather than a first course, leave the meat in big pieces rather than bite-size chunks. I can imagine my grandmother serving this soup with rye bread spread with fresh butter. | SERVES 6 TO 8

BROTH

1 WELL-RAISED LARGE ROASTING CHICKEN, QUARTERED

3 OR 4 FLAT-LEAF PARSLEY SPRIGS

2 OR 3 CELERY STALKS WITH LEAVES,
    EACH CUT INTO 3 OR 4 PIECES

1 YELLOW ONION, HALVED AND EACH HALF
    STUCK WITH 1 WHOLE CLOVE

2 CARROTS, PEELED AND EACH CUT INTO 3 OR 4 PIECES

4 QUARTS CHICKEN STOCK (PAGE 59)
    OR STORE-BOUGHT REDUCED-SODIUM BROTH

1 TEASPOON SEA SALT

1½ TEASPOONS BLACK PEPPERCORNS

To make the broth, combine all of the ingredients in a large pot and bring to a boil over medium-high heat. Decrease the heat to a gentle simmer and cook, skimming off any foam that rises to the surface, for 30 minutes. Turn off the heat and let sit undisturbed for 1 hour, then remove the chicken from the pot.

When the chicken is cool enough to handle, remove the meat from the bones and peel away the skin. Break up the meat into chunky spoon-size pieces and set aside. If the broth is not as strongly flavored as you would like, return the skin and bones to the pot and bring the broth back to a boil. Decrease the heat to a steady simmer and cook, skimming as needed, until reduced by one-fourth to one-third. Then strain the broth through a fine-mesh sieve and reserve. (The broth may be made up to 1 day ahead; cover and refrigerate the chicken and the broth separately.)

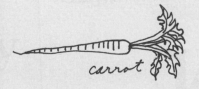

carrot

yellow onion

CONTINUED

Chicken Noodle Soup, *continued*

NOODLES

2 CUPS [8 OUNCES] BREAD FLOUR
   OR OTHER HIGH-GLUTEN FLOUR

$1/2$ TEASPOON SEA SALT

2 EGGS

$1 1/2$ TEASPOONS WATER

2 CELERY STALKS, SLICED

2 CARROTS, PEELED AND SLICED

2 LEEKS, WHITE AND LIGHT
   GREEN PARTS ONLY, THINLY SLICED

2 TO 3 TEASPOONS SEA SALT

FRESHLY GROUND BLACK PEPPER

2 TO 3 TABLESPOONS MINCED FRESH FLAT-LEAF PARSLEY,
   LEAVES, RINSED AND SQUEEZED DRY [SEE PAGE 83], OR
   1 TABLESPOON MINCED FRESH TARRAGON, FOR GARNISH

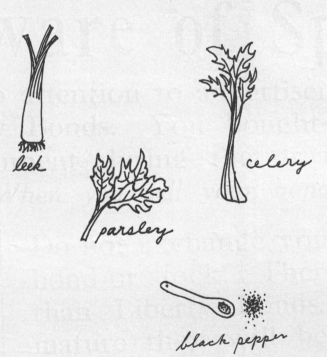

eggs

leek

parsley

celery

black pepper

To make the noodles, in a large bowl, stir together the flour and salt. In a small bowl, whisk together the eggs and water until blended. Create a well in the center of the flour mixture and pour in the eggs. With a fork, gradually combine the wet ingredients with the dry ingredients until a rough dough forms. Turn the dough out onto a floured work surface and knead for about 5 minutes, until smooth. Shape into a ball, cover with an overturned bowl, and let rest for 20 minutes.

Lay a few kitchen towels flat on a work surface that you can dedicate to pasta drying and dust the towels lightly with flour. Anchor a standard manual pasta machine to your work surface and set the rollers at the widest setting. Cut the dough into 5 equal pieces and slip 4 pieces back under the bowl. Hand flatten the fifth piece to about $1/2$ inch thick and run it through the rollers of the pasta machine. Fold the dough into thirds, like a business letter, dust it with a little flour to prevent sticking, and run it through the rollers again. Repeat until the dough is smooth and somewhat silky. Reset the rollers to the next narrowest setting and pass the dough through the rollers and then pass it through the same setting again. Continue passing the dough through progressively narrower settings, lightly dusting the dough or rollers with flour as needed to prevent sticking, until the dough sheet is about $1/4$ inch thick. Lay the sheet on a flour-dusted work surface and repeat with the remaining dough pieces.

You can cut the dough sheets into thin ribbons by hand or by machine. To cut by hand, dust a dough sheet lightly with flour and fold it over itself to form a manageable rectangle. Using a very sharp knife, cut the rectangle crosswise into $1/8$-inch-wide strips, then shake the strips free. If using a pasta machine, secure the strand-cutting attachment to the machine (make sure it will cut the noodles about $1/8$ inch wide), lightly dust a dough sheet, and pass it through the cutters. As soon as the noodles are cut, lay them on the flour-dusted towels, dust them with a little flour, and lightly run your fingers through them to make sure all of the surfaces get coated. Don't worry about getting too much flour on the noodles. You can shake off any excess when you are ready to cook them. Repeat until you have cut all of the dough sheets into noodles.

When the noodles are dry to the touch, gather them up onto a rimmed baking sheet and cover them with a kitchen towel to keep the dust off. Leave them out on the counter until needed (do not put them in the refrigerator). They will keep for up to 1 day.

To make the soup, if you like, skim off the fat from the top of the broth and discard. In a large pot, combine the celery, carrots, and reserved broth and bring to a boil over high heat. Decrease the heat to a simmer and cook for 10 to 15 minutes, until the vegetables are tender. Add the reserved chicken, the noodles (shake off the excess flour), and the leeks and cook, maintaining a steady simmer, until the soup is bubbly hot and the noodles are cooked through. This should take about 5 minutes. (If the chicken is straight from the refrigerator, add it to the pot a minute or two ahead of the noodles so you don't overcook the noodles.) Season the soup to taste with the salt and with the pepper. (It will probably need more salt than you think it will.)

Ladle the soup into warmed bowls and garnish with the parsley. Serve at once.

garlic

CHICKEN STOCK

MAKES 4 TO 6 QUARTS

3 TO 5 POUNDS CHICKEN BACKS, NECKS, AND/OR WINGS, PLUS SOME FEET, IF POSSIBLE
2 CARROTS, CHOPPED
2 OR 3 CELERY STALKS, CHOPPED
1/2 HEAD GARLIC, CLOVES SEPARATED AND LIGHTLY SMASHED (SEE PAGE 172), WITH LOOSE SKINS REMOVED
1 LARGE YELLOW ONION, COARSELY CHOPPED, WITH 1 WHOLE CLOVE STUCK INTO 2 OF THE PIECES
3 BAY LEAVES
STEMS FROM 1/4 BUNCH FLAT-LEAF PARSLEY
3 OR 4 THYME SPRIGS
1 TABLESPOON BLACK PEPPERCORNS

Remove as much visible fat from the chicken pieces as possible. In a stockpot, combine the chicken with cold water to cover (preferably filtered water) and bring to a rolling boil over high heat. Add the carrots, celery, garlic, onion, bay, parsley, thyme, and peppercorns and decrease the heat to a simmer. Cook at a steady simmer, uncovered, for 3 hours. Check frequently and skim off any foam that rises to the surface (one of the secrets of a good stock is to skim often).

Remove from the heat and strain through a fine-mesh sieve. For a more concentrated flavor, return the strained stock to the pot and simmer until reduced by one-fourth to one-third. Let cool, cover, and refrigerate for up to 1 week or freeze for up to 2 months. Lift off and discard the fat from the surface before using.

peppercorn

bay leaves

RABBIT WITH SOUR CREAM
WITH STEAMED POTATOES AND BACON RED CABBAGE

The casserole part of this recipe is best cooked in a big cast-iron or enameled cast-iron Dutch oven. If you have neither, choose any big, heavy pot with a tight-fitting lid that will hold all of the ingredients.

Your butcher will probably be happy to break down the rabbit for you, but if you want to give it a try yourself, I have included some tips (see page 64). The marinade works equally well with chicken or with game birds such as pheasant or quail. The spiced cabbage may be made a day or two ahead, so you can make it on the same day you put the rabbit in the marinade. The cabbage is also good with sausage and pork chops. Double-smoked bacon, which is a specialty of Polish and German smokehouses, is bacon that is left in the smoker much longer than regular American bacon, usually at least four times the normal amount of time. Nowadays, some American companies are producing it. If you cannot locate it, regular bacon may be substituted.

If your steamer is big enough, I recommend cooking extra potatoes and serving them the next day using this simple preparation: Melt about 4 tablespoons unsalted butter with some first-rate extra virgin olive oil in a sauté pan over medium-high heat, add the potatoes, and toss them until they are nice and hot and lightly browned. Transfer them to a bowl, roll them around in some chopped fresh chives or tarragon, and pour any butter and oil remaining in the pan over the top. This preparation is too much with the rich rabbit dish, but it is perfect with simple grilled fish. Among my favorite potato varieties for this dish are Caribe, Cranberry Red, Red Sangre, French Fingerling, Desiree, and Russian Banana. | SERVES 6 TO 8

MARINADE
2 CUPS RED WINE VINEGAR
2 CUPS DRY RED WINE
2 CUPS WATER
4 TEASPOONS BLACK PEPPERCORNS, SMASHED
2 TEASPOONS JUNIPER BERRIES, SMASHED
4 BAY LEAVES

To make the marinade, combine all of the ingredients in a saucepan, bring to a boil over high heat, and boil for 5 minutes. Remove from the heat and let cool completely.

Lay the rabbit pieces in a single layer in a glass or ceramic baking dish. Pour the cooled marinade over the rabbit and turn the pieces as needed to coat on all sides. Cover and refrigerate for 48 hours, turning the pieces occasionally.

peppercorn

CONTINUED

juniper berries

Rabbit with Sour Cream, *continued*

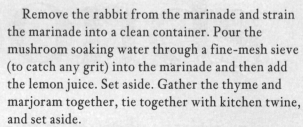

shiitake

2 [3- TO 4-POUND] RABBITS, CUT INTO
   SERVING PIECES [SEE PAGE 64]

3 OUNCES DRIED PORCINI OR SHIITAKE
   MUSHROOMS, SOAKED IN HOT WATER TO
   COVER FOR 15 TO 20 MINUTES, DRAINED,
   AND SOAKING WATER RESERVED [PAGE 101]

JUICE OF 2 LEMONS

6 FRESH THYME SPRIGS

STEMS FROM 1/3 BUNCH FRESH MARJORAM OR
   FLAT-LEAF PARSLEY SPRIGS

OLIVE OIL, FOR BROWNING

6 SLICES DOUBLE-SMOKED BACON OR OTHER
   SMOKY BACON, CUT CROSSWISE INTO NARROW STRIPS

2 YELLOW ONIONS, SLICED

4 CARROTS, PEELED AND SLICED

SPICED CABBAGE

3 SLICES DOUBLE-SMOKED BACON OR OTHER SMOKY BACON,
   CUT CROSSWISE INTO NARROW STRIPS

1 LARGE RED ONION, SLICED

2 CLOVES GARLIC, MINCED

1 LARGE HEAD RED CABBAGE, CORED
   AND THINLY SLICED OR SHREDDED

1 TABLESPOON CARAWAY SEEDS

2 LARGE APPLES OR PEARS, PEELED, CORED, AND CHOPPED

GRATED ZEST AND JUICE OF 1 LEMON

2 CUPS DRY RED WINE

3 TO 4 TABLESPOONS RED WINE VINEGAR

3 TO 4 TABLESPOONS HONEY

SEA SALT AND FRESHLY GROUND BLACK PEPPER

12 SMALL FRENCH FINGERLING OR OTHER WAXY POTATOES

SEA SALT

MINCED FRESH FLAT-LEAF PARSLEY OR FRESH TARRAGON
   OR CHOPPED CHIVES, FOR GARNISH

1 CUP SOUR CREAM OR CRÈME FRAÎCHE, OR A MIXTURE

Remove the rabbit from the marinade and strain the marinade into a clean container. Pour the mushroom soaking water through a fine-mesh sieve (to catch any grit) into the marinade and then add the lemon juice. Set aside. Gather the thyme and marjoram together, tie together with kitchen twine, and set aside.

Have ready one or more big plates or platters for holding the meats and vegetables as are they are browned. Coat the bottom of a Dutch oven lightly with olive oil and heat over medium-high heat. Working in batches, add the bacon, rabbit, onion, and carrots to the pot and brown well on all sides, transferring each batch to the plate as it is finished. Add more oil between batches if necessary.

If the shiitakes are whole, quarter them or for smaller mushrooms cut in half; the pieces should be sized to eat easily. Return the browned meats and vegetables to the pot; add the rehydrated mushrooms, the strained marinade mixture, and the herb bundle. Bring to a boil and reduce the heat to a simmer, skimming off any foam that rises to the surface. Cover and cook gently, checking occasionally and skimming off any foam, for 45 minutes, until the vegetables are tender and the rabbit is done. Alternatively, once all of the ingredients are in the pot and are at a boil, cover the pot, transfer it to a preheated 325°F oven, and cook for about 1 hour.

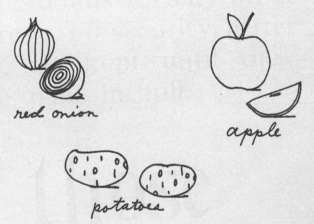

red onion

apple

cabbage

potatoes

To make the cabbage, in a big sauté pan, fry the bacon in its own fat until crisp. Add the onion and garlic and cook, stirring occasionally, for 5 to 8 minutes, until soft. Add the cabbage and cook, stirring and tossing, for 3 to 5 minutes, until nicely wilted. Add the caraway, apples, lemon juice and zest, wine, vinegar, and honey. Bring to a boil, decrease the heat to a simmer, cover, and cook for 45 minutes to 1 hour. If near the end of cooking it is too juicy for your liking, uncover the pan to allow the liquid to reduce. When the cabbage is ready, it should be tender and glistening and taste nicely sweet and sour. Season with salt and pepper, cover, and set aside off the stove, and then reheat just before serving. (This cabbage may be cooked a day ahead, cooled, covered, and refrigerated and then reheated just before serving.)

About 25 minutes before serving, pour water into a steamer pot, place over medium-high heat, and set the rack in place. Add the potatoes to the rack and liberally sprinkle them with salt. If you need to layer the potatoes, sprinkle each layer with salt. Cover the steamer and as soon as the water is boiling, decrease the heat to a simmer and steam for 15 to 20 minutes, until the potatoes are fork-tender. Remove the steamer from the heat and let the potatoes rest for at least 3 minutes before removing them from the steamer. Transfer the potatoes to a nice bowl or platter, garnish with the parsley, and keep warm.

To finish the rabbit and vegetables, using a slotted spoon, transfer the meat and vegetables to a serving platter and keep warm. Discard the herb bundle. Increase the heat under the pot and bring the juices to a boil. Cook until they are thick enough to coat a spoon nicely. Taste and adjust the seasoning with salt and pepper.

To serve, spoon some of the sauce over the rabbit and vegetables and set the platter on the table. Spoon the sour cream into a small bowl and place the sour cream, potatoes, and cabbage alongside the rabbit and vegetables. Invite your guests to spoon sour cream onto the stew to their taste.

CONTINUED

chives

caraway seeds

lemon

RED Wine

Honey

TIPS AND TRICKS
How to Cut Up a Rabbit into Serving Pieces

1 USING A BONING KNIFE, CUT EACH HIND LEG OFF AT THE JOINT.

2 LAY EACH LEG ON THE CUTTING BOARD, INNER THIGH FACING UP.

3 STARTING AT THE BALL JOINT, CUT DOWN ALONG THE SEAM OF THE LEG TO EXPOSE THE THIGH BONE.

4 SET EACH BONELESS LEG AND THIGH ASIDE AS YOU WORK ON THE REST.

5 CUT EACH OF THE FRONT LEGS OFF AT THE JOINT. THE BEST WAY TO DO THIS IS TO LIFT THE LEG UP AND AWAY FROM THE BODY AND THEN CUT UNDER AND OFF.

6 CUT THE LOIN SECTION OF THE BODY INTO TWO PIECES, CUTTING WHERE THE RIB CAGE ENDS (FRONT END) SO YOU HAVE TWO BONE-IN PIECES.

7 TRIM OFF ANY EXCESS BACKBONE FROM THE FRONT PORTION OF THE BODY AND THE HIP SOCKETS FROM THE BACK-LEG PORTION OF THE BODY.

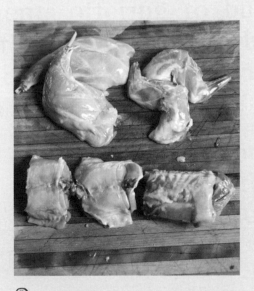

8 ALTERNATIVELY, YOU CAN BONE THE LOINS FROM THE BACKBONE. YOU WOULD THEN COOK THE LOIN LESS TIME, BROWNING IT AND THEN ADDING IT BACK TO THE STEW FOR ONLY 6 TO 8 MINUTES.

RASPBERRY-CURRANT LINZER TORTE

I started making this dessert, named for the Austrian city of Linz, in the 1970s. The first time was for my sister Mary's wedding. It was the groom's cake and I think I added whole wheat flour for nuttiness. In the early days I used almonds, but I now think that hazelnuts are more "authentic." My old brown *Gourmet* cookbook from the 1970s says to use almonds and does not include cocoa. It tastes great either way.

If possible, use homemade jam. Raspberry or currant would be the classic choice. But in early summer, I often make a quick jam from a combination of whatever is ripe in the garden: raspberries, currants, *fraises des bois*, and strawberries. I have included the instructions for a quick raspberry-currant jam here, but if you decide to buy the jam, you will need 1 to 1 1/2 cups. Whether you use homemade or store-bought jam, just make the torte!

The crust is basically a cookie dough that you press into a tart pan. Grind the nuts in an old-fashioned nut grinder, if you are lucky enough to have one, which makes them flaky and light. Otherwise, chop them by hand, shred them by the handful on a box grater, or pulse them in a food processor. If you use a food processor, be sure to use short pulses and stop the moment the consistency is correct or you will end up with a nut paste. If you want a more refined lattice top, grind the nuts finer. I prefer some coarseness because it improves the taste and texture.

To suggest ice cream is gilding the lily, but a little vanilla ice cream alongside each slice would be nice with this, along with a cup of Viennese-style coffee. | MAKES 1 [8-TO 9-INCH] TORTE; SERVES 6 TO 8

CRUST

1 CUP ALL-PURPOSE FLOUR

1/2 CUP WHOLE WHEAT FLOUR

1/4 TEASPOON SEA SALT

1 1/2 TABLESPOONS NATURAL UNSWEETENED DUTCH-PROCESS COCOA POWDER

1/2 TEASPOON GROUND GINGER, OR 2 TEASPOONS PEELED AND GRATED FRESH GINGER

1/2 TEASPOON GROUND CINNAMON

1/4 TEASPOON GROUND CLOVES

1 CUP ALMONDS OR HAZELNUTS, FLAKED, FINELY SHREDDED, OR PULSED IN A FOOD PROCESSOR

1 CUP GRANULATED SUGAR

1 CUP UNSALTED BUTTER

3 EGG YOLKS

GRATED ZEST OF 1 LEMON

To make the crust, in a medium bowl, stir together the all-purpose flour, whole wheat flour, salt, cocoa powder, ginger, cinnamon, cloves, and almonds until well mixed. In a large bowl combine the granulated sugar and butter and beat with a handheld mixer on medium-high speed or with a wooden spoon until light and fluffy. Add the egg yolks and lemon zest and stir until incorporated. Add the flour mixture to the butter mixture and stir until thoroughly combined and a soft dough forms.

Divide the dough into 2 portions, one twice as large as the other. Press out each portion like a thick hamburger patty, wrap separately in plastic wrap, and refrigerate for at least 30 minutes, until chilled, or up to 24 hours.

ginger

almonds

CONTINUED

Raspberry-Currant Linzer Torte, *continued*

raspberries

RASPBERRY-CURRANT JAM

1 POUND FRESH RASPBERRIES AND RED CURRANTS,
   PREFERABLY IN EQUAL PARTS

1 1/2 CUPS GRANULATED SUGAR

GRATED ZEST OF 1 LEMON

2 TABLESPOONS FRESHLY SQUEEZED LEMON JUICE

1 EGG WHITE WHISKED WITH 1 TEASPOON WATER,
   FOR EGG WASH

CHOPPED HAZELNUTS OR SLICED ALMONDS, FOR GARNISH

CONFECTIONERS' SUGAR, FOR DUSTING

To make the jam, remove any stems from the currants. In a nonreactive pot, combine the currants and raspberries, granulated sugar, and lemon zest and juice and bring to a boil over high heat. Decrease the heat to a simmer and cook, stirring often, for 15 to 20 minutes, until thick and jammy and a candy thermometer registers 228°F. Be sure to cook the jam long enough (being careful not to scorch) for it to thicken. Remove from the heat and let cool. You should have 1 to 1 1/2 cups.

To bake the torte, preheat the oven to 375°F. Remove only the larger dough portion from the refrigerator and press it onto the bottom and sides of an 8- or 9-inch round tart pan with a removable bottom. Pour in the cooled jam and then refrigerate while you make the lattice for the top.

On a lightly floured work surface, roll out the second dough portion to match the diameter of your pan. With a table knife or a pastry or pizza cutter, cut the dough into 1/2- to 3/4-inch-wide strips. For the fanciest lattice top, lay half of the strips parallel to one another across the tart, spacing them about 1/2 inch apart. Lay the remaining strips perpendicular to the first strips, spacing them about 1/2 inch apart and gently weaving them over and under the first strips. If a strip breaks, just press the broken edges

back together. Alternatively, for a simple lattice, place half of the strips parallel to one another across the tart, spacing them about 1/2 inch apart. Then lay the remaining strips on top of and perpendicular to the first strips, spacing them about 1/2 inch apart. Press the ends of each strip onto the edge of the bottom crust.

Brush the lattice strips with the egg wash, then sprinkle the hazelnuts evenly around the outside edge. Bake for 40 to 50 minutes, until the crust is golden brown. (Start checking after 30 minutes and decrease the heat to 350°F if the crust seems to be browning too fast.) Let cool completely on a wire rack, then remove the pan sides. Using a wide metal spatula, carefully slide the torte onto a serving plate. Liberally dust the top of the torte with confectioners' sugar and cut into wedges to serve.

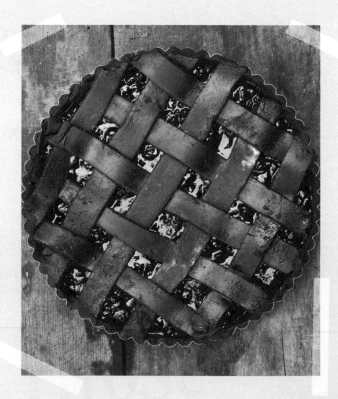

jam

BELGIUM

My Belgian friend Anne de Lovinfosse inspired this menu. One day we sat together at the bar at Cindy's Backstreet Kitchen and I asked her what here favorite meal was from home. This menu includes some of the dishes we spoke about that afternoon. Mussels and French fries are a classic Belgian pairing and make a wonderful first course. Add a strong Dijon-flavored mayonnaise to dip the fries in and you have a match made in heaven. It might have been more traditional to make *waterzooi*, a popular chicken and cream stew, or *carbonade flamande*, sweet-and-sour beef stew made with beer rather than the red wine used in the *carbonades* of France, but I found a gravy-topped meat loaf and because it was divine, I decided to include it. I hope you will enjoy it! Dessert was a toss-up between crepes, which require no special pan, and Belgium waffles, which require a special pan, so I went for the equipment-easy crepes. Later I made a batch of Belgium waffles in a regular waffle iron and they were great, so I will save them for the next book.

MUSSELS STEAMED IN BELGIAN BEER

WITH FRENCH FRIES

You will need a large, deep sauté pan or large braising pan with a lid for steaming the mussels. They will cook best if they fit in a single layer. A little overlap is okay, but make sure they are not piled on top of one another or they won't have enough room to shake around and open. If necessary, use two pans and add a little more butter and beer.

Try to cook the French fries at the same time the mussels are steaming so they are hot out of the oil when you serve them, though you can keep them in a warm oven briefly. If you want to cheat a little, cut the potatoes into thin matchsticks, fry them until crisp, and cool them in a single layer. They will become like shoestring fries and may be made up 2 hours in advance and served at room temperature. If you are wary of deep-frying, the mussels are also wonderful with grilled bread or garlic bread. And if you want to simplify your menu, the mussels will serve four as a main course. | SERVES 6

AIOLI
1 EGG YOLK
1 TO 2 TABLESPOONS ICE WATER
2 OR 3 CLOVES GARLIC, POUNDED INTO A PASTE [SEE PAGE 26]
SEA SALT
PINCH OF FRESHLY GROUND BLACK PEPPER [OPTIONAL]
¼ CUP EXTRA VIRGIN OLIVE OIL
½ TO ¾ CUP OLIVE OIL

MUSSELS
2 TABLESPOONS UNSALTED BUTTER
3 SHALLOTS, MINCED, OR 1 SMALL RED ONION, THINLY SLICED
4 POUNDS BLACK MUSSELS, SCRUBBED AND DEBEARDED
1 OR 2 CLOVES GARLIC, MINCED
2 TABLESPOONS COGNAC
1 TO 1½ CUPS BELGIAN OR OTHER
    WHEAT BEER OR DRY WHITE WINE
1 CUP CRÈME FRAÎCHE
3 TABLESPOONS CHOPPED FRESH FLAT-LEAF PARSLEY
    LEAVES, RINSED AND SQUEEZED DRY [SEE PAGE 83]
SEA SALT AND FRESHLY GROUND BLACK PEPPER

FRENCH FRIES [PAGE 72]

To make the aioli, in a bowl, whisk together the egg yolk, 1 tablespoon of the ice water, garlic, salt, and pepper until thick and light. Begin adding the extra virgin olive oil a drop at a time while whisking constantly. As the mixture begins to thicken, begin adding the extra virgin oil in a slow, thin, steady stream while continuing to whisk constantly. When all of the extra virgin oil has been added, begin adding the olive oil in a slow, steady stream, stopping when the egg yolk can absorb no more oil and you have a thick, creamy emulsified sauce. If the sauce begins to break (the oil and egg yolk separate), add a few more drops of ice water. (If you don't feel like employing so much elbow grease, use a blender, processing the egg yolk, ice water, garlic, salt, and pepper until thick and light and then adding the oils in a thin, steady stream with the motor running.)

To cook the mussels, in a large sauté pan or braising pan, melt the butter over high heat. When the butter is hot, add the shallots and cook, stirring, for a few minutes, until the shallots begin to soften. Add the mussels, garlic, and Cognac and pour in the beer to a depth of about 1 inch. Cover the pan, bring the liquid to a simmer, and cook, shaking the pan back and forth, for about 5 minutes, until the mussels begin to open. Uncover, and when the mussels have opened, add the crème fraîche and parsley, and swirl

CONTINUED

Mussels Steamed in Belgian Beer, *continued*

FRENCH FRIES

One of the tricks to making great fries is using the right kind of potato. You want a potato with high starch and low sugar, otherwise the sugar in the potato will caramelize and become bitter before the fries are cooked. Winnemucca and Kennebec are two excellent choices and some russet varieties also work well. Although you cannot always know where a potato has been before you buy it, try to purchase potatoes that have not been refrigerated, which can cause the starch to turn to sugar. The other trick is to keep the oil at the correct temperature. If the temperature drops, the fries will be greasy. See page 276 for more thoughts on deep-frying. | SERVES 6

5 POUNDS POTATOES, PREFERABLY KENNEBEC OR WINNEMUCCA

PEANUT OIL, FOR DEEP-FRYING

SEA SALT

to combine. Continue to cook until everything is piping hot. Season with salt and pepper, being conservative with the salt because mussels can be salty.

To serve, pile the fries on a big plate and place in the center of the table. Divide the mussels evenly among deep bowls, being sure to get a nice amount of broth in the bottom of each bowl and discarding any mussels that failed to open. Serve aioli on the side for guests to enjoy as they like. I don't use it for the mussels. I use it for the fries!

Using a long, sharp knife, cut the unpeeled potatoes lengthwise into slices $1/2$ inch thick. Then cut the slices lengthwise into strips $1/2$ inch wide. In a large bowl, soak the potato strips in water to cover for a few minutes to remove excess surface starch. Drain and dry thoroughly with kitchen towels.

Pour the peanut oil to a depth of 2 to 3 inches into a deep, heavy saucepan and heat to 375°F on a deep-frying thermometer. While the oil is heating, place a wire cake rack over a baking sheet and place them next to the stove.

When the oil is ready, add about 2 handfuls of the fries to the hot oil and fry for 3 to 5 minutes, until golden brown and crisp. Using a wire skimmer, transfer to the prepared baking sheet to drain. Repeat with the remaining fries, always making sure the oil returns to 375°F before you add a new batch. Serve the fries piping hot, sprinkled with the salt.

Kennebec potatoes

FLEMISH MEAT LOAF
WITH SPICY TOMATO GRAVY

In Belgium's northern region of Flanders, the locals enjoy a wide variety of ground meat dishes, from pâtés and terrines to homey meat loafs that make the child in all of us happy. The meat mixture can also be used to make meatballs or *boulettes* (small meat patties). When you crave this meat loaf on a simpler menu, serve it with mashed potatoes and your favorite green vegetable. | SERVES 6

GRAVY
2 TABLESPOONS VEGETABLE OIL

1/2 YELLOW ONION [CUT THROUGH THE STEM END],
    THINLY SLICED INTO CRESCENTS

2 CLOVES GARLIC, MINCED

1 SERRANO CHILE, STEMMED, SEEDED IF
    DESIRED, AND SLICED

1 FRESH CAYENNE CHILE, STEMMED, SEEDED IF DESIRED,
    AND SLICED [OR OTHER SPICY CHILE OF YOUR LIKING]

2 CUPS PEELED TOMATO WEDGES [SEE PAGE 181]

1/4 TEASPOON GROUND CINNAMON

PINCH OF GROUND CLOVES

1/2 TEASPOON CUMIN SEEDS, TOASTED IN A DRY PAN
    UNTIL FRAGRANT AND THEN GROUND [SEE PAGE 23]

SEA SALT AND FRESHLY GROUND BLACK PEPPER

2 CUPS CHICKEN STOCK [PAGE 59] OR VEAL STOCK OR
    STORE-BOUGHT REDUCED-SODIUM CHICKEN BROTH

MEAT LOAF
3/4 POUND GROUND VEAL

3/4 POUND GROUND BEEF

3/4 CUP FRESH BREAD CRUMBS

1 EGG, LIGHTLY BEATEN

1/2 YELLOW ONION, MINCED

2 CLOVES GARLIC, MINCED

JUICE OF 1/2 TO 1 LIME, DEPENDING ON JUICINESS OF LIME

1-INCH PIECE FRESH GINGER, PEELED AND GRATED

1/4 TO 1/2 TEASPOON CUMIN SEEDS, TOASTED IN A DRY
    PAN UNTIL FRAGRANT AND GROUND [SEE PAGE 23]

1/8 TEASPOON GROUND CINNAMON

PINCH OF GROUND CLOVES

1/2 TO 1 TEASPOON SEA SALT

1 TO 1 1/2 TEASPOONS FRESHLY
    GROUND BLACK PEPPER

tomatoes

To make the gravy, in a sauté pan, heat the oil over medium to medium-low heat. Add the onion, garlic, and both chiles, cover, and cook for 10 to 15 minutes, until the onion is caramelized (see page 14 for more on caramelizing onions). Go slowly, stir occasionally, and reduce the heat if the garlic starts to brown. Add the tomatoes, re-cover, and cook, stirring occasionally, for 10 to 15 minutes, until they begin to break down. Add the cinnamon, cloves, and cumin, season with salt and pepper, and cook for 2 to 3 minutes longer, until nicely aromatic. Stir in the stock, increase the heat to medium-high, and cook for about 10 minutes, until the liquid in the pan is reduced by half. Remove from the heat. (The gravy may be made up to 2 days ahead, cooled, covered, and refrigerated. Bring to room temperature before using.)

To make the meat loaf, preheat the oven to 375°F. In a large bowl, combine all of the ingredients, using the smaller amounts of cumin, salt, and pepper, and mix thoroughly but gently. In a small sauté pan, fry a nugget of the meat mixture, taste, and adjust the seasoning if needed with more cumin, salt, and pepper. Pile the meat mixture into an oval or rectangular baking dish just large enough to accommodate it and have room for the sauce and shape into a loaf. Crosshatch the top of the loaf, and then pour the gravy over and around the loaf.

Bake the meat loaf, basting occasionally with the sauce surrounding it, for 45 to 50 minutes, until cooked through when tested with a thin knife blade. Let sit for 5 to 10 minutes before slicing, then slice and arrange on a warmed platter to serve. Be sure to serve plenty of gravy with each piece.

GRATIN OF BELGIAN ENDIVE AND HAM

My Belgian friend Anne says that in Belgium this gratin is served with mashed potatoes and a green salad for a satisfying and simple supper. It also makes a rich, warming appetizer, portioned at one-half endive per person. In this menu, it plays the role of a hearty side dish. It may be assembled in advance and then baked just before serving, which makes it ideal for entertaining. It also holds well for 5 to 10 minutes in a warm oven if the timing of dinner needs to be adjusted.

This gratin may be baked in a single large dish and then plated for serving or baked in individual dishes. For the latter, I like to use either classic white French porcelain dishes or Spanish earthenware *cazuelas* (see page 142). | SERVES 6

4 TO 6 TABLESPOONS UNSALTED BUTTER

9 HEADS BELGIAN ENDIVE, HALVED LENGTHWISE
   AND STEM ENDS TRIMMED BUT NOT CORED

JUICE OF 1/2 LEMON

1/2 TEASPOON SEA SALT

FRESHLY GROUND BLACK PEPPER

BÉCHAMEL

3 TABLESPOONS UNSALTED BUTTER

1/4 CUP ALL-PURPOSE FLOUR

3 CUPS WHOLE MILK

SEA SALT AND FRESHLY GROUND BLACK PEPPER

FRESHLY GRATED NUTMEG, FOR SEASONING

A FEW DASHES OF TABASCO SAUCE

1 1/2 CUPS GRATED AGED GRUYÈRE CHEESE

6 LARGE SLICES COOKED HAM [SUCH AS BLACK FOREST
   OR HONEY-CURED]

1/4 TO 1/2 CUP GRATED AGED GRUYÈRE CHEESE

1/4 TO 1/2 CUP GRATED PARMESAN CHEESE

endive

In a large sauté pan, melt 4 tablespoons of the butter over medium heat. When the butter is hot, place the endive halves, cut side down, in the pan and sauté for 5 minutes, until the edges are caramelized. Turn the endive halves and cook, adding some or all of the remaining 2 tablespoons butter if the endives threaten to scorch, for 3 to 5 minutes, until the outer leaves are tender. Season with the lemon juice, salt, and pepper and continue to cook for 8 to 10 minutes, until just tender. Remove from the heat and reserve until needed.

To make the béchamel, in a sauce pan, melt the butter over medium-low heat. Sprinkle in the flour and cook, stirring constantly with a wooden spoon, until aromatic and the raw smell of flour is gone. Do not allow the roux to brown. Slowly pour in the milk while stirring constantly, and then cook, continuing to stir, for 5 to 8 minutes, until thickened to the consistency of thick cream and it coats the back of the spoon. Season with the salt, pepper, nutmeg, and Tabasco. Add the Gruyère cheese and stir just until melted. Remove from the heat and let cool slightly.

To assemble the gratin(s), butter 1 large or 6 small gratin dishes. (The large dish should accommodate the endives, snuggly but not crowded, in a single layer.) Cut the ham slices in half crosswise, and wrap a piece of ham around the center of each endive half. Place the endive halves, cut side up, in the prepared dish(es). Pour the béchamel evenly over the top and sprinkle with the Gruyère and Parmesan. (At this point, the dish may be covered and refrigerated for up to 2 hours before baking.)

Preheat the oven to 400°F. Bake until golden brown and yummy. This could take anywhere from 15 to 30 minutes, or more, depending on how cold everything is when you put the dish(es) in the oven. If everything looks cooked through, but the top is not nicely browned, pop the dish(es) under the broiler (make sure they are broiler safe) for a few minutes to finish caramelizing around the edges. The dish should be hot and bubbling when served.

CARAMELIZED APPLE CREPES
WITH BITTERSWEET CHOCOLATE SAUCE
AND VANILLA ICE CREAM

The Belgians are serious crepe makers—as serious as their French neighbors—and they are also serious apple growers, making this a perfect dessert for a Belgian menu. I like to serve two crepes per person for this dessert. My dad always rolled crepes, so that is what I tend to do, but they may also be folded into quarters. Even for seasoned professionals, the first crepe often doesn't work, so don't get discouraged if this happens. If you have dogs, they will love it.

For a simpler variation, skip the apples and serve the warm crepes with chocolate sauce and ice cream. The crepes and the chocolate sauce may be made ahead. Although the chocolate sauce will keep for up to 2 weeks, I don't make it too long before I need it because it has a tendency to disappear. | SERVES 6

CREPES

1/3 CUP ALL-PURPOSE OR WHOLE WHEAT FLOUR

1 CUP WHOLE MILK OR BEER

1/4 CUP BRANDY OR COGNAC

3 EGGS

1 TABLESPOON SUGAR

PINCH OF SEA SALT

1 TABLESPOON OLIVE OIL OR MELTED BUTTER

UNSALTED BUTTER OR NONSTICK
    COOKING SPRAY, FOR COOKING

CARAMELIZED APPLES

3 TO 5 TABLESPOONS UNSALTED BUTTER

4 TO 6 APPLES, HALVED, PEELED, CORED,
    AND THICKLY SLICED

6 TABLESPOONS SUGAR

GRATED ZEST AND JUICE OF 1 LEMON

1/4 TEASPOON PURE VANILLA EXTRACT

CHOCOLATE SAUCE

5 OUNCES BITTERSWEET CHOCOLATE, FINELY CHOPPED

2 TABLESPOONS UNSALTED BUTTER

2 TABLESPOONS DARK RUM

1/2 CUP HEAVY CREAM OR WATER

1 QUART PREMIUM VANILLA ICE CREAM

bittersweet chocolate

To make the crepe batter, in a bowl, whisk together the flour, milk, brandy, eggs, sugar, salt, and oil until smooth. (Alternatively, whirl the ingredients together in a blender.) If necessary, strain the batter through a fine-mesh sieve to remove any lumps. (The batter may be covered and refrigerated for up to 8 hours before cooking.)

Heat an 8-inch sauté pan over medium-high heat and coat it liberally with butter. When the butter is hot, fill a 1 1/2-ounce (3-tablespoon) ladle with batter, lift the pan off of the heat, and starting at the side opposite the handle, slowly pour the batter into the pan, tilting and rotating the pan as you go to get a thin, even layer across the bottom. (You might only need 1 ounce—you want the crepes very thin.) Return the pan to the heat and cook for 1 1/2 to 2 minutes, until the batter is set and the crepe is starting to caramelize in areas on the underside. Using a thin metal spatula or your favorite spatula, turn the crepe and cook for just a moment or two longer on the second side, until cooked but not brown, 30 seconds more. Transfer the crepe to a plate. Repeat with the remaining batter, stacking the crepes as they are finished. Cover the stack with a kitchen towel until needed. You should have 12 crepes.

Preheat the oven to 350°F. Butter a baking dish.

To prepare the apples, melt 3 tablespoons of the butter in a large sauté pan over medium heat. When the butter is hot, add the apples and sauté, shaking the pan, for just a minute or two. Sprinkle the sugar over the apples and let the apples caramelize slowly, shaking the pan often, for 6 to 8 minutes. (Depending on how juicy the apples are, you might need to reduce the heat to cook them through and add the remaining butter to properly caramelize them.) When the apples are nicely caramelized, stir in the lemon zest and juice and the vanilla. Remove from the heat.

Fill the crepes with the apples, using about 2 to 3 tablespoons for each crepe and either rolling them or folding them (see at right). Arrange the crepes in the prepared baking dish. (If the crepes are rolled, place them seam side down in the dish.) They should fit in a relatively snug single layer but not be too crowded. Bake for 8 minutes, until hot and golden.

While the crepes are baking, make the chocolate sauce. Pour water to a depth of about 1 inch into a large, shallow pan and bring to a simmer. Place the chocolate, butter, and rum in a heatproof bowl that will sit nicely over the pan with the simmering water. Place over the water and heat, stirring often, until the chocolate and butter are melted and the mixture is smooth. Stir in the cream, remove from the heat, and keep warm. (The sauce may be made up to 1 week ahead, cooled, covered, and refrigerated. Reheat in a water bath just before serving.)

To serve, place 2 crepes on each plate and top with a big scoop of ice cream and some warm chocolate sauce.

TIPS AND TRICKS

HOW TO STUFF A CREPE THE CLASSIC WAY
THE FIRST SIDE OF THE CREPE COOKS LONGER, SINCE THE SECOND SIDE IS JUST FINISHED; AS A RESULT, THE FIRST SIDE HAS NICER COLOR, SO YOU WANT TO ALWAYS PLACE THE FILLING ON THE SECOND SIDE. LAY THE CREPE IN FRONT OF YOU AND SPOON SOME OF THE FILLING ON THE TOP HALF, KEEPING THE FILLING AWAY FROM THE TOP, LEFT, AND RIGHT EDGES. FOLD THE BOTTOM HALF OF THE CREPE UP OVER THE TOP, AND THEN FOLD THE CREPE IN HALF AGAIN, LEFT TO RIGHT. YOU WILL END UP WITH A QUARTER CIRCLE.

HOW TO STUFF A CREPE DAD'S WAY
LAY THE CREPE IN FRONT OF YOU AND SPOON THE FILLING IN A LINE ACROSS THE CREPE, POSITIONING IT ABOUT ONE-THIRD OF THE WAY ABOVE THE CREPE EDGE NEAREST YOU. KEEP THE FILLING AWAY FROM THE LEFT AND RIGHT EDGES OF THE CREPE. WORKING FROM THE CREPE EDGE NEAREST YOU, ROLL UP THE CREPE AROUND THE FILLING.

milk

apples

lemon zest

wheat BEER

sugar

ENGLAND

When I was sixteen, my sister Mary wanted to study textile dying in Peru, but our father could not see sending her to South America because a civil war was raging there at the time. Mary did a lot of research and instead went to England to join a group of women who had studied weaving and working with natural dyes and had set up a cottage industry in Sussex County. I got to visit her (I'm still amazed that my dad let me go) and fell in love with the country the minute I stepped off the plane. I still like everything about England, especially London—the people, the culture, the aesthetic—and I go there as often as I can.

The food in London was not nearly as good on that first trip as it is now, and some of the best changes have taken place in the gastropubs, the inspiration for this menu. These lively gathering places, which first appeared in the early 1990s and combine high-quality food and high-end beer, remind me of Mustards Grill. When Mustards opened in 1983, our customers came in still wearing their winery boots and blue jeans.

I always liked the idea of people being able to sit down to a great meal without having to dress up. The gastropubs feel the same way. They are full of young, hip chefs who, instead of doing the Michelin-star thing, are focusing on making great food in a comfortable, easygoing spot that makes you want to settle in and stay until the doors close for the night.

PEA SOUP

WITH SERRANO HAM

Basically, with this recipe, you make a potato-leek soup and then add the peas at the very end. Cook the peas separately and shock them in ice water to keep the soup bright green. Fresh English peas taste great, but frozen peas can be used in a pinch. Add them to the blender straight from the freezer with some of the hot soup. This soup is delicious hot or chilled. | SERVES 6 TO 8

2 TABLESPOONS UNSALTED BUTTER, OR 1 TABLESPOON
    EACH BUTTER AND EXTRA VIRGIN OLIVE OIL

1 SMALL YELLOW ONION, DICED

1 SMALL LEEK, WHITE AND LIGHT GREEN PARTS ONLY, DICED

5 CUPS CHICKEN STOCK [PAGE 59] OR STORE-BOUGHT
    REDUCED-SODIUM BROTH

1 LARGE RUSSET OR YUKON GOLD POTATO, PEELED AND DICED

1/2 TEASPOON SEA SALT

1/4 TEASPOON FRESHLY GROUND BLACK PEPPER

4 OR 5 MACE BLADES, FINELY CHOPPED OR GROUND

3 CUPS FRESH OR FROZEN ENGLISH PEAS

1 TABLESPOON EXTRA VIRGIN OLIVE OIL

3 SLICES SERRANO HAM

CRÈME FRAÎCHE, FOR GARNISH

WHOLE CHERVIL LEAVES, JULIENNED MINT LEAVES, OR
    MINCED TARRAGON, FOR GARNISH

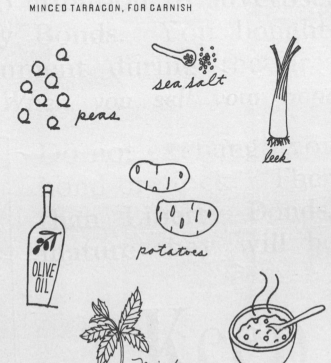

In a large pot, melt the butter over medium heat. When the butter is hot, add the onion and leek, cover, and cook, stirring occasionally, for about 8 minutes, until tender. Do not let the vegetables caramelize. If they begin to color, decrease the heat slightly. Add the stock, potato, salt, pepper, and mace, re-cover, and cook for 15 to 20 minutes, until the potato is tender. To check for doneness, see if you can easily mash a piece against the side of the pot. Remove from the heat and reserve. Let cool for 1 to 2 hours if you want a chilled soup.

If using fresh peas, bring a saucepan filled with water to a boil. Have ready an ice bath. Add the peas to the boiling water and cook for 3 to 5 minutes, just until tender. Using a slotted spoon or wire skimmer, transfer the peas to the ice bath and leave until cool, then drain the peas. If serving the soup cold, transfer the peas to a blender or food processor and process until a smooth puree forms. Add the reserved soup once it is cool and blend. Cover and refrigerate for at least 1 to 2 hours, until chilled. If serving the soup hot, blend the reserved soup with an immersion blender or in a standard blender. Just before serving, swirl in the pea puree and heat until hot but still a vibrant green. If you prefer a rustic texture, add the puree to the soup as is. For a smooth, elegant soup, pass the puree through a fine-mesh sieve.

In a sauté pan or skillet, heat the olive oil over high heat. When the oil is hot, add the ham and fry for 1 to 2 minutes, until crispy. Using tongs, transfer the ham to paper towels to drain and then crumble when cool enough to handle.

Ladle the soup into bowls—warmed or chilled—and garnish with the ham, crème fraîche, and chervil. Serve right away.

DEEP-FRIED SMELT

WITH PAPRIKA AIOLI

At the restaurant, we call these "fries with eyes" because we buy small smelt—about the size of your little finger—and leave them whole. You can also use the larger Lake Superior fish, but you have to cut off their heads, gut them (see opposite), and fry fewer in each batch. This is also a great way to prepare calamari and fresh anchovies.

The trick to getting an ultracrispy crust is to dust the fish with a dry mix of cornstarch and chickpea flour or semolina before frying and to fry in oil that is hot enough. Before I fry the dusted fish, I like to place them in a big sieve with a handle and shake them to release the excess dry mix. For additional thoughts on deep-frying, see page 276. | SHOWN PAGE 85 | SERVES 6 TO 8

PAPRIKA AIOLI
2 EGG YOLKS
JUICE OF 1/2 LEMON [ABOUT 2 TABLESPOONS]
1 TABLESPOON DRY SHERRY
4 OR 5 CLOVES GARLIC, MINCED
1 TABLESPOON SPANISH SMOKED PAPRIKA
1 TEASPOON CUMIN SEEDS, TOASTED IN A DRY PAN
    UNTIL FRAGRANT AND THEN GROUND [SEE PAGE 23]
1/2 TEASPOON SEA SALT
1/4 TEASPOON FRESHLY GROUND BLACK PEPPER
3/4 CUP TO 1 CUP EXTRA VIRGIN OLIVE OIL

1 CUP CORNSTARCH
1 CUP CHICKPEA FLOUR OR SEMOLINA
1/2 TEASPOON SEA SALT
1/4 TEASPOON FRESHLY GROUND BLACK PEPPER
CORN, CANOLA, OR PEANUT OIL, FOR DEEP-FRYING
1 POUND TINY SMELT, ANCHOVIES, OR WHITEBAIT,
    CLEANED [SEE PAGE 81]
2 TABLESPOONS MINCED FRESH FLAT-LEAF PARSLEY
    LEAVES, RINSED AND SQUEEZED DRY [SEE PAGE 83]
LEMON OR LIME WEDGES, FOR GARNISH

To make the aioli, in a blender, combine the egg yolks, lemon juice, sherry, garlic, paprika, cumin, salt, and pepper and process at high speed until smooth, 1 to 2 minutes. With the motor running, pour in 3/4 cup of the olive oil in a thin, slow, steady stream and process just until the oil is incorporated. Taste and if the taste is good—not too eggy and not too oily—blend for about 1 minute longer, until thick and creamy. If it tastes too eggy, add up to 1/4 cup of the remaining oil to your liking (again with the motor running and in a thin, steady stream). If it tastes too oily, add a few drops of lemon juice, ice water, or vinegar. When you are happy with the taste, put the aioli in a serving dish and refrigerate until needed. (You can also make the aioli by hand. In a bowl, whisk together the eggs yolks and seasonings until thick and smooth, and then whisk in the oil, a drop at a time at first and then in a thin, slow, steady stream. Transfer to a bowl, cover, and refrigerate until the fish is ready.)

Line a baking sheet with parchment paper and place it next to the stove. (Do not use paper towels; the fish will stick to them.) In a large bowl, whisk together the cornstarch, chickpea flour, salt, and pepper. Alternatively, pass the ingredients together through a sifter to ensure that everything is well mixed and free of lumps. Pour the oil to a depth of 2 to 3 inches into a deep, wide, heavy saucepan and heat to 375°F on a deep-frying thermometer.

cumin

Sherry

sea salt

lemon

Working in small batches, dust the fish with the cornstarch mixture, shaking off the excess, and drop into the hot oil. Fry for about 2 minutes for small fish or 3 minutes for larger fish, until golden brown. Using a wire skimmer or slotted spoon, transfer to the prepared baking sheet. Repeat with the remaining fish, always making sure the oil returns to 375°F before you add a new batch.

To serve, line a plate with a paper cocktail napkin, pile the crispy fish on the plate, and sprinkle with the parsley. Serve the aioli and the lemon wedges on the side.

TIPS AND TRICKS
PREPARING SMALL FISH

TO CHECK FOR SCALES ON A SMALL FISH, RUN YOUR FINGER FROM TAIL TO HEAD ALONG BOTH SIDES OF THE FISH. IF THE SKIN FEELS SMOOTH, YOU'RE GOOD TO GO. BUT IF YOU FEEL SHARP LITTLE SCALES (LARGER FISH WILL DEFINITELY HAVE THEM), YOU WILL NEED TO REMOVE THEM. TO DO THIS, USE EITHER A FISH SCALER OR THE DULL SIDE OF THE BLADE OF A SMALL PARING KNIFE (MAKE SURE YOU USE THE DULL SIDE AND NOT THE SHARP EDGE). GENTLY RUN THE SCALER OR KNIFE FROM THE TAIL TOWARD THE HEAD. YOU SHOULD SEE SCALES POPPING OFF (IT IS A GOOD IDEA TO DO THIS OVER A SHEET OF NEWSPAPER FOR EASY CLEANUP). IF YOU ARE GOING TO BE CUTTING THE FISH, RINSE IT UNDER COLD RUNNING WATER AND PAT DRY WITH PAPER TOWELS.

IF THE FISH ARE SMALL—NO BIGGER THAN YOUR LITTLE FINGER—YOU CAN FRY THEM WHOLE. IF THEY ARE ANY BIGGER THAN THAT, YOU WILL HAVE TO CUT OFF THE HEAD AND CUT EACH FISH. THIS SOUNDS HARDER THAN IT IS. JUST SLICE OFF THE HEAD AND THEN MAKE AN INCISION ALONG THE BELLY, FROM THE CHIN (OR WHERE THE CHIN USED TO BE) TO THE TAIL. USE YOUR THUMB TO SLIDE OUT THE ENTRAILS AND THEN DISCARD THEM. (IT IS IMPORTANT TO SCALE THE FISH BEFORE CUTTING IT BECAUSE YOU NEED THE FIRMNESS OF AN INTACT FISH FOR DOING THIS PART.) RINSE THE FISH UNDER COLD RUNNING WATER AND PAT DRY WITH PAPER TOWELS.

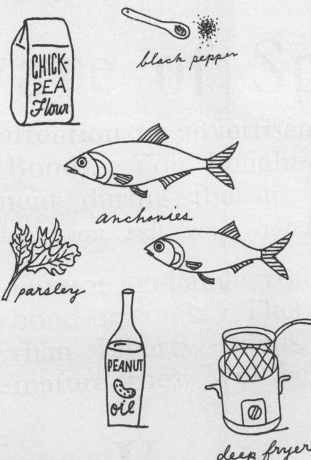

black pepper

CHICK-PEA Flour

anchovies

parsley

PEANUT oil

deep fryer

smelt

SOMERSET ROASTED CHICKEN

WITH BACON, DIJON, AND
CARAMELIZED APPLES BRAISED IN CIDER

When I made this dish for my husband, John, he said it was the best chicken he had ever tasted. The flavors of the apples, onion, and bacon coming together are what make this dish, a favorite of cooks in southwestern England, memorable. My friend Laura Chenel, who almost singlehandedly put fresh goat cheese in the American larder, gave me Lady Apples for Christmas one year, so I used them here, but this is good with any sweet-tart apple such as Braeburn or Gravenstein. I like to core the apples and leave the skin on. If you prefer to peel them, go ahead, but make sure you leave the chunks good size so the apples don't end up as applesauce.

Select a roasting pan with low sides so that all of the ingredients brown nicely. The directions call for finishing the sauce in the roasting pan on the stove top. This ensures that every last bit of the flavor that developed in the roasting pan gets into the sauce. If you prefer, you can finish the sauce in a saucepan, but you need to scrape up every bit possible from the roasting pan and transfer it to the new pan. | SHOWN PAGE 84 | SERVES 6 TO 8

MARINADE
LEAVES FROM 2 LONG ROSEMARY SPRIGS
2 CLOVES GARLIC, COARSELY CHOPPED
1 TEASPOON GROUND CUMIN
1 TEASPOON SEA SALT
2 TABLESPOONS FRESHLY GROUND BLACK PEPPER

1 WELL-RAISED CHICKEN, ABOUT 4 POUNDS
3 OR 4 ROSEMARY SPRIGS
UNSALTED BUTTER, FOR THE CHICKEN

To make the marinade, using a mortar and pestle, mash together the rosemary, garlic, cumin, salt, and pepper into a paste. Rub the paste evenly over the inside and outside of the bird, cover, and marinate in the refrigerator for at least 2 hours.

To roast the chicken, preheat the oven to 400°F. Truss the bird or tuck the wings under and tie the legs together. Break the rosemary sprigs into smaller pieces and tuck them into the cavity of the bird and in the wing and leg crevices. Rub butter on the bottom of a shallow roasting pan and then on the entire outside of the chicken.

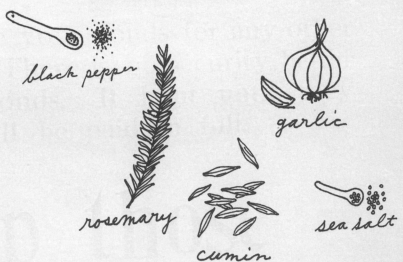

black pepper

garlic

rosemary

cumin

sea salt

1¹/₂ TABLESPOONS EXTRA VIRGIN OLIVE OIL

2 TABLESPOONS PURE MAPLE SYRUP

2 TEASPOONS SUGAR

1 SHALLOT, THINLY SLICED

2 LARGE YELLOW ONIONS, HALVED THROUGH THE STEM
   END AND THINLY SLICED INTO CRESCENTS

2 CLOVES GARLIC, MINCED

12 SMALL, FIRM APPLES (SUCH AS LADY APPLE), OR 4 LARGE
   APPLES (SUCH AS BRAEBURN OR GRAVENSTEIN),
   QUARTERED IF SMALL OR CUT INTO SIXTHS IF LARGE

3¹/₂ CUPS HARD CIDER

4 CUPS CHICKEN STOCK (PAGE 59) OR STORE-BOUGHT
   REDUCED-SODIUM BROTH

8 OUNCES BACON, DICED

2 TEASPOONS FRENCH DIJON MUSTARD

1 TO 2 TEASPOONS MINCED FRESH ROSEMARY

1 TO 2 TABLESPOONS MINCED FRESH FLAT-LEAF PARSLEY
   LEAVES, RINSED AND SQUEEZED DRY (SEE BELOW)

In a bowl, stir together the olive oil, maple syrup, sugar, shallot, onions, garlic, and apples. Pour the mixture into the bottom of the prepared roasting pan. Place the bird, breast side down, on the apple mixture. Pour 2 cups of the hard cider into the pan. In a bowl, stir together the remaining 1¹/₂ cups cider and the stock.

Pop the pan into the oven and roast the chicken, basting the bird with no more than ¹/₂ cup of the cider-stock mixture every 15 to 20 minutes, for 35 minutes. Then carefully flip the chicken breast side up, decrease the oven temperature to 375°F, and continue to roast, basting one more time, for 20 to 30 minutes, until the juices run clear when a thigh is pierced and the skin is a rich caramel color and crisp.

While the chicken is roasting, in a sauté pan, fry the bacon over medium heat until crisp. Using a slotted spoon, transfer the bacon to paper towels to drain.

When the chicken is ready, remove the pan from the oven and transfer the chicken to a platter. Tent the chicken with aluminum foil and let rest for about 15 minutes to allow the juices to settle back into the meat. To finish the sauce, first tilt the roasting pan at an angle and spoon off as much of the fat that rises to the surface as possible. Then put the roasting pan over 1 or 2 burners and turn on the heat to medium-high. Stir in the remaining stock-cider basting mixture, bring to a boil, and lower the heat to a simmer. Cook, scraping up all of the flavorful bits from the pan bottom, until the liquid is reduced by about one-third and is a nice juicy, but not watery, consistency. At the last minute, stir in the bacon, mustard, and rosemary and parsley to taste, mixing well.

To serve, pour some of the sauce onto a deep serving platter and place the bird on top. (Don't put any of the sauce on top of the bird because it will ruin the crispiness of the skin.) Pour the remaining sauce into a gravy boat. Carve the chicken and serve. Pass the sauce at the table.

TIPS AND TRICKS

A PARSLEY TRICK

I LIKE TO MINCE AND THEN RINSE MY PARSLEY. THIS MEANS THAT AFTER I MINCE IT, I SWEEP IT INTO A PAPER TOWEL, GIVE IT A GOOD RINSE IN COOL WATER, AND THEN WRING IT OUT. THIS REMOVES ANY HINT OF A GRASSY TASTE.

maple syrup

parsley

shallots

SOMERSET ROASTED
CHICKEN

FIGS POACHED
IN WHISKEY
AND HONEY

PAPRIKA AIOLI

DEEP-FRIED
SMELT

SIMPLE ROASTED
CARROTS
AND POTATOES

85

SIMPLE ROASTED CARROTS AND POTATOES

I wrote this recipe with the roasted chicken (see page 82) in mind, but one of my testers also liked it with pork chops. The carrots take longer to cook than the potatoes, so they need to be cut smaller. Tender, young carrots can be roasted whole. When I can find young rainbow carrots—red, yellow, white, and light and dark orange—I like to use them because all the different colors look wonderful. I scrub them well but don't peel them and I roast them whole. Put them in the baking dish with a little water, cover the dish, and place them in the oven for 15 to 20 minutes to get them going, then uncover, add the potatoes, dress with the olive oil and salt and pepper, add the wine, and continue as directed. | SHOWN PAGE 85 | SERVES 6 TO 8

8 TO 12 MEDIUM-SIZE POTATOES (SUCH AS YUKON GOLD, GERMAN BUTTERBALL, FRENCH FINGERLING, RUSSIAN FINGERLING, OR YELLOW FINN)

8 TO 12 BABY OR MIDSIZE CARROTS, ABOUT AS THICK AS YOUR THUMB, PEELED AND CUT INTO STICKS 4 TO 5 INCHES LONG

2 TO 3 TABLESPOONS OLIVE OIL

SEA SALT AND FRESHLY GROUND BLACK PEPPER

1/4 CUP DRY WHITE WINE OR WATER

1 TABLESPOON MINCED FRESH FLAT-LEAF PARSLEY, RINSED AND SQUEEZED DRY (SEE PAGE 83)

Preheat the oven to 375°F. (If you are cooking these in the same oven as the chicken, simply pop them into the oven when you decrease the heat to 375°F.)

Cut the potatoes in half, or quarter them if they are large. In a baking dish, combine the potatoes and carrots and spread in a single layer. Drizzle with 2 tablespoons of the olive oil, season with salt and pepper, and toss to coat, adding the remaining 1 tablespoon oil if needed to coat evenly. Pour in the wine.

Roast the vegetables until tender when pierced with a knife. The timing depends on the size of the vegetables, so begin checking after 10 to 15 minutes.

Remove from the oven, sprinkle with the parsley, and serve directly from the baking dish.

parsley

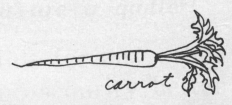
carrot

black pepper

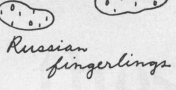
Russian fingerlings

olive oil

FIGS POACHED IN
SCOTCH WHISKY AND HONEY
WITH VANILLA ICE CREAM

High-quality dried figs have been slowly and evenly dried in the sun, so pass up dried figs with uneven dry patches or sunburned spots. You can make this dish with fresh figs, too, but I like keeping dried Turkish figs on hand for using up leftover wine. The flavor of the honey is important here, as well. Wildflower, orange blossom, or blackberry is a good choice. Chestnut honey would be too strong.

If you are cooking on a gas stove, use caution when adding the whisky. The alcohol will catch fire if it (or its vapors) comes into contact with the flame. Move the pan away from the burner before you add the whisky, and take care not to slosh the whisky-honey mixture over the side of the pan while you are cooking. | SHOWN PAGE 85 | SERVES 6 TO 8

2 CUPS DRY WHITE WINE

1/2 CUP FRESHLY SQUEEZED LEMON JUICE
   [FROM ABOUT 4 LEMONS]

1/2 LEMON, THINLY SLICED

18 DRIED FIGS

1/2 CUP MILD-FLAVORED HONEY

2 TABLESPOONS SCOTCH WHISKY,
   OR MORE IF YOU LIKE A STRONGER FLAVOR

1 QUART PREMIUM VANILLA ICE CREAM OR FROZEN YOGURT

To poach the figs, in a saucepan, combine the wine, lemon juice, and lemon slices and bring to a boil over high heat. Add the figs, decrease the heat to a simmer, and cook for 10 to 15 minutes for dried figs or 2 to 4 minutes for fresh, until the figs are tender. The timing will vary depending on the dryness of the figs.

Using a slotted spoon, transfer the figs to a plate and let cool. Add the honey and whisky to the pan off the heat and then return the pan to high heat. Bring to a boil and cook until reduced to a syrup. (At this point the figs and the syrup may be cooled, covered, and refrigerated overnight before continuing.)

Preheat the oven to 375°F. Cut the figs in half lengthwise and arrange them, cut side up and in a single, snug layer, in a gratin dish. Drizzle the figs with half of the syrup.

Bake the figs for 15 to 25 minutes, until they are caramelized and their edges are brown. About halfway through the baking, tilt the gratin dish, scoop up some of the sauce, and spoon it over the figs to moisten them. Move the figs a bit, too, to make sure they are not sticking, and then rotate the pan back to front to ensure even baking.

When the figs are ready, remove from the oven and let cool for a few minutes. To serve, place 1 or 2 scoops of ice cream in each serving dish and spoon the figs over the top. Drizzle the remaining syrup over the figs and ice cream and serve at once.

fig

IRELAND

My nephew Kristofer Hall now calls Ireland home. He fell in love with Emer Lang, married her, and moved to the Emerald Isle. So I have another excuse to eat Irish butter on potatoes, soda bread, and everything else butter is good with!

Ireland has the most beautiful dairy country—bright green grass carpeting gently undulating pastureland—the polar opposite of the golden brown hills and valleys of my California summers. It is also home to countless foragers in search of a wealth of wild greens, such as borage, sorrel, dandelions, garlic scapes, and arugula. They collect vegetables at the seaside, too, including carrageen, used primarily for desserts; dulse, which is transformed into a crisp snack food; and sea lettuce, which is tossed into salads or used as a garnish. Irish waters also deliver pristine oysters, scallops, salmon, turbot, Arctic char, and more, which made my decision on what to serve here difficult. For dessert, I crossed the border into Scotland and borrowed a classic scone recipe, knowing that the Irish are as crazy about scones as the Scots are, and dressed it up with Irish rolled oats.

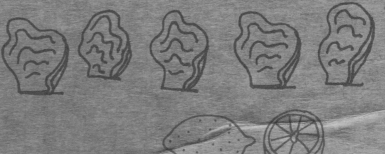

OYSTERS WITH IRISH SODA BREAD

AND GUINNESS STOUT

I like to eat this combination on the patio if it is a nice day, which in Ireland often means wearing a winter jacket. I have wonderful memories of being on holiday in Ireland and eating oysters with my family at picnic tables while looking out at the crashing waves. You can dress up the oysters in individual porcelain oyster plates or lay them on crushed ice on a big platter and have everyone gather around. Either way, make sure you shuck the oysters as close as possible to the time of serving. The soda bread is great with any Irish meal—or any other dish, for that matter.

Because I live on the West Coast, I use Skookum or Sweetwater, but every oyster region has its stars. For the mignonette, use the best-quality malt or cider vinegar you can find. Oddly enough, cheap malt vinegar is invariably either too high in acid and harsh or too bland. You want one that is bright and refreshing with medium acidity. My favorite brand is Sarson's, which is made in England and is 100 percent malted barley. The best cider vinegars are aromatic and taste like apples. Try as many as you can until you find one that suits your palate. | SERVES 6

SODA BREAD
2 1/2 CUPS WHOLE WHEAT FLOUR
1/2 CUP ALL-PURPOSE OR PASTRY FLOUR
1 TEASPOON BAKING SODA
1 TEASPOON SALT
2 CUPS BUTTERMILK
1 EGG
1 TABLESPOON VEGETABLE OIL
1 TEASPOON HONEY

Preheat the oven to 375°F. Butter a 9 by 5-inch loaf pan.

To make the soda bread, in a large bowl, stir together the flours, baking soda, and salt, mixing well. In a separate bowl, whisk together the buttermilk, egg, oil, and honey until well blended. Pour the buttermilk mixture into the flour mixture and stir until a dough forms.

Pour the dough into the prepared loaf pan and smooth the top as well as you can. Bake for 45 to 60 minutes, until a toothpick inserted into the center comes out clean and dry. Alternatively, protecting your nondominant hand with a hot pad, invert the loaf onto the pad and tap the bottom with your other hand. If the loaf sounds hollow, it is ready. Let the loaf cool completely on a rack.

CONTINUED

Oysters with Irish Soda Bread, *continued*

MIGNONETTE

1 CUP MALT OR CIDER VINEGAR [OR CHAMPAGNE
    VINEGAR OR RED WINE VINEGAR IF YOU CANNOT
    FIND THE OTHERS]
3/4 CUP MINCED SHALLOT
1/4 TEASPOON SEA SALT
1 TO 1 1/2 TABLESPOONS COARSELY CRACKED
    BLACK PEPPERCORNS

CRUSHED ICE, FOR SERVING
36 FRESH OYSTERS, SCRUBBED
LEMON WEDGES, FOR SERVING
TABASCO SAUCE, FOR SERVING
1/2 CUP BUTTER, FOR SERVING WITH THE SODA BREAD
GUINNESS STOUT, FOR SERVING

To make the mignonette, in a small bowl, whisk together the vinegar, shallot, salt, and pepper to taste. Cover and refrigerate until serving.

To prepare the oysters, line a large platter with a layer of crushed ice. Using an oyster knife, shuck each oyster carefully: protect the hand that is holding the oyster with a thick towel and position the oyster with the flatter side up, the rounded end pointing toward your thumb and fingers, and the pointed end—the hinged end—pointing toward you. Insert the knife at the oyster's hinge and twist sharply to snap the hinge. Slip the knife along the inside of the top shell and lift off and discard the shell. Then slide the knife under the oyster to sever the adductor muscle, freeing the oyster from the shell. Leave the oyster in the bottom (deeper) shell and try not to spill any of the oyster liquid. Check for shell fragments and remove any that you find. Nest the oyster in the bed of ice and shuck the remaining oysters the same way.

Serve the oysters with the lemon wedges and Tabasco on the side. Demitasse spoons are handy for spooning on the Tabasco. Seafood forks are optional, as the oysters have been freed from the shells. Slice the soda bread and place in a bread basket or let your guests slice their own pieces, as you see fit. Serve with plenty of Irish butter and Guinness Stout!

peppercorns

shallots

sea salt

VINEGAR

GUINESS

lemon

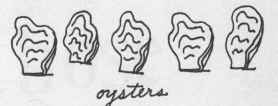

oysters

IRISH BUTTER-POACHED SCALLOPS

WITH LEEKS AND SWEET GARDEN PEAS

Irish butter is much richer and has fewer milk solids than the everyday butter sold in the United States. You can substitute the more widely available European-style butter, which, like Irish butter, is higher in butterfat than standard U.S. butter. Kerrygold brand is my favorite, and Plugrá is a popular brand. I like to use big scallops for this dish because they are easier to cook all at once in a couple of big pans. While looking for a vegetable to go with the scallops, I found two recipes, one for butter-cooked leeks and one for milk-cooked leeks, both of them in Coleman Andrews's excellent *The Country Cooking of Ireland*. They were so similar to my mom's creamed peas—butter, salt, and pepper—that I went in the kitchen and made this combination of leeks and peas with what I had on hand. Use some Irish Soda Bread (see page 89) to mop it all up. | SERVES 6

GREMOLATA

1 CUP COARSELY SHREDDED DRIED BREAD CRUMBS

2 TO 3 TABLESPOONS OLIVE OIL

SEA SALT AND FRESHLY GROUND BLACK PEPPER

1 CLOVE GARLIC, FINELY MINCED

GRATED ZEST OF 1 LEMON

1/2 CUP CHOPPED FRESH FLAT-LEAF PARSLEY OR CHIVES

LEEKS AND PEAS

1 LARGE LEEK, WHITE AND LIGHT GREEN PARTS ONLY, OUTER LAYERS DISCARDED AND THINLY SLICED (3 TO 3 1/2 CUPS)

2 TABLESPOONS UNSALTED BUTTER

3 TABLESPOONS CRÈME FRAÎCHE OR HEAVY CREAM

1/4 CUP WATER

1/2 TEASPOON SEA SALT

7 GRINDS OF BLACK PEPPER

1 3/4 TO 2 CUPS SHELLED FRESH OR FROZEN ENGLISH PEAS

12 TO 18 JUMBO SCALLOPS, DEPENDING ON EVERYONE'S APPETITE

SEA SALT AND FRESHLY GROUND BLACK PEPPER

1 CUP CLARIFIED IRISH BUTTER (SEE PAGE 255)

GRATED ZEST AND JUICE OF 2 LEMONS

WATERCRESS SPRIGS, FOR GARNISH

To make the *gremolata*, preheat the oven to 350°F. Put the bread crumbs in a small bowl, drizzle with the olive oil, season with salt and pepper, and toss to coat evenly. Spread in a pie pan or small baking sheet and toast for 7 to 8 minutes, until golden brown. Remove from the oven and let cool completely. Just before serving, stir in the garlic, lemon zest, and parsley.

To prepare the leeks and peas, in a saucepan, combine the leek, butter, crème fraîche, water, salt, and pepper and bring to a boil. Reduce the heat to a simmer and cook for 1 to 2 minutes, until the leeks are a little tender and the sauce is reducing. Use your best judgment as to when to add the peas. If they are fresh but starchy they may take some time, so add them as soon as the leeks start to soften. If they are frozen, they may take just 2 to 3 minutes, so add them at the end. Shake the pan occasionally during cooking to change what is on the bottom of the pan with what is on the top. Cook until the vegetables are tender.

Once the vegetables are cooking, season the scallops on both sides with salt and pepper. In a big sauté pan (large enough to hold all of the scallops in a single layer), melt the butter over medium heat. When the butter is hot and foamy, add the scallops and poach gently for 3 to 5 minutes, basting as needed, until just done. They are ready when they feel just firm to the touch.

To serve, spoon the vegetables into individual deep plates or shallow soup bowls and top with the scallops. Add the lemon zest and juice to the butter from the scallop pan, then drizzle over the scallops. Sprinkle with some of the *gremolata* and garnish with the watercress.

FORAGER'S SALAD

The Irish climate is perfect for cultivating many different kinds of wonderful greens, but foraging for wild greens is also a national tradition, and many of the Irish cookbooks I have describe how to make delicious salads and other dishes from them. I know we cannot all go out into the woods and meadows to find our greens, but I do want to encourage you to put on the forager's cap to find new additions to your salads. Even if you never leave the island of Manhattan, you can find interesting salad candidates at local farmers' markets, upscale produce shops, and everyday grocery stores.

Have fun when you prepare this salad. Go for a variety of flavors and textures to keep it interesting, and be creative when you cut the vegetables: chop some small, leave some in big, dramatic pieces, shred some on a box grater, and so on. A Japanese mandoline-style slicer, a Mouli Julienne slicer (hard to find nowadays, except in secondhand stores), or the grater-slicer attachment of a stand mixer makes quick work of cutting the ingredients. | SERVES 6

VINAIGRETTE
2 TABLESPOONS CIDER, RED, OR WHITE WINE VINEGAR OR
    FRESHLY SQUEEZED LEMON JUICE
1 TABLESPOON DIJON MUSTARD (OPTIONAL)
1 SHALLOT OR CLOVE GARLIC, MINCED
SEA SALT AND FRESHLY GROUND BLACK PEPPER
6 TABLESPOONS EXTRA VIRGIN OLIVE OIL

4 TO 6 CUPS GREENS (SUCH AS BABY BEET GREENS, KALE,
    AND CHARD; WATERCRESS; ARUGULA; DANDELION GREENS;
    BUTTER LETTUCES; MUSTARD GREENS; AND CHICORIES)

VEGETABLES
CARROTS, PREFERABLY A MIX OF COLORS,
    PEELED AND SLICED
TURNIPS, PEELED AND GRATED
FENNEL BULB, THINLY SLICED, AND FRONDS
CELERY, THINLY SLICED
BEETS, COOKED AND SLICED OR
    FINELY SHAVED OR JULIENNED RAW
FINELY SHAVED CUCUMBER
GREEN ONIONS, WHITE AND LIGHT GREEN
    PARTS ONLY, SLICED
SUGAR SNAP PEAS, BLANCHED AND SLICED
BOILING POTATOES, COOKED AND CUBED OR SLICED
PEA SHOOTS, TRIMMED

celery

SOFT HERBS SUCH AS TARRAGON, BASIL, MINT, AND CHIVES,
    SMALL LEAVES LEFT WHOLE AND LARGE LEAVES STEMMED
    AND CHOPPED
FLOWERS SUCH AS BORAGE, VIOLETS, NASTURTIUMS, AND
    CHIVE BLOSSOMS, FOR SPRINKLING
1 CUP WALNUTS OR HAZELNUTS, TOASTED (SEE PAGE 23),
    FOR GARNISH
6 OUNCES ARTISANAL IRISH OR AMERICAN BLUE CHEESE,
    CRUMBLED, FOR GARNISH

To make the vinaigrette, in a small bowl, whisk together the vinegar, mustard, shallot, and a pinch each of salt and pepper until the salt dissolves. Gradually whisk in the olive oil in a slow, steady stream and continue to whisk until well emulsified. Set aside.

Select an assortment of 3 to 5 greens and place in a large mixing bowl. Select a few of the vegetable suggestions and a few of the herbs suggestions and add to the bowl. Whisk the vinaigrette briefly to recombine, drizzle over the greens and vegetables, and toss to coat lightly and evenly. Sprinkle a handful of flowers over the top, garnish with the nuts and cheese, and serve right away.

beets

SHORTCAKES
WITH STRAWBERRY SAUCE

This recipe makes more than you need for your dinner party guests, because I like to eat leftover shortcakes the next morning. Split them, toast them, and eat 'em with butter and jam or jam and whipped cream, as my stepkids do. For a perfect dessert make these oat-rich shortcakes and top them with the ruby red strawberry sauce and crème fraîche. | SERVES 10 TO 12

3 CUPS ALL-PURPOSE FLOUR

1 CUP WHOLE WHEAT FLOUR

1/2 CUP ROLLED OATS

1/4 CUP WHEAT GERM

6 TABLESPOONS GRANULATED SUGAR

4 TEASPOONS BAKING POWDER

1 TEASPOON BAKING SODA

1 TEASPOON SALT

1 1/2 CUPS COLD UNSALTED BUTTER, CUT INTO 1/2-INCH PIECES

2 1/4 CUPS SOUR CREAM, OR 2 CUPS SOUR CREAM
    AND 1/4 CUP WHOLE MILK OR HEAVY CREAM

2 EGG YOLKS

2 EGG WHITES MIXED WITH 2 TABLESPOONS
    WATER, FOR AN EGG WASH

CRYSTAL SUGAR [OPTIONAL]

STRAWBERRY SAUCE

2 PINTS FRESH STRAWBERRIES, HULLED

1/4 CUP GRANULATED SUGAR

JUICE OF 1 ORANGE

SEEDS SCRAPED FROM 1/2 VANILLA BEAN

2 CUPS CRÈME FRAÎCHE OR WHIPPED CREAM

Preheat the oven to 375°F. Line a rimmed baking sheet with parchment paper.

In a large bowl, stir together both flours, and the rolled oats, wheat germ, granulated sugar, baking powder, baking soda, and salt. Scatter the butter over the top and, using a pastry blender or a pair of knives, cut in the butter until it is the size of peas.

In a medium bowl, whisk together the sour cream and egg yolks until blended. Make a well in the center of the flour mixture and pour in the sour cream mixture. Using a wooden spoon, stir until a rough dough forms.

Turn the dough out onto a lightly floured work surface and knead gently a few times until it comes together. Form the dough into a disk about 10 inches in diameter and 1 1/2 to 2 inches thick. Cut the disk in half and then cut each half into 6 wedges. Transfer the wedges to the prepared baking sheet. Brush lightly with the egg wash. Sprinkle with the crystal sugar, if desired.

Bake for about 20 minutes, until golden. Transfer the cakes to a rack and let cool.

To make the sauce, halve or quarter lengthwise 1 pint of the berries, depending on their size. In a food processor or blender, combine the remaining 1 pint of berries, the granulated sugar, and the orange juice. Using the tip of a knife, scrape the seeds from the vanilla bean into the processor. Process until a smooth puree forms. Transfer to a bowl. If you prefer a very smooth sauce, pass it through a fine-mesh sieve into the bowl. (Sometimes, I just put the berries in a bowl, mash them with the back of a fork, and then mix in the sugar, orange juice, and vanilla seeds.) Add the cut berries to the puree, stir to mix, and reserve until needed.

To serve, preheat the oven to 350°F. Return the cakes to the baking sheet and place in the oven for about 5 minutes, until hot and just beginning to get toasty. Remove from the oven, and when cool enough to handle, split each cake horizontally with a fork. Place the bottom of each cake on a dessert plate and top with a liberal amount of the strawberry sauce and a healthy dollop of the crème fraîche. Cover with the cake tops and spoon the remaining strawberry sauce on top. Finish with a dollop of crème fraîche. Serve right away.

SWEDEN AND NORWAY

This Scandinavian supper reminds me of nights when my mother would serve "chilled" canned salmon, fresh-dug potatoes with dill or chive butter, and tomatoes with vinaigrette. I also remember only spelling out my last name when asked. I knew if I just said it, it would be spelled wrong (Paulson or Paulsen). And once I spelled and pronounced it, the Norwegians and Swedes of Minnesota—the state that proudly calls itself the center of Scandinavian American culture—would say, "What? That's not how you spell it!"

And then there were Mrs. Nelson's cookies. She was the mother of my science teacher in both grade school and junior high and she lived down the street. She baked incredible Christmas cookies—tables and tables of them. When you went into her house at holiday time, just about every flat surface would be covered with beautiful glass and ceramic plates, some of them three tiers tall, full of cookies of all sizes, shapes, and types. It was the Santa Claus land of cookies; in fact, it was better than a visit to Santa Claus.

But Mrs. Nelson's extraordinary display is not my only childhood cookie memory. Cookies seemed to be everywhere in the Minnesota of the 1950s and 1960s. At Halloween, Thanksgiving, and Easter, after school, and at Girl Scout meetings, there were always cookies. If someone dropped in for a visit, you would put on a pot of coffee and bring out something baked. My mom made "egg coffee" by boiling water, mixing the ground coffee with egg, and then stirring the ground coffee into the boiling water. After it steeped for five minutes, it was ready and you poured it through a tiny strainer into a cup. It was a somewhat complicated process and it was very special. The result was a rich, mild coffee that seemed to taste best in the good china cups stored at the back of the cupboard. It was made with bottled spring water, never tap water, yet more evidence of how special it was. I have never forgotten egg coffee, and now my home has filtered water for coffee and tea—and plenty of cookies for every occasion. Some things are in the hardwiring. This menu includes three of my favorites.

SWEDISH MEATBALLS

Before I cook these meatballs, I gently press a little indentation in the top of each one, to make a little holder for some of the fruit sauce. After they are cooked, I roll them lightly in the "gravy" (as my Minnesota Swedish neighbors called it), then spoon a little cranberry into the indentations. The trick is to have the gravy and the cranberry sauce ready and waiting for the meatballs the moment they come out of the oven. I prefer cranberry sauce, but lingonberry jam is classic and any tart jelly or jam would be good. I like the hint of allspice in meatballs. That spice isn't used much anymore, and it should be. Here, the meatballs are a first course, but they would make a good main course, too, accompanied with steamed wild rice and a green salad. | MAKES ABOUT 3 DOZEN 1½-INCH MEATBALLS; SERVES 12 AS AN APPETIZER, 6 AS AN ENTREE

GRAVY

2 TABLESPOONS UNSALTED BUTTER
2 TABLESPOONS ALL-PURPOSE FLOUR
1½ CUPS CHICKEN STOCK [PAGE 59] OR
    STORE-BOUGHT REDUCED-SODIUM BROTH
½ CUP WHOLE MILK OR HEAVY CREAM
1 TABLESPOON CHOPPED FRESH DILL

unsalted butter

CRANBERRY SAUCE

1 POUND FRESH OR FROZEN CRANBERRIES
GRATED ZEST AND JUICE OF 1 LEMON
½ CUP SUGAR, PLUS MORE IF NEEDED
¼ CUP WATER, PLUS MORE IF NEEDED

MEATBALLS

1 TO 2 TABLESPOONS UNSALTED BUTTER
¼ CUP MINCED YELLOW ONION
⅔ POUND GROUND BEEF
⅔ POUND GROUND VEAL
⅔ POUND GROUND PORK
1½ CUPS FRESH BREAD CRUMBS
1½ TEASPOONS SALT
FRESHLY GROUND BLACK PEPPER
¼ TEASPOON FRESHLY GRATED NUTMEG
¼ TEASPOON GROUND ALLSPICE
¾ CUP WHOLE MILK
2 EGG YOLKS, OR 1 WHOLE EGG
CHOPPED FRESH DILL, FOR GARNISH

allspice

cranberries

To make the gravy, in a saucepan, melt the butter over medium heat. Sprinkle in the flour and then stir with a whisk or wooden spoon until the mixture is smooth and the color of caramel. Pour in the stock in a slow, steady stream while whisking or stirring constantly and bring to a boil. Add the cream and reduce over high heat, stirring occasionally, for 10 to 15 minutes, until the gravy is a nice thick consistency. Stir in the dill and set the sauce aside until you are ready to serve the meatballs.

To make the cranberry sauce, in a saucepan, combine all of the ingredients over medium-high heat and cook for about 15 minutes, until every cranberry has burst. Add more sugar if you like and more water if the pot seems dry. Remove from the heat and reserve.

To make the meatballs, in a large sauté pan, melt 1 tablespoon of the butter over medium heat. When the butter stops foaming, add the onion and sauté for about 5 minutes, until soft. If the pan seems too dry, add the remaining 1 tablespoon butter. When the onion is ready, set it aside to cool.

In a big bowl, combine the meats, bread crumbs, salt, a few grinds of pepper, nutmeg, allspice, milk, and egg yolks and mix together gently with your hands until the ingredients are evenly distributed. When the onion is cool, work it into the meat mixture.

CONTINUED

Swedish Meatballs, *continued*

Preheat the oven to 425°F. Line 2 baking sheets with parchment paper and lightly brush with canola oil or olive oil, or coat with nonstick cooking spray.

In a small skillet, sauté a little nugget of the meat mixture and then taste and adjust the seasoning of the mixture. When you are happy with the flavor, form the meat mixture into balls 1½ to 2 inches in diameter and place them on the prepared baking sheets, spacing them about 1 inch apart. You should get about 36 meatballs. Press a little indentation in the top of each meatball to form a spot to hold the cranberry sauce later.

Place in the oven and bake for about 20 minutes, until lightly browned all the way around but still tender and pink on the inside.

To serve, bring the gravy back to a simmer. Arrange the meatballs attractively in a casserole dish or other deep-sided serving platter and pour some of the sauce over and around them. Top some of them with a bit of cranberry sauce (in the little indentation), leaving some without for variety. Sprinkle with the dill and serve any additional gravy and/or cranberry sauce on the side.

SWEDISH SALTED CUCUMBER

cucumber

This is a simple and tasty side or condiment. I use an English (hothouse), Armenian, Lebanese, or Japanese cucumber, all of which are nearly seedless, rather than the "burpy"—as my dad used to call them—American cucumber that is loaded with seeds. (The Lebanese cucumber is smaller than the others, so you will need to use a couple of them here.) If you use the standard American cucumber, halve it lengthwise, scoop out the seeds, and then thinly slice into half-moons. | SERVES 6

1 CUCUMBER, PEELED AND THINLY SLICED
1 TEASPOON SEA SALT
⅓ CUP CHAMPAGNE VINEGAR OR RICE VINEGAR
2 TABLESPOONS SUGAR
¼ TEASPOON FRESHLY GROUND WHITE PEPPER
2 TABLESPOONS CHOPPED FRESH DILL

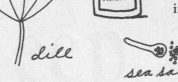

dill   sea salt

Put the cucumber slices in a shallow bowl, sprinkle with the salt, toss to coat evenly, and let sit for 20 minutes or so. Just before serving, rinse briefly under running cold water and squeeze gently to remove the excess moisture. Place in a serving bowl.

To make the dressing, whisk together the vinegar, sugar, pepper, and dill until well mixed. Pour over the cucumbers and toss to mix. You can make this ahead and chill until ready to serve, if you wish.

HALIBUT WITH WILD MUSHROOMS
and Horseradish Dilled Creamy Green Beans

I have broiled the halibut here, but it is also a great fish for cooking on a griddle. The surface caramelizes and keeps the interior moist. Both wild-caught Alaskan halibut, which has a high fat content (and is thus rich and moist) and wild-caught San Francisco halibut, which is leaner, would be good. San Francisco halibut, which is actually a type of flounder, should be cooked for less time than the Alaskan halibut or it will dry out. California white bass or black cod would also be good selections.

I used baby green beans from the garden. If you would like to simplify the vegetable step, you can finish the beans in the pan with the mushrooms instead of doing them in a separate pan. The dish won't look quite as fancy, but it will still taste good. If you feel like cooking a batch of mashed or steamed potatoes, they would be good with the halibut and beans. | SERVES 6

DILL BUTTER
3 TABLESPOONS UNSALTED BUTTER, AT ROOM TEMPERATURE
1 TABLESPOON MINCED FRESH DILL
1 TABLESPOON PREPARED OR GRATED FRESH HORSERADISH
SEA SALT AND FRESHLY GROUND BLACK PEPPER

6 (6-OUNCE) SKINLESS HALIBUT FILLETS
1 TO 2 TABLESPOONS OLIVE OIL, FOR BRUSHING THE FISH
SALT AND FRESHLY GROUND BLACK PEPPER
3 TABLESPOONS UNSALTED BUTTER
1/4 RED ONION, MINCED
12 TO 14 OUNCES FRESH WILD MUSHROOMS OR A MIXTURE
    OF FRESH CULTIVATED AND REHYDRATED DRIED
    WILD MUSHROOMS [SEE PAGE 101], TORN OR CUT INTO
    BITE-SIZE PIECES
4 TO 6 TABLESPOONS GRATED FRESH HORSERADISH,
    OR 2 TO 3 TABLESPOONS PREPARED HORSERADISH
2 TABLESPOONS AQUAVIT OR VODKA
1 CUP DRY WHITE WINE OR VERMOUTH
A FEW GRATINGS OF NUTMEG
1 1/2 TO 2 TABLESPOONS MINCED FRESH FLAT-LEAF PARSLEY
    LEAVES, RINSED AND SQUEEZED DRY [SEE PAGE 83]
6 TABLESPOONS HEAVY CREAM
12 OUNCES VERY YOUNG GREEN BEANS, STEMMED AND
    BLANCHED, OR REGULAR GREEN BEANS,
    TOPPED AND TAILED, STRINGED IF NECESSARY,
    CUT IN HALF, AND BLANCHED
1 TO 1 1/2 TABLESPOONS MINCED FRESH DILL

To make the dill butter, in a small bowl, mix together the butter, dill, and horseradish and season with salt and pepper. Reserve until needed.

Preheat the broiler. Brush both sides of the fish fillets with olive oil, season both sides with salt and pepper, and arrange on a broiler pan or rimmed baking sheet. Set aside.

In a large sauté pan, melt 1 tablespoon of the butter over medium-low heat. Add the onion, stir to coat, cover, and cook for about 5 minutes, until tender but not caramelized. Uncover the pan, stir in the mushrooms, and increase the heat to medium-high. Cook for 8 to 10 minutes, until the mushrooms have released and then reabsorbed their juices and are just beginning to caramelize around the edges.

black pepper

red onion

dill

parsley

Stir in the horseradish and then pour in the aquavit and cook for 3 to 5 minutes, until most of the alcohol has burned off. If you have a gas burner and are familiar with the technique, you can swirl the pan so that a little alcohol splashes over and ignites the vapors to burn the alcohol off more quickly. Add the wine and nutmeg and simmer for another 3 to 5 minutes, until the pan juices are mostly reduced. Season with salt and pepper, remove from the heat, and reserve until needed. (The mushrooms may be prepared up to this point up to 1 hour in advance, and set aside at room temperature.)

Measure the fish at the thickest point, then place under the broiler and broil for 7 minutes per inch of thickness, being careful not to overcook it. Finish the mushrooms and the green beans as the fish cooks.

To finish the mushrooms, reheat gently and stir in 1 tablespoon of the remaining butter and the parsley to taste. To finish the beans, in a separate sauté pan, heat the cream over medium-high heat and cook until reduced by half. Stir in the beans, dill, and the remaining 1 tablespoon butter. Season with salt and pepper and cook until the beans are heated through.

To serve, put a healthy pool of the mushrooms in the center of each warmed plate, push them out with the back of a spoon to make space for some green beans in the middle, and pile in some beans. Arrange the fish attractively down the side of the beans. Smear the fish with some of the dill butter and let it melt into the surface. Serve immediately.

TIPS AND TRICKS
REHYDRATING DRIED MUSHROOMS

THE PROCESS FOR REHYDRATING DRIED MUSHROOMS IS VERY SIMPLE. PUT THE DRIED MUSHROOMS IN A LARGE BOWL AND POUR ENOUGH BOILING WATER OVER TO COVER THEM. IF THEY TRY TO FLOAT UP, WEIGHT THEM DOWN WITH A BOWL OR A PLATE. ALLOW TO SOAK UNTIL SOFT. THE SOAKING TIME WILL VARY DEPENDING UPON THE DENSITY OF WHAT YOU ARE REHYDRATING: PORCINI WILL BE REHYDRATED WITHIN 10 TO 12 MINUTES, WHEREAS SHIITAKE MUSHROOMS CAN TAKE UPWARD OF 30 MINUTES. CHECK FOR PLIABILITY, AND WHEN SOFT LIFT THE REHYDRATED MUSHROOMS UP AND OUT OF THE SOAKING LIQUID WITH YOUR FINGERS OR A SLOTTED SPOON. IT IS ESPECIALLY IMPORTANT WITH THE MUSHROOMS THAT YOU DO NOT POUR THE LIQUID OVER THE REHYDRATED MUSHROOMS BECAUSE ALL OF THE DIRT AND GRIT HAS SETTLED TO THE BOTTOM—LEAVE IT THERE. ONCE STRAINED, THE SOAKING LIQUID MAKES A GREAT ADDITION TO SAUCES AND A WONDERFUL BASE FOR VEGGIE STOCK.

morel

king trumpet

halibut

white WINE

PEPPERKAKER

Most Norwegian Americans know these as ginger cookies. But when I was growing up in Minnesota, we got gingersnaps from my German grandmother and my half-Norwegian mother made these cookies and called them *pepperkaker*. Despite what you might assume from the name, the batter includes no pepper but does have a lot of spices. I normally would never use as much as I have listed here, but Beatrice Ojakangas, a well-respected Scandinavian food writer and cook, calls for the same amount in her recipe for the cookies. I found recipes for these cookies in four of my Scandinavian cookbooks and all of them were about the same. The main difference is that some call for dark corn syrup and some for dark molasses. I chose to go with the molasses because it has more iron than corn syrup (and to me, more flavor). Some of my tasters said they would prefer less clove, so cut back on it if you like. | MAKES ABOUT 60 COOKIES

2 CUPS ALL-PURPOSE FLOUR

SCANT 1 TEASPOON GROUND CLOVES

1 TEASPOON GROUND GINGER

1 TEASPOON GROUND CARDAMOM

2 TEASPOONS GRATED LEMON OR ORANGE ZEST

1 TEASPOON BAKING SODA

2/3 CUP UNSALTED BUTTER, AT ROOM TEMPERATURE

3/4 CUP PACKED DARK BROWN SUGAR

3 TABLESPOONS DARK MOLASSES

1 1/2 TABLESPOONS WATER, PLUS MORE IF NEEDED

CHOPPED ALMONDS OR MINCED CANDIED GINGER,
    FOR GARNISH [OPTIONAL]

POWDER SUGAR, FOR GARNISH

Preheat the oven to 350°F. Have ready 2 ungreased baking sheets or line each sheet with silicone baking mats or parchment paper.

In a medium bowl, stir together the flour, spices, lemon zest, and baking soda until well mixed. In a large bowl, using a wooden spoon, beat together the butter and brown sugar until light and creamy. Add the molasses and water and mix well.

Add the flour mixture to the butter mixture and mix until incorporated. If the dough is not coming together, add a tiny bit more water. Do not add too much or the dough will be a sticky mess when you try to roll it out. Gather the dough into a ball, divide

it in half, and flatten each half into a disk. Wrap separately in plastic wrap and chill for about 1 hour, until firm.

Remove 1 disk from the refrigerator. On a lightly floured work surface, roll out the dough 1/4 inch thick. (Alternatively, dust the disk with flour and roll out between 2 sheets of waxed paper.) Using a 2 1/2-inch round cookie cutter (or any shape you like), cut out as many cookies as possible. Transfer the cookies to a baking sheet, spacing them about 1 inch apart. Sprinkle each cookie with a pinch of almonds. Gather up the scraps, press into a disk, and refrigerate.

Bake the cookies for about 10 minutes, until set but not brown. Do not overbake. Let cool for a few minutes on the baking sheet and then transfer to racks to cool completely. While the first batch is baking, repeat the rolling and cutting with the second dough disk and then with the dough scraps, and then bake the second batch when the first batch comes out of the oven. If you like, roll or dust the cookies with powder sugar.

The cooled cookies may be stored in an airtight tin at room temperature for up to 1 week.

lemon zest

MOM'S SPRITZ COOKIES
WITH MOM'S HOT CHOCOLATE

These cookies are made with a cookie press, which you can find in most hardware or cookware stores. The press comes with nozzles or disks to make cookies in different shapes. I remember my mother making S-shaped cookies and sprinkling them with green or red sugar. She would occasionally make "wreaths," too, and sprinkle them with colored sugars. I consider these cookies Norwegian because my mother was half Norwegian, but they may be German, as she was half German, too.

A couple tips: The dough must not be too warm when you try to press it through the disk or it will come out mushy. Also, press the cookies out onto a cool baking sheet or they will lose their shape before they can be baked. When my mom and her girlfriends sent one another cards with cookie or other recipes written on them, they always wrote "good luck" on the card. So I am wishing you good luck, too. | SHOWN PAGE 103 | MAKES 45 TO 60 COOKIES, DEPENDING ON SHAPE

1 CUP UNSALTED BUTTER, AT ROOM TEMPERATURE
2/3 CUP SUGAR
3 EGG YOLKS
1 TEASPOON PURE ALMOND EXTRACT
2 1/2 CUPS ALL-PURPOSE FLOUR
RED OR GREEN CRYSTAL SUGAR, FOR SPRINKLING
MOM'S HOT CHOCOLATE (OPPOSITE), FOR SERVING

vanilla extract

sugar

unsalted butter

egg yolks

In a bowl, using a wooden spoon, beat together the butter and sugar until light and fluffy. Add the egg yolks and almond extract and beat until combined. Then add the flour and stir until well mixed. Gather the dough into a ball, divide into 4 equal pieces, wrap separately in plastic wrap, and refrigerate for at least 30 minutes, until chilled.

Preheat the oven to 400°F. Have 2 ungreased baking sheets ready or line each baking sheet with a silicone baking mat.

Read the manufacturer's directions for the cookie press before you begin. Remove 1 piece of dough from the refrigerator. To ease packing the dough into the press, shape it into a log slightly smaller in diameter than the press, and then slip it into the tube. Select a disk and secure it in place. Holding the press upright, and applying even pressure to the handle, press out cookies onto a baking sheet, spacing them about 1 inch apart. Repeat with a second dough piece. Sprinkle the cookies with red or green crystal sugar.

Bake the cookies for about 8 minutes, until golden. Let cool for a few minutes on the baking sheet, then transfer to racks to cool completely. While the first batch is baking, repeat with the remaining 2 dough pieces, pressing the cookies onto the second baking sheet, and then bake the second batch when the first batch comes out of the oven.

Put a handful of the cooled cookies on a plate and serve with the hot chocolate. Store the remaining cookies in an airtight tin at room temperature for up to 1 week.

MOM'S HOT CHOCOLATE

Everybody likes hot chocolate and cookies. This is how my mother made hot chocolate when I was kid—the perfect antidote to a Minnesota winter. Now that I am older, I sometimes use strong brewed coffee in place of the water and I add a shot of brandy when it's icy cold outside. Mom always made this in small batches, but feel free to double or triple the recipe if you have a crowd. | SERVES 2

4 TEASPOONS DUTCH-PROCESS UNSWEETENED COCOA
    POWDER (DROSTE BRAND IS MOM'S CHOICE)
5 TEASPOONS SUGAR
1/4 CUP WATER
1 1/2 CUPS WHOLE MILK
2 BIG MARSHMALLOWS, FOR SERVING

In a small, heavy saucepan, stir together the cocoa, sugar, and water and bring to a boil over medium heat. Add the milk and whisk continuously until hot. Do not allow it to boil. Pour into warmed mugs and top each mug with a marshmallow. Serve piping hot.

LEMON-LIME TARTLETS WITH BERRIES

I adapted the recipe for the tartlet shells from a recipe for *sandbakelse* (sand tarts) in *Swedish Recipes Old and New*, published by the American Daughters of Sweden in 1955, and the lemon-lime filling from a recipe in *Desserts* by Nancy Silverton. If you can find the traditional 2-inch, fluted *sandbakelse* molds, use them. If not, any tartlet pan of the same size will work. You can even use a full-size tart pan for the recipe. If you end up with extra filling, it is delicious tucked into crepes, served over vanilla ice cream, or, if feeling blue, eaten straight from a spoon.

If you want the curd perfectly smooth (and you live near a place that sells fresh duck eggs), use 2 duck egg yolks in place of the 3 chicken egg yolks. | SHOWN PAGE 103 | MAKES 25 TO 30 TARTLETS

TARTLET SHELLS
2 CUPS SIFTED ALL-PURPOSE FLOUR

2/3 CUP SUGAR

14 TABLESPOONS COLD UNSALTED BUTTER,
    CUT INTO 1/2-INCH CUBES

1 EGG, BEATEN

LEMON-LIME CUSTARD
1 LIME

7 TO 8 LEMONS

3 WHOLE EGGS

3 EGG YOLKS

3/4 CUP SUGAR

1/2 CUP UNSALTED BUTTER, AT ROOM TEMPERATURE,
    CUT INTO SMALL CUBES

FRESH SEASONAL BERRIES (SUCH AS RASPBERRY,
    BLACKBERRY, OR BLUEBERRY), FOR GARNISH

To make the tartlet shells, preheat the oven to 400°F. Have ready thirty 2-inch *sandbakelse* molds or fluted tartlet pans and a large rimmed baking sheet.

In a large bowl, stir together the flour and sugar. Add the butter and toss to coat with the flour mixture. Add the egg and mix together with your fingers or a spoon until a smooth, thick dough forms. To shape each shell, place a small ball of the dough into a mold, and with floured thumbs, press the dough thinly over the bottom and up the sides. Be sure to get the dough very thin so that the shells will bake up crisp. As the molds are lined, put them on the baking sheet. You may not need all of the molds.

Bake the shells for 8 to 10 minutes, until the dough looks set and is just starting to brown at the edges. Let cool slightly in the molds, then carefully remove the shells to racks and let cool completely.

To make the custard, grate the zest from the lime into a 1/4-cup measure, then grate the zest from the lemons into the same measure until you have 1/4 cup grated zest. Juice the lime and pour the juice into a 1-cup measure, then juice the lemons into the same measure until you have 1 cup juice.

unsalted butter

egg yolks

ALL-PURPOSE *Flour*

Pour water to a depth of about 3 inches into a wide, large pot and bring to a boil over high heat. Select a stainless-steel bowl that will rest in the rim of the pot. Add the citrus zest and juice, whole eggs, egg yolks, and sugar to the bowl and whisk until blended. Set the bowl over (not touching) the boiling water and whisk vigorously, incorporating as much air as possible. Rotate the bowl from time to time to prevent the eggs from cooking around the sides. Continue to cook, whisking constantly, for 5 to 10 minutes, until the foam disappears and the mixture has thickened. The mixture will not curdle, so don't be afraid to cook it until it is very thick. Remove from the heat and beat in the butter, a cube at a time, beating well after each addition.

Strain the mixture through a fine-mesh sieve into a bowl with a spout or into a large glass liquid measuring cup. Arrange the cooled tartlet shells on a tray or rimmed baking sheet, and pour the custard into the shells, filling them nearly to the rim. Top each tartlet with a few berries and then refrigerate for at least 2 hours, until firm and set. Serve chilled.

TIPS AND TRICKS
ALMOND COOKIE VARIATION

ADD 1 CUP FINELY GROUND BLANCHED ALMONDS AND ABOUT 1/4 TEASPOON [MAYBE A BIT MORE] PURE ALMOND EXTRACT TO THE DOUGH JUST BEFORE ADDING THE FLOUR. WHEN YOU PRESS THE DOUGH INTO THE MOLDS, MAKE THE BOTTOM AND SIDES AS YOU WOULD FOR A TART, OR THE THICKNESS OF A COOKIE. BAKE AS DIRECTED, THEN REMOVE FROM THE MOLDS AND LET COOL COMPLETELY. TO SERVE, PLACE THE COOKIES UPSIDE ON A PLATTER AND DUST WITH CONFECTIONERS' SUGAR. FOR A FANCIER PRESENTATION, LEAVE THEM RIGHT SIDE UP, FILL EACH ONE WITH A LITTLE BIT OF VERY GOOD JAM, AND DUST WITH CONFECTIONERS' SUGAR.

almonds

blueberries

lime

FRANCE

My early culinary training was in French food. In the 1970s, I got excited about the cooking of Richard Olney, Simone Beck, Julia Child, Elizabeth David, and Alma Lach (from Chicago, of all places) and then the Troisgros brothers and on to Mireille Johnston, Paul Bocuse, and Jacques Pépin. Nowadays, when I read through recipes for some of the dishes that captivated me then, I find some of them too fussy, and yet they brought a certain generation of American cooks forward from casserole-blighted lives.

My mom's theory of raising kids was to keep us busy, so starting when I was thirteen years old, I took all of the classes offered at the brilliant, though now-defunct, La Cuvette cooking school. I ended up doing retail for Lois Lee, who was the owner of the shop where the classes were held and my first and foremost culinary mentor. Verna Meyers, the teacher, kept telling me that I was too small and couldn't lift the stockpots. But she kept teaching me because I set up the equipment for all of her classes. She set high standards and always told me to work with the best—people and ingredients—one of the most important pieces of advice I have ever been given. I have tried to put those words of wisdom to work in this and every menu in this book.

This country French menu is one of my favorites in the book, and it is good even if you make only one of the dishes. The peppers and eggs make a great supper dish or a Sunday brunch, and the quail are a satisfying twist on grilling when you are not in the mood for a classic American barbecue. And I like to make the charlotte at least once each apple season. I usually pour a little extra crème fraîche on top and eat the charlotte while curled up by the fire reading a book.

HERBED ROASTED PEPPERS
WITH ONION AND "UNDEVILED" EGGS

This luscious combination is beautiful brought to the table right in the pot it was braised in, with some toasted bread on the side. It is good served hot or at room temperature. You can instead put a dollop of the pepper mixture on top of hard-boiled egg halves for simple "undeviled" eggs, or you can serve the pepper mixture in the gratin dish topped with soft-boiled or poached eggs sprinkled with Maldon sea salt and grilled crunchy bread, all garnished with minced chives and chive blossoms. You can also transform it into a sauce by simply dicing the bell pepper and onion instead of slicing them.

The pepper and onion mixture may be made up to 1 day in advance, covered, and refrigerated. If you are feeling lazy, you can even skip roasting the peppers and use sliced raw peppers, skin and all. Leftovers (or if you decide to make extra on purpose) are good on grilled fish or chicken and would brighten up a sandwich or a baked potato. | SERVES 6

1½ TABLESPOONS EXTRA VIRGIN OLIVE OIL
    OR UNSALTED BUTTER
1 RED BELL PEPPER, ROASTED (SEE PAGE 29), PEELED,
    SEEDED, AND CUT LENGTHWISE INTO WIDE STRIPS
1 ORANGE OR YELLOW BELL PEPPER, ROASTED (SEE PAGE 29),
    PEELED, SEEDED, AND CUT LENGTHWISE INTO WIDE STRIPS
½ RED ONION, JULIENNED
1 CLOVE
3 TABLESPOONS DRY WHITE WINE
½ CUP CHIFFONADE-CUT FRESH BASIL, MINT,
    OR SAGE LEAVES
1 LOAF COUNTRY-STYLE FRENCH BREAD SUCH AS
    PAIN AU LEVAIN OR BAGUETTE, THINLY SLICED
OLIVE OIL, FOR TOASTING THE BREAD
SEA SALT AND FRESHLY GROUND BLACK PEPPER
SHAVED PARMESAN, AGED DRY JACK,
    OR RICOTTA SALATA CHEESE (OPTIONAL)
3 HARD-BOILED EGGS,
    HALVED LENGTHWISE (OPTIONAL)

Preheat the oven to 350°F.

In a cast-iron or other heavy pot, heat the olive oil over medium-high heat. Add the bell peppers and onion and stir to coat. Cook for a minute or two, to get the vegetables hot throughout, and then add the clove and wine. Reduce the heat to the lowest setting, cover, and let cook for 30 minutes to 1 hour, until the peppers and onion are nicely melted into the oil. It is important to cook this slowly, so use a heat diffuser (see page 187) if necessary. Stir in half of the basil near the end of the cooking time.

While the vegetables are cooking, brush the bread slices on both sides with olive oil and arrange them on a baking sheet. Bake for 7 to 10 minutes, until golden brown and crispy on both sides. Reserve until needed.

When the peppers and onions are melted and luscious, turn up the heat and reduce any pan juices to a syrup. Season with salt and pepper.

To serve, top the toasted bread slices with the pepper-onion mixture, scatter a little cheese on top, and then a sprinkling of the remaining basil. Or, nestle the egg halves, cut side up, in the pepper-onion mixture and serve directly from the braising pot, with the toasted bread on the side.

bell peppers

GRILLED QUAIL SALAD
WITH ROASTED MUSHROOMS
AND HONEY COFFEE VINAIGRETTE

This salad could be made with Cornish game hens, pheasant, or squab in place of the quail, though you will have to adjust the cooking time according to the bird. I like how the white of the button mushrooms contrasts with the shiitake, and I think their different textures play nicely off of each other. Other mushrooms, such as cremini, would work fine, as well. You want to use only the white and pale green parts of the frisée here, but the green trimmings can be saved for soup or for sautéing. If you are not fond of bitter greens, substitute a lettuce of your choice. | SERVES 6

HONEY COFFEE VINAIGRETTE
2 TO 3 TABLESPOONS BREWED ESPRESSO
    OR DOUBLE-STRENGTH REGULAR COFFEE
1/4 CUP AGED SPANISH SHERRY VINEGAR
2 TEASPOONS HONEY
1 SHALLOT, MINCED
1/2 TEASPOON SEA SALT
1/4 TEASPOON FRESHLY GROUND BLACK PEPPER
1/2 CUP EXTRA VIRGIN OLIVE OIL

1 TABLESPOON MINCED FRESH ROSEMARY
1 TABLESPOON MINCED FRESH THYME
4 CLOVES GARLIC, MINCED
4 TABLESPOONS EXTRA VIRGIN OLIVE OIL,
    PLUS MORE IF NEEDED
6 PARTIALLY BONED OR BONE-IN QUAIL
SEA SALT AND FRESHLY GROUND BLACK PEPPER
8 OUNCES SHIITAKE MUSHROOMS, STEMMED AND QUARTERED
8 OUNCES BUTTON MUSHROOMS, STEMMED AND QUARTERED
GRATED ZEST AND JUICE OF 1/2 LEMON
4 TO 6 CUPS FRISÉE OR CURLY ENDIVE OR ESCAROLE
    CHICORY LEAVES, WHITE AND LIGHT GREEN PARTS ONLY
2 CUPS WILD OR CULTIVATED ARUGULA OR
    WATERCRESS, TOUGH STEMS REMOVED
ABOUT 1 TABLESPOON COFFEE BEANS, CRUSHED,
    OR COCOA NIBS, FOR GARNISH

To make the vinaigrette, in a small bowl, whisk together the espresso, vinegar, honey, shallot, salt, and pepper until the honey is well incorporated and the salt is fully dissolved. Gradually whisk in the olive oil in a slow, steady stream and continue to whisk until well emulsified. Reserve until needed.

To make the marinade, mix together half each of the rosemary, thyme, garlic, and olive oil. Rinse the birds under cold running water and pat dry with paper towels. Season the birds with salt and pepper and rub well with the marinade. Cover and refrigerate for several hours. This is a strong marinade so they won't need a lot of time.

While the birds are marinating, cook the mushrooms. In a large, heavy sauté pan, heat the remaining 2 tablespoons oil (or more if needed to coat the pan lightly) over high heat. Tilt the pan to spread the oil. In rapid succession, add the mushrooms, lemon juice, and lemon zest, then cover and cook, shaking the pan, for 3 to 5 minutes, until the mushrooms begin to brown around the edges. Add the remaining rosemary, thyme, and garlic and cook for another minute or two, being careful not to burn the garlic. Add half of the vinaigrette and cook until the liquid in the pan is almost completely absorbed by the mushrooms. Remove from the heat and reserve until ready to serve.

To cook the quail, prepare a medium-hot charcoal and/or wood fire in a grill. If you are working with bone-in birds, split them at the backbone so they can be laid flat on the grill; if the breastbones have been removed, tuck the wing tips behind the shoulders to keep the breasts uncovered for nice grilling.

CONTINUED

Grilled Quail Salad, *continued*

Place the birds on the grill rack directly over the fire and grill, turning once, for 2¹/₂ to 3 minutes on each side, until the skin is well caramelized. As the birds cook on each side, rotate each one a quarter turn after the first minute or so to create attractive crosshatching. A little charring on the skin here and there isn't bad. Alternatively, you could cook the quail on a stove-top grill pan over medium-high heat.

Just before the quail are ready to come off the grill, in a small saucepan, bring the remaining half of the vinaigrette to a boil over high heat. Place the frisée and arugula in a bowl, pour the hot vinaigrette over the top, and toss to mix. Reheat the mushrooms until hot.

To serve, divide the greens among individual plates, placing them in the center. Sprinkle the mushrooms over the greens, dividing them evenly, and place a quail in the center of each plate. Garnish each serving with no more than ¹/₂ teaspoon of the coffee beans and serve.

GRILLED ASPARAGUS OR FAVA BEANS
WITH RICOTTA SALATA

fava beans

Darren McRonald, a former chef at Cindy's Backstreet Kitchen, taught me this dish. If you want to be authentic, you can use a French cheese (they make literally hundreds of different kinds), but I have found that mildly salty *ricotta salata* is an excellent choice. You might instead opt for a French or American fresh goat cheese, a good feta, or even crumbled Roquefort. | SERVES 6

2 POUNDS ASPARAGUS (ABOUT 24 SPEARS), TOUGH ENDS
    SNAPPED OFF, OR YOUNG, TENDER FAVA BEANS IN THE POD
4 TABLESPOONS EXTRA VIRGIN OLIVE OIL
SEA SALT AND FRESHLY GROUND BLACK PEPPER
2 OUNCES RICOTTA SALATA CHEESE

Prepare a medium-hot charcoal and/or wood fire in a grill. Place the asparagus or fava beans in a flat, shallow dish, drizzle with 2 tablespoons of the olive oil, and season with salt and pepper. Toss to coat evenly.

asparagus

Place the asparagus or fava beans on the grill rack directly over the fire and grill, turning as needed to cook evenly, for 2 to 4 minutes, until they turn a brighter shade of green and are just starting to become tender. A grilling basket or perforated tray helps keep the vegetables from falling through the grill grates.

Transfer to a serving platter. Drizzle with the remaining 2 tablespoons olive oil, season with salt and pepper, and crumble or coarsely grate the cheese over the top. Very young, tender fava beans can be eaten pod and all, though some diners may choose to squeeze the steamed beans free of the pods.

APPLE CHARLOTTE
WITH CRÈME FRAÎCHE OR WHIPPED CREAM

When selecting apples for this classic French dessert, pick larger ones. Smaller apples have more core by weight. A sweet-tart variety like McIntosh would be good. If you do not have a traditional charlotte mold, just about any straight-sided pot or mold with a cover will work. I used a Le Creuset mold for this recipe and have also used a terrine covered with aluminum oil in the past; soufflé dishes would also work. | SERVES 6 TO 8

3 TO 4 POUNDS COOKING APPLES

1/2 CUP APRICOT JAM OR ORANGE MARMALADE

1/4 TO 1/3 CUP SUGAR, DEPENDING ON SWEETNESS OF APPLES

2 TO 4 TABLESPOONS DARK RUM

1 1/2 TABLESPOONS UNSALTED BUTTER

1 TEASPOON PURE VANILLA EXTRACT

1 [1 1/2-POUND] LOAF BRIOCHE, CHALLAH, OR OTHER EGG
    BREAD, CUT INTO 1/4- TO 1/3-INCH-THICK SLICES

1 CUP CLARIFIED BUTTER [SEE PAGE 255], MELTED

CRÈME FRAÎCHE OR LIGHTLY SWEETENED WHIPPED CREAM,
    FOR GARNISH

Peel and core the apples but leave them whole. Put them in a heavy saucepan, place over low heat, cover, and cook slowly, letting them steam in their own juices, for 15 to 20 minutes, until very soft and mashable.

Add 1/4 cup of the jam, the sugar, rum to taste, the butter, and the vanilla to the apples and mash together all of the ingredients until well mixed. Then continue to cook over low heat, uncovered, until very thick. The timing will vary depending on the type of apple used. Remove from the heat and reserve.

Preheat the oven to 350°F.

Have ready an 8-cup charlotte mold. Cut the bread slices into rectangles that can be easily fit in the mold. One at a time, dip one side of each bread rectangle into the clarified butter and arrange the bread over the entire bottom and sides of the mold, with the buttered side against the mold.

apples

CONTINUED

Apple Charlotte, *continued*

Pack the apple mixture into the bread-lined mold and then top with a layer of butter-dipped bread rectangles, with the buttered side up. Cover the mold. (At this point, the charlotte may be covered and refrigerated for 1 day before continuing. Remove from the refrigerator about 30 minutes before baking to take off some of the chill.)

Bake for 45 minutes, until golden brown and very aromatic. Transfer to a rack, uncover, and let cool for about 15 minutes. Meanwhile, in a small saucepan, combine the remaining $1/4$ cup jam and a few spoonfuls of water and heat, stirring, until warm and the consistency of a nice glaze.

To unmold the charlotte, invert a serving plate over the top of the mold and carefully flip the mold and plate together, and then carefully lift off the mold. Drizzle the warm jam glaze evenly over the charlotte and carry your masterpiece to the table so your guests can see it before it is cut. Pass a bowl of crème fraîche at the table.

sugar

apricot jam

unsalted butter

GREECE

I have been fascinated with Greece, both ancient and modern, for nearly my whole life. I regularly read about it in books, newspapers, and magazines; watch programs about it on television, and have studied it in classrooms. My associations range from its crowded pantheon of gods and goddesses and extraordinary archaeological sites to Jacqueline Kennedy's second husband, a shipping tycoon. Despite decades of fascination with everything Greek, I didn't actually see the country in person until John and I went there on our honeymoon.

It was a boat trip—a summer cruise—and most of our time was spent island hopping alongside crowds of other vacationers. In fact, we never set foot on the mainland. But we did have a particularly wonderful—and iconic—meal one night of grilled fresh fish with lightly cooked greens and delicious honeyed fruits—a simple and delightful Mediterranean feast. Greek cooks draw on the same ingredients as their neighbors— fish, fresh vegetables, olive oil, olives, cheeses, lamb, poultry, grains—but prepare their bounty in uniquely Greek ways.

CRETAN MIXED-VEGETABLE CASSEROLE

This Cretan dish has the unusual name of *symbetheri*, or "in-laws," most likely because it brings lots of unrelated vegetables together, much like in-laws at a wedding. It can be served hot, at room temperature, or chilled, and I always make it in big batches because it comes in handy for a quick lunch, plus it tastes better the day after it is made. It is a rustic dish, so do not cut any of the vegetables too precisely and do include a mix of shapes and sizes. It is ideally made in summertime when fresh tomatoes and summer squashes are at their best, but you can substitute canned tomatoes for the fresh and 2 cups of peeled and diced winter squash (kabocha, butternut, acorn) for the summer squash in the cool months. Kalamata olives are the traditional choice here, but sometimes I find them too briny and instead opt for another Mediterranean olive. Use any olive that you like. In the menu, I am serving this dish as a first course, but it would make a wonderful main course or a side dish to grilled or roasted fish or chicken. | SERVES 6

OLIVE OIL, FOR SAUTÉING

8 VERY SMALL GLOBE EGGPLANTS, OR 4 ASIAN EGGPLANTS, TRIMMED AND HALVED OR IN BIG CHUNKS

3 YELLOW SUMMER OR PATTYPAN SQUASHES, CUT INTO 2-INCH CHUNKS

3 SMALL ZUCCHINI, ROLL CUT INTO 2-INCH CHUNKS [SEE OPPOSITE], OR 12 BABY ZUCCHINI, TRIMMED AND LEFT WHOLE

2 SMALL RED OR SWEET ONIONS, FINELY CHOPPED

2 OR 3 CARROTS, PEELED AND CUT INTO ANGLED CHUNKS

4 TO 6 MEDIUM TO SMALL POTATOES [SUCH AS RUSSIAN FINGERLING OR YUKON GOLD], PEELED AND HALVED OR QUARTERED, DEPENDING ON SIZE

4 LARGE TOMATOES, PEELED [SEE PAGE 181] AND QUARTERED, OR 1½ TO 2 CUPS CANNED TOMATOES, QUARTERED

1 TO 2 TABLESPOONS MINCED FRESH FLAT-LEAF PARSLEY, RINSED AND SQUEEZED DRY [SEE PAGE 83]

2 TO 3 TABLESPOONS MINCED FRESH OREGANO

SEA SALT AND FRESHLY GROUND BLACK PEPPER

4 CLOVES GARLIC, SLICED

1 BUNCH COLLARD GREENS, MUSTARD GREENS, SWISS CHARD, OR RAINBOW CHARD, STEMMED AND CUT INTO 2-INCH PIECES

4 TO 6 OUNCES FETA CHEESE, CRUMBLED, FOR GARNISH

LEMON WEDGES, FOR GARNISH

BLACK OLIVES, FOR GARNISH

GRILLED OR WARMED CRUSTY BREAD SLICES, FOR SERVING

Coat a large saucepan with olive oil and heat over medium-high heat. Add the eggplant and cook, turning as needed, for 10 to 12 minutes, until caramelized on all sides. Transfer to a plate. Repeat with the summer squashes and then with the zucchini, adding more oil to the pan if needed to prevent scorching and transferring the vegetables to a plate as each batch is done. The timing for the squashes and zucchini will be shorter.

Pour a little more oil into the pan and add the onions, carrots, and potatoes and stir to coat lightly with the oil. Decrease the heat to medium-low, cover, and cook for about 10 minutes, until tender but not browned. Uncover, add the tomatoes and half of the parsley and oregano, and season with salt

black pepper

Tomatoes

and pepper. Bring to a boil and add the garlic and the reserved caramelized vegetables. Decrease the heat to a simmer, cover, and cook for 10 minutes. Add the greens and cook for 10 to 20 minutes longer, until the greens are wilted to your liking. In Crete, the vegetables are cooked until completely tender, but if you prefer your vegetables a bit firmer, shorten the cooking time.

To finish, transfer the vegetables to a large, deep platter, sprinkle with the remaining parsley and oregano, and serve hot or let rest before serving. This dish reheats well (it may be kept overnight in the refrigerator) and is also delicious cold. Garnish with the feta, lemon wedges, and olives just before serving and pass the bread at the table.

TIPS AND TRICKS

HOW TO DO A ROLL CUT

A ROLL CUT IS GOOD FOR CYLINDRICAL VEGETABLES, SUCH AS ZUCCHINI, ASPARAGUS, CUCUMBERS, OR CARROTS WITH THE VEGETABLE ON A CUTTING BOARD, MAKE THE FIRST CUT AT ONE END AT ABOUT A 45-DEGREE ANGLE. ROLL THE VEGETABLE A QUARTER TURN TOWARD YOU AND MAKE A SECOND CUT AT A 45-DEGREE ANGLE. CONTINUE TO ROLL THE VEGETABLE A QUARTER TURN AND CUT AT A 45-DEGREE ANGLE EACH TIME UNTIL YOU REACH THE OPPOSITE END OF THE VEGETABLE.

zucchini

pattypan squash

EXTRA VIRGIN olive Oil

lemon

Russian fingerlings

black olives

LAMB STEW
WITH GARLIC, PARSLEY, AND VINEGAR

You can enjoy this stew any time of year. In winter, the beet salad on page 120 is the perfect dish to precede it. In summer, use the dressing for the beet salad on a first-course salad of sliced assorted heirloom tomatoes. In fall, serve baked acorn, butternut, or kabocha squash alongside the stew. Or, for an even simpler supper, accompany the stew with crusty bread and a tumbler of red wine.

I have used lamb from the leg here, but it can made with shank or shoulder meat, too. Generally, I like to trim off excess fat and sinew, although the meat is always more tender when I haven't removed the fat. If you choose not to trim the fat, you will need to skim more often. | SERVES 6

2 OR 3 SMALL TO MEDIUM EGGPLANTS,
    TRIMMED AND CUT INTO 1/2-INCH DICE
SEA SALT
1/2 CUP DRIED CURRANTS OR RAISINS
1/3 CUP RED WINE VINEGAR
1/4 CUP DRY RED WINE
1/3 TO 1/2 CUP OLIVE OIL
3 1/2 POUNDS BONELESS LAMB FROM THE LEG, TRIMMED
    OF FAT AND SINEW AND CUT INTO 2-INCH CUBES
FRESHLY GROUND BLACK PEPPER
2 LARGE YELLOW ONIONS, DICED
2 TO 4 CLOVES GARLIC, MINCED
2 TO 2 1/2 POUNDS FRESH TOMATOES, PEELED [PAGE 181]
    AND CHOPPED; 4 TO 5 CUPS CANNED TOMATOES,
    CHOPPED; OR 4 TO 5 CUPS CANNED TOMATO PUREE
SCANT 1 TABLESPOON HONEY
1 1/2 TEASPOONS GROUND CINNAMON
1 1/2 TEASPOONS GROUND CUMIN
4 TABLESPOONS MINCED FRESH MINT
4 TABLESPOONS MINCED FRESH FLAT-LEAF PARSLEY LEAVES,
    RINSED AND SQUEEZED DRY [SEE PAGE 83]

In a colander, toss the eggplant with enough salt to coat it lightly and let drain for 30 minutes. In a small bowl, combine the currants, vinegar, and wine and leave to soak until needed. Preheat the oven to 350°F.

To brown the meat, place a large, ovenproof braising pan or flameproof terra-cotta casserole over medium-high heat and pour in enough of the olive oil to coat the bottom nicely. Season the lamb with salt and pepper. When the oil is hot, add some of the lamb to the pan, being careful not to crowd the pan.

(Work in small batches to ensure caramelization—not steaming.) If you didn't hear a sizzle when the lamb hit the oil, increase the heat. Sear the meat, stirring occasionally and scraping up any brown bits that stick to the pan bottom, until browned on all sides. Using a slotted spoon, transfer to a plate to drain. Brown the remaining meat in batches the same way.

If the pan is dry, add a little more oil. Then add the onion and garlic and cook over medium-high heat, stirring occasionally, for about 10 minutes, until the onion is caramelized and has softened (see page 14). If the garlic looks as if it might burn, decrease the heat slightly. Using the slotted spoon, transfer the onion and garlic to the plate with the lamb.

To start building the stew, add a little more oil to the pan if it is dry. Gently squeeze the excess moisture from the eggplant, put the eggplant in the pan, and stir to coat with the oil. Sauté the eggplant for a few minutes and then stir in the tomatoes, honey, cinnamon, cumin, and 2 tablespoons each of the mint and parsley. Bring to a boil, return the lamb and the onion and garlic to the pan, add the currants and their soaking liquid, and stir to mix well.

Cover the pan and transfer it to the oven. Braise for 1 to 1 1/2 hours, checking from time to time and skimming off any fat as needed, until the lamb is tender and the juices have reduced to a saucelike consistency. When the meat is tender, take out the solids and reduce the liquid on the stove top, then recombine. Transfer the stew to a warmed serving dish, sprinkle with the remaining 2 tablespoons each mint and parsley, and serve at once.

WINTER DOUBLE-BEET SALAD

Here in California, I can find the ingredients for this easy salad from late fall until early spring, so I named it after the season in which it fits best. The red and golden beets and the salad greens will brighten a winter table. The same dressing complements a tomato salad in summer. | SERVES 6

3 MEDIUM-LARGE RED BEETS
3 MEDIUM-LARGE GOLDEN BEETS
3 TABLESPOONS OLIVE OIL
1 TEASPOON SEA SALT
1 CUP WATER

DRESSING
1 SHALLOT, MINCED
2 TABLESPOONS RED WINE VINEGAR
7 TO 9 TABLESPOONS EXTRA VIRGIN OLIVE OIL
1 TABLESPOON CHOPPED FRESH DILL
1 TABLESPOON CHOPPED FRESH MINT
SEA SALT AND FRESHLY GROUND BLACK PEPPER

1 HEAD FRISÉE, WHITE AND PALE GREEN LEAVES ONLY,
    CUT CROSSWISE INTO 1-INCH PIECES
1 HEAD TREVISO RADICCHIO,
    CUT CROSSWISE INTO 1½-INCH PIECES
1 HEAD ESCAROLE, TRIMMED OF ALL GREEN, CHOPPED
    INTO 1- TO 1½-INCH PIECES
½ CUP CRUMBLED FETA, FOR GARNISH
½ SMALL RED ONION, THINLY SLICED INTO HALF RINGS,
    FOR GARNISH
FRESHLY GROUND BLACK PEPPER

Preheat the oven to 375°F. If the beet greens are still attached, trim them off, leaving ½ inch of the stem intact, and reserve for another use. In a roasting pan just large enough to accommodate the beets in a single layer, combine the beets, olive oil, salt, and water. Swish everything around so that the oil, salt, and water are well mixed and all of the beets are coated with some of the mixture.

Pop the pan into the oven and roast the beets for 1½ to 2 hours, until fork-tender. The timing will depend on their size.

To make the dressing, in a small bowl, whisk together the shallot and vinegar. Gradually whisk in 7 tablespoons of the oil in a slow, steady stream and continue to whisk until well emulsified. Whisk in the dill and mint and season with salt and pepper. Taste and if it is too tart, add some or all of the remaining 2 tablespoons oil, a little at a time, until you arrive at the balance you like.

When the beets are ready, remove from the oven. When they are cool enough to handle, peel them, cut into ¼-inch-thick slices, and place in a bowl. Pour about one-third of the dressing over the beets (reserve the remainder for the greens) and marinate for at least 20 minutes.

To serve, arrange the beets, overlapping the slices slightly, on a nice plate. Place the greens in a bowl, drizzle with the remaining two-thirds dressing, and toss to coat. Pile the dressed greens in the center of the beets. Garnish the greens and the beets with the feta and onion and grind some pepper over the top.

beets

mint

POTATOES, TOMATOES, AND GREENS

Yahnera, a Cretan dish, combines potatoes, leeks, onions, and fennel. *Tsigarelli*, a specialty of Corfu, mixes greens with onion, garlic, and fennel and sometimes a touch of tomato. In this recipe, I have joined elements from both dishes along with what I had on hand the day I made it. For the greens, assemble a mixture that will impart a flavor that is a nice mix of mild and bitter. Rather than toss out the trimmed tough stems from the greens, you can chop them and tenderize them along with the onions.

If you use vegetable stock rather than chicken stock, this dish will make a nice main course for vegetarians. To turn it into a tasty appetizer, sprinkle it with feta cheese and serve it with grilled bread. And if you have leftovers, add some cooked dried heirloom beans and their broth or more stock to make a soup. | SERVES 6

1/4 CUP OLIVE OIL

1 LEEK, WHITE AND LIGHT GREEN PARTS ONLY, CUT INTO 1/2-INCH-THICK SLICES

1 YELLOW ONION, DICED

2 TO 4 SMALL HEIRLOOM POTATOES, FINELY DICED

1 CUP CHICKEN STOCK [PAGE 59] OR VEGETABLE STOCK, STORE-BOUGHT REDUCED-SODIUM CHICKEN OR VEGETABLE BROTH, OR WATER

1 TEASPOON FENNEL SEEDS, CRUSHED IN A MORTAR

2 CUPS PEELED [SEE PAGE 181] AND DICED FRESH OR CANNED TOMATOES

1 FENNEL BULB, BULB DICED AND FRONDS CHOPPED AND RESERVED FOR GARNISH

1 TEASPOON GROUND ALEPPO OR ESPELETTE PEPPER

2 BUNCHES KALE, CHARD, AND/OR MUSTARD GREENS, TOUGH STEMS REMOVED [SEE HEADNOTE] AND LEAVES TORN INTO BITE-SIZE PIECES

SEA SALT AND FRESHLY GROUND BLACK PEPPER

JUICE OF 1/2 TO 1 LEMON

EXTRA VIRGIN OLIVE OIL, FOR DRIZZLING

In a small Dutch oven or other heavy pot, heat the olive oil over high heat. When the oil is hot, add the leek and onion (and the chopped stems from the greens, if using), cover, and cook slowly, stirring occasionally, for about 20 minutes, until the vegetables are soft and starting to caramelize (see page 14 for more on caramelizing onions).

Add the potatoes, stock, and fennel seeds and cook, stirring, for about 5 minutes. Add the tomatoes, fennel bulb, and Aleppo pepper, stir well, cover, and cook for about 5 minutes, until the potatoes are half-cooked (test with a fork). Add the greens and continue to cook, covered, for 5 to 8 minutes, until the potatoes and greens are tender and the juices have reduced and are syrupy.

If the vegetables are cooked to your liking but the dish is too brothy, using a slotted spoon, transfer the vegetables to a plate, increase the heat to high, and boil until the juices are reduced. Return the vegetables to the pan, stir to coat with the reduced juices, and season with salt, pepper, and lemon juice to taste. Transfer to a serving dish, garnish with the fennel fronds, and drizzle with the extra virgin olive oil. Serve hot or at room temperature. It is also very tasty chilled.

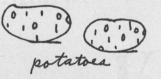

potatoes

leek

yellow onion

fennel

WALNUT CAKE
WITH CITRUS SPOON SWEET

This combination is often eaten during Lent because it contains neither eggs nor butter. Spoon sweets, which are like jams that you eat with a spoon instead of smear on your morning toast, are very good but very sweet. This is an authentic recipe and the fruit must be cooked very slowly for the best result. Use a wide, heavy pan to ensure even evaporation, and cook the fruit until it is the consistency of a heavy syrup, rather than of a marmalade. Depending on the time of year and how juicy the fruits are, you may need to add more water toward the end of cooking.

Unless all of your guests have a serious sweet tooth, you will have some of the spoon sweet left over. It is good folded into an ice cream base, warmed and spooned on top of oatmeal, or served with pound cake and tea. You can also pack it into tightly capped small canning jars for gift giving. It will keep in the refrigerator for a couple of months. Just be careful to use a clean spoon to dish it out each time.

The walnut cakes go together quickly, which makes them a good choice for dessert even when you are not making spoon sweets. They make an excellent base for any seasonal fruit when you are pressed for time. You can forgo making the spoon sweets and instead heat up some high-quality orange or lemon marmalade for soaking the cakes and a good apricot jam to spoon on top. I used $^1/_2$-cup custard cups for baking the cakes, but you can also use miniature angel food cake pans or individual soufflé dishes, adjusting the cooking time as necessary. | MAKES 6 SMALL CAKES

SPOON SWEET
2 ORANGES
3 LEMONS
2 CUPS SUGAR
1 CUP WHITE WINE
2 CUPS WATER
$^1/_2$ CUP HONEY
1 CINNAMON STICK

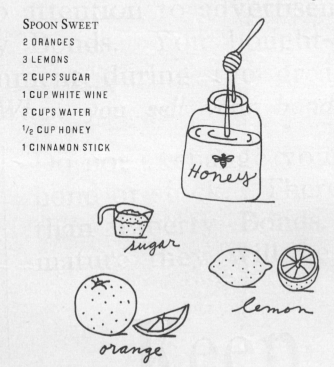

To make the spoon sweet, slice off the stem end of each citrus fruit. Place the fruits in a saucepan, add water to cover, and bring to a full rolling boil over high heat. Boil for 1 minute and drain. Repeat this step 3 to 5 times, always starting the fruits in cold water, until they are very tender (this both tenderizes the fruits and removes some of their bitterness). Let the fruits cool until they can be handled.

Cut each fruit in half through its equator (not through the stem end). Cut each half into quarters and remove the white membrane connector (in the center of the orange) and seeds. Then finely cut each quarter into either perfect squares or rustic pieces. Both end up looking and tasting great.

CONTINUED

Walnut Cake, *continued*

WALNUT CAKE

1/2 CUP FRANGELICO OR BRANDY

1 TEASPOON BAKING SODA

1 CUP SEMOLINA

1 CUP FINELY CHOPPED WALNUTS

1/3 CUP SUGAR

1 TEASPOON BAKING POWDER

1 TEASPOON GROUND CINNAMON

1/4 TEASPOON GROUND CLOVES

GRATED ZEST AND JUICE OF 2 ORANGES [1/2 CUP JUICE]

1/4 CUP WALNUT OIL OR VERY FRUITY EXTRA
   VIRGIN OLIVE OIL

GREEK-STYLE PLAIN YOGURT, FOR GARNISH

WALNUT HALVES, TOASTED [SEE PAGE 23], FOR GARNISH

Return the fruit pieces to the pan, add the sugar, wine, water, honey, and cinnamon, and stir to mix well. Bring to a boil over medium-high heat and then decrease the heat to a very slow simmer. Cook uncovered, stirring occasionally and skimming off any foam that rises to the surface, for 1 1/2 to 2 hours. Remember, the slower you go the better. I often put a heat diffuser (see page 187) under the pan to avoid scorching. The mixture is ready when it is the consistency of a thick syrup and the skin of the fruit is tender and beginning to become translucent. If the mixture thickens too much and becomes like a marmalade before it is the correct consistency, add a bit more water and keep cooking. Remove from the heat, remove and discard the cinnamon stick, and reserve until needed.

To make the cake, preheat the oven to 325°F. Spray six 1/2-cup custard cups or similar molds with nonstick cooking spray and set them on a rimmed baking sheet.

In a small bowl, combine the Frangelico and baking soda and set aside. In a food processor, combine the semolina, nuts, sugar, baking powder, cinnamon, and cloves and process until fluffy and almost powdery. Pour into a big bowl. (It is okay to do this part by hand; the cakes will just have a little more "texture" from the hand-chopped walnuts.) Make a well in the center of the dry ingredients and pour in the orange zest and juice, the Frangelico mixture, and the walnut oil. Using a wooden spoon, mix just until all of the ingredients are evenly moistened.

Fill each prepared mold three-fourths full (the cakes need room to expand in the heat of the oven). Bake for about 20 minutes, until a toothpick inserted into the center of a cake comes out dry and the top springs back when gently pressed. Remove from the oven.

While the cakes are still hot from the oven, prick the top of each one about a dozen times with a toothpick or skewer. Spoon a little of the syrupy part of the spoon sweet (no more than a scant tablespoon) over the top of each cake. Let the cakes cool completely.

To serve, turn each cooled cake out onto a dessert plate. Top each cake sparingly with the spoon sweet and add a dollop of yogurt and the walnuts. Be sure to be generous with the yogurt. It is a welcome contrast to the sweetness of the dessert and it brightens the palate.

ITALY

American cooks have been in love with Italian food for four decades. But until recently, they were content with exploring the cuisines of the mainland, of Tuscany and Emilia-Romagna, Piedmont and Lombardy, Liguria and Lazio. Only now are they turning their attention to Sicily, where an abundance of seafood, fruits, and vegetables and a rich mix of cultures have contributed to an extraordinary and varied table.

Over the centuries, many different cultures—Greek, Roman, Arab, Norman, Lombard, French, Spanish, Bourbon—have left their mark on Sicilian cuisine. The Greeks began colonizing Sicily around 800 BCE, bringing grapes and olives. The Arabs, who arrived in the ninth century ACE, carried eggplant, lemons, oranges, apricots, sugar, citrus, raisins, nutmeg, clove, pepper, cinnamon, and pine nuts, among other foodstuffs. In the sixteenth century, the Spanish introduced the foods of the Americas: cocoa, corn, tomatoes, peppers, and turkey. Even a small culinary treasure from North Africa, couscous, found its way to the island and settled in Trapani. Not surprisingly, this bountiful pantry has produced a complex and endlessly delicious cuisine, making it difficult to decide which dishes to include here.

BROCCOLI RABE, ARUGULA, AND PROSCIUTTO

WITH WALNUT PESTO

If you prepare the pesto, dressing, and broccoli rabe ahead of time, this dish comes together quickly just before serving. In spring, broccolini, broccoli, asparagus, or English peas may be substituted for the rabe. I recommend leaving some texture in the pesto. A smooth pesto would still taste good, but a little texture will help it stand out more. Any leftover pesto would be delicious on pasta or on a green bean and potato salad.

   Some stores carry already-sliced prosciutto, but if possible, ask for the prosciutto to be freshly sliced. You can use an expensive or an everyday but still good-quality balsamic vinegar for the vinaigrette. Of course, the better the vinegar, the better the dish will be, and a rich artisanal vinegar will make a big difference. | SERVES 6

WALNUT PESTO
3 CLOVES GARLIC, PEELED
1/2 CUP EXTRA VIRGIN OLIVE OIL
1/4 CUP WALNUT OIL
3/4 CUP WALNUTS, TOASTED [SEE PAGE 23]
1/4 CUP GRATED PARMIGIANO-REGGIANO CHEESE
3/4 CUP LIGHTLY PACKED FRESH BASIL LEAVES
GRATED ZEST AND JUICE OF 1 LEMON
   [ABOUT 2 TABLESPOONS]
1/4 TO 1/2 TEASPOON SEA SALT
1/4 TEASPOON FRESHLY GROUND BLACK PEPPER

VINAIGRETTE
1 TABLESPOON AGED SPANISH SHERRY VINEGAR
1 TABLESPOON BALSAMIC VINEGAR
1/2 SHALLOT, MINCED [1 TABLESPOON AT MOST]
1/2 TEASPOON SEA SALT
1/4 TEASPOON FRESHLY GROUND BLACK PEPPER
2 TABLESPOONS WALNUT OIL
3 TABLESPOONS EXTRA VIRGIN OLIVE OIL

1 TO 1/2 POUNDS BROCCOLI RABE, TOUGH STEM ENDS TRIMMED
OLIVE OIL, FOR BRUSHING
SEA SALT AND FRESHLY GROUND BLACK PEPPER
3 TO 4 CUPS ARUGULA, TOUGH STEMS REMOVED
18 THIN SLICES PROSCIUTTO OR SERRANO HAM [ABOUT 5 OUNCES]
6 TO 8 TABLESPOONS FRESH MILD GOAT CHEESE, CRUMBLED
TOASTED WALNUTS [SEE PAGE 23], FOR GARNISH
FRESHLY GROUND BLACK PEPPER

broccoli rabe

To make the pesto, in a food processor, combine the garlic, olive and walnut oils, walnuts, cheese, and basil and process until everything is well mixed and coarsely chopped. Add the lemon zest and juice, 1/4 teaspoon of the salt, and the pepper and process until the pesto is the texture you like. Taste and stir in more salt if needed.

   To make the vinaigrette, in a small bowl, whisk together the vinegars, shallot, salt, and pepper until the salt is fully dissolved. Gradually whisk in the oils in a slow, steady stream and continue to whisk until well emulsified. Reserve until needed.

   Place the broccoli rabe in a shallow dish. Drizzle with the olive oil, season with salt and pepper, and turn to coat evenly. Let marinate for at least 10 minutes or up to 1 hour. Prepare a medium-hot charcoal and/or wood fire in a grill.

   Place the broccoli on the grill rack directly over the fire and grill, turning once, until just tender and nicely grill marked. This should take 1 1/2 to 3 minutes on each side. Or, sauté the broccoli rabe in a cast-iron skillet over high heat.

   To serve, place the arugula in a bowl, drizzle with the vinaigrette, and toss to coat evenly. Arrange 3 prosciutto slices flat on each plate and top with the broccoli rabe. Drizzle with a good dose of the pesto and then sprinkle on some dressed arugula, goat cheese, and walnuts. Finish each plate with a couple grinds of pepper.

SOUR-AND-SWEET STUFFED SARDINES

For the past twenty years, I have been working at becoming "greener" in my personal and professional life. Some practices are simple, like working with the local waste management company to turn all of the food waste in my restaurants into compost. Other actions present more complex issues. For example, longfin squid is caught sustainably, but it is then shipped to China for processing, frozen, and shipped back to the United States for distribution. In other words, it is caught in an eco-friendly manner, but its processing and distribution produce a huge carbon footprint. Fortunately, sardines, the star of this first course, do not present the same dilemma. They reach maturity and reproduce quickly, are harvested in nondetrimental ways, and are sold fresh.

This dish is perfect for entertaining. It can be served hot, chilled, or at room temperature. You can bake this dish two or three days in advance, refrigerate it, and then serve it chilled or at room temperature. It is ideal picnic food, or with the addition of a nice big green salad and some warm garlic bread, it would make a satisfying light supper.

If you don't want to make the sauce from scratch, you can add anchovies to a simple jarred tomato sauce, or easier still, you can use a nice store-bought puttanesca sauce that already has anchovies in it. Manicaretti brand makes a good one. I prefer "canned" items in glass jars because I find the taste is much better than the same food sold in cans.

I have called for a Rangpur lime here, also known as a mandarin lime, which is a cross between a mandarin orange and a lemon and has a highly tart, acidic flavor. I used it because I have a Rangpur lime tree growing in my garden and I like the way its juice balanced the sweetness of the orange in the recipe. If you cannot find a Rangpur lime, use whatever tart citrus you like, such as grapefruit, lemon, or Persian lime. | SERVES 6

SAUCE

2 TO 3 TABLESPOONS OLIVE OIL

½ YELLOW ONION, MINCED

3 TO 6 ANCHOVY FILLETS, MINCED

2 CLOVES GARLIC, MINCED

¼ CUP DRY WHITE WINE

3 CUPS PUREED OR FINELY CHOPPED
   FRESH OR CANNED TOMATOES

SEA SALT AND FRESHLY
   GROUND BLACK PEPPER

To make the sauce, in a large sauté pan over medium-low heat, heat the olive oil. Add the onion, anchovies, and garlic, stir well, cover, and cook, shaking the pan occasionally, for 5 to 8 minutes, until the onion is translucent and tender. Add the wine, increase the heat to medium-high, and cook until the pan is nearly dry. Add the tomatoes, stir well, and heat until the sauce is hot and bubbly. Lower the heat to a simmer and cook for a few more minutes, until thick and luscious looking. Season with salt and pepper and reserve until needed.

CONTINUED

anchovies

Sour-and-Sweet Stuffed Sardines, *continued*

FILLING

3 TABLESPOONS EXTRA VIRGIN OLIVE OIL

1/2 YELLOW ONION, MINCED

1 CLOVE GARLIC, MINCED

1 SMALL OR 1/2 LARGE SHALLOT, MINCED

5 TABLESPOONS GOLDEN RAISINS

5 TABLESPOONS PINE NUTS

2 TABLESPOONS MINCED FRESH FLAT-LEAF PARSLEY
   LEAVES, RINSED AND SQUEEZED DRY [SEE PAGE 83]

1 TABLESPOON MINCED FRESH MINT

1 TO 1 1/2 CUPS FRESHBREAD CRUMBS

JUICE OF 1 ORANGE OR 2 TANGERINES

JUICE OF 1 RANGPUR LIME OR OTHER TART CITRUS FRUIT

8 TO 10 FRESH SARDINES

3 TABLESPOONS EXTRA VIRGIN OLIVE OIL

SEA SALT AND FRESHLY GROUND BLACK PEPPER

CRUSHED BAY LEAVES, FOR SPRINKLING

To make the filling, in a large sauté pan, heat the olive oil over medium heat. Add the onion, garlic, and shallot and cook, stirring occasionally, for about 5 minutes, until soft. Stir in the raisins, pine nuts, parsley, and mint and cook for a minute or two, until the raisins have plumped a bit. Add the bread crumbs and cook for a minute more. Stir in the orange and lime juices, remove from the heat, and let cool completely.

Preheat the oven to 375°F. Select a baking dish just large enough to hold the sardines snugly in a single layer. Oil the dish with olive oil.

To clean the sardines, scale each fish with a fish scaler or the dull side of the blade of a small paring knife, gently running the scaler or knife from the tail toward the head of the fish (you should see scales popping off). Cut off the head and then make an incision along the belly from the chin (or where the chin used to be) to the tail. Use your thumb to slide out the entrails and then discard them. Repeat with the remaining sardines and then rinse each fish under cold running water and pat dry with paper towels.

When the filling has cooled, stuff each sardine belly with 1 to 1 1/2 tablespoons. Reserve the remaining filling.

In a large sauté pan, heat the olive oil over medium-high heat. When the oil is hot, add the fish and cook, turning once, for about 1 1/2 minutes on each side, until crispy on both sides. You may need to do this in batches to avoid crowding the pan. (If this step seems too difficult, you can skip it. Instead, arranged the stuffed fish in the prepared baking dish, sprinkle with salt and pepper, brush with a little olive oil, and bake in the preheated oven for 5 to 10 minutes, then continue with the next step at the point at which you add the sauce.)

Carefully transfer the sardines to the prepared baking dish, packing them close together, and season with salt and pepper. Spoon the tomato sauce over the fish, getting some on each of the fish but not covering them completely. Sprinkle the remaining filling over the fish and then tuck the bay leaves in between the fish.

Pop the pan into the oven and bake the sardines for 15 to 20 minutes, about 10 minutes per inch of thickness, until tender when gently pressed. Serve hot, at room temperature, or chilled.

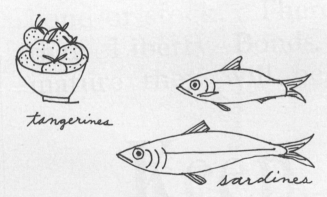

tangerines

sardines

black pepper

SWORDFISH INVOLTINI
WITH CRISPY BREAD CRUMBS AND HERBS

Darren McRonald, who was the chef at Cindy's Backstreet Kitchen while I was working on this book, is a fantastic Italian cook and this is one of my favorite of his many excellent fish dishes. It is wonderful as part of this menu, but it is also good on its own with a simple spinach salad or braised chard or with the Potatoes, Tomatoes, and Greens on page 121. These tasty stuffed rolls also make a good small first course, with just one roll per person.

When shopping for the fish, look for Pacific swordfish that has been sustainably caught, either by harpoon on longline, rather than by trawling. Try to find a chunk that has been cut from the loin and has a large eye. The eye of the loin is the center part that is usable when sliced, not the trim that you would scrape and use for a dumpling filling, for example. Ideally, you want to start with a triangular piece of fish that is 4 inches along the bottom and 6 inches to the tip. If you cannot find good swordfish, tuna or skinless sole fillets can be used. If you use sole, lay the stuffing on the skinned side of the fillet. The muscle structure of the skinned side will help hold everything together after rolling. The fish may be stuffed earlier in the day and kept covered in the refrigerator. Return the dish to room temperature before baking. Reserve the leftover stuffing for toasting in the oven alongside the fish. As Darren showed me, it makes a great garnish. | SERVES 6

STUFFING

3 TABLESPOONS OLIVE OIL

1/2 WHITE ONION, MINCED

1/4 CUP PINE NUTS, TOASTED [SEE PAGE 23]

1/4 CUP DRIED CURRANTS, SOAKED IN WARM WATER TO
COVER UNTIL SOFT [ABOUT 30 MINUTES] AND DRAINED

3 CUPS FINE FRESH BREAD CRUMBS
[FROM CRUST-FREE BREAD]

1/3 CUP MINCED FRESH FLAT-LEAF PARSLEY LEAVES,
RINSED AND SQUEEZED DRY [SEE PAGE 83]

LEAVES FROM 2 TO 3 THYME SPRIGS, MINCED
[ABOUT 1 TABLESPOON]

LEAVES FROM 2 TO 3 MINT SPRIGS, MINCED
[ABOUT 2 TABLESPOONS]

1/4 CUP DRY WHITE WINE

SEA SALT AND FRESHLY GROUND BLACK PEPPER

1 1/2-POUND PIECE SWORDFISH LOIN, 4 BY 6 INCHES

1 LEMON, HALVED LENGTHWISE,
CUT INTO 12 HALF-MOONS, AND SEEDED

3 TABLESPOONS OLIVE OIL

To make the stuffing, in a small sauté pan, heat the olive oil over medium-high heat. Add the onion and sauté for about 5 minutes, until it is tender but has not taken on any color. Remove from the heat and add the pine nuts, currants, bread crumbs, parsley, thyme, mint, and wine and season with salt and pepper. Stir to mix well and reserve until needed.

Thinly slice the fish loin into 12 equal slices (about 2 ounces each). To make the slices a little thinner and easier to roll, lay each slice between lightly dampened sheets of plastic wrap and pound them to thin slightly.

Preheat the oven to 375°F. Select a baking dish just large enough to accommodate the fish rolls in a single layer, without crowding, and rub the dish with olive oil.

To make the rolls, position a slice of fish with the long side (bottom of the triangle) facing you. Place 1 1/2 to 2 tablespoons of the stuffing near the edge of the fish nearest you and gently roll the fish around the stuffing like a cannoli. Place the roll, seam side down, in the prepared baking dish. Repeat with the

CONTINUED

Swordfish Involtini, *continued*

swordfish

remaining fish slices. You will not need all of the stuffing. Do not crowd the rolls in the dish. They need space to expand during cooking or they will cook unevenly. Place the lemon slices between the rolls, and then drizzle the olive oil over the rolls. Line a rimmed baking sheet with parchment paper and spread the leftover stuffing on the parchment.

Place the fish in the oven and roast for 8 to 12 minutes, until done. It should feel slightly firm to the touch when pressed gently. It will continue to cook when removed from the oven, so be careful not to overcook it. Put the stuffing in the oven at the same time to toast. If the fish rolls look a bit pale to you, pop the dish (make sure it is broiler safe) under the broiler for a bit to brown the top before taking it out of the oven. Transfer the rolls to a warmed platter or individual plates and sprinkle liberally with the toasted stuffing. Serve right away.

CHESTNUT AND GREEN OLIVE PORK STEW

After the initial steps, this stew can be finished on the stove top, in the oven, or in a slow cooker. It tastes even better on the second night, so I encourage you to make it a day ahead of serving. If you do refrigerate it overnight, remove the fat that will have solidified on the surface before reheating. I like this stew spooned over a mound of mashed or steamed potatoes or over plain or buckwheat polenta. You can make your own buckwheat polenta by adding 1 tablespoon buckwheat to each $^1/_2$ cup polenta before cooking, or you can purchase premixed buckwheat polenta from Manicaretti.

Unlike most Sicilian cooks, I prefer to use pitted olives in this stew, because I worry about someone chipping a tooth. In winter, vacuum-packed chestnuts, which are peeled, roasted, and ready to go, are easy to find in grocery stores. Fresh chestnuts are a lot of trouble, so if you cannot find vacuum-packed chestnuts, add a handful of toasted almonds just before the end of cooking. The stew is also good without any nuts. | SERVES 6

4 TO 4$^1/_2$ POUNDS BONELESS PORK BUTT, TRIMMED OF
  EXCESS FAT AND CUT INTO LARGE CHUNKS
2 TEASPOONS SEA SALT
1 TEASPOON FRESHLY GROUND BLACK PEPPER
OLIVE OIL, FOR BROWNING

1 TO 2 YELLOW ONIONS, CUT INTO CHUNKS
1 TO 2 CLOVES GARLIC
1 TO 2 CARROTS, PEELED AND CUT INTO CHUNKS
2 CUPS DRY WHITE WINE
3 TO 4 CUPS CHICKEN STOCK [PAGE 59] OR STORE-BOUGHT
  REDUCED-SODIUM BROTH

3 OR 4 BAY LEAVES

2 ROSEMARY OR SAGE SPRIGS

3/4 CUP BIG, MEATY GREEN OLIVES (SUCH AS PICHOLINE OR
   CASTELVETRANO), PITTED IF DESIRED

3/4 CUP VACUUM-PACKED CHESTNUTS

LEAVES AND TENDER STEMS FROM 1/2 BUNCH FLAT-LEAF
   PARSLEY, MINCED, RINSED, AND SQUEEZED DRY (SEE PAGE 83)

Season the pork with the salt and pepper. Place a large plate next to the stove for resting the browned meat. Coat a large, heavy pot with just enough olive oil to cover the bottom nicely and heat over medium-high heat. Working in batches to avoid overcrowding the pan, add the pork and sear, turning as needed, until browned on all sides. Using a slotted spoon or tongs, transfer to the plate to drain and rest while you brown the remaining meat.

When the final batch of pork has been transferred to the plate, add the onions, garlic, and carrots to the pot and cook over medium-high heat, stirring occasionally, for about 10 minutes, until browned. Using the slotted spoon, transfer the browned vegetables to the plate holding the meat. Add the wine to the pan, bring to a boil, and boil, scraping up any browned bits stuck to the pot bottom, until the liquid is reduced by half. Return the meat and vegetables to the pot and stir in 3 cups of the stock, the bay leaves, and the rosemary.

To finish the stew on the stove top, bring to a boil and decrease the heat to a simmer. Cook uncovered, skimming off any foam that rises to the surface, for 1 1/2 to 2 hours, until the pork is tender. If the stew seems to be getting too dry, add some or all of the remaining 1 cup stock. During the last 20 minutes of cooking, stir in the olives and chestnuts.

To finish the stew in the oven, bring to a boil on the stove top, cover, and place in a preheated 300°F oven for 2 1/2 to 3 hours. To finish the stew in a slow cooker, transfer the stew to the cooker and cook

on the medium setting for 6 hours. In either case, if the stew seems to be getting too dry, add some or all of the remaining 1 cup stock. During the last 20 minutes of cooking, stir in the olives and chestnuts.

Remove and discard the bay leaves and rosemary sprigs. Serve piping hot, garnished liberally with the parsley.

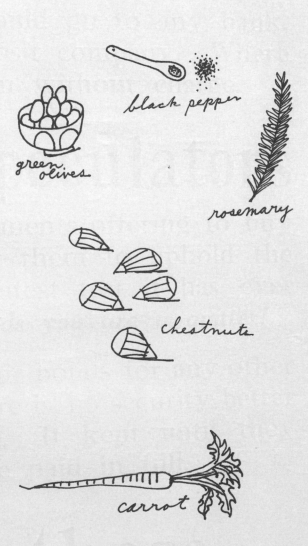

green olives

black pepper

rosemary

chestnuts

carrot

LIMONCELLO-DRENCHED BABAS
WITH WHIPPED CREAM AND CANDIED PISTACHIOS

It seems like every family with a Meyer lemon tree in the Napa Valley makes limoncello, the popular lemon liqueur of southern Italy. It is simple to make, requiring more time than effort, and homemade is more delicious than store-bought. If you decide to make it, consider doubling the batch and use the extra for gifts or for personal consumption (a little added to a martini or margarita never hurts). It is always a good idea to use organic ingredients, but it is especially important for limoncello because you are using the skins of the lemons. If you cannot find Meyer lemons, use whatever lemon variety you can find. You can also substitute tangerines or mandarin oranges for the lemons.

The babas are yeast-raised cakes, a dessert that you don't see often nowadays. To make them, you will need up to twelve $^1/_2$-cup baba molds or custard cups or a single 12-cup Bundt pan. I rarely end up with leftover babas, but when I do, I use them to make a trifle. | SERVES 8 TO 12

LIMONCELLO SYRUP
1 CUP SUGAR
2 CUPS WATER
$^3/_4$ CUP LIMONCELLO, HOMEMADE
    [PAGE 135] OR STORE-BOUGHT

BABAS
1 TABLESPOON ACTIVE DRY YEAST
$^1/_4$ CUP WARM WATER [105°F]
2 CUPS ALL-PURPOSE FLOUR
2 TABLESPOONS SUGAR
$^1/_8$ TEASPOON SALT
4 EGGS, AT ROOM TEMPERATURE
SEEDS SCRAPED FROM 1 VANILLA BEAN
$^2/_3$ CUP UNSALTED BUTTER, AT ROOM TEMPERATURE,
    CUT INTO SMALL PIECES
4 TO 5 TABLESPOONS GOLDEN RAISINS OR DRIED
    CURRANTS, SOAKED IN A LITTLE LIMONCELLO

CANDIED PISTACHIOS
$^3/_4$ CUP PISTACHIOS
1 EGG WHITE
SUGAR, FOR COATING

2 CUPS HEAVY CREAM
LIME OR LEMON MARMALADE,
    FOR GLAZE [OPTIONAL]
SPLASH OF LIMONCELLO [OPTIONAL]

vanilla beans

pistachios

To make the syrup, in a small saucepan, combine the sugar and water and bring to a boil over high heat. Decrease the heat to medium and reduce for 8 to 10 minutes, until thick. Take the pan off the heat, stir in the limoncello, and set aside until you are ready to glaze the babas.

To make the babas, in a small bowl, sprinkle the yeast over the warm water and let stand for 5 minutes, until foamy. Add $^1/_4$ cup of the flour to the yeast mixture and stir well.

In a stand mixer fitted with the paddle attachment, mix together the remaining $1^3/_4$ cups flour, the sugar, and the salt on medium-high speed for 20 to 30 seconds. On medium speed, add the eggs, vanilla seeds, and yeast mixture and beat until combined. Remove the bowl from the stand, cover with a wet towel (or a clean shower cap), and let the dough rise for about 1 hour, until doubled in size.

When the dough has almost doubled, preheat the oven to 350°F. Butter twelve $^1/_2$-cup baba molds or custard cups and place on a rimmed baking sheet. Or, butter one 12-cup Bundt pan.

When the dough has doubled, sprinkle the butter and soaked raisins over it and return the bowl to the mixer stand fitted with the paddle attachment. (Make sure the butter is soft at room temperature, so that it will combine easily.) On medium speed, beat until the butter is thoroughly incorporated.

Pour the batter into the prepared molds, filling them no more than two-thirds full, or into the Bundt pan. Bake for 15 to 20 minutes, if using small molds, or 40 to 50 minutes, if using a Bundt pan, until puffed and golden. The babas are done when a toothpick inserted into the center comes out clean and they spring back when pressed gently; once turned out of the molds, they will sound hollow when tapped on the bottom.

Meanwhile, make the pistachios. Line a rimmed baking sheet with parchment paper or a silicone baking mat. In a small bowl, toss the pistachios with the egg white and sugar, coating evenly. Pour the coated nuts out onto the prepared baking sheet and spread them in a single layer. Bake for about 7 minutes, until lightly browned. Let cool completely on the pan.

When the babas are done, remove them from the oven and immediately invert onto a rack. Let them cool slightly. While the cakes are still warm, arrange them in a large, shallow dish. With a toothpick or skewer, prick each cake in a number of places. Drizzle the cakes with about half of the syrup, turn the cakes over, and drizzle with the remaining syrup. Let the babas sit in the dish to absorb any syrup that wasn't soaked up right away and let cool before serving. If you have used a Bundt pan, invert the cake onto the rack, let cool slightly, then while still warm, place the rack and cake over a baking sheet. Prick the Bundt cake repeatedly, and pour the syrup over. Or, after thoroughly pricking the cake, place it back in the Bundt pan and pour the syrup over. (If it cools too much and won't release from the pan, reheat in the oven for 5 minutes.)

At least 15 minutes before serving, put a bowl and a whisk or the beaters for a handheld mixer into the freezer. Just before serving, pour the cold cream into the chilled bowl and whisk or beat with a handheld mixer on medium-high speed until the cream has doubled in volume. Do not overbeat.

To serve, divide the babas among individual plates, spoon the whipped cream on top or alongside, then sprinkle with the candied nuts. Serve the Bundt cake sliced on a large plate, topped with whipped cream and sprinkled with the candied nuts. For a fancy finish, melt a little lime or lemon marmalade over low heat, thin with a splash of limoncello, and brush a little of the glaze on the top of each baba before topping with the cream and nuts.

LIMONCELLO

4 LEMONS, PREFERABLY MEYER,
   WELL SCRUBBED, PLUS
   JUICE OF 2 LEMONS, STRAINED
2 CUPS (90 PROOF) VODKA
1 CUP SUGAR
1 CUP WATER

Have ready a sterilized pint (or larger) glass jar with a tight-fitting lid (see page 278 for instructions on how to sterilize the jar).

Using a vegetable peeler, peel the 4 lemons, removing only the zest and none of the bitter white pith. Put the peels in the sterilized jar and pour in the vodka. Cover and let sit at room temperature for 10 days. Juice the 4 lemons and use the juice to make lemonade or for another use.

When the 10 days have passed, in a small saucepan, combine the sugar, water, and the juice from 2 lemons and bring to a rolling boil over high heat, stirring to dissolve the sugar. Boil for 5 minutes, then remove from the heat and let cool completely.

Add the cold syrup to the lemon peel–vodka mixture in the jar and re-cover. Shake to mix. Let the jar sit in a cool cupboard or other dark spot for at least 10 days. Strain through a fine-mesh sieve before using. Store in a dark cupboard for up to 6 months.

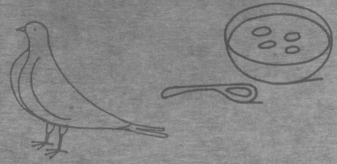

SPAIN

My first trip to Spain was in 1993, not long after opening Roti, in San Francisco. I was in the restaurant one afternoon, when the phone rang, and a man who introduced himself as Juan said he would like to send me a ticket to Spain. My response was quick: "I don't have time for this," I said, thanked him, and hung up. He called back immediately, told me I would be receiving a first-class ticket to Spain the next day, and that he hoped to see me and a lot of other American chefs in Spain in two weeks.

The Spanish government felt that Americans were so focused on Italy and France that they were missing the marvelous cuisine of Spain, and that the only way to change that was to invite American chefs to explore the country. When I arrived in Madrid, a big, handsome Spaniard came up to me and said, "Hello, Cindy." I recognized his voice—it was Juan. We were soon joined by a half dozen other chefs and we set out on our journey. We visited the buildings of Gaudí, the art of Dalí, and the works of many other Spanish forward-thinkers. We went from city— Madrid, Segovia, Barcelona, San Sebastián— to countryside—craggy mountains, arid plains, lush forests, sandy beaches—and each stop was pure chef heaven to me. Every city and every region had its own culinary traditions, its own flavors, and even the most elegant meals had an intensity of flavor and a sense of fun and warmheartedness. When I returned home, I couldn't wait to start cooking Spanish food.

Several years later, when friends from Spain were visiting, forty people came to my home for dinner. One of them, Juan Suarez (a different Juan), asked if he could help me with the cooking. In his professional life, Juan is a well-respected lawyer, but as with many men in Spain, he is also a true culinarian. *Ajo blanco*, a white gazpacho made with bread and almonds, was the evening's first course, and Juan made it the traditional way, slowly pounding the nuts and bread in a mortar. He prepared it alone, with no help from me or from an electric appliance, and the amount of pounding that that single dish demanded to feed my forty guests was extraordinary. That's why the opening course of this menu has to be *ajo blanco*.

WHITE GAZPACHO
WITH PEELED WHITE GRAPES

When you taste this velvety chilled soup, you won't believe that it contains no cream. The texture comes from finely ground almonds and bread. I've researched several recipes for this soup, as I love it, and it seems that people are split half and half on whether to soak the bread in water or in milk. I like to soak the bread in milk (whole, low fat, whatever you have) but I do it in water for my vegan guests. Use your very best olive oil, almonds, sherry, and bread for this dish. Every ingredient has to shine.

The classic garnish for this soup is peeled grapes. Yes, it is like the days of ancient Rome, but it is such a perfect garnish that it is worth the effort. Use a sharp paring knife and sit down for a few minutes to do it. Peel at least three grapes per serving.

I use raw (skin-on) almonds for most dishes because I prefer their appearance, but for this one, I buy blanched almonds. You can skin natural almonds yourself: Bring them to a boil in water to cover, boil for a few minutes, and drain well. Rub them in a tea towel until the skins slip off and then toss the skins. Some people prefer to roast the nuts and steam them wrapped in a towel to loosen the skins. If you do it this way, be sure not to brown them!

You can make this soup the day before the meal (but wait to peel the grapes the day of serving). It will separate but you can whisk it back together in about three seconds. Serve the soup in well-chilled bowls, either by putting the bowls in the refrigerator for 30 minutes before serving or by filling them with ice for about 10 minutes before serving and then tossing out the ice just before ladling in the soup. A $^{1}/_{2}$-cup portion is plenty if you are serving the whole menu, as the soup is quite rich. I often serve it in espresso cups or demitasses to guests while they are still milling around before dinner. It looks especially stunning in dark bowls. This recipe makes more soup than you'll need if making the rest of the menu, but be sure to keep the leftovers because it's fantastic the next day for lunch. | SERVES 6 TO 8

1/2 LOAF DAY-OLD ARTISANAL WHITE BREAD [ABOUT 7 OUNCES]

1 CUP MILK [OR WATER FOR A VEGAN SOUP]

18 TO 30 LARGE WHITE SEEDLESS GRAPES

1 1/3 CUPS [7 OUNCES] BLANCHED WHOLE ALMONDS

2 TO 4 CLOVES GARLIC, COARSELY CHOPPED

3/4 CUP EXTRA VIRGIN OLIVE OIL

1 CUP ICE MIXED WITH 2 1/2 CUPS WATER [THE MEASURING CUP SHOULD READ 3 1/2 CUPS]

2 TABLESPOONS AGED SPANISH SHERRY VINEGAR

SEA SALT

grapes

Trim off the crust from the bread and tear the bread into even-sized chunks. Put the chunks in a bowl, pour the milk over them, and let soak for 1 hour. While the bread is soaking, peel the grapes, place in a bowl, cover, and refrigerate.

After 1 hour, squeeze the milk from the bread and discard the liquid. In a food processor, combine the nuts, garlic, and bread. With the motor running, slowly add the olive oil in a thin, steady stream. Then, with the motor still running, slowly add the ice water and then the vinegar. Season with salt.

CONTINUED

White Gazpacho, *continued*

In Spain, this soup is typically perfectly smooth. To achieve that texture, process the pureed soup in small batches, running each batch for at least 1 minute. Strain the blended soup through a chinois (ultrafine-mesh conical sieve) or a double-mesh sieve. When you taste the soup, it should be velvety, without any graininess at all.

Refrigerate the soup until very cold, at least 30 minutes or up to overnight, and chill the bowls for at least 30 minutes. Just before serving, cut the grapes in half lengthwise. Ladle the soup into the cold bowls, and float some grape halves on top of each serving. Refrigerate any leftover soup in an airtight container for up to 2 days.

SHERRIED SQUAB LIVERS ON TOAST

While the squabs are roasting in the oven (see page 142), make this simple, delicious first course from the reserved livers for guests to enjoy with a good Pinot Noir while they wait for the main course. (If your butcher will be cleaning the birds for you, be sure to ask him or her to save the livers for you.) This could also be done with chicken livers, although they will take a little longer to cook.

Use great bread to make the toast. And because the livers will cook very quickly and are best served warm, be sure to have the toast ready before you begin cooking them. You could dress this up with chopped parsley or chervil, but I like to keep it simple: just bite-size toasts topped with the liver cooked in butter and sherry. | SHOWN PAGE 141 | SERVES 4

1 TO 2 TABLESPOONS UNSALTED BUTTER

4 SQUAB LIVERS

1 TABLESPOON DRY SHERRY, PLUS MORE IF NEEDED

4 SLICES COUNTRY-STYLE BREAD, TOASTED
    AND THEN CUT INTO A SLICE JUST LARGE
    ENOUGH TO HOLD A LIVER

Heat a small sauté pan over medium heat and add 1 tablespoon of the butter. When the butter is hot, add the livers and cook, turning once, for 30 seconds on each side. Pour in the sherry and continue to cook for 1 to 1$\frac{1}{2}$ minutes, until medium-rare or no more than medium. If the pan seems dry, add the remaining 1 tablespoon butter or pour in another splash of sherry. Let cook for 10 seconds more, then remove from the heat.

Place each toast on a plate, top each toast with a liver, and spoon the pan juices over the livers. Serve right away.

ROASTED STRIPED BASS
WITH POTATOES AND TOMATOES

I wish Americans were not so afraid of fish. A big fish like a striped bass is easy to cook once it has been cut into steaks (bone in and with skin intact for flavor), which is what I am using here. Once you arrange all of the ingredients in a *cazuela* (see page 142) or shallow ceramic or glass baking dish and slip it into the oven, you only have to baste it a few times and sip wine. You can use skinless fish fillets, but you will need to baste the fish a little more often.

If you are lucky enough to have a wood-burning oven, use it to cook this dish, increasing the cooking time to 25 minutes. You can also try a different type of potato, such as German Butterball, French fingerling, or other yellow-fleshed variety. Do not use new potatoes, however, as they are too waxy and won't cook up creamy and delicious in the oven. The herb paste may be made the night before and refrigerated. And the entire dish may be assembled ahead of time and kept in the refrigerator under plastic wrap for up to 6 hours. Bring it back to room temperature before placing in the hot oven. | SHOWN PAGE 141 | SERVES 4

HERB PASTE
SEA SALT AND FRESHLY GROUND BLACK PEPPER
4 LARGE OR 6 SMALL CLOVES GARLIC, COARSELY CHOPPED
4 GREEN ONIONS, WHITE AND PALE GREEN PARTS ONLY, MINCED
3 TABLESPOONS CHOPPED FRESH FLAT-LEAF ITALIAN
    PARSLEY LEAVES, RINSED AND SQUEEZED DRY [SEE PAGE 83]
LEAVES FROM 1-INCH ROSEMARY SPRIG, COARSELY CHOPPED
LEAVES FROM 3 FRESH THYME SPRIGS, COARSELY CHOPPED

3 LARGE YUKON GOLD POTATOES, THINLY SLICED
4 [6-OUNCE] STRIPED BASS STEAKS, 3/4 TO 1 INCH THICK
4 TOMATOES, PEELED [SEE PAGE 181] AND HALVED THROUGH
    THE EQUATOR
SEA SALT AND FRESHLY GROUND BLACK PEPPER
4 TO 6 TABLESPOONS EXTRA VIRGIN OLIVE OIL

Fill a saucepan with salted water and bring to a boil over high heat. While the water is heating, make the herb paste. In a mortar, combine a small amount each of salt and pepper and the garlic and grind together with a pestle until a paste forms. Add the green onions, parsley, rosemary, and thyme and work together with the garlic paste. Alternatively, in a blender, combine all of the paste ingredients and process until everything is well chopped and mixed together. Do not overprocess the paste. It should have some texture. Set the paste aside.

Preheat the oven to 425°F. Oil the bottom of a 12-inch-diameter and 3-inch-deep *cazuela* with olive oil.

When the water is boiling, add the potato slices and boil for 8 to 10 minutes, until barely cooked. Drain the potatoes in a colander and then lay them in a single layer on a kitchen towel to cool.

Arrange the potato slices in the bottom of the prepared *cazuela*, covering it completely and evenly. Place the fish steaks on top the potatoes and tuck the tomato halves, cut side up, between the pieces of fish. Sprinkle with salt and pepper and drizzle with olive oil. Spoon some of the herb paste onto each tomato half and fish steak.

Roast the fish and potatoes, basting the fish 3 or 4 times during cooking, for 15 to 20 minutes, until the potatoes are fork-tender and the fish is just falling off the bone. If the fish is ready and the potatoes have a way to go, transfer the fish to a warmed platter and keep warm while you finish cooking the potatoes. It is better if the potatoes are overdone and the fish is underdone, so always blanch the potatoes more than you think you should.

Serve the fish and potatoes directly from the *cazuela*. Be sure to spoon some of the sauce from the bottom of the *cazuela* over the fish and potatoes on each diner's plate.

ROASTED SQUAB

ROASTED
STRIPED BASS

RICOTTA CHEESE

SHERRIED SQUAB LIVERS ON TOAST

141

ROASTED SQUAB

WITH GARLIC, ONIONS, AND SHERRY

If you are a hunter, this is a great way to cook game birds. You can make this recipe with any medium or small birds or bird parts: pigeons, ducks, quail, partridge, pheasant breasts, Cornish game hens, bone-in chicken breasts, or chickens split into halves or quarters. Roasting the meat over sherry-braised onions and garlic makes it juicy and flavorful. Cooking times will, of course, vary. Quail will cook the fastest, it depends on size with squab and pheasant, and wild duck will cook much quicker than domestic duck.

Cooking in a *cazuela* is something you want to do on a slow, lazy cooking-at-home day. If you are in a hurry, you can prepare this dish in a covered sauté pan over medium heat. The onions should be ready in no more than 10 to 15 minutes. Just remember to uncover the pan and give them a stir every now and again. If you don't have a *cazuela* and you are not in a rush, use a paella pan or a large sauté pan. You want something with short sides for evaporation and large enough so that the birds are not too crowded.

When the thyme in my garden is in bloom, I stuff handfuls of it into the cavities of the birds. When you serve the birds, you can pull out the darkened thyme sprigs or leave them in. You can also choose to reduce the braising juices or leave them lighter, more like a broth. I prefer a broth consistency so that I can sop it up with slices of crusty bread. | SHOWN PAGE 140 | SERVES 4

4 SQUABS, LIVERS RESERVED FOR SERVING ON TOAST
    [PAGE 138] AND GIZZARDS, HEARTS, WING TIPS,
    AND NECKS RESERVED FOR STOCK [SEE PAGE 143]
SEA SALT AND FRESHLY GROUND BLACK PEPPER
16 TO 24 FRESH THYME SPRIGS [4 TO 6 SPRIGS PER BIRD]
6 TABLESPOONS EXTRA VIRGIN OLIVE OIL
1 HEAD GARLIC, SEPARATED INTO CLOVES, LOOSE SKINS
    REMOVED, AND ROOT END ON EACH CLOVE TRIMMED
2 YELLOW ONIONS, HALVED THROUGH THE STEM END AND
    THINLY SLICED INTO CRESCENTS [ABOUT 1½ CUPS]
1½ CUPS DRY SHERRY
EXTRA VIRGIN OLIVE OIL, UNSALTED BUTTER,
    OR RENDERED DUCK FAT, FOR THE BIRDS

Rinse each bird under cold running water and pat dry with paper towels. Season the birds inside and out with salt and pepper and place 4 to 6 thyme sprigs in the cavity of each bird. Let the birds rest at room temperature for 30 minutes before cooking, or cover and refrigerate overnight.

Set a large *cazuela* on the stove top, turn on the heat to the lowest setting, and pour in the olive oil. Add the garlic and onions, sprinkle with a little salt, and cook, stirring occasionally, for 45 minutes to 1½ hours, until sweet and lightly golden. If you are using a sauté pan or paella pan, start the garlic and onions over medium heat and cook for about 10 minutes, until the onions are sweet and slightly golden, then decrease the heat and continue to cook for about 15 minutes, until tender.

sea salt

garlic

Sherry

cazuela

clove

About 20 minutes before the garlic and onions are ready, preheat the oven to 450°F. If you have a convection oven, prehcat it to 425°F. (I have also cooked these birds in a covered Big Green Egg barbecue grill and in a wood-fired oven.)

Pour in the sherry and increase the heat a little. When the sherry comes to a boil, remove from the heat and arrange the birds, breast side down, on top of the onions and garlic. Drizzle olive oil over each bird or smear with butter or duck fat and pop into the oven. Roast for 20 minutes, then flip the birds over and roast for another 10 to 15 minutes, basting at least 3 or 4 times during cooking. Remove the birds from the oven when they are golden brown and delicious.

You can plate each bird with a mound of onions and several spoonfuls of the sauce, or you can arrange the birds and onions on a large platter and pass the sauce separately. Alternatively, place the *cazuela* right on the table, being sure to protect the tabletop from the hot dish.

TIPS AND TRICKS
USING EVERY PART

BECAUSE I DON'T LIKE TO WASTE ANY PART OF THE BIRD, I MAKE A STOCK FROM THE SQUAB TRIMMINGS. FIRST, RINSE THE RESERVED TRIMMINGS UNDER COLD WATER AND PLACE THEM IN A SMALL SAUCEPAN. ADD WATER OR CHICKEN STOCK [PAGE 59] JUST TO COVER [1 TO 2 CUPS]. ADD A FEW YELLOW ONION SLICES, A BAY LEAF OR TWO, A FEW PEPPERCORNS, AND THE STEMS OF ANY HERBS FROM A DISH YOU MIGHT ME MAKING AT THE SAME TIME. BRING TO A BOIL OVER HIGH HEAT, DECREASE THE HEAT TO LOW, AND SIMMER FOR 30 MINUTES OR SO. IF YOU DON'T NEED THE BROTH RIGHT AWAY, LET IT COOL AND STORE IT IN THE FREEZER FOR UP TO 2 MONTHS.

IF THE SAUCE STARTS TO REDUCE TOO MUCH WHEN YOU ARE ROASTING THE SQUABS, ADD SOME OF THIS STOCK. IF YOU NEED A THICKER SAUCE, KEEP THE BIRDS WARM, POUR THE JUICES INTO A LITTLE SAUCEPAN, ADD SOME OF THIS STOCK, AND REDUCE OVER HIGH HEAT. YOU CAN FINISH THE SAUCE WITH A LITTLE BUTTER, BUT THAT TAKES THE DISH TO A DIFFERENT LEVEL—NO LONGER SIMPLE AND RUSTIC.

yellow onion

bay leaves

RICOTTA CHEESE
WITH WARM HONEY AND WALNUTS

It seems in every country you can find a dish that combines cheese or a fermented milk product, honey, and nuts. Here, I mix fresh ricotta cheese with crème fraîche to make a light dessert that has a consistency reminiscent of cheesecake but without all of the work. You will need to use a high-quality ricotta. On the West Coast, Bellwether Farms makes two types, from Jersey cow's milk and from sheep's milk, either of which would be good. Top-quality farmer cheese can be used in place of the ricotta.

Warm the honey just before serving and give the nuts a hint of toasting. Don't brown the nuts too much or you won't taste the cheese. Walnuts are traditional, but you can also use salted Marcona almonds. Their saltiness delivers a nice contrast to the sweet honey and rich ricotta cheese.

In summer, serve this with fresh berries scattered about or strawberry jam or orange marmalade instead of the honey, if you prefer. For serving, I use shallow, miniature *cazuelas* from Spain that hold just 1/3 cup. I like the contrast of the caramel color of the *cazuelas* against the white cheese, but any small ramekins or cups will work. You can make this dessert the night before serving, but it goes together so quickly that you won't feel pressured making it just before dinner.

SHOWN PAGES 140–141 | SERVES 4

1 CUP FRESH RICOTTA CHEESE

1/3 CUP CRÈME FRAÎCHE

1/2 CUP FLAVORFUL HONEY [SUCH AS BLACKBERRY, POPULAR IN NAPA, OR ORANGE BLOSSOM]

1/2 CUP WALNUTS, LIGHTLY TOASTED [SEE PAGE 23]

In a bowl, whisk together the ricotta and crème fraîche just until combined. Spoon into ramekins and smooth the tops, then cover and chill until serving.

When ready to serve, heat the honey just until warm. Pour a little of the warm honey over each filled ramekin and top with the nuts. Serve while the honey is warm.

cazuela

Blackberry Honey

ricotta cheese

walnuts

HUNGARY

In the 1960s, according to George Lang in *The Cuisine of Hungary*, the Gallup Poll listed *gulyás* as one of the five most popular meat dishes in the United States. What happened? We all went Italian and French. But *gulyás*, or goulash as Americans call it, is still a great dish, as you will discover when you make the recipe I have included here.

Paprika is indispensable in goulash and in many other Hungarian dishes, though the bright red pepper is not native to Hungary and the details of its arrival are clouded in disagreement. Some believe that the peppers are native to India and to East and Central Africa and were brought by the conquering Turks in the sixteenth century; others insist they were carried to Europe from America. Whenever they arrived, they are now an indispensable ingredient of the cuisine. Hungarian paprika comes in several different grades, ranging from very mild, very sweet, and bright red to mildly pungent and pale red to hot and light brown. For the most authentic taste, use Hungarian paprika in the dishes in this chapter, preferably one that is a blend of sweet and mildly pungent and is a rich red. The "rose" grade is a good choice and widely available in the United States.

Goulash, which some food scholars date to the ninth century, was originally a shepherd's dish that was cooked over an open fire wherever the herdsman and his flock settled for the night. I dream of making it that way someday—in a big iron kettle resting in a three-sided stand over a wood fire—and then eating it outdoors at tables covered with red-patterned cloths, much like you see in the Hungarian countryside, where families regularly dine outdoors in the warm summer months. That's the perfect centerpiece and the perfect setting for an alfresco Supper Club feast.

MUSHROOM FRITTERS

A combination of mushrooms is nice here to ensure a variety of textures and tastes. Try to include a mix of small, leggy types that grow in clumps, a medium-size variety, and a meaty large type. Clean the mushrooms by gently wiping them with barely damp paper towels. Do not dunk them in water or they will soak it up and become soggy. The batter here is similar to a crepe batter: eggy, milky, and light, rather than a heavier classic fritter batter. You can make the batter a few hours ahead up to the point at which you whisk in the egg whites, and then finish it just before you are ready to begin frying. Although I have used canola oil here, Hungarian cooks traditionally use lard. See page 276 for more thoughts on deep-frying. | SHOWN PAGE 150 | MAKES ENOUGH FOR A BIG FRITTER PARTY

1½ POUNDS MUSHROOMS (SUCH AS SHIITAKE, MOREL,
    CHANTERELLE, KING TRUMPET, YELLOW FOOT, CREMINI,
    AND PORCINI), STEMMED AND HALVED IF LARGE
2 TABLESPOONS FRESHLY SQUEEZED LEMON JUICE
SEA SALT AND FRESHLY GROUND BLACK PEPPER

VINAIGRETTE
1 SHALLOT, MINCED
JUICE OF ½ LEMON
1 TABLESPOON CHAMPAGNE VINEGAR
¼ TEASPOON SEA SALT
PINCH OF FRESHLY GROUND BLACK PEPPER
6 TABLESPOONS EXTRA VIRGIN OLIVE OIL
SCANT 1 TABLESPOON CHOPPED FRESH DILL

BATTER
2 TABLESPOONS EXTRA VIRGIN OLIVE OIL
2 EGGS, SEPARATED
1 CUP WHOLE MILK
¾ CUP ALL-PURPOSE FLOUR

CANOLA OIL, FOR DEEP-FRYING
2 TABLESPOONS ALL-PURPOSE FLOUR
SEA SALT
3 CUPS WILD ARUGULA OR OTHER INTERESTING,
    FLAVORFUL GREEN, TOUGH STEMS REMOVED
DILL FRONDS, FOR GARNISH

Place the mushrooms in a large bowl, drizzle with the lemon juice, season with salt and pepper, and toss to mix. Let the mushrooms sit for 30 minutes or so.

To make the vinaigrette, in a small bowl, whisk together the shallot, lemon juice, vinegar, salt, and pepper until the salt dissolves. Gradually whisk in the olive oil in a slow, steady stream and continue to whisk until well emulsified. Whisk in the dill and set aside.

To make the batter, in a bowl, whisk together the olive oil, egg yolks, and milk until blended and then whisk in the flour until smooth. In a separate bowl, whisk the egg whites until thick and frothy (but not forming peaks). Fold the egg whites into the yolk mixture just until combined.

Preheat the oven to warm. Line a plate or two with paper towels for draining the mushrooms when they come out of the oil. Pour the canola oil to a depth of 4 inches into a deep, heavy saucepan

Chanterelle

and heat to 350°F to 365°F on a deep-frying thermometer. Dust the mushrooms with the flour.

When the oil is ready, dip a handful of the mushrooms into the batter, lift them out, allowing the excess batter to drain off, and carefully placing them in the hot oil. (Do not crowd the pan or the mushrooms will turn into oil sponges.) Fry the mushrooms, making sure they do not touch one another, for 3 to 4 minutes, until the batter has puffed up a bit and is a crispy golden brown. Using a wire skimmer, transfer to a towel-lined plate and keep them warm in the oven while you fry successive batches. Repeat with the remaining mushrooms, always skimming away any stray fried bits and making sure the oil returns to 350°F to 365°F before you add a new batch. Salt the fritters to taste as they come out of the pan.

To serve, place the greens in a bowl and dress with just enough of the vinaigrette to coat lightly. Mound the greens in the center of a large serving plate. Arrange the fritters around the greens, drizzle a little extra vinaigrette around the edge of the plate, and sprinkle dill fronds sparingly about. Go easy on the dill; less is more here. Or, you can plate individual servings.

king trumpet

morel

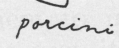

porcini

cremini

shiitake

PAPRIKA CHICKEN
WITH BUTTERED EGG DUMPLINGS

This comes together nicely if you cook the chicken, slip it into a warm oven, and then finish the sauce and boil the dumplings. If you are short on time, you can simplify the recipe by serving store-bought egg noodles in place of the dumplings, but do try the dumplings at least once. This dish makes a nice main course, accompanied with a green salad. | SHOWN PAGE 151 | SERVES 6

6 CHICKEN DRUMSTICKS, SKINNED IF DESIRED

6 CHICKEN THIGHS, SKINNED IF DESIRED

SEA SALT AND FRESHLY GROUND BLACK PEPPER

2 TABLESPOONS OLIVE OIL

1 LARGE YELLOW ONION, SLICED

1 RED BELL PEPPER, STEMMED, SEEDED,
    AND SLICED LENGTHWISE

3 TO 4 TABLESPOONS HUNGARIAN PAPRIKA

1/8 TO 1/4 TEASPOON CAYENNE PEPPER

1/2 CUP WATER

1 LARGE TOMATO, PEELED [SEE PAGE 181] AND DICED

DUMPLINGS

2 EGGS

3/4 CUP WATER

2 TABLESPOONS OLIVE OIL

1/2 TEASPOON SEA SALT

2 1/3 CUPS ALL-PURPOSE FLOUR

1/2 TEASPOON BAKING POWDER

2 TABLESPOONS SOUR CREAM

MELTED UNSALTED BUTTER, FOR DRESSING THE DUMPLINGS

2 TO 3 TABLESPOONS CHOPPED FRESH FLAT-LEAF
    PARSLEY LEAVES, RINSED AND SQUEEZED DRY [SEE PAGE 83],
    FOR GARNISH

1 GREEN BELL PEPPER, STEMMED, SEEDED, AND CUT INTO
    RINGS, FOR GARNISH

Season the chicken pieces with salt and pepper. In a large skillet, heat the olive oil over medium-high heat. Add the chicken pieces and cook, turning as needed, until lightly browned on both sides. Transfer the chicken to a plate to drain. Add the onion and red bell pepper to the pan and stir to coat with the oil. Decrease the heat to medium, cover, and sweat for 20 to 30 minutes, until the onion is tender and translucent but not browned. Uncover and stir occasionally and decrease the heat to low if the onion starts to brown.

Stir in the paprika and cayenne and cook, stirring, for 1 minute longer. Return the chicken to the pan and stir in the water and tomato. Adjust the heat to maintain a simmer, cover, and cook for about 30 minutes, until the chicken is opaque throughout.

While the chicken is cooking, make the dough for the dumplings. In a big bowl, whisk together the eggs, water, olive oil, and salt until blended. In a separate bowl, stir together the flour and baking powder. Add 1/2 cup of the flour mixture to the egg mixture and whisk until blended. Then add the remaining flour mixture and mix with a wooden spoon until you have a smooth, thick dough that holds together and can be rolled out. You may need to turn the dough out onto a floured work surface and knead it a few times for it to come together. If it is too wet and sticky, add a little more flour, a tablespoon at a time.

tomato

Lightly flour a large baking sheet or tray. On a lightly floured work surface, roll out the dough into a large rectangle or square $1/4$ to $1/3$ inch thick. (You may find it easier to divide the dough in half and roll out half at a time.) Using a sharp knife or a bench (or board) scraper, cut the dough into nonuniform 1- to 2-inch-wide strips, and then cut the strips crosswise to make free-form 1- to 2-inch shapes. Transfer the dumplings to the prepared pan and let them air-dry for several minutes before cooking. Bring a large pot filled with salted water to a rolling boil, for cooking the dumplings.

When the chicken is done, transfer the pieces to a nice platter and keep it in a warm oven while you finish the sauce and cook the dumplings.

To finish the sauce, scoop out about 1 cup of the broth from the skillet, stir the sour cream into it, and stir the mixture back into the skillet. (This is to temper the sour cream so it is not too cold when it hits the hot sauce.) Taste the sauce and adjust the seasoning with salt and pepper. Bring the sauce just to a boil over medium heat, decrease the heat to low, and keep it warm while you cook the dumplings.

yellow onion

To cook the dumplings, shake the excess flour from them, carefully drop them into the boiling water, and then stir a few times to make sure they are not sticking together. Cook until they float to the surface and then cook for 1 to 2 minutes longer and taste one. If it does not tasty doughy, the dumplings are ready. Scoop them out with a wire skimmer or large slotted spoon, shaking off the excess water, and transfer to a warmed serving bowl. Drizzle with the melted butter, sprinkle with some of the parsley, season with salt and pepper, and toss to coat evenly.

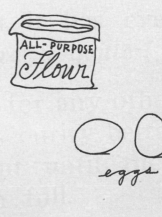

eggs

To serve, pour the steaming-hot sauce over the chicken and garnish the chicken with the green bell pepper and the remaining parsley. Serve the buttered dumplings on the side.

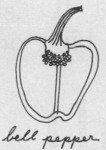

bell pepper

DIOTORTA

MUSHROOM
FRITTERS

PAPRIKA CHICKEN

151

GULYÁS

(GOULASH)

I have served this dish both as a main course and as a first course followed by a light main. To serve it as a main, leave the meat and vegetables in bigger pieces, cook the broth down to a thick, stewy consistency, and include dumplings (page 148). When serving the dumplings, it is traditional to use water rather than stock for the *gulyás*, but if you would like a richer broth, use stock. Time the dumplings so that you can transfer them directly to the hot finished stew. In Hungary, *gulyás* typically includes lard or suet, beef or mutton, and sometimes organ meats. My more "domestic" version is made with lamb shank, beef stew meat, and olive oil. Finally, although sour cream is not at all traditional, my husband, John, loves this dish with a dollop of sour cream, so I have included it as garnish. | SERVES 6

3 TO 4 TABLESPOONS OLIVE OIL [ENOUGH TO COAT BOTTOM
    OF A LARGE, WIDE PAN]

1¼ TO 1½ POUNDS BEEF STEW MEAT, CUT INTO BIG CHUNKS

2 SMALL LAMB SHANKS, ABOUT 1 POUND EACH, OR 2 POUNDS
    BONELESS LAMB SHOULDER MEAT, CUT INTO BIG CHUNKS

1 VERY LARGE YELLOW ONION, DICED

1 OR 2 CELERY STALKS, CUT INTO CHUNKS

2 MEDIUM OR 3 SMALL CARROTS, PEELED AND DICED

1 CLOVE GARLIC, CHOPPED AND THEN MASHED IN A MORTAR

1½ TEASPOONS CARAWAY SEEDS

¼ CUP HUNGARIAN PAPRIKA

SEA SALT

4 VERY RIPE TOMATOES, PEELED [SEE PAGE 181] AND DICED,
    OR 2 CUPS CANNED TOMATO SAUCE

4 TO 6 CUPS CHICKEN STOCK [PAGE 59] OR BEEF STOCK, STORE-
    BOUGHT REDUCED-SODIUM CHICKEN BROTH, OR WATER

5 MEDIUM YUKON GOLD OR RUSSET POTATOES [OR OTHER
    NONWAXY POTATO], DICED OR CUT INTO CHUNKS

1 TO 2 PARSLEY ROOTS OR 1 PARSNIP, PEELED AND DICED

2 GREEN BELL PEPPERS, STEMMED, SEEDED, AND DICED

1 TEASPOON CAYENNE PEPPER [OPTIONAL]

2 ANAHEIM CHILES, STEMMED, SEEDED, AND THINLY SLICED,
    FOR GARNISH

3 TABLESPOONS CHOPPED FRESH FLAT-LEAF PARSLEY LEAVES,
    RINSED AND SQUEEZED DRY [SEE PAGE 83], FOR GARNISH

SOUR CREAM, FOR SERVING

Set a large, wide, heavy pan over medium-high heat and pour in enough oil to coat the bottom. When the oil is hot, add the beef and cook, turning as needed, until the meat is nicely browned on all sides. Using a slotted spoon, transfer to a plate to drain. You may need to do this in batches so as not to crowd the pan. Then add the lamb shanks and cook, turning as needed, until nicely browned on all sides. Transfer to a plate.

Add the onion, celery, and carrots to the fat remaining in the pan and cook over medium-high heat, stirring, for about 10 minutes, until browned. Stir in the garlic and cook for a minute. Add the caraway and paprika, season with salt, and cook, stirring, for 1 to 2 minutes, until the caraway and paprika are fragrant. Return all of the meat to the pan and stir in the tomatoes and stock. Bring just to a boil, decrease the heat to a vigorous simmer, cover, and cook for 1½ to 2 hours, until the lamb and beef are tender when pierced with a fork. Check occasionally and skim off any foam that rises to the surface. (If you use lamb shoulder meat, the cooking time will probably be closer to 1 hour.)

When the meat is tender, transfer it to a large platter. Add the potatoes, parsley roots, and bell peppers to the pan and simmer for 15 to 20 minutes, until the potatoes and parsley roots are fork-tender.

While the vegetables are cooking, pull the meat from the shank bones and discard the bones. If you opt to make this as a soup, you will need to cut the lamb into smaller pieces. The beef will break into smaller pieces on its own. When the vegetables are almost tender, return the meat to the pan and add the cayenne.

Transfer the stew to a warmed large serving dish and garnish with the chiles and parsley. Pass the sour cream at the table for guests to dollop on top.

potatoes

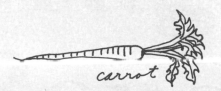

carrot

TIPS AND TRICKS

A DRAINING TIP

I DON'T LIKE TO DRAIN BROWNED MEATS AND VEGETABLES ON PAPER TOWELS BECAUSE THEY IMPART A CHEMICAL TASTE AND THEY SOAK UP JUICES THAT COULD BE RETURNED TO THE DISH. INSTEAD, I LIKE TO DRAIN MEATS AND VEGETABLES ON AN INVERTED PLATE (WITH A NICE SLOPING RIM) SET ON TOP OF A LARGER PLATE OR PLATTER. THIS WAY THE JUICES AND/OR FAT CAN DRAIN DOWN AND BE RETURNED TO THE PAN.

BEET SALAD GELLÉRT

Beets and beet greens are two of my favorite winter vegetables. In the cold months, we need color to wake up our appetites and beets always come through with color. If your beet greens are tender and young, add them to the salad or save them for a sautéed vegetable accompaniment. I named this simple but elegant salad for the celebrated Hotel Gellért, a stunning Art Nouveau structure in central Budapest that opened in 1918 and is famous for its handsome design and its thermal baths, complete with wave bath and sun-bathing terrace. | SERVES 6

1 BUNCH SMALL RED BEETS

1 BUNCH SMALL GOLDEN BEETS

SEA SALT

VINAIGRETTE

1/4 CUP CHAMPAGNE VINEGAR

1 TEASPOON DIJON MUSTARD

1 TABLESPOON PREPARED HORSERADISH

1/8 TEASPOON CARAWAY SEEDS

1 1/2 TEASPOONS SUGAR

1 TEASPOON SEA SALT

1/2 CUP EXTRA VIRGIN OLIVE OIL

beet

1 LARGE OR 2 SMALL HEADS BUTTER LETTUCE, LEAVES SEPARATED AND LEFT WHOLE IF SMALL OR TORN INTO PIECES IF LARGE

1 LARGE OR 2 SMALL HEADS FRISÉE, WHITE AND PALE GREEN LEAVES ONLY, CUT CROSSWISE INTO 1-INCH PIECES

Preheat the oven to 375°F.

Trim the greens off the beets, leaving 1/2 inch of the stem intact, and set the greens aside. Place the beets in a baking dish just large enough to accommodate them in

a single layer and add water to a depth of about 1 inch. Sprinkle some salt around the beets and cover the dish. Roast the beets for 45 minutes to 1 hour for beets that are 1 to 2 inches in diameter, until fork-tender. The timing will depend on the size of the beets.

While the beets are cooking, make the vinaigrette. In a small bowl, whisk together the vinegar, mustard, horseradish, caraway, sugar, and salt until the sugar and salt dissolve. Gradually whisk in the olive oil in a slow, steady stream and continue to whisk until well emulsified. Reserve until needed.

When the beets are ready, let them cool until they can be handled and then peel and julienne them and place in a bowl. Pour about one-third of the vinaigrette over the warm beets (reserve the remainder for the greens) and toss to coat.

Place the greens in a bowl, dress as needed with the remaining vinaigrette, and then divide among individual plates. Top with the beets, dividing them evenly, and serve immediately.

DIOTORTA

This special-occasion cake is made for baptisms, weddings, Christmas celebrations, and the like. It takes work and time to make, but it is so delicious and beautiful that it is worth the effort. If you are not up to the task, however, the walnut cake on its own, dusted with confectioners' sugar and each slice topped with a dollop of whipped cream, is a respectable stand-in.

Before you begin whipping the egg whites for the cake, have the other ingredients mixed together, as you must combine them the minute the whites are ready. A copper bowl is the best choice for whipping egg whites (copper chemically interacts with the whites, making them more stable and satiny), with stainless steel the next-best choice. A glass or ceramic bowl has slippery sides, which can restrict climbing, and plastic bowls can have traces of oil, which inhibit volume. Make sure the bowl and the whisk or mixer attachment are clean and dry.

If you cannot find chestnut puree for the chestnut cream, you can make your own. Buy chestnuts in simple syrup (look for them in jars in specialty food stores), drain off and reserve the syrup, and then combine the chestnuts with just enough of the simple syrup to process into a nice puree.

| MAKES ONE 9- OR 10-INCH CAKE; SERVES 10 TO 12

CAKE
4 EGGS, SEPARATED
1 CUP GRANULATED SUGAR
1 CUP WALNUTS, FINELY GROUND
1 TEASPOON BAKING POWDER
1/2 CUP ALL-PURPOSE FLOUR
1 TABLESPOON PURE VANILLA EXTRACT
1/2 TEASPOON PURE ALMOND EXTRACT
1/2 CUP PLUS 3 TABLESPOONS UNSALTED BUTTER, MELTED
SCANT 1/4 TEASPOON CREAM OF TARTAR
PINCH OF SALT

vanilla

COFFEE CREAM
3/4 CUP WHOLE MILK
1/2 CUP BREWED ESPRESSO
1 1/2 CUPS CONFECTIONERS' SUGAR
3 TABLESPOONS ALL-PURPOSE FLOUR
2 TEASPOONS PURE VANILLA EXTRACT
1 1/2 CUPS UNSALTED BUTTER,
    AT ROOM TEMPERATURE

espresso

Preheat the oven to 300°F. Butter and flour a 10-inch springform cake pan.

To make the cake, in a large bowl, using a stand mixer or handheld mixer on medium-high speed or a whisk, beat together the egg yolks and 1/2 cup of the granulated sugar until smooth, light, and fluffy. In a small bowl, stir together the walnuts, the remaining 1/2 cup sugar, and the baking powder until well combined. Slowly mix the walnut mixture into the yolk mixture in 3 batches, alternating with the flour in 2 batches, just until combined. Try not to deflate the yolks too much. Stir the vanilla and almond extracts into the melted butter, and then add the butter to the walnut-yolk mixture, stirring just until well mixed.

In a clean, dry bowl, combine the egg whites, cream of tartar, and salt and whisk on high speed with the mixer or vigorously by hand for 3 to 5 minutes, until soft peaks form. Transfer the beaten whites to the walnut mixture and fold them in gently, folding just until no white streaks are visible. Pour the batter into the prepared pan.

CONTINUED

Diotorta, *continued*

CHESTNUT CREAM
1 CUP [7 TO 8 OUNCES] SWEET CHESTNUT PUREE

²/₃ CUP UNSALTED BUTTER, AT ROOM TEMPERATURE

1 CUP CONFECTIONERS' SUGAR

2 TEASPOONS PURE VANILLA EXTRACT

2 TABLESPOONS DARK RUM

3 OUNCES SEMISWEET CHOCOLATE, CHOPPED

10 TO 12 PERFECT WALNUT HALVES

1 TO 1¹/₂ CUPS WALNUTS, TOASTED [SEE PAGE 23]
    AND FINELY CRUSHED [OPTIONAL]

Bake for 30 to 40 minutes, until the cake springs back when touched gently in the middle. This is meant to be a moist cake, so be careful not to over-bake it. Let the cake cool completely in the pan on a rack. When cool, run a knife around the inside edge of the pan to loosen the cake sides and then unclasp the pan sides and lift them off.

To make the coffee cream, set up an ice bath. In a heavy saucepan, combine the milk, espresso, confectioners' sugar, flour, and vanilla over low heat and cook, stirring constantly, for about 5 minutes, until a thick custard forms. (Alternatively, combine the ingredients in a baine marie over low heat.) Transfer the custard to a bowl, place the bowl in the ice bath, and stir the custard until cool.

Using a stand mixer fitted with the paddle attach-ment or a wooden spoon, beat the butter into the cooled custard until smooth. Cover and refrigerate for 20 minutes or so before frosting the cake. Do not refrigerate the mixture too long or the butter will harden and the coffee cream will be difficult to spread on the cake.

To make the chestnut cream, in a bowl, stir the chestnut puree to loosen it, so it will be easier to mix. In a bowl, using a mixer on medium-high speed or a wooden spoon, cream together the butter and confectioners' sugar until smooth and fluffy. Add the chestnut puree, vanilla, and rum and mix until combined.

Place the chocolate in a small heatproof bowl, place the bowl over (not touching) simmering water in a saucepan, and heat, stirring occasionally, until the chocolate melts and is smooth. Remove the bowl from the heat. One at a time, dip the walnut halves into the chocolate, coating evenly, and set the coated walnuts aside on a sheet of waxed paper or parchment paper. Let stand undisturbed for at least 10 minutes, until the chocolate hardens.

To assemble the cake, carefully slide it off the pan bottom onto a work surface. Using a long serrated knife and a sawing motion, cut the cake horizontally into 3 equal layers. Transfer 1 layer to a cake plate, top with half of the coffee cream, and spread evenly to the edges with an offset spatula. Place a second layer on top and spread the remaining coffee cream evenly over the layer. Place the third layer on top and refrigerate the cake for about 10 minutes to chill.

When the cake is cool, mound about two-thirds of the chestnut cream on the top, and using broad strokes, spread the cream evenly over the top and sides of the cake. Spoon the remaining chestnut cream into a pastry bag fitted with a ¹/₂-inch star tip and pipe 10 to 12 rosettes along the top edge of the cake, spacing them evenly around the entire cake (when you cut the cake, each slice will have a rosette). Nestle a chocolate-dipped walnut in the center of each rosette. Using your palm, carefully pat the crushed walnuts around the sides of the cake, pressing them firmly enough so that they adhere to the chestnut cream. Chill until ready to serve, but bring to room temperature 2 hours before serving. Cut into slices to serve. Store any leftover cake in the refrigerator for a couple of days.

chestnuts

RUSSIA AND GEORGIA

This menu is politically volatile. I wanted to include some Russian dishes in the book because my paternal grandfather was from Russia, and I have always loved Georgian food. But I have a limited number of pages, so I decided to combine Russia and Georgia in a single chapter in the hope that they will coexist happily here despite their tumultuous history.

Sadly, I have never been to Georgia, though I have long studied its cuisine, which is a heady mix of influences from the kitchens of the Middle East, Armenia, Azerbaijan, and Europe. I first went to Russia when I was in college and found myself in a world totally different from the Midwest of my childhood. Some of those days are a blur now, but I do remember eating smoked sturgeon every night and thinking that maybe it was the only way to use up all of the fish caught to sustain the country's profitable caviar industry.

Choosing just four dishes from my large cache of recipes from these two great cuisines was difficult. Sorrel is a popular soup green in Russia, and while the soup recipe in this chapter acknowledges that tradition, it was also inspired by the need to use up the sorrel that threatens to over-take my garden each spring. The Georgian "pressed" chicken, known as *tabaka*, after the traditional pan (*tapha*) in which it is cooked, was a relatively easy choice because it is so well known in both Georgia and Russia. In fact, it is so popular in Moscow that it is sometimes mistakenly identified as a Russian dish. Pancakes rolled around a savory or a sweet filling and mushrooms in countless guises are both common on the Russian table, so I decided to combine them here. And the pudding made from dried sour cherries and black bread was such a big hit with the Supper Club crowd one winter that I knew it had to be on this menu.

157

RUSSIAN POTATO, SPINACH, AND SORREL SOUP

This light, bright green soup is similar to French and English sorrel soups but made with a meat broth. It is best prepared in early spring when sorrel is at its tenderest. You can also use nettles, if you are lucky enough to find them in the forest or at a farmers' market. The base of the soup may be made a day ahead, covered, and refrigerated, and then the sorrel, spinach, spring onions, cream, and dill added just before serving. The cream is optional; leave it out if you want a lighter, brighter broth. Sometimes I like to whip the cream and add a dollop to every portion. If you are making the soup the day of serving, do not add the sorrel until the last minute, as it darkens once it is cooked. Serve the soup hot or chilled; it is delicious either way. | SERVES 6

3 TABLESPOONS CLARIFIED BUTTER [PAGE 255]

2 OR 3 LEEKS, WHITE AND LIGHT GREEN PARTS ONLY, SLICED

4 CUPS CHICKEN STOCK [PAGE 59] OR BEEF STOCK OR
    STORE-BOUGHT REDUCED-SODIUM CHICKEN BROTH

2 POTATOES, PEELED AND DICED

2 POUNDS MIXED SORREL AND SPINACH, PREFERABLY
    IN EQUAL PARTS, TOUGH STEMS REMOVED AND CHOPPED

3 OR 4 SPRING ONIONS OR GREEN ONIONS, WHITE
    AND LIGHT GREEN PARTS ONLY, MINCED

¼ TO ⅓ CUP HEAVY CREAM [OPTIONAL]

1 TABLESPOON CHOPPED FRESH DILL, 2 TEASPOONS DRIED
    DILL, OR 3 TABLESPOONS MINCED FRESH CHERVIL

SEA SALT AND FRESHLY GROUND BLACK PEPPER

In a soup pot, heat the butter over medium-high heat. When the butter is hot, stir in the leeks, decrease the heat to medium-low, and cook slowly for 5 to 8 minutes, until the leeks are beginning to soften. Pour in the stock, increase the heat to high, and bring just to a boil. Add the potatoes, adjust the heat to maintain a steady simmer, and cook for 15 to 20 minutes, until the potatoes are fork-tender.

Add the sorrel and spinach and cook for a few minutes, just until wilted and tender. Stir in the onions, cream, and dill, mixing well. Season with salt and pepper. Ladle into warmed bowls and serve right way. Or, let cool, cover, and refrigerate and serve in chilled bowls. For an alternate garnish, reserve the cream and whip it, then spoon it over each serving.

heavy cream

sorrel

green onions

potatoes

black pepper

dill

leek

GRATINÉED PANCAKES FILLED WITH MUSHROOMS

Despite the name, these Russian pancakes are not like the thick flapjacks served in American diners. Instead, they are delicate like French crepes, although they are a bit thicker. I grew up eating crepes, which I attribute to my dad's Russian heritage; I didn't have my first pancakes until I was a teenager. For the mushrooms, use a combination of your favorite wild and cultivated varieties, keeping in mind that you need some rich, flavorful mushrooms in the mix. I have included some dried mushrooms along with the fresh to intensify the overall flavor of the filling. And be sure to overseason the stuffing slightly, as the crepes will absorb some of the flavor. Depending on how many you snack on while making them, you'll probably have extra crepes. I always like to make extras for breakfast or to use for dessert later in the week. | SERVES 6

CREPES

2 EGGS, SEPARATED

1½ TEASPOONS UNSALTED BUTTER, MELTED, PLUS MORE FOR COOKING, AT ROOM TEMPERATURE (OR PAN SPRAY FOR COOKING)

½ TEASPOON SEA SALT

½ TEASPOON SUGAR

3 CUPS WHOLE MILK

2 CUPS ALL-PURPOSE FLOUR

To make the crepe batter, in a bowl, whisk together the egg yolks, butter, salt, and sugar until smooth. Add the milk and flour and whisk until smooth. In a separate bowl, beat the egg whites with a whisk or a handheld mixer on medium-high speed until firm peaks form. Using a rubber spatula, fold the whites into the yolk mixture just until no white streaks remain.

To cook the crepes, heat an 8-inch crepe or sauté pan over medium-high to high heat and coat with butter or spray with pan spray. Fill a 2-ounce (4-tablespoon) ladle with batter, lift the pan off of the heat, and starting at the side opposite the handle, slowly pour the batter into the pan, tilting and rotating the pan as you go to get a thin, even layer across the bottom. Return the pan to the heat and cook for 1 to 1½ minutes, until the batter is set and the crepe is golden brown on the underside. Using a thin metal spatula, turn the crepe and cook for 30 seconds on the second side, until golden brown. Transfer the crepe to a plate. Repeat with the remaining batter, stacking the crepes as they are finished. Cover the stack with a tea towel to keep them warm until you fill them. You should have 12 crepes.

FILLING

UNSALTED BUTTER, FOR SAUTÉING

1 POUND MIXED WILD AND CULTIVATED FRESH MUSHROOMS, TRIMMED AND CUT SMALL

ABOUT 1/4 OUNCE DRIED MUSHROOMS (SUCH AS PORCINI OR MOREL), SOAKED IN HOT WATER TO COVER FOR 5 MINUTES, DRAINED, AND MINCED (SEE PAGE 101)

1 YELLOW ONION, CUT SMALL

2 TEASPOONS FRESH THYME LEAVES, COARSELY CHOPPED

1 CARROT, PEELED AND FINELY GRATED

2 TABLESPOONS DRY SHERRY

1/2 CUP COOKED WHITE RICE

SEA SALT AND FRESHLY GROUND BLACK PEPPER

1 EGG, LIGHTLY BEATEN

1/2 CUP GRATED PARMESAN CHEESE

3 TO 4 TABLESPOONS UNSALTED BUTTER, MELTED

3 TABLESPOONS FINE DRIED BREAD CRUMBS

1/4 CUP GRATED PARMESAN OR OTHER AGED CHEESE

SOUR CREAM, FOR SERVING

MINCED FRESH CHIVES, FOR SERVING

To make the filling, heat a large sauté pan over medium-high heat and add just enough butter to coat the bottom liberally. Wait until the butter has foamed and is beginning to brown and then add the mushrooms and cook, stirring, for 5 to 8 minutes, until they begin to release their juices. Stir in the onion and thyme and cook, stirring, for about 3 minutes, until the onion is tender. Add the carrot and cook for just 1 minute more, then pour in the sherry and deglaze the pan, stirring to scrape up any browned bits. Stir in the rice, mixing well, and season with salt and pepper. Transfer the filling to a bowl and let cool for just a bit. Mix the egg into the cooled filling and then fold in the Parmesan.

Preheat the oven to 375°F. Butter a baking dish just large enough to accommodate the rolled crepes in a single layer.

To fill the crepes, lay a crepe in front of you. Spoon about 1/3 cup (3 heaping tablespoons) of the filling in a line across the crepe, positioning it about one-third of the way above the edge nearest you and keeping it away from the left and right edges. Working from the crepe edge nearest you, roll up the crepe around the filling and place it, seam side down, in the baking dish. Repeat until you have used up all of the filling. The crepes should fit in a relatively snug single layer but not be too crowded.

In a bowl, drizzle the bread crumbs with the butter and stir to coat evenly. Sprinkle over the crepes then sprinkle the Parmesan evenly over the top. Bake for 15 to 20 minutes, until bubbly and crisp. If the crepes are bubbly but are not browned and crisp, pop them under the broiler (make sure the baking dish is broiler safe) for a few minutes. Transfer to individual plates and serve right away, with the sour cream and chives on the side.

yellow onion

morel

porcini

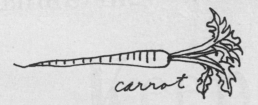

carrot

CLASSIC GEORGIAN "PRESSED" CHICKEN

WITH WALNUT AND BEET SAUCES

I made this with poussins, but it could easily be made with chicken thighs or breasts, boneless half chickens, or Cornish hens. If you use poussins or Cornish hens, you will need one bird per person, unless you are doing the whole menu, in which case, half a bird per person will be plenty. The parchment paper keeps the skin of the birds from sticking to the pan you are using as a weight. If you don't have a pan to use as a weight, use a couple of bricks wrapped in aluminum foil. You can also skip the pressing step, though the dish won't be authentic. If you opt not to press, make sure the skin still gets very crispy.

The pan juices are finished with a little water or stock and parsley. You can use the backbones and wing tips that you removed from the birds to make a quick stock to use for the liquid. The walnut sauce and the beet sauce are delicious with these birds, but it is fine to make just one of them. Both of them may be made a day ahead and refrigerated, saving you time on serving day. You can also serve the walnut sauce on other types of poultry and on fish and vegetables. If you only have sweet paprika on the shelf, add a touch of cayenne pepper along with the paprika. The sauce needs a little heat to counter the richness of the nuts. I love the beet sauce on grilled fish as well. | SERVES 6

WALNUT SAUCE
1 CUP WALNUTS
1 OR 2 CLOVES GARLIC
1½ TO 2 TEASPOONS GROUND CORIANDER
1 TEASPOON HOT PAPRIKA
2 TO 3 TEASPOONS CIDER VINEGAR
UP TO 1 CUP WATER
SEA SALT

BEET SAUCE
2 BEETS, BOILED OR ROASTED, PEELED,
    AND FINELY GRATED
1 SMALL CLOVE GARLIC, MINCED
1 TABLESPOON OLIVE OR WALNUT OIL
2 TABLESPOONS CIDER OR RICE VINEGAR
3/4 CUP SOUR CREAM, OR 6 TABLESPOONS
    EACH GREEK-STYLE PLAIN YOGURT AND CRÈME FRAÎCHE
SEA SALT
1 TO 2 TABLESPOONS MINCED FRESH CILANTRO

To make the walnut sauce, in a blender, combine the walnuts, garlic, coriander, paprika, and 2 teaspoons of the vinegar. With the motor running, slowly add the water, stopping when the sauce is the consistency of thick cream. It should be thinner than mayonnaise but thicker than a rich broth. Taste and season with the remaining 1 teaspoon vinegar and coriander, if needed, and with salt. Set aside.

To make the beet sauce, in a bowl, combine all of the ingredients and mix well. Cover and chill before serving.

CONTINUED

walnuts

beets

Classic Georgian "Pressed" Chicken, *continued*

6 POUSSINS

6 TABLESPOONS UNSALTED BUTTER

SEA SALT AND FRESHLY GROUND BLACK PEPPER

2 OR 3 CLOVES GARLIC, MASHED IN A MORTAR

SCANT 1 CUP WATER OR STOCK

1 CUP FRESH FLAT-LEAF PARSLEY LEAVES, MINCED,
   RINSED, AND SQUEEZED DRY [SEE PAGE 83]

3 TOMATOES, CUT INTO WEDGES AND LIGHTLY SALTED

To prepare the poussins, remove the backbones and wing tips from each bird (see page 165) or ask your butcher to do it for you. Turn each bird breast side up, and using both hands, press firmly on the breast to break the breastbone and flatten the bird.

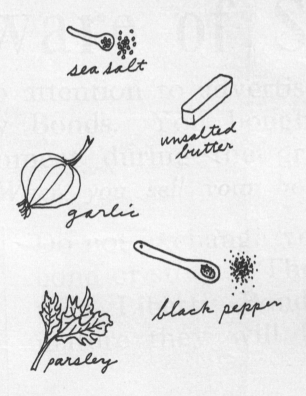

Place 2 very large sauté pans (big enough to hold all of the birds with a little space left over) over medium-low heat and add the butter (dividing it if using 2 pans). While the butter melts, season the birds on both sides with salt and pepper. When the butter is nice and foamy, place the birds, bone side down, in the pan(s). Cover just the birds, not the pan, with parchment paper, and place a second pan on top of the parchment. Fill the top pan with water (or a weight) to press the birds down, and then "fry" the birds slowly for 25 minutes. Remove the top pan(s), being careful not to slosh any water into the cooking pan(s), flip the birds over skin side down, and replace the parchment and the top pan(s) and the weight. Cook for another 15 to 20 minutes to crisp the skin and finish cooking the meat.

If you don't want to be bothered with pressing the birds on both sides, you can add the birds, bone side down, to the melted butter and cook for about 10 minutes, until seared. Then flip the birds skin side down, cover with parchment paper, top with a weighted pan, and cook for 10 to 15 mintues, until done (no additional turning needed).

When the birds are ready, pull them out of the pan(s), put them on a large platter, and keep them warm. Add the garlic and water to the pan juices (dividing them if using 2 pans), increase the heat to high, and cook, stirring to scrape up any browned bits on the pan bottom(s), until reduced by two-thirds. Stir in the parsley and remove from the heat.

Spoon the pan sauce over the birds and place the tomatoes wedges here and there around the platter. Serve the walnut and beet sauces on the side.

TIPS AND TRICKS
HOW TO REMOVE THE BACKBONE AND WINGS TIPS OF A BIRD

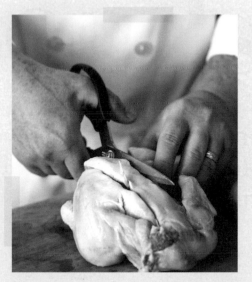

1 TO REMOVE THE BACKBONE, TURN THE BIRD BREAST SIDE DOWN. USING POULTRY SHEARS OR A SHARP KNIFE AND STARTING AT THE NECK, CUT ALONG ONE SIDE OF THE BACKBONE.

2 GENTLY OPEN THE BIRD UP, CUT ALONG THE OTHER SIDE OF THE BONE, AND THEN LIFT THE BONE AWAY FROM THE BODY. TO REMOVE EACH WING TIP, PULL THE WING OUT FROM THE BODY AND CUT RIGHT THROUGH THE MIDDLE OF THE EXTENDED JOINT WITH THE KNIFE OR SHEARS.

RUSSIAN SOUR CHERRY PUDDING

This is a great dessert for a party. Both the pudding and the sauce may be made earlier in the day and warmed just before serving. The puddings can be warmed in a 375°F oven for about 8 minutes and the sauce can be reheated over low heat.

Hearty, dense Russian black bread is made from a mix of wheat and rye flours and includes coffee and cocoa powder. It can often be found in specialty food stores and in some bakeries, or if you are an adventurous baker, you can try to make a loaf. If you cannot find black bread, you can substitute a dark pumpernickel, made without caraway seeds. | SERVES 8

PUDDING
10 EGGS, SEPARATED
5 CUPS GRANULATED SUGAR
1/2 CUP UNSALTED BUTTER, AT ROOM TEMPERATURE
3 SLICES STALE BLACK BREAD [ABOUT 3 OUNCES], FINELY CRUMBLED
1 CUP GROUND ALMONDS
3/4 CUP ALL-PURPOSE FLOUR
3/4 TEASPOON GROUND CINNAMON
2 LOOSELY PACKED CUPS DRIED SOUR CHERRIES [12 OUNCES], SOAKED IN HOT WATER TO COVER FOR 30 MINUTES AND DRAINED

SAUCE
2 CUPS DRIED SOUR CHERRIES
2/3 CUP WATER
1/2 CUP DRY RED WINE
1/4 CUP GRANULATED SUGAR
2 TEASPOONS CORNSTARCH

CHANTILLY CREAM
1 CUP HEAVY CREAM
1/4 CUP CONFECTIONERS' SUGAR
1/2 TEASPOON PURE VANILLA EXTRACT

CONFECTIONERS' SUGAR, FOR DUSTING

cinnamon

Preheat the oven to 400°F. Liberally butter eight 3/4-cup soufflé dishes or similar molds. Place the molds on a large rimmed baking sheet.

To make the pudding, in a stand mixer fitted with the paddle attachment, or in a large bowl with a handheld mixer, beat together the egg yolks, granulated sugar, and butter on medium speed until well mixed and foamy. On low speed, beat in the bread crumbs, almonds, flour, and cinnamon until well combined.

In a separate bowl, using the whisk attachment on the stand mixer or clean beaters on the handheld mixer, whip the egg whites on medium-high speed until firm peaks form. Fold the egg whites into the yolk mixture, mixing just until no white streaks are visible.

Pour a thin layer of the batter, about 1/2 inch deep, into the bottom of each mold. Bake for 12 to 15 minutes, until firm. Remove from the oven. Divide half of the cherries evenly among the molds, top with another thin layer of the batter, and return the molds to the oven. Bake again for 10 to 12 minutes, until firm. Remove from the oven. Divide the remaining cherries evenly among the molds and top with the remaining batter, dividing it evenly. (Each mold should have 3 layers of batter and 2 layers of cherries, ending with batter.) Return the molds to the oven and bake for 10 to 12 minutes. The puddings are ready when they crest about the rim of the molds a bit, like a soufflé, and the tops are a little crispy. Remove from the oven.

While the puddings are baking, make the sauce. In a saucepan, combine the cherries and $^1/_3$ cup of the water and bring just to a boil over medium-high heat. Add the wine and granulated sugar, decrease the heat to a simmer, and cook, stirring occasionally, for 10 minutes, until the cherries are plump. In a small bowl, stir together the cornstarch and the remaining $^1/_3$ cup water until the cornstarch dissolves. Stir the cornstarch mixture into the simmering sauce, increase the heat to high, and bring to a boil. Cook for about 2 minutes, until the cornstarch is thoroughly combined and the sauce has thickened slightly. Remove from the heat and keep warm.

To make the chantilly cream, in a bowl, whisk together the cream, confectioners' sugar, and vanilla until thickened to the consistency of smooth whipped cream. Be careful not to overmix; it should be firm but not dry.

To serve, using a small spoon, poke a hole in the top of each warm pudding and push down the top a bit. Place a spoonful of the sauce into the opening in each pudding. Top each pudding with a healthy dollop of the cream and a dusting of confectioners' sugar and serve warm.

dried cherries

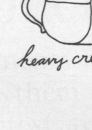

heavy cream

almonds

RED Wine

sugar

ALL-PURPOSE Flour

AFRICA AND
THE MIDDLE EAST

ETHIOPIA

I once spent three weeks in Kenya and Tanzania, where I saw and ate a lot, but I have never been to Ethiopia. Oddly enough, I have never even eaten in an Ethiopian restaurant in this country. The inspiration for all of these recipes comes from the many African cookbooks that I have collected and cooked from over the years and from my sister Mary, who lives in Minneapolis. For years, Mary raved about an Ethiopian food truck she frequents and we finally tried it together on one of my visits. I ate *injera* (flat bread) and *wot* (stew) from the truck, which parks on Nicollett Mall in downtown Minneapolis.

After that food-truck experience, I tried to make *injera* several times, even tracking down the traditional teff (a cereal grass) flour that it calls for, but every attempt was a miserable failure. Then I found a recipe in Peter Reinhart's *Whole Grain Breads, New Techniques, Extraordinary Flavor* and I decided to give *injera* one more try. I restocked my teff flour and whipped up a batch of the flat bread, following Peter's excellent directions. This time I was successful—great *injera* and very easy to make. You can seek out Peter's *injera* recipe, though you may want to save time and buy the bread from an Ethiopian restaurant or bakery, which is what the recipe testers did.

This chapter does not include a dessert. That's because the traditional Ethiopian meal does not finish with a pastry or other sweet. Some books suggest serving chilled fresh fruits, which is one of my favorite ways to end a dinner. The fruits help cleanse the palate and settle the stomach after the spicy foods. Ethiopians then cap the meal with small cups of strong coffee. If you crave something sweet, you can serve a honey or custard filo pastry from North Africa, Egypt, or even the Middle East.

SWISS CHARD
WITH COTTAGE CHEESE AND SPICED BUTTER

Collard greens are the typical choice for this dish, but I have found that rainbow chard is equally good prepared this way. Traditionally, this dish is served with *injera*, which is soft and crepelike, but it is also great with crisp flat bread, crackers, or pita.

Look for a European-style butter, which has a higher butterfat content and less water than standard U.S. butter, to clarify for making the spiced butter. As mentioned earlier, Plugrá is a popular U.S. brand. Or, pick up some Irish butter, such as Kerrygold brand. It is important to start with one of these denser butters because butter loses its water when you clarify it. Any butter will work, but a less dense, more watery butter will take longer to clarify and will yield a smaller amount of clarified butter.

You will need to use a heat diffuser (see page 187) when flavoring the butter with the spices. The heat diffuser, which allows for very slow, gentle cooking, will ensure that the milk solids in the butter won't burn while the spices are flavoring the oil in the butter. If you will be making the lentil stew that goes with this menu, you will need all of the butter this recipe yields. But don't worry if you have some left over. I find it quite addictive and a delicious way to dress up everything from popcorn to mixed nuts to a broiled fish fillet. In fact, you may want to make extra on purpose; it will keep in the freezer for 4 to 6 weeks. | SERVES 6

SPICED BUTTER
1 POUND EUROPEAN-STYLE UNSALTED BUTTER
1/4 CUP MINCED YELLOW ONION
1 CLOVE GARLIC, MINCED
1 TABLESPOON PEELED AND GRATED
    FRESH GINGER
1/2 TEASPOON GROUND CINNAMON
3 GREEN CARDAMOM PODS, CRUSHED
1-INCH PIECE CINNAMON STICK
2 WHOLE CLOVES
SEVERAL NUTMEG GRATINGS OR MACE BLADES

unsalted butter

TOPPING
1 1/2 CUPS SMALL-CURD COTTAGE CHEESE OR
    GREEK-STYLE PLAIN YOGURT
2/3 CUP SPICED BUTTER [ABOVE]
2 CLOVES GARLIC, LIGHTLY SMASHED [PAGE 172]
SEA SALT AND FRESHLY GROUND BLACK PEPPER

cardamom pods

To make the butter, in a saucepan, melt the butter over medium-high heat. When it has fully melted, add the onion, garlic, ginger, ground cinnamon, cardamom, cinnamon stick, cloves, and nutmeg and heat just until the butter comes to a boil. Move the pan to a burner covered with a heat diffuser and cook over the lowest heat setting for 45 minutes.

Line a fine-mesh sieve with cheesecloth. Strain the butter through the sieve into a container with a tight-fitting lid. You should have 1 cup. Let cool before using in the topping. Cover and refrigerate or freeze the remainder.

To make the topping, in a bowl, stir together the cottage cheese, spiced butter, garlic, 1/4 to 1/2 teaspoon salt, and 1/4 teaspoon pepper. Taste and adjust the seasoning with salt and pepper if needed. Let the mixture sit at room temperature for at least 20 minutes to allow the flavors to develop. If you like, fish out and discard the garlic clove just before serving.

CONTINUED

Swiss Chard, *continued*

garlic

GREENS

2 POUNDS RAINBOW CHARD

SCANT 1/3 TO 1/2 CUP SPICED BUTTER [PAGE 170]

1 TABLEPOON PEELED AND MINCED FRESH GINGER

2 SMALL CLOVES GARLIC, MINCED

1/3 CUP MINCED YELLOW ONION

SEA SALT AND FRESHLY GROUND BLACK PEPPER

To make the greens, trim any rough ends off of the chard stems and then tear the leaves from the stems. Cut the stems crosswise into thin strips (matchsticks) and cut the leaves crosswise into 1/2-inch-wide ribbons. Keep the stems and leaves separate.

In a large sauté pan, heat the spiced butter over medium heat. Add the chard stems, ginger, garlic, and onion and cook, stirring occasionally, for about 8 minutes, until the stems are tender. Add the leaves and cook, stirring occasionally, for 5 to 8 minutes, until wilted. Season with salt and pepper.

To serve, pile the greens on a warmed platter and spoon the topping over them. Serve right away.

TIPS AND TRICKS
SMASHING GARLIC

THE BEST TOOLS FOR SMASHING GARLIC ARE A MORTAR AND PESTLE AND A CHEF'S KNIFE. I ALWAYS USE THE SIDE OF THE CHEF'S KNIFE [THIS IS THE KNIFE WITH THE TRIANGULAR BLADE, RANGING IN LENGTH FROM 6 TO 12 INCHES LONG]. TO SMASH GARLIC THIS WAY, WITH THE BLADE FACING AWAY FROM YOU, SET THE SIDE OF THE KNIFE [AT ITS WIDE END] ON TOP OF A CLOVE OF GARLIC. PLACE THE HEEL OF YOUR HAND ON THE FLAT SIDE OF THE KNIFE, AND APPLY FIRM PRESSURE DOWNWARD AND FORWARD; ALTERNATIVELY, YOU COULD SMACK THE SIDE OF THE BLADE FIRMLY WITH THE SIDE OF YOUR FIST. YOU CAN DO THIS WITH PEELED OR UNPEELED CLOVES. [ACTUALLY IT'S A PRETTY HANDY WAY TO PEEL A GARLIC CLOVE BECAUSE, WITH SOME PRACTICE, THE CLOVE WILL SPLINTER AND SEPARATE FROM ITS SKIN BUT REMAIN MOSTLY IN ONE PIECE.]

CENTRAL AFRICAN-INSPIRED SPINACH

I have used spinach here, but Swiss chard or beet or mustard greens would also be excellent prepared this way. I prefer my greens wilted and just tender, so I add them near the end of cooking. This dish is good over brown rice. | SERVES 6

2 TABLESPOONS CANOLA OR OTHER NEUTRAL OIL

2 SMALL RED ONIONS, MINCED

2 TOMATOES, PEELED [SEE PAGE 181] AND DICED

1 POBLANO [PASILLA] CHILE, STEMMED, SEEDED
   IF DESIRED, AND DICED

1 TEASPOON SEA SALT

1/2 TEASPOON CAYENNE PEPPER

1/4 CUP SMOOTH PEANUT BUTTER MIXED WITH
   2 TO 3 TABLESPOONS BOILING WATER UNTIL SMOOTH

4 POUNDS SPINACH, TOUGH STEMS REMOVED

In a large sauté pan, heat the canola oil over medium-high heat. When hot, add the onions and sauté for 5 to 10 minutes, until golden. Add the tomatoes, chile, salt, and cayenne and cook, stirring occasionally, for 2 to 3 minutes. Add the peanut butter mixture and the spinach and cook, stirring, until the greens are wilted to your liking. Transfer to a warmed serving bowl or platter and serve.

poblano chile

SPICED RED LENTIL STEW

The spice mix is what makes this dish so good. Depending on your tolerance for spicy food, include or leave out the seeds of the árbol chiles. If you like a lot of heat and spice, include every last chile seed and finish the dish with 1 tablespoon of the spice mix combined with 2 tablespoons of the spiced butter, stirring it into the stew or serving it on the side. (If you prefer, you can add the spice mix to warmed extra virgin olive oil, rather than the spiced butter.) You can also put some of the spice mix on the table for guests to add as they like. Any leftover spice mix is good on almonds or olives or in scrambled or deviled eggs. I have yet to find a premade spice mix, but I'm sure one is out there. It's so tasty that I'm sure you will find many uses for it. | SERVES 6

SPICE MIX
1 TEASPOON CUMIN SEEDS
1/2 TEASPOON FENUGREEK SEEDS
2 WHOLE CLOVES
SEEDS FROM 3 GREEN CARDAMOM PODS
1/8 TEASPOON ALLSPICE BERRIES
1/4 TEASPOON BLACK PEPPERCORNS
1/2 OUNCE DRIED ÁRBOL CHILE [ABOUT
    18 DRIED CHILES], GROUND
1/4 CUP SWEET PAPRIKA
1/4 TEASPOON GROUND GINGER
1/8 TEASPOON GROUND TURMERIC
2 TABLESPOONS CAYENNE PEPPER

árbol chiles

6 TABLESPOONS SPICED BUTTER [PAGE 170]
1 YELLOW ONION, MINCED
4 TO 6 CLOVES GARLIC, MINCED
2 TABLESPOONS SPICE MIX [ABOVE]
1 1/2 CUPS RED LENTILS, RINSED AND PICKED OVER FOR DEBRIS
2 TOMATOES, PEELED [SEE PAGE 181] AND MINCED
2 CUPS WATER
1 TEASPOON SEA SALT
WHISKED GREEK-STYLE PLAIN YOGURT, FOR GARNISH
CHIFFONADE-CUT FRESH MINT LEAVES, FOR GARNISH

To make the spice mix, in a sauté pan, combine the cumin, fenugreek, cloves, cardamom, allspice, and peppercorns over medium-high heat and toast, shaking the pan frequently, for 1 to 2 minutes, until very aromatic. Pour onto a plate and let cool and then finely grind in a spice grinder or a well-cleaned coffee grinder. Pass the freshly ground spices and the chile, paparika, ginger, turmeric, and cayenne through a fine-mesh sieve (make sure it is completely dry) or through a sifter into a bowl. You should have 1/2 to 2/3 cup. Store in a tightly capped container until needed.

To make the stew, in a large saucepan, melt 4 tablespoons of the spiced butter over medium-high heat. When the butter is hot, stir in the onion and garlic, decrease the heat to low, cover, and cook, stirring now and then, for 6 to 8 minutes, until the onion is translucent. Stir in 1 tablespoon of the spice mix and cook uncovered, stirring occasionally, for 1 to 2 minutes, until aromatic. Increase the heat to medium-high and add the lentils, tomatoes, and water. Bring to a boil, decrease the heat to a simmer, and cook uncovered for 12 to 20 minutes, until the lentils are very tender. The timing will depend on the age of the lentils.

For a spicier stew, while the lentils are cooking, melt the remaining 2 tablespoons spiced butter in a small sauté pan over medium-high heat. Add the remaining 1 tablespoon spice mix, decrease the heat to medium-low, and cook, stirring, for several minutes, until the spice mix is well incorporated and the butter is aromatic. Remove from the heat.

When the lentils are ready, add the salt and stir in the spiced butter–spice mix combination, if using. Transfer to a warmed serving bowl, top with a drizzle of yogurt and a sprinkle of mint for a cooling garnish, and serve.

CHICKEN AND EGG STEW

This is one of the most frequently ordered dishes at Ethiopian restaurants in America. I like the fact that you get both the chicken and the egg at the same time, throwing into turmoil the question of which came first. (If you have extra company, or just an odd number, you can add another egg.) You want the eggs to be soft-boiled after their first cooking so they can finish in the stew. In the United States, cooks don't often prepare eggs this way, which makes this dish a nice change. I especially like the textures of the egg and chicken combining in the same bite. The spices add depth and the ginger adds brightness, making this an addictive dish. If you don't feel up to making Peter Reinhart's *injera* from *Whole Grain Breads*, serve the stew with white or brown rice. | SERVES 6

6 EGGS

SEA SALT AND FRESHLY GROUND BLACK PEPPER

4 TO 6 TABLESPOONS UNSALTED BUTTER OR
    SPICED BUTTER [PAGE 170]

2 LARGE YELLOW ONIONS, FINELY CHOPPED

3 CLOVES GARLIC, MINCED

1 TABLESPOON PEELED AND GRATED FRESH GINGER

3 TABLESPOONS SPICE MIX [PAGE 173]

1 [3- TO 3½-POUND] WELL-RAISED CHICKEN, SKINNED
    AND CUT INTO 6 SERVING PIECES

3 TO 4 TABLESPOONS TOMATO PASTE

2 TO 3 CUPS CHICKEN STOCK [PAGE 59]
    OR STORE-BOUGHT REDUCED-SODIUM BROTH

Have ready an ice bath. In a saucepan, combine the eggs with water to cover by 1 inch and 2 teaspoons salt. Bring to a boil over medium-high heat, decrease the heat to a simmer, and cook for 5 minutes. Using a slotted spoon, immediately transfer the eggs to the ice bath and let cool completely. Tap with a spoon, then one at a time, gently peel the eggs under cold running water and reserve. They're just soft-cooked at this stage, so do be gentle.

In a large sauté pan, melt the butter over medium-high heat. (The amount of butter will depend on the size and depth of your pan; add the minimum first, then increase the amount to coat the bottom of the pan.) Add the onions, garlic, ginger, and spice mix, decrease the heat to low,

and cook slowly, stirring occasionally, for 10 to 12 minutes, to develop the flavors.

Meanwhile, season the chicken pieces on both sides with salt and pepper. When the onion mixture is ready, increase the heat to medium-high, stir in the tomato paste (add the larger amount for a more tomatoey flavor), and cook for 1 to 2 minutes. Add the chicken pieces and coat well with the onion mixture. Pour in 2 cups of the stock, mix well, and then add more stock if needed to achieve a soupy stew consistency. Bring to a boil, decrease the heat to a simmer, and cook for 20 minutes.

Add the eggs to the pan and continue to cook for 8 to 10 minutes, until the sauce is nicely thickened and the egg yolks have more fully set. Taste and adjust the seasoning with salt and pepper. Remove the stew from the heat and let rest for 5 to 10 minutes before serving while you remove the eggs from the pan and slice them in half lengthwise. Transfer the stew to a nice serving bowl then tuck the egg slices back into the stew.

WARMING WINTER VEGETABLE STEW

WITH PEANUT SAUCE

You can adapt this stew to your liking with different vegetables you have on hand or with what looks good at the market. For a vegan stew, substitute canola oil for the butter. The spicy heat comes from the chiles, but you can add a spoonful of the spice mix in the lentil stew on page 173 in place of the chiles. The peanut butter can be smooth or crunchy—chef's choice. Serve the stew over rice or baked or grilled sweet potatoes. Leftovers are good the next day at room temperature. | SERVES 6

4 TABLESPOONS UNSALTED BUTTER OR
   SPICED BUTTER [PAGE 170]

1 LEEK, WHITE AND LIGHT GREEN PARTS ONLY, SLICED,
   OR 1 YELLOW ONION, COARSELY CHOPPED

2 OR 3 DRIED ÁRBOL OR OTHER DRIED HOT CHILES, STEMMED,
   SEEDED IF DESIRED, AND CRUSHED

2 TABLESPOONS TOMATO PASTE

2 SMALL RUTABAGAS, TURNIPS, OR CARROTS,
   PEELED AND CUT INTO CHUNKS

8 OUNCES CABBAGE [1/4 HEAD] OR PEELED WINTER SQUASH
   [1/2 AVERAGE-SIZE SQUASH], CUT INTO CHUNKS

2 TOMATOES, PEELED [SEE PAGE 181] AND CHOPPED,
   OR 2 CUPS CANNED TOMATOES

3 TO 4 CUPS COARSELY CHOPPED BEET, RUTABAGA,
   OR TURNIP GREENS

1 CUP [8 OUNCES] PEANUT BUTTER MIXED
   WITH 1 1/2 CUPS BOILING WATER UNTIL SMOOTH

1 FULLY RIPENED [BLACK] PLANTAIN, PEELED AND DICED

SEA SALT

SALTED ROASTED PEANUTS, FOR GARNISH

In a large sauté pan, melt the butter over medium-high heat. Add the leek and cook, stirring often, for 3 to 5 minutes, until tender. Add the chiles and tomato paste and cook, stirring, for 1 to 2 minutes to brown slightly and heighten the flavor. Add the rutabagas, cabbage, and tomatoes and cook for 10 to 12 minutes, until the rutabagas are almost tender. Fold in the greens and continue to cook until the greens are wilted to your liking.

Stir in the peanut butter mixture and cook until piping hot and the vegetables can be easily pierced with a fork. Mix in the plantain and season with salt. Transfer to a warmed serving bowl or platter, garnish with the peanuts, and serve.

rutabaga

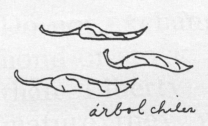

árbol chiles

cabbage

peanuts

MOROCCO

The food of Morocco combines flavors and textures that are soothing, familiar, and irresistible: spicy *harissa* (hot chile sauce), rich lamb *tagine* (stew), and bright vegetable salad—dishes that I could live on all summer long (and all winter, too). Over the centuries, Moroccan cuisine has been influenced by the kitchens of the Arabs and the Berbers, the Spanish and the Portuguese, the Persians and the Senegalese, the French and more. The country itself is blessed with broad swaths of fertile land, towering mountain ranges, and both an Atlantic and a Mediterranean coast, all of which deliver an abundance of fine ingredients. It has three great culinary capitals—Marrakesh, Fez, and Tetúan—and many regional specialties tucked into geographical pockets large and small around the county.

Not surprisingly, Morocco's culinary bounty made deciding which dishes to include in this menu challenging. Also, I find the cuisine a good match to every season, so I have provided both summer and winter recipes or variations for you to mix and match according to the time of year you are serving your Moroccan Supper Club feast.

MARINATED OLIVES

Both the green and the black olives benefit from sitting in their marinade for several days before serving so they can soak up the flavor. But if you have not planned ahead, they will still taste good after just a day in the marinade. Although the olives are fine served at room temperature, I often gently warm them in a sauté pan. That little bit of heat brings out their flavors.

GREEN OLIVES WITH HERBS

Although these olives will keep for weeks, I have always eaten them or used them up in sauces much sooner, and the seasonings do dissipate over time. Any of these green olives that are not eaten with your Moroccan meal are delicious in salads, as a garnish for fish or chicken, or pitted and slipped into roasted lamb sandwiches. | MAKES ABOUT 3 CUPS

3 CUPS BRINED GREEN OLIVES (SUCH AS CASTELVETRANO, PICHOLINE, OR MOROCCAN GREEN)
2 CLOVES GARLIC, SMASHED (SEE PAGE 172)
6 TABLESPOONS CHOPPED FRESH CILANTRO, LEAVES AND TENDER STEMS ONLY
6 TABLESPOONS CHOPPED FRESH FLAT-LEAF PARSLEY, LEAVES, RINSED AND SQUEEZED DRY (SEE PAGE 83)
1 TO 2 TABLESPOONS HARISSA (PAGE 179)

In a bowl, combine the olives and cold water to cover and let soak overnight.

Drain the olives in a colander, shaking the colander well to release as much liquid as possible, and transfer to a bowl. Add the garlic, cilantro, parsley, and *harissa* and stir to coat evenly. Cover and refrigerate for at least overnight or preferably up to several days. Bring to room temperature or warm gently in a sauté pan before serving.

BLACK OLIVES WITH PRESERVED LEMON

Like the green olives, these black olives will keep for several weeks. If you are lucky enough to have some black olives left over, they are delicious smashed and smeared on grilled garlic bread, tossed into pasta, scattered atop pizza, or made into tapenade for serving as is or for mixing with odd bits of cheese as a spread for vegetables or grilled breads. | MAKES ABOUT 3 CUPS

1 PRESERVED LEMON (PAGE 179)
1 TO 2 TEASPOONS DRIED OREGANO
JUICE OF 1/2 LARGE LEMON
1/4 CUP EXTRA VIRGIN OLIVE OIL
2 TEASPOONS HARISSA (PAGE 179), OR 1 TEASPOON RED PEPPER FLAKES
3 CUPS OIL-CURED BLACK OLIVES

black olives

Cut or pull away any pulp from the preserved lemon and discard it. Finely julienne or mince the peel and place in a small bowl. Crumble the dried oregano over the lemon peel. Add the lemon juice, olive oil, and *harissa* and stir to mix. Put the olives in a bowl, pour the lemon peel mixture over the top, and stir to combine.

Cover and refrigerate for at least overnight or preferably up to several days. Bring to room temperature or warm gently in a sauté pan before serving.

green olives

lemon

PRESERVED LEMONS

It is good to use organic produce whenever possible, but it is particularly important with this recipe because you will be eating the peel. | MAKES ABOUT 1 QUART

12 TO 14 LEMONS
2 TO 3 CUPS KOSHER SALT
1 TABLESPOON BLACK PEPPERCORNS, COARSELY CRACKED
1 TABLESPOON RED PEPPER FLAKES
1 CINNAMON STICK
1 TO 2 CUPS FRESHLY SQUEEZED LEMON JUICE

Have ready a sterilized quart (or larger) glass jar with a tight-fitting lid (see page 278 for instructions on how to sterilize the jar).

Rinse the lemons well. Working with 1 lemon at a time, cut in half from the top (stem end) to the bottom three-fourths of the way through, keeping the base intact. Then cut in half again from the top to the bottom three-fourths of the way through, keeping the base intact. When pulled open gently, the lemon should look like a four-petaled flower. Repeat with the remaining lemons.

Sprinkle the inside of each lemon liberally with some of the salt. Pack a layer of lemons, standing them upright with the cut end up, into the sterilized jar. Sprinkle liberally with the salt and then with some of the peppercorns and red pepper flakes. Add additional layers in the same manner, packing each layer tightly and seasoning with the salt, peppercorns, and red pepper flakes. As the lemons climb up the sides of the jar, tuck the cinnamon stick down the side of the jar. Be sure to pack the lemons firmly. Don't worry about keeping the lemons perfect, as you will cut away the pulp and use only the peel.

Once all of the lemons are packed into the jar, pour in enough lemon juice to fill all of the spaces around them, wiggling the lemons as you pour to make sure you eliminate all of the air pockets. A chopstick comes in handy for this task. Seal the jar tightly and let rest at cool room temperature or wine-cellar temperature for 4 to 6 weeks (out of direct sunlight). To help the salt dissolve, turn the jar upside down a couple of times a day during the first week and once or twice a week for the rest of the time.

The lemons are ready when the peels are tender (only the peels are used in recipes that call for preserved lemon). Once the jar has been opened, refrigerate and take out just what you need using tongs or a spoon to avoid contaminating the remaining contents of the jar.

CLASSIC HARISSA

I have used this traditional North African condiment in the marinades for olives on page 178, but it can used in many ways: on scrambled eggs; mixed into butter or olive oil and drizzled over panfried or grilled steaks, lamb chops, or chicken breasts; or alongside grilled fish with couscous. Or, for a tasty vegetarian main dish, whisk a couple of spoonfuls into a lemon vinaigrette (3 parts extra virgin olive oil, 1 part freshly squeezed lemon juice, sea salt, and freshly ground black pepper) and spoon the vinaigrette over roasted potatoes or sweet potatoes with or without fresh goat cheese or feta cheese and grilled onions. | MAKES ABOUT 1/3 CUP

2 TO 4 SERRANO OR FRESNO CHILES AND 1 TO 3 FRESH RED
    CHILES (SUCH AS CAYENNE OR THAI BIRD), STEMMED AND
    SEEDED IF DESIRED; OR 10 DRIED ÁRBOL OR OTHER DRIED
    HOT CHILES, STEMMED, SEEDED IF DESIRED, SOAKED IN
    HOT WATER TO COVER FOR 5 TO 10 MINUTES, AND DRAINED

CONTINUED

Marinated Olives, *continued*

¼ CUP EXTRA VIRGIN OLIVE OIL,
    PLUS MORE FOR STORAGE IF NEEDED

4 CLOVES GARLIC

GRATED ZEST AND JUICE OF ½ LEMON

1 TABLESPOON SWEET OR HOT PAPRIKA

1 TEASPOON CUMIN SEEDS, TOASTED IN A DRY PAN
    UNTIL FRAGRANT AND THEN GROUND [SEE PAGE 23]

½ TEASPOON SEA SALT

½ TEASPOON CAYENNE PEPPER [OPTIONAL]

In a food processor, combine the chiles and oil and process until no large chunks of chile remain. Add the garlic, lemon zest and juice, paprika, cumin, salt, and cayenne and process until a paste forms. Use immediately, or transfer to a container with a tight-fitting lid, pour a thin layer of olive oil on top, cover, and refrigerate. It will keep for up to several weeks.

lemon zest

HARIRA SOUP

This soup, which is one of the dishes in the traditional meal that breaks the Ramadan fast, typically includes lamb, but I have a vegetarian version here. What makes the soup so special is the date and lemon garnish.

The recipe calls for cooked and cooled chickpeas and lentils. You can cook the chickpeas the same way you cook the pot beans on page 22, minus the epazote sprig, or you can use canned chickpeas. If you opt for the latter, you should still rub the skins off the beans. To do that, rub them gently between your palms, or place them on half of a large clean kitchen towel, cover with the other half of the towel, and gently roll the chickpeas back and forth, using your palms, until you see the skins separating, then pick the skins off. Don't apply too much pressure or you will end up with chickpea paste. I like to use red lentils, which are easily cooked in boiling water to cover for about 15 minutes, depending on their age. If you cannot find them, any color lentil will do.

I like the robust flavor of this dish when using the authentic amount of spices, but I've included the key spices as a range below; you can opt for the smaller amount if that better suits your guests' tastes. | SERVES 6 TO 8

3 TABLESPOONS OLIVE OIL

2 YELLOW ONIONS, SLICED

3 CELERY STALKS, SLICED CROSSWISE

½ TO 1 TABLESPOON GROUND TURMERIC

cumin

½ TO 1 TEASPOON CUMIN SEEDS, TOASTED IN A DRY
    PAN UNTIL FRAGRANT AND THEN GROUND [SEE PAGE 23]

1 TEASPOON SEA SALT

½ TEASPOON FRESHLY GROUND BLACK PEPPER

JUICE OF 2 LEMONS [ABOUT ¼ CUP]

4 TO 6 TOMATOES [2 TO 2½ CUPS], PEELED [SEE BELOW]
AND GRATED ON THE LARGE HOLES OF A BOX GRATER,
WITH JUICE RESERVED

4 CUPS WATER OR VEGETABLE STOCK

2 CUPS [4 OUNCES] DRIED CHICKPEAS, COOKED, COOLED,
AND TOUGH SKINS RUBBED OFF, OR 1 [15-OUNCE]
CAN CHICKPEAS, DRAINED, RINSED, AND TOUGH SKINS
RUBBED OFF

¾ CUP [4 OUNCES] LENTILS, PREFERABLY RED

2 TABLESPOONS MINCED FRESH CILANTRO

5 TABLESPOONS MINCED FRESH FLAT-LEAF PARSLEY
LEAVES, RINSED AND SQUEEZED DRY [SEE PAGE 83]

2 TABLESPOONS SEMOLINA

4 OUNCES THIN VERMICELLI, BROKEN INTO
SPOON-SIZE LENGTHS

½ CUP CHOPPED PITTED DATES, FOR GARNISH

LEMON WEDGES, FOR GARNISH

In a soup pot, heat the olive oil over medium-high heat. Add the onions and celery and cook, stirring occasionally, for about 10 minutes, until tender but not browned. Decrease the heat if the vegetables begin to brown. Add the turmeric, cumin, salt, and pepper and cook for about 1 minute. Add the lemon juice, tomatoes and their juice, water, chickpeas, lentils, cilantro, and 2 tablespoons of the parsley and bring to a boil. Decrease the heat to a quiet simmer and cook for 20 minutes, skimming off any foam that rises to the surface.

Ladle out about 1 cup of the hot soup and whisk the semolina into it until dissolved. Whisk the semolina mixture back into the pot. Add the vermicelli and cook just until tender. Watch closely as the noodles cook very quickly.

Put the dates, lemon wedges, and the remaining 3 tablespoons parsley in separate small bowls. Ladle the soup into warmed bowls and serve. Pass the garnishes at the table.

TIPS AND TRICKS
PEELING TOMATOES

TO PEEL TOMATOES, SELECT A POT THAT'S LARGE ENOUGH TO COMFORTABLY HOLD ALL YOUR TOMATOES, FILL WITH WATER, AND BRING TO A BOIL. MEANWHILE, SET UP A BIG BOWL OF ICE WATER. CORE THE TOMATOES, THEN TURN THEM OVER AND CUT AN X INTO THEIR SKINS AT THEIR BOTTOMS. PLACE THE TOMATOES IN THE BOILING WATER FOR 5 TO 10 SECONDS, JUST UNTIL THE SKINS START TO PUCKER. TRANSFER IMMEDIATELY TO THE ICE BATH. THE SKINS SHOULD PEEL OFF EASILY.

vermicelli

parsley

cilantro

lemon

tomatoes

HOMEMADE
DATE CANDY

WINTER SQUASH AND EGGPLANT TAGINE

BACHELOR'S LAMB TANGIA

SUMMER AND WINTER BELL
PEPPER SALADS

WINTER SQUASH AND EGGPLANT TAGINE

WITH COUSCOUS

You can serve this vegetable stew as a lovely simple meal on its own, or with a roasted leg of lamb for a more elaborate supper. The term *tagine* is used both for a slowly simmered stew and for the round earthenware dish with a conical lid in which the stew is cooked. A gratin dish or a roasting pan can be used in place of the classic *tagine*. To save steps, I roast the vegetables in a big gratin dish, rather than sauté them in batches. This method also uses less oil.

If you have ever made chickpeas from fresh, you will appreciate how much work they are. Fresh chickpeas are small, hard-to-open pods that require careful shucking before they can be cooked. I have also used fresh shelling beans, such as cranberry beans, in this recipe with great success. They are easily found at farmers' markets in fall. Both the sauce and the *harissa* may be made a day or two ahead and kept tightly covered in the refrigerator. | SHOWN PAGE 182 | SERVES 6 TO 8

GREEN HARISSA

2 CLOVES GARLIC

2 JALAPEÑO CHILES, STEMMED, SEEDED IF DESIRED

1 TEASPOON CUMIN SEEDS, TOASTED IN A DRY PAN
   UNTIL FRAGRANT AND THEN GROUND [SEE PAGE 23]

JUICE OF 1 LEMON

6 TO 8 TABLESPOONS OLIVE OIL

2 PINCHES OF SEA SALT

1 CUP CHOPPED FRESH CILANTRO

cumin

SAUCE

1 1/2 TEASPOONS CORIANDER SEEDS

1 1/2 TEASPOONS CUMIN SEEDS

1 TEASPOON CARAWAY SEEDS

1 TEASPOON SWEET PAPRIKA

1 TEASPOON GROUND GINGER

1 TEASPOON RED PEPPER FLAKES

1/2 TEASPOON GROUND ALLSPICE

2 TO 3 TABLESPOONS OLIVE OIL

1 LARGE YELLOW ONION, MINCED

2 CLOVES GARLIC, MINCED

1 JALAPEÑO CHILE, STEMMED, SEEDED IF
   DESIRED, AND MINCED

2 TO 3 CUPS TOMATO PUREE

1 TABLESPOON HONEY

1 TEASPOON SEA SALT

1/2 TO 1 CUP WATER

allspice

coriander

To make the *harissa*, in a blender or food processor, combine the garlic, chiles, cumin, lemon juice, 6 tablespoons of the oil, salt, and cilantro and process until well mixed. Add some or all of the remaining 2 tablespoons oil, a little at a time, until the mixture is the consistency you like. (If you want to dollop it on at the end, use less oil, and if you want drizzle it on, use more oil.) Reserve until needed.

To make the sauce, in a mortar, combine the coriander, cumin, and caraway seeds and grind with a pestle until pulverized. Add the paprika, ginger, red pepper flakes, and allspice and mix well. Reserve until needed.

In a saucepan, heat 2 tablespoons of the olive oil over medium-high heat. When the oil is hot, add the onion and garlic and cook, stirring, for 6 to 8 minutes, until soft and translucent. Add the chile and the reserved spice mixture and cook, stirring, until fragrant. Add the tomato puree (use the larger amount if you want a saucier dish), honey, salt, and 1/2 cup of the water. Cook, adding some or all of the remaining 1/2 cup water if the pan begins to dry out, for 20 to 30 minutes, until the flavors have developed and melded nicely. If the pan seems to be drying out too quickly, lower the heat to slow the cooking. You want to give all of the ingredients enough time to develop fully.

BEANS

1 1/3 CUPS [8 OUNCES] DRIED CHICKPEAS, OR 3 CUPS FRESH
    SHELLING BEANS [SUCH AS FRESH CRANBERRY BEANS]
    OR CHICKPEAS, RINSED AND PICKED OVER FOR DEBRIS
1 CARROT, PEELED AND CUT INTO 4 CHUNKS
1 CELERY STALK, CUT INTO 4 CHUNKS
ZEST OF 1 LEMON, PEELED WITH A VEGETABLE PEELER
    IN 1 LONG STRIP AND KEPT INTACT, IF POSSIBLE

VEGETABLES

2 SMALL TO MEDIUM EGGPLANTS, TRIMMED AND
    CUT INTO 2-INCH PIECES
2 OR 3 SMALL ZUCCHINI, CUT INTO 1 1/2-INCH-THICK ROUNDS
SEA SALT AND FRESHLY GROUND BLACK PEPPER
2 POUNDS KABOCHA, RED KURI, OR OTHER
    TASTY WINTER SQUASH, PEELED, SEEDED, AND DICED
4 TO 6 TABLESPOONS OLIVE OIL
2 CUPS DRAINED, COOKED BEANS [ABOVE]
1/4 CUP OIL-CURED BLACK OLIVES, PITTED

SIMPLE COUSCOUS

1 1/2 CUPS QUICK-COOKING COUSCOUS
1 1/2 CUPS VEGETABLE STOCK OR WATER
PINCH OF GROUND CINNAMON [OPTIONAL]
3/4 TEASPOON SEA SALT
1 1/2 TABLESPOONS UNSALTED BUTTER,
    AT ROOM TEMPERATURE, OR OLIVE OIL

GREEK-STYLE PLAIN YOGURT, FOR GARNISH

To cook the beans, in a large saucepan, combine the beans, carrot, celery, and lemon zest with water to cover generously (4 to 5 cups) and bring to a boil over medium-high heat. Decrease the heat to a simmer, cover, and cook until the beans are tender. The timing will depend on the age of the beans. The fresh shelling beans will cook in about 20 minutes and the dried beans will take about twice as long, around 40 minutes. Drain the beans and discard the carrot, celery, and lemon zest. If you won't be using the beans right away, refrigerate them once they have cooled, as the starches in cooked beans sour quickly.

Preheat the oven to 400°F. To prepare the vegetables, in a colander, toss the eggplant and zucchini with enough salt to coat them lightly and leave to drain for 30 minutes. Gently squeeze the excess moisture from the eggplant and zucchini, place in a large bowl, and add the winter squash. Drizzle with 4 tablespoons of the olive oil, sprinkle with pepper and a little additional salt, and toss to coat the vegetables evenly, adding some or all of the remaining 2 tablespoons oil if needed to coat everything. Be cautious with the salt, as the eggplant and zucchini will still have some salt in them.

Transfer the vegetables to a large gratin dish, spreading them in a single layer, and roast for 15 minutes. Give the vegetables a good stir and roast for 15 minutes longer. Remove the dish from the oven, add the beans, reserved sauce, and olives, and stir to mix well. Return the dish to the oven and cook for 30 minutes longer, until the winter squash is fork-tender.

When the vegetables are nearly ready, prepare the couscous. Put the couscous in a saucepan with a tight-fitting lid. Bring the stock to a boil over high heat. Pour the stock over the couscous, cover, and let sit for 5 minutes. In a small bowl, mix together the cinnamon and salt. Uncover, fluff the couscous, and mix in the butter and cinnamon mixture.

Serve the couscous on a large platter or divide among individual plates. With the back of a spoon, make a well in the center of the couscous. Scoop the vegetables into the well. Drizzle with some of the yogurt and top with some of the *harissa*. Pass the remaining yogurt and *harissa* at the table.

eggplant

BACHELOR'S LAMB TANGIA

This is a compilation of a handful of different recipes, but it is inspired by a *tangia*, which, like *tagine*, is the name for both the meat stew and the earthenware vessel in which it is cooked. It is a specialty of Marrakesh and the dish is cooked by and for men. The cooking vessel is jar shaped, broader at the center and narrower at the top and bottom. The ingredients for the stew are put into the jar and the top of the jar is covered with parchment paper that is secured in place with string. Traditionally, the filled jar is carried to the local *hammam* (bathhouse) and buried in the hot ashes of the furnace that heats the baths, where it is left to cook for several hours.

The stew can be made with lamb, beef, or goat. When we made it for the Supper Club, we used local Napa Valley spring lamb from Don Watson's Wooly Weeders. If you want to simplify the menu, you can serve this stew with one of the pepper salads on page 188 and the couscous that accompanies the vegetable *tagine* on page 185. Set out plenty of bread for sopping up the juices. Ciabatta, which is crisp on the outside and light and airy on the inside, is ideal.

I have experimented with a number of different vessels for cooking this dish, including a Le Creuset enameled cast-iron *doufeu*, a big cast-iron pot, and an antique cassoulet dish. Whichever type of pot you use, make sure it has a tight-fitting lid to preserve the delicious juices. The directions here are for slowly cooking the stew in the oven, but you can prepare it on the stove top, using a heat diffuser (see page 187) to keep the heat gentle and steady. It can also be cooked in a wood-burning oven, an "egg cooker" barbecue grill, or even a slow cooker.

The *ras el hanout* (spice mixture) is critical to this dish, but if you don't have a full spice cabinet or you just want to reduce the number of ingredients, you can use a mixture of 1 tablespoon ground cumin, $\frac{1}{2}$ teaspoon ground allspice, and $\frac{1}{4}$ teaspoon saffron threads. Or, you can buy a premade mix; Kalustyan's in New York City carries a good one (order online at www.kalustyans.com). Preserved lemons can vary in size, which is why I have suggested 1 to 2 lemons in the ingredients list. If the preserved lemons you have are large, a single one will be sufficient. | SHOWN PAGE 183 | SERVES 6 TO 8

RAS EL HANOUT

1½ TEASPOONS BLACK PEPPERCORNS

1½ TEASPOONS CUMIN SEEDS,
   TOASTED IN A DRY PAN UNTIL FRAGRANT [SEE PAGE 23]

1 TEASPOON GROUND GINGER

1 TEASPOON GROUND CINNAMON

1 TEASPOON GROUND CORIANDER

½ NUTMEG, GRATED

¼ TEASPOON CAYENNE PEPPER OR HOT CHILE POWDER

4 GREEN CARDAMOM PODS, SEEDS GROUND

4 CLOVES, GROUND

To make the *ras el hanout*, combine the peppercorns, cumin, ginger, cinnamon, coriander, nutmeg, cayenne, cardamom, and cloves in a spice grinder or well-cleaned coffee grinder and grind to a powder. Or, grind together in a mortar with a pestle. Reserve until needed.

To cook the stew, preheat the oven to 275°F to 300°F (remember, the oven is low because this stew must cook very slowly).

peppercorn

STEW

3½ POUNDS BONELESS LAMB SHOULDER,
    CUT INTO 12 TO 14 PIECES
¼ CUP UNSALTED BUTTER, PREFERABLY
    CLARIFIED BUTTER [SEE PAGE 255]
¼ CUP EXTRA VIRGIN OLIVE OIL
2 YELLOW ONIONS, COARSELY CHOPPED
CLOVES FROM 1 HEAD GARLIC, HALVED IF LARGE
½ BUNCH CILANTRO, LEAVES AND TENDER
    STEMS ONLY, MINCED
½ BUNCH FLAT-LEAF PARSLEY, LEAVES AND
    TENDER STEMS ONLY, MINCED, RINSED,
    AND SQUEEZED DRY [SEE PAGE 83]
1 TO 2 PRESERVED LEMONS [PAGE 179], PEEL ONLY,
    RINSED AND QUARTERED
1½ TEASPOONS SEA SALT, PLUS MORE TO TASTE
1 TEASPOON GROUND GINGER
2 LARGE FRESH TOMATOES, PEELED [SEE PAGE 181] AND
    GRATED ON THE LARGE HOLES OF A BOX GRATER, OR
    1½ TO 2 CUPS CANNED TOMATOES, GRATED OR CHOPPED
1 TO 1½ CUPS WATER OR LOW-SODIUM CHICKEN OR
    LAMB STOCK

In a heavy ovenproof pot with a tight-fitting lid, combine the lamb, butter, olive oil, onions, garlic, cilantro, parsley, lemon, 1½ teaspoons of the salt, the ginger, 1 teaspoon of the *ras el hanout*, the tomatoes, and 1 cup of the water and mix well. Add the remaining ½ cup water if it seems too dry. Cover and place in the oven for 2½ to 3 hours, until the lamb is very tender. Taste and adjust the seasoning with additional salt, if necessary

Transfer the stew to a warmed serving dish or serve directly from the pot. This is best eaten from a bowl with a soup spoon or dessert spoon, since the sauce is juicy. Pass the remaining *ras el hanout* at the table for diners to add as desired.

TIPS AND TRICKS
HEAT DIFFUSER
A HEAT DIFFUSER IS A DISK MADE FROM TWO SHEETS OF PERFORATED METAL WITH A SLIM CHANNEL OF SPACE BETWEEN THEM, AND IS USED TO DIFFUSE THE INTENSITY OF DIRECT HEAT ON THE STOVE TOP. IF YOU DON'T HAVE ONE, YOU CAN FASHION A HEAT DIFFUSER FROM ALUMINUM FOIL. BEFORE YOU START COOKING, FORM A THICK DOUGHNUT OUT OF ALUMINUM FOIL AND REST YOUR PAN ON THE MAKESHIFT DIFFUSER TO MAKE SURE IT IS STABLE. I HAVE ALSO STACKED TWO BURNER GRATES TO INCREASE THE DISTANCE BETWEEN THE HEAT AND THE PAN.

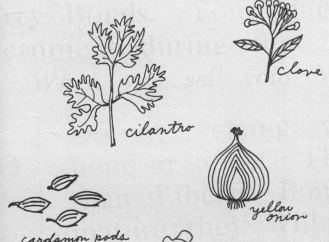
cilantro

clove

lemon

tangia jars

cardamon pods

yellow onion

ginger

cast iron pot

SUMMER AND WINTER BELL PEPPER SALADS

I like to peel my roasted peppers over a bowl to catch the flavorful juices. I also squeeze the juice and seeds from the tomatoes into a fine-mesh sieve placed over a bowl to capture the juices. Both the pepper juice and the tomato juice go into the pan with the other ingredients. If you want to skip roasting the pepper, you can buy jarred roasted peppers, though the flavor will not be as good.

| SHOWN PAGE 183 | EACH SALAD SERVES 6 TO 8

SUMMER BELL PEPPER SALAD

4 RED BELL PEPPERS, ROASTED [SEE PAGE 29],
   PEELED, STEMMED, AND SEEDED
3 TABLESPOONS OLIVE OIL
1 POUND TOMATOES, PEELED [SEE PAGE 181], HALVED
   THROUGH THE STEM END, HALVES SQUEEZED OF SEEDS
   AND JUICE, AND CUT LENGTHWISE INTO WIDE STRIPS
2 CLOVES GARLIC, SLICED
1 OR 2 SERRANO CHILES, STEMMED, SEEDED IF DESIRED,
   AND SLIT OR SLICED
1/4 TO 1/2 TEASPOON SEA SALT

Tear each bell pepper lengthwise into its natural segments, then tear each segment into halves or thirds, depending on the size of the peppers.

In a large sauté pan, heat the olive oil over medium-high heat. When the oil is hot, add the bell peppers, tomatoes (and all of the pepper and tomato juices), garlic, and chiles and simmer for 10 to 20 minutes, until the flavors have blended. Add 1/4 teaspoon of the salt, then taste and add more salt if needed.

Spread the vegetables on a platter and let cool. Cover and chill before serving.

WINTER BELL PEPPER SALAD

4 GREEN BELL PEPPERS OR MIXTURE OF GREEN BELL
   PEPPERS AND POBLANO [PASILLA] PEPPERS, ROASTED
   [SEE PAGE 29], PEELED, STEMMED, AND SEEDED
1 TEASPOON GROUND CUMIN
2 TABLESPOONS OLIVE OIL
JUICE OF 1/2 LEMON
1 PRESERVED LEMON [PAGE 179], PEEL ONLY,
   RINSED AND MINCED
1/4 TO 1/2 TEASPOON SEA SALT

Tear each pepper lengthwise into its natural segments, then tear each segment lengthwise into nice-size strips. In a bowl, combine the peppers, cumin, olive oil, lemon juice, preserved lemon, and 1/4 teaspoon of the salt and mix well. Taste and add more salt if needed. Cover and refrigerate for at least 30 minutes to allow the flavors to blend. Serve chilled.

pasillas

bell pepper

cumin

garlic

olive oil

HOMEMADE DATE CANDY
WITH Tangerines

In winter, one of my favorite ways to end a Moroccan meal is with a mint tisane, tangerines, dates, and toasted almonds. For each serving, I plan on $1^{1}/_{2}$ tangerines, 2 dates, and 2 tablespoons toasted raw (skin-on) almonds. There is also a date candy available that is quite nice with tangerines. This is my version of it. The candied rose petals that accompany the peach dessert on page 190 would also be nice with the candy and tangerines. Orange blossom water is distilled, and can be found at Indian and/or Arabic markets, other specialty markets, big-city grocery stores, and online. Make sure your dates are moist and fresh. When chopping dates, coat your knife blade with oil so the pieces won't stick. | SHOWN PAGE 182 | SERVES 6 TO 8

$^{2}/_{3}$ TO $^{3}/_{4}$ CUP GROUND TOASTED NATURAL ALMONDS
1 POUND DATES, PITTED, AND DICED
6 TABLESPOONS PEANUT OR VEGETABLE OIL
2 TABLESPOONS HONEY
1 TO 2 TABLESPOONS ORANGE BLOSSOM WATER
$^{1}/_{2}$ TEASPOON GROUND CINNAMON
SCANT 1 CUP CONFECTIONERS' SUGAR,
    PLUS MORE IF NEEDED
9 TANGERINES

cinnamon

In a large bowl, combine $^{2}/_{3}$ cup of the almonds, the dates, oil, honey, orange blossom water to taste, and cinnamon and mix well, adding more ground almonds if the mixture is too wet to hold together. Shape the mixture into 2-teaspoon-size balls or ovals. Roll the balls or ovals in the confectioners' sugar, coating lightly and evenly, and place on a rack. Let rest for about 1 hour to dry. If all of the confectioners' sugar is absorbed, re-roll them in more sugar just before serving.

Arrange the candies on an attractive plate and accompany with a bowl of tangerines on ice and let guests peel their own.

Honey

almonds

tangerines

DELIGHTFUL SUMMER PEACH DESSERT

It is important to have delicious, perfectly ripe peaches for this dessert. I often combine two different varieties. Suncrest, Summerset, and Flavorcrest are among the best choices. I like to serve the peaches in small, clear glass bowls to show them off.

The candied rose petals will keep for several days in an airtight container at room temperature (unless they are at my house and at dog level—my dogs love them). They also go well with the date candy on page 189, the Moroccan winter dessert. Rose water is distilled, and can be found at Indian and/or Arabic markets, other specialty markets, big-city grocery stores, and online.

A platter of fruits on ice is another nice way to end a Moroccan meal in summer. I prefer whole individual small fruits or cut larger fruits rather than a "fruit salad." Melon, such as watermelon or cantaloupe, and figs are a must. Peaches and grapes round out the platter. A shaker of confectioners' sugar, flavorful honey, dates, cinnamon sugar, raw (skin-on) almonds and walnuts (toasted, if you like), and lemon wedges are good accompaniments. | SERVES 6 TO 8

CANDIED ROSE PETALS
1 EGG WHITE
PETALS FROM 2 OR 3 PESTICIDE-FREE,
    JUST-OPENED VERY FRESH ROSEBUDS
SUPERFINE SUGAR, FOR DUSTING

4 TO 6 LARGE, RIPE PEACHES, PEELED
2 TABLESPOONS SUPERFINE SUGAR
3 TABLESPOONS ROSE WATER
SMALL FRESH MINT LEAVES, FOR GARNISH
GROUND CINNAMON, FOR GARNISH
A REALLY DELICIOUS VANILLA ICE CREAM,
    FOR SERVING (OPTIONAL)

To make the candied rose petals, in a small bowl, lightly beat the egg white with a few drops of water. One at a time, dip each rose petal into the egg white (or brush with a small, fine pastry brush), covering the petal with a thin, even coat. Lightly dust the petal with the superfine sugar, coating it evenly and gently shaking off the excess sugar. Place the petal on a rack and repeat with the remaining petals. Let sit for about 2 hours, until dry and crisp.

Cut the peaches into sixths or quarters, depending on their size, and place in a bowl. Sprinkle with the sugar, drizzle with the rose water, and toss gently to mix. Cover and chill for 2 hours before serving.

To serve, top the peaches with a few mint leaves, a little cinnamon, the candied rose petals, and a scoop of vanilla ice cream.

sugar

egg yolk

peach

mint

SOUTH AFRICA

I have always been fascinated by the layering of different culinary traditions in a single place, which is why South Africa, a star of the Supper Club, made it into this book. The cuisine is a varied and delicious mix of the foods of the indigenous peoples, the Xhosa and the Zulu, the Sotho and the Tsonga, the Venda and others, and of a long list of colonizers and other settlers, including the Dutch, British, French, Portuguese, German, Malaysian, Indian, Indonesian, and more. The indigenous peoples brought myriad native fruits, nuts, and wild game to the national table, and the newcomers contributed cookery styles, from the stews, breads, and soups of Europe to the curries, pickles, chutneys, and sambals of Asia.

The South African menu here can draw on only a few of these many influences. For example, the hearty *bobotie*, a curry-spiced ground lamb dish topped with an egg custard, originated with the country's Indonesian settlers, while the creamy milk tart, a standard at bake sales and afternoon teas, comes from the Dutch community. I could have included a British-style meat pie, an Indian-inspired curry, a German pastry, a Xhosan cornmeal porridge, or many other dishes, but they must wait for another menu.

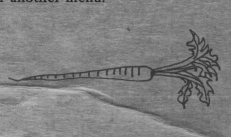

GREEN CORN SOUP

In South Africa, fresh sweet corn is known as green mealies and grilled corn on the cob is a typical summertime snack. This corn soup is popular throughout the country and is seasoned in many different ways. I decided on mace here, finding that it nicely complemented the natural sweetness of the corn. I have used chicken stock as the base, but if you prefer a vegetarian soup, you can make a quick corn stock: Reserve the corn cobs after stripping them of their kernels. Sweat chopped yellow onion in a little butter or olive oil, add the corncobs and water to cover, and simmer for about 40 minutes, then strain and use in place of the chicken stock. The white wine you use will vary depending on how sweet your corn is; if it's very sweet, balance it with drier wine. | SERVES 6 TO 8

3 TABLESPOONS UNSALTED BUTTER OR OLIVE OIL

1 YELLOW ONION OR LEEK [WHITE
    AND LIGHT GREEN PARTS ONLY], SLICED

KERNELS FROM 10 TO 12 EARS CORN

2 OR 3 THYME SPRIGS, OR ½ TO 1 TEASPOON DRIED THYME

¼ TEASPOON GROUND MACE, 2 SMALL MACE BLADES,
    OR A FEW NUTMEG GRATINGS

1 CUP WHITE WINE

1 BAY LEAF

4 CUPS CHICKEN STOCK [PAGE 59] OR STORE-BOUGHT
    REDUCED-SODIUM BROTH

SEA SALT AND FRESHLY GROUND BLACK PEPPER

PINCH OF SUGAR, IF NEEDED

MINCED FRESH FLAT-LEAF PARSLEY LEAVES, RINSED
    AND SQUEEZED DRY [SEE PAGE 83], FOR GARNISH

CHOPPED FRESH CHIVES, FOR GARNISH

In a soup pot, melt the butter over medium-high heat. When the butter is hot, add the onion, decrease the heat to medium-low, and sweat for about 20 minutes, until tender. Add the corn kernels, thyme, and mace, increase the heat to medium-high, and cook, stirring, for 2 to 3 minutes. Add the wine and bay leaf and cook until the wine is reduced by half. Add the stock, bring to a boil, and decrease the heat to a simmer. Cook uncovered, skimming off any foam that rises to the surface, for 15 to 20 minutes, until the corn is tender. Remove and discard the bay leaf and thyme sprigs.

At this point, I like to transfer half of the soup to a blender, process it until smooth, and then swirl it back into the soup in the pot. But you may decide to keep it all in the pot or blend it all smooth. Season with salt and pepper and add the sugar if the sweetness level of the corn needs a little help.

Ladle the soup into warmed bowls and garnish with the parsley and chives. Serve right away.

black pepper

OLIVE OIL

leek

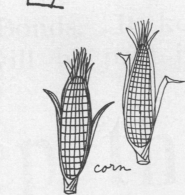
corn

chicken stock

BOBOTIE
WITH BAKED SWEET POTATOES

This South African comfort food has been compared to moussaka, meat loaf, and English shepherd's pie, though its origin lies in Southeast Asia, evidenced by the use of curry, turmeric, and fruits. It originally came about on the Cape of Good Hope as a use for leftover roasted meats, but now it is often made from scratch.

Yellow rice (flavored with turmeric, cinnamon, and raisins) is the traditional accompaniment, but I prefer sweet potatoes because the combination reminds me of my mom's meat loaf and baked potatoes. | SERVES 6 TO 8

CUSTARD

2 EGGS

1¼ CUPS WHOLE MILK

2 PINCHES OF SEA SALT

¾ CUP SLICED ALMONDS

1 TO 2 TABLESPOONS CANOLA, PEANUT, OR SUNFLOWER OIL

2 SMALL YELLOW ONIONS, THINLY SLICED
   THROUGH THE STEM END

1 TO 2 CLOVES GARLIC, MINCED

1 TO 2 TABLESPOONS CURRY POWDER

1 TEASPOON GROUND TURMERIC

1 LARGE CARROT, PEELED AND GRATED

1 LARGE GRANNY SMITH OR
   OTHER TART GREEN APPLE, GRATED

8 OR 9 DRIED APRICOTS, THINLY SLICED OR FINELY DICED

⅓ CUP (2 OUNCES) FIRMLY PACKED GOLDEN RAISINS

2 SLICES STALE WHITE BREAD, CRUSTS REMOVED, TORN
   INTO PIECES, AND SOAKED IN ¼ CUP WHOLE MILK

1½ TEASPOONS SEA SALT

½ TEASPOON FRESHLY GROUND BLACK PEPPER

2 POUNDS GROUND LAMB, OR 1 POUND EACH GROUND LAMB
   AND GROUND BUFFALO OR BEEF

3 OR 4 BAY LEAVES

Preheat the oven to 350°F.

While the oven is heating, make the custard. In a bowl, whisk together the eggs, milk, and salt until smooth. Cover and refrigerate until needed.

Spread the almonds on a rimmed baking sheet, pop the pan into the oven, and toast for about 7 minutes, until golden brown. Pour onto a plate and let cool. Leave the oven set at 350°F.

In a large sauté pan, heat 1 tablespoon of the oil over medium-low heat. Add the onions, stir to coat with the oil, cover, and cook, shaking the pan frequently, for 7 to 10 minutes, stirring frequently, until translucent, very tender, and just beginning to caramelize (see page 14 for more on caramelizing onions). If the onions begin to scorch, add the remaining 1 tablespoon oil. Add the garlic and cook for 1 minute. Add the curry powder (use the smaller amount if you like less spice) and turmeric and cook, stirring, for 30 to 60 seconds, until nicely aromatic. Remove from the heat, cool slightly, then combine with the toasted almonds, carrot, apple, apricots, raisins, the soaked bread and any remaining milk, and the salt and pepper in a big bowl, and mix well. Add the meat and mix well. Fry a nugget of the mixture in a little oil, taste, and adjust the seasoning of the mixture.

CONTINUED

almonds

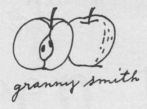

granny smith

Bobotie, *continued*

SWEET POTATOES
8 UNIFORM-SIZE SWEET POTATOES
OLIVE OR PEANUT OIL, FOR RUBBING
SEA SALT

TOMATO AND ONION SMOOR [PAGE 196], FOR SERVING
CARROT SAMBAL [PAGE 197], FOR SERVING
APRICOT CHUTNEY [PAGE 197], FOR SERVING

Transfer the mixture to a large *cazuela* (see page 142) or other large round or oval baking dish and pat down to even the surface and remove any air pockets. Spear the bay leaves into the dish at regular intervals, leaving them exposed enough so that you can pull them out after baking. Bake for 35 to 40 minutes, until it is just firming up. Carefully remove the dish from the oven and drain off any excess fat that has risen to the surface. Pour the custard evenly over the top, return the dish to the oven, and bake for about 20 minutes more, until the custard is set.

Once the *bobotie* has begun baking, rub the sweet potatoes with oil and salt and prick each potato in a couple of places with fork tines. Place the sweet potatoes on a rimmed baking sheet and slip them into the oven after the *bobotie* has been cooking for 15 to 20 minutes. Bake for 35 to 45 minutes, until fork-tender.

To serve, place the *bobotie* on the table in the dish in which it was baked. Arrange the sweet potatoes on a platter and set the sweet potatoes, *smoor*, sambal, and chutney alongside the *bobotie*.

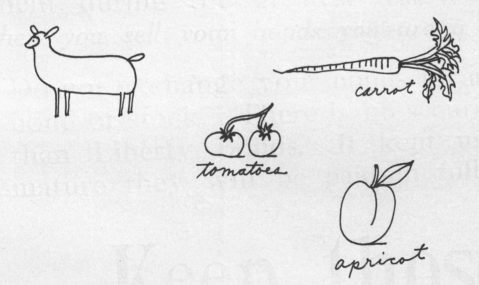

TOMATO AND ONION SMOOR

Sugar is traditionally added to this dish, but I don't use it and my version turns out quite tasty. Whether you need it will depend on how sweet the tomatoes are. An alternative way to make this dish is to cook the caramelized onions as directed. Then cut the tomatoes in half through the equator, place cut side up in a baking dish, season with the chile, sugar (if using), and salt, and top with the onions. Bake in a preheated 350°F oven until hot throughout but not falling apart. This usually takes about 20 minutes. The tomatoes look nice and hold their shape this way. | SERVES 6 TO 8

2 TABLESPOONS OLIVE OIL

1 LARGE YELLOW ONION, CUT INTO ¼-INCH-THICK SLICES

6 TO 8 TOMATOES, PEELED [PAGE 181] AND
    COARSELY CHOPPED

1 SMALL JALAPEÑO CHILE, STEMMED, SEEDED
    IF DESIRED, AND MINCED

UP TO 1 TABLESPOON SUGAR [OPTIONAL]

1 TO 1½ TEASPOONS SEA SALT

In a large sauté pan, heat the olive oil over medium-high heat. When the oil is hot, add the onion, stir to coat with the oil, and cook, stirring occasionally, for 5 to 10 minutes, until the onion starts to turn golden. Decrease the heat to medium-low and continue to cook slowly for 10 to 15 minutes, until the onion is nicely browned on the edges. Stir more frequently as the onion begins to caramelize to prevent burning (see page 14 for more on caramelizing onions).

Add the tomatoes, chile, and sugar, stir well, and cook over the lowest heat setting for 15 to 20 minutes, until well heated. Do not cook the mixture so long that you end up with a sauce. If you cannot set the heat low enough, use a heat diffuser (see page 187). Season to taste with the salt, transfer to a bowl, and serve hot or warm.

sea salt

yellow onion

EXTRA VIRGIN Olive Oil

sugar

tomatoes

CARROT SAMBAL

If you can, make this sambal several days ahead, as the flavor improves with sitting. I serve it along-side *bobotie*, but it is also a great condiment in sandwiches, with roasted pork or chicken, or with most curries. Adjust the amount of sugar according to the sweetness of the carrots. | MAKES ABOUT 1½ CUPS

SEEDS FROM 2 GREEN CARDAMOM PODS

2 DRIED ÁRBOL OR OTHER HOT DRIED CHILES, STEMMED, SEEDED IF DESIRED, AND CHOPPED

1 POUND CARROTS, PEELED AND GRATED

1 TABLESPOON PEELED AND MINCED OR GRATED FRESH GINGER

2 CLOVES GARLIC, MINCED

1 TEASPOON SEA SALT

½ TO ¾ CUP SUGAR

½ CUP WATER

¼ CUP DISTILLED WHITE VINEGAR

sea salt

carrot

Smack the cardamom seeds with the side of a chef's knife to pulverize, or grind in a spice grinder, a well-cleaned coffee grinder, or a mortar with the chiles until pulverized.

In a heavy, nonreactive pot, combine the carrots, ginger, garlic, salt, ½ cup of the sugar, the water, and the cardamom and chile. Bring to a boil over high heat, decrease the heat to a simmer, and cook, stirring occasionally, for 30 minutes. Add the vinegar and cook for about 30 minutes more. The carrots are ready when they are translucent and a bit spicy. Taste for sweetness and add some or all of the remaining sugar, if needed. Serve chilled or at room temperature.

sugar

APRICOT CHUTNEY

apricot

In spring and early summer, when fresh apricots are available, I use them for this chutney. But I have also made it with 1 mango, peeled and diced, or 2 large or 4 small tomatoes, peeled and quartered, at other times of the year. | MAKES ABOUT 1 CUP

1½ CUPS DRIED APRICOTS

4 FRESH APRICOTS, PEELED AND DICED

3 BIRD CHILES, OR 2 SERRANO AND 1 JALAPEÑO CHILE, STEMMED, SEEDED IF DESIRED, AND MINCED

2-INCH PIECE FRESH GINGER, PEELED AND FINELY GRATED

1 LARGE CLOVE GARLIC, SMASHED [SEE PAGE 172] AND THEN MINCED

½ CUP CIDER VINEGAR

2 TO 4 TABLESPOONS SUGAR

¼ CUP WATER

In a heavy, nonreactive saucepan, combine the dried apricots with water to cover and bring to a boil over high heat. Remove from the heat and let soak for 10 minutes. Drain the apricots and dice.

In a heavy, nonreactive saucepan, combine the rehy-drated dried apricots, fresh apricots, chiles, ginger, garlic, vinegar, 2 tablespoons of the sugar, and the water and bring to a boil over medium-high heat, stirring occasion-ally. Decrease the heat to a simmer and cook for 30 to 60 minutes, until thick and wonderful. Taste about half-way through cooking and add some or all of the remaining 2 tablespoons sugar, if necessary. Stir the chutney off and on as it cooks and take care that it doesn't scorch on the pan bottom. Serve chilled or at room temperature.

MILK TART
WITH BLOOD ORANGE COMPOTE

I found only one recipe for this typical South African tart in my cookbook collection, so I turned to the Internet for more ideas. In the end, I used the pastry recipe that I included in my *Fog City Diner Cookbook* because it comes out so nice and flaky. But I have added a style variation that I discovered in a South African recipe: grating the frozen butter into the flour mixture. It works great. Just make sure that you put the flour into the bowl first and grate the butter on top, or the butter will be difficult to mix evenly.

Although milk tarts are sometimes made without a crust, I prefer them with the pastry shell. Otherwise, the dessert seems too much like a dish of baked milk. I have used blood oranges for the compote, but any good oranges or even raspberries or strawberries would be delicious. Both the filling and the tart shell can be made up to a day ahead, which makes this a great party dessert. Keep the filling in the refrigerator and the tart shell chilled until just before baking, and then combine them and put the tart in the oven to bake while you sit down to the main course. This way, the tart will be warm when you are ready to serve it. I think it tastes best warm, but it can also be served hot, at room temperature, or chilled.

This is not a sweet dessert. David Gold, a local veterinarian who is from South Africa, told me that my milk tart tasted like home. It is sort of a nursery school tart—that is, it is geared toward a little kid's palate. Some of the testers thought it needed more sugar. If you like your desserts sweet, add more sugar to the filling and accompany the tart with the chantilly cream. | MAKES ONE 9-INCH TART; SERVES 6 TO 8

TART SHELL
2 CUPS ALL-PURPOSE FLOUR
1/2 TEASPOON SEA SALT
1 TEASPOON GRANULATED SUGAR [OPTIONAL]
1 CUP PLUS 2 TABLESPOONS UNSALTED BUTTER, FROZEN
3 TO 5 TABLESPOONS ICE WATER

sea salt

sugar

unsalted butter

To make the tart shell, in the bowl of a stand mixer, whisk together the flour, salt, and granulated sugar. Using the large holes on a box grater, grate the frozen butter onto the flour mixture and toss to mix lightly. Fit the mixer with the paddle attachment and beat together the flour and butter on medium speed just until combined. On low speed, add the ice water, a little at a time, and mix just until the dough comes together in a rough mass. (Add the water slowly because you may not need it all.)

Transfer the dough to a large piece of plastic wrap, shape it into a disk about 1 inch thick, and wrap in the plastic wrap. Refrigerate for 30 minutes.

Preheat the oven to 450°F. Butter a 9-inch fluted classic pie dish.

FILLING

¼ CUP CAKE FLOUR

¾ TEASPOON BAKING POWDER

½ TEASPOON SEA SALT

3 EGGS

¾ CUP GRANULATED SUGAR

2 CUPS WHOLE MILK

1 TEASPOON PURE VANILLA EXTRACT

⅛ TEASPOON PURE ALMOND EXTRACT

2 TABLESPOONS UNSALTED BUTTER, MELTED

1½ TEASPOONS GRANULATED SUGAR MIXED

    WITH ½ TEASPOON GROUND CINNAMON

blood orange

CHANTILLY CREAM (OPTIONAL GARNISH)

1 CUP HEAVY CREAM

¼ CUP CONFECTIONERS' SUGAR

½ TEASPOON PURE VANILLA EXTRACT

BLOOD ORANGE COMPOTE

5 OR 6 BLOOD ORANGES

½ VANILLA BEAN, SPLIT LENGTHWISE,

    OR ½ TEASPOON PURE VANILLA EXTRACT

2 TO 4 TABLESPOONS GRANULATED SUGAR

⅓ CUP SLICED ALMONDS, TOASTED [OPTIONAL; SEE PAGE 23]

On a lightly floured work surface, roll out the dough into an 11-inch round about ¼ inch thick. Roll the dough around the pin, position the pin over the prepared pie dish, and then unroll the dough, centering it over the dish. Gently press the dough snuggly into the bottom and sides of the dish. Take care not to stretch the dough, as it will shrink during baking. Turn the edge under on the rim and flute. Line the tart shell with a piece of aluminum foil and fill with pie weights or dried beans.

Place the tart shell in the oven and bake for 15 minutes. Decrease the heat to 350°F, remove the weights and foil, return to the oven, and bake for 4 to 7 minutes longer, until golden. Let cool on a rack. Leave the oven set at 350°F.

To make the filling, in a small bowl, stir together the flour, baking powder, and salt. In a large bowl, whisk together the eggs and granulated sugar until light and fluffy. Pour in the milk and the vanilla and almond extracts and whisk to combine. Then slowly sprinkle the flour mixture into the egg mixture, stirring as you go and mixing well. Stir in the butter and pour the filling into the cooled, prebaked shell. Sprinkle the cinnamon sugar evenly over the top and bake for about 45 minutes, until set. Transfer to a rack.

While the tart is baking, make the chantilly cream. In a bowl, whisk together the cream, confectioners' sugar, and vanilla until thickened to the consistency of whipped cream. Cover and refrigerate until needed.

To make the compote, working with 1 orange at a time, cut a slice off the top and bottom just to reveal the flesh. Stand the orange upright on a cutting board and slice off the peel, pith, and membrane in wide strips, working from the top to the bottom and following the contour of the fruit. Holding the fruit in one hand over a bowl, cut along either side of each section to free it from the membrane, and allow the sections to drop into the bowl. Repeat with the remaining oranges.

Using the tip of a paring knife, scrape the seeds from the vanilla bean onto the oranges, and then add the spent pod halves, or drizzle the vanilla extract over the oranges. Sprinkle with the granulated sugar to taste and mix well. Let sit for a while to allow the flavors to develop. If you have used the vanilla bean, remove the pod halves before serving.

Cut the warm tart into slices and transfer to individual plates. Top each serving with some of the compote and chantilly cream and a sprinkle of the almonds.

almonds

LEBANON

Among the first people I met when I moved to the Napa Valley in 1979 was the Doumani family, whose ancestry is Lebanese. Carl, the patriarch, once brought a still-warm deer liver to me at Mustards and asked me to cook it for him. He was quite the sight walking in the front door clutching a dripping liver. His daughter Lissa convinced me to open Cindy's Backstreet Kitchen, which means she has had a role in making this book happen, too. She and her husband, Hiro Sone, own the celebrated restaurant Terra, next door to Cindy's. Not surprisingly, the Doumani family piqued my interest in Lebanese food soon after I met them.

In 2000, I was fortunate to meet Anissa Helou, a wonderful food writer and art historian whose book, *Lebanese Cuisine*, is both a culinary history and a comprehensive collection of recipes of her birthplace. That book proved the perfect starting point for my research into this rich and varied Mediterranean cuisine built on an abundance of vegetables, citrus and other fruits, nuts, olives and olive oil, herbs, seafood, poultry, and lamb. This simple menu represents just a sliver of the wealth of the Lebanese table.

SPICED WALNUTS AND OLIVES

These quick and easy treats are addictive. Serve them with pre-dinner cocktails to heighten your guests' appetite for what is to follow.

Zatar, an herb and spice mix common throughout much of the Middle East, is used to season both the walnuts and the olives. The mix varies by region and even by cook, but thyme, sumac, and sesame seeds are common to nearly every blend. Penzeys Spices carries a good-quality store-bought version. You can also whip up your own mix. I use equal amounts of dried thyme, toasted sesame seeds, and dried sumac. If you use 1 tablespoon of each, you will have enough for this menu, with some extra to try in other dishes. It's great on grilled corn with butter and lemon or lime juice. | SHOWN PAGE 205 | MAKES 2 CUPS WALNUTS AND 2 CUPS OLIVES

WALNUTS
2 CUPS WALNUT HALVES
2 TABLESPOONS ZATAR
1/2 TEASPOON SEA SALT
3 TABLESPOONS OLIVE OIL OR SESAME OIL

OLIVES
2 TO 3 TABLESPOONS OLIVE OIL
3 OR 4 THYME SPRIGS
1 TO 2 TABLESPOONS ZATAR
ZEST OF 1 LEMON, IN WIDE STRIPS
2 CUPS OIL-CURED BLACK OLIVES

To prepare the walnuts, preheat the oven to 350°F. In a big bowl, toss together the walnuts, *zatar*, salt, and oil. Pour the nuts out onto a rimmed baking sheet and bake for 7 to 10 minutes, until nicely toasted.

To make the olives, in a large sauté pan, heat the olive oil over medium-high heat. Add the thyme, *zatar*, and lemon zest and then toss in the olives. Sauté for 5 to 7 minutes, until hot.

Serve the nuts at room temperature and the olives warm. You can mix them together, but I like to keep them separate. Remember to set out a dish for the olive pits.

walnuts

black olives

GARLIC CHICKEN
WITH GARLIC AND POTATO SAUCE

The marinade on this dish was inspired by a recipe in *Lebanese Cuisine*, by my friend Anissa Helou. I adapted the sauce to include less garlic. All of the Lebanese recipes I have found use almost twice as much garlic as I would typically add. Everyone to whom I have served this dish has liked it, but you may want to double the garlic for a more authentic experience.

I cook the potatoes for the sauce in salted water and then reserve some of the water for moistening the "mash." Passing the cooked potatoes through a potato ricer or a food mill (harder to clean) will give you the best texture, and the smoother the mash the smoother the sauce.

I use the marinade on a whole chicken and cook the bird in a covered grill. I feel that chicken cooked over a charcoal and/or wood fire is superior to chicken roasted in the oven, but you can opt to do the latter. The chicken can also be cooked in a wood-burning oven or in an "egg cooker" barbecue grill. | SHOWN PAGE 204 | SERVES 6

8 CLOVES GARLIC, SMASHED [SEE PAGE 172]

1 TEASPOON ALLSPICE BERRIES

1/2 TO 1 TEASPOON WHITE OR BLACK PEPPERCORNS
    [DEPENDING ON YOUR TASTE]

1/2 TO 1 TEASPOON SEA SALT [DEPENDING ON YOUR TASTE]

1/4 TEASPOON CAYENNE PEPPER

1/8 TEASPOON GROUND CINNAMON

GRATED ZEST AND JUICE OF 1 LEMON

2 TABLESPOONS OLIVE OIL

1 [4- TO 5-POUND] WELL-RAISED CHICKEN

GARLIC AND POTATO SAUCE

4 CLOVES GARLIC

1/4 TEASPOON SEA SALT

1 EGG YOLK

1 TO 2 TABLESPOONS LEMON JUICE
    [ABOUT 1/2 TO 1 LEMON]

1 TO 2 TABLESPOONS DRAINED AND WHISKED
    GREEK-STYLE PLAIN YOGURT [SEE PAGE 217]

1/2 TO 3/4 CUP OLIVE OIL

1 CUP MASHED POTATO [SUCH AS KENNEBEC,
    RUSSET, OR YUKON GOLD]

To make the marinade, combine the garlic, allspice, peppercorns, salt, cayenne, and cinnamon in a mortar and smash and pound with a pestle until everything is pretty well mixed. Add the lemon zest and juice and the oil and smash again until you have thickish paste that is loose enough to smear on the bird. (Or, use a blender for this step.)

Rinse the chicken with cold water, drain well, and pat dry with paper towels. Smear the bird inside and out with the marinade, trying to get some under the skin as well. Cover and marinate in the refrigerator for 2 to 4 hours.

egg yolk

lemon zest

peppercorn

olive oil

To make the sauce, in a food processor, combine the garlic, salt, egg yolk, and 1 tablespoon of the lemon juice and process until the garlic has been reduced to small bits. Add the yogurt, 1/2 cup of the oil, and the mashed potato and process until almost smooth. Add the remaining oil 1 tablespoon at a time, until the sauce reaches a texture you like. Add the remaining 1 tablespoon lemon juice to taste. Cover and reserve at room temperature or refrigerated until needed. If refrigerated, bring back to room temperature before serving.

Prepare a medium-hot charcoal and/or wood fire for indirect-heat cooking in a grill. To do this, bank all of the hot charcoal and/or wood to one side. (When testing this recipe for the book, we used 10 pieces of mesquite wood and 20 pieces of charcoal briquette.) Place the chicken, breast side up, on the grill rack away from the fire, cover, and grill for 10 minutes. Turn the chicken breast side down, re-cover, and continue to cook for another 10 minutes. Then turn the chicken breast side up one more time and cook for 10 to 20 minutes, depending on the heat of the grill, until the juices run clear when a thigh joint is pierced with a knife. If the chicken seems to be browning and cooking too quickly, decrease the temperature of the fire by closing down the vents on the grill. When the chicken is ready, transfer to a platter and let rest for 10 to 15 minutes in a warm spot to allow the juices to settle back into the meat.

garlic

Carve the chicken and serve it on individual plates or carve it at the table. Pass the sauce at the table.

Kennebec potatoes

GARLIC CHICKEN

CRISPY WALNUT TRIANGLES
SPICED WALNUTS AND OLIVES
ZUCCHINI

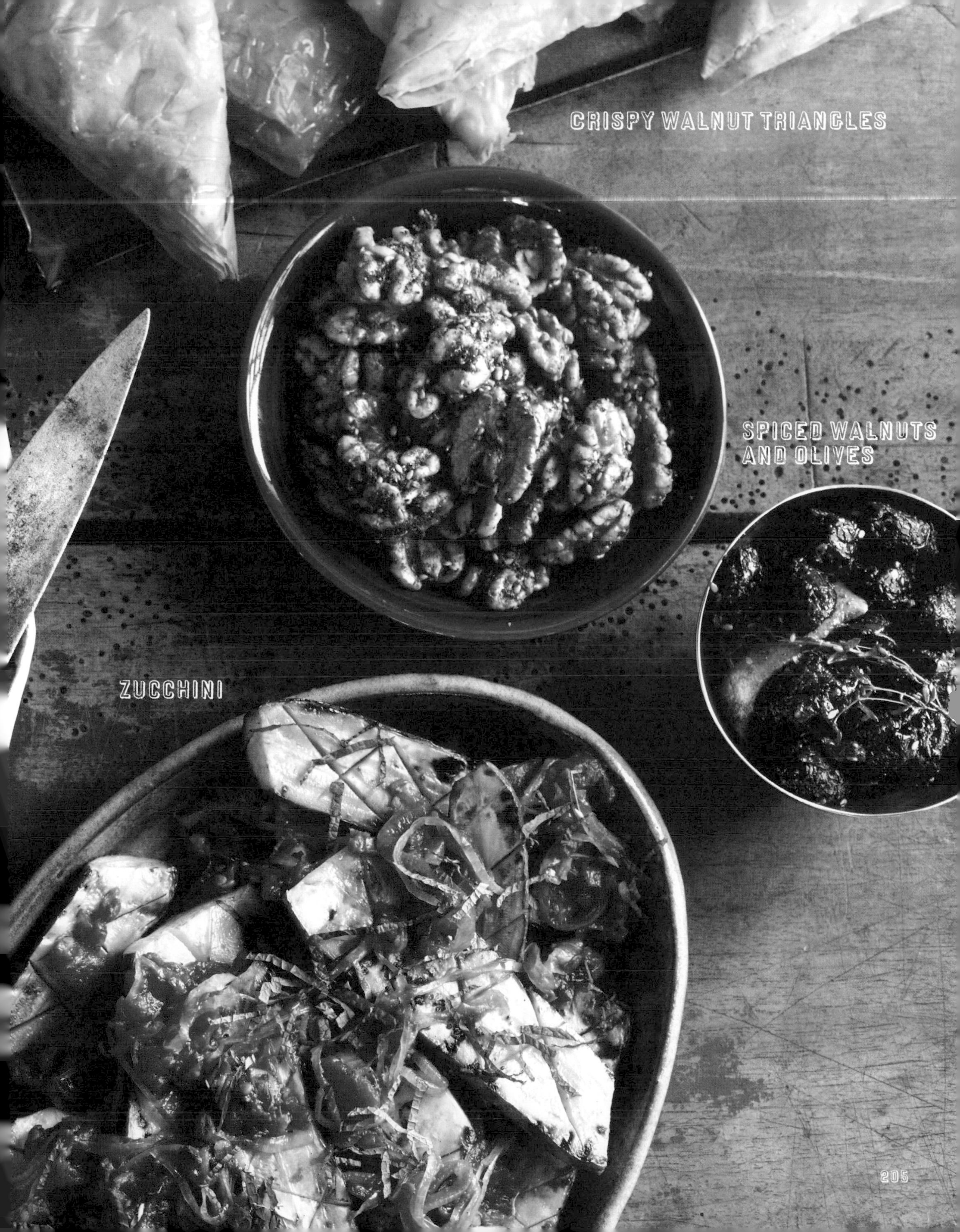

ZUCCHINI
WITH TOMATO AND MINT

Cook this dish at the height of summer when gardens and farmers' markets are full of the three main ingredients: zucchini, tomatoes, and mint. In this menu, it is a side dish to the garlic chicken, but it would also be a wonderful first course.

In traditional Lebanese cooking, the zucchini would be fried or boiled before they are added to the sauce. I always do the garlic chicken on the grill, so I usually put the zucchini on the grill, which is nontraditional but delicious. If you want to add another vegetable, grilled eggplant would be good. | SHOWN PAGE 205 | SERVES 6

2 TABLESPOONS OLIVE OIL, PLUS MORE FOR BRUSHING

1 LARGE OR 2 SMALL ONIONS, HALVED THROUGH THE STEM
    END AND THINLY SLICED INTO CRESCENTS

2 TO 3 TABLESPOONS CHIFFONADE-CUT FRESH MINT LEAVES
    OR CHOPPED FRESH CILANTRO, FOR GARNISH

1 1/2 POUNDS TOMATOES, PEELED [SEE PAGE 181]
    AND COARSELY DICED

SEA SALT AND FRESHLY GROUND BLACK PEPPER

12 TINY OR 6 SMALL ZUCCHINI [1 TO 1 1/2 POUNDS]

2 TO 3 TABLESPOONS DRAINED AND WHISKED GREEK-STYLE
    PLAIN YOGURT, FOR GARNISH [OPTIONAL; SEE PAGE 217]

CAYENNE PEPPER, FOR GARNISH [OPTIONAL]

Preheat a medium-hot charcoal and/or wood fire in a grill.

In a large sauté pan, heat the olive oil over medium heat. Add the onions, cover, and cook for 15 to 20 minutes, until very tender. Add half of the mint, the tomatoes, 1/2 teaspoon salt, and 1/4 teaspoon pepper and cook slowly for about 15 minutes, until thick and saucelike. The sauce could be made up to this point 1 day ahead, covered, and refrigerated, and then reheated just before serving.

Trim off the stem and blossom ends of each zucchini and split each squash in half lengthwise. Brush both sides with olive oil and sprinkle with salt and pepper.

When ready to serve, place the zucchini on the grill rack directly over the fire and grill for 2 to 3 minutes on each side, until nicely charred on the outside and just tender inside.

Spoon the warm sauce onto a platter and arrange the zucchini on top. Sprinkle with the remaining mint and garnish with the yogurt and cayenne pepper.

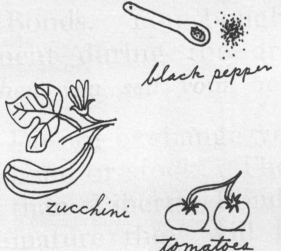

black pepper

zucchini

tomatoes

mint

CRISPY WALNUT TRIANGLES

These triangles are delicious, but they are also very rich, so you won't be able to eat that many. Because the syrup is dense, only a little is needed. Any extra syrup is great for seasoning iced or hot herb tisanes or black teas. | SHOWN PAGE 205 | SERVES 8

SYRUP
3/4 CUP SUGAR

5 TABLESPOONS WATER

1/2 TO 1 TEASPOON FRESHLY SQUEEZED LEMON JUICE [DEPENDING ON YOUR TASTE]

1 1/2 TEASPOONS ROSE WATER

1 1/2 TEASPOONS ORANGE BLOSSOM WATER

FILLING
1/2 CUP WALNUTS

1 TABLESPOON SUGAR

1/4 TEASPOON GROUND CINNAMON

1/2 TEASPOON ROSE WATER

1/2 TEASPOON ORANGE BLOSSOM WATER

8 SHEETS PHYLLO DOUGH, KEPT UNDER A DAMPENED KITCHEN TOWEL TO PREVENT DRYING [SEE PAGE 208]

1/4 CUP UNSALTED BUTTER, MELTED

walnuts

sugar

Preheat the oven to 400°F. Generously butter a rimmed baking sheet or line with parchment paper or a silicone baking mat.

To make the syrup, in a heavy saucepan, combine the sugar, water, and lemon juice and bring to a boil, stirring to dissolve the sugar. Boil for 3 minutes and then remove from the heat. Stir in the rose water and orange blossom water. Reserve until needed.

To make the filling, in a food processor, combine the walnuts, sugar, and cinnamon and process until finely ground. Pour into a bowl and stir in the rose water and the orange blossom water.

Lay a phyllo sheet horizontally on a work surface, with a long side facing you. Brush the right one-third of the pastry with some of the butter. Fold the buttered third in and then brush the top of the folded flap with butter. Fold the left third of the sheet over on top of the first fold. Lay out a second phyllo sheet and repeat the buttering and folding. Now brush the top of one of the folded sheets with butter and stack the other folded sheet on top. You now have 6 layers. Cut this stack into 2 squares. Place 1 tablespoon or so of filling off-center on each square, brush the edge around the filling with a little butter, and fold each square into a triangle. Less is more on the filling; the triangles should be flat. This dessert is mostly about the buttery, crispy phyllo. Place the triangles on the prepared baking sheet, and repeat until all of the pastry and filling are used up. You should have 8 triangles.

Bake for 8 to 10 minutes, until golden brown and crispy on top. Transfer the triangles to a rack placed over a tray (to collect any syrup that drips from the triangles). Drizzle the syrup over the warm triangles. Serve warm or at room temperature.

CONTINUED

Crispy Walnut Triangles, *continued*

TIPS AND TRICKS

PHYLLO SAVVY

MOST PHYLLO DOUGH IS SOLD FROZEN AND MUST
BE THAWED SLOWLY. ONE OF THE BEST WAYS
TO DO THIS IS TO LAY IT, STILL FOLDED IN ITS
PLASTIC, BETWEEN TWO DAMP TOWELS AND LET
IT THAW AT ROOM TEMPERATURE. THEN, WHEN
YOU ARE READY TO START WORKING WITH THE
PHYLLO, TAKE OFF THE CELLOPHANE WRAPPING
AND GENTLY LAY OUT THE SHEETS BETWEEN THE
DAMP TOWELS. MAKE SURE THE TOWELS THAT
THE PHYLLO COMES INTO CONTACT WITH ARE LINT
FREE, AND REMOVE EACH SHEET FROM UNDER
THE TOP TOWEL AS NEEDED.

1 BRUSH THE RIGHT ONE-THIRD OF THE
PASTRY WITH SOME OF THE BUTTER.

2 FOLD THE BUTTERED THIRD IN AND
THEN BRUSH THE TOP OF THE FOLDED
FLAP WITH BUTTER.

3 NOW BRUSH THE TOP OF ONE OF THE FOLDED SHEETS WITH BUTTER AND STACK THE OTHER FOLDED SHEET ON TOP.

4 YOU NOW HAVE 6 LAYERS. CUT THIS STACK INTO 2 SQUARES.

5 PLACE 1 TABLESPOON OR SO OF FILLING OFF-CENTER ON EACH SQUARE, AND BRUSH THE EDGE AROUND THE FILLING WITH A LITTLE BUTTER.

6 FOLD EACH SQUARE INTO A TRIANGLE. PLACE THE TRIANGLES ON THE PREPARED BAKING SHEET, AND REPEAT UNTIL ALL OF THE PASTRY AND FILLING ARE USED UP.

TURKEY

I did not travel to Turkey until I was in my fifties, and when I got there, I could not figure out why I had waited so long. I loved being near the Bosporus, watching the boats and eating dinner in cafés on the banks and bridges of Istanbul. The flavors, colors, and aromas of the cooking and the natural light of the setting make this one of the best places in the world to eat.

Like so many cuisines in this part of the world, the Turkish table is an intriguing amalgam of different influences, with the Middle East, Central Asia, and the Balkan Peninsula the primary players. The ingredients are as heady as the influences, with most of them harvested from the great agricultural belts and bountiful waters that punctuate Turkey's geography. I have chosen four simple yet iconic dishes to show off this culinary abundance, hoping that they will inspire you to investigate further on your own.

LAMB CHOPS
WITH BULGUR PILAF

You don't need to make a fancy sauce to go with these simply prepared chops. They are wonderfully flavorful on their own, especially if they are grilled over a charcoal and/or wood fire. You can ask your butcher to french the chops (trim away the meat to expose the ends of the bones) or you can do it yourself.

Bulgur pilafs came to Turkey from Armenia. Before then, rice was the staple grain on the Turkish table. If you are faced with diners who suffer from gluten intolerance, you could substitute a mixture of chickpeas and lentils or rice in place of the bulgur and omit the pasta. If you prepare rice, you will need to increase the liquid to 2 cups and you will need to cover the pan once the rice and stock have been added. If you opt for chickpeas and lentils, you can cook the lentils in the liquid and add cooked chickpeas at the end just to warm. In both cases, you will need to omit the pasta, of course.

I enjoyed working on these recipes because they reminded me how different cultures use the same ingredients and cooking techniques to make completely different meals. And when making the pilaf I had a fond recollection of one of the first chefs I worked for, Gabino Soletino, browning his rice and noodles before cooking. | SERVES 6

12 TO 18 SINGLE-BONE LAMB RIB CHOPS, FRENCHED
1/2 TEASPOON SEA SALT
FRESHLY GROUND BLACK PEPPER

MARINADE
1 SHALLOT, VERY THINLY SLICED OR MINCED
1 CLOVE GARLIC, SMASHED [SEE PAGE 172]
JUICE OF 1 LEMON [ABOUT 2 TABLESPOONS]
2/3 CUP OLIVE OIL
1/2 TEASPOON GROUND SUMAC
LEAVES FROM 2-INCH ROSEMARY SPRIG, MINCED
LEAVES FROM 5 OR 6 OREGANO SPRIGS, MINCED

garlic

Season the lamb chops on both sides with salt and pepper and reserve until needed.

To make the marinade, in a small bowl, stir together the shallot, garlic, lemon juice, olive oil, sumac, rosemary, and oregano, mixing well. Smear this mixture all over the lamb chops, pressing into the meat well. Let the marinade work its magic for at least 30 minutes.

CONTINUED

sea salt

lamb chops

OLIVE OIL

rosemary

Lamb Chops, *continued*

BULGUR PILAF

4 TABLESPOONS UNSALTED BUTTER

1 SMALL RED ONION, MINCED

3 FRESH CHILES (SUCH AS JALAPEÑO, SERRANO,
  OR POBLANO), STEMMED, SEEDED IF DESIRED, AND
  MINCED, OR 1 RED BELL PEPPER, SEEDED AND
  MINCED, PLUS 1 TEASPOON OR SO CAYENNE PEPPER

1 OUNCE CAPELLINI OR THIN VERMICELLI
  (ABOUT 3/4-INCH-THICK BUNDLE), BROKEN INTO SHORT,
  UNEVEN PIECES

SCANT 2 CUPS BULGUR, RINSED IN COLD WATER AND
  WELL DRAINED

1 1/4 CUPS STOCK (SUCH AS CHICKEN, BEEF, OR VEGETABLE)
  OR WATER

2 TO 3 TABLESPOONS GOLDEN RAISINS

1/2 TEASPOON GROUND ALLSPICE

1/8 TEASPOON GROUND CLOVES

1/2 TO 3/4 TEASPOON SEA SALT, DEPENDING
  ON SALTINESS OF STOCK

2 TO 3 TABLESPOONS CHIFFONADE-CUT FRESH MINT

To make the pilaf, in a large sauté pan, melt 2 tablespoons of the butter over medium-high heat. When the butter is hot, add the onion and sauté for several minutes, until golden. Add the chiles and cook, stirring, for several minutes more, until softened. Add the noodles and cook, stirring to coat with the butter, for 1 minute. Add the bulgur and cook, stirring, for 2 minutes. Stir in the stock, raisins, allspice, cloves, and 1/2 teaspoon of the salt. Bring to a boil, decrease the heat to a simmer, and cook for 15 minutes. Fluff with a fork and check for doneness. The grains should be tender and the liquid should be absorbed. If done, remove from the heat, cover with a tea towel, and let rest until serving. If the grains are too firm, continue to cook until tender.

While the bulgur is cooking, prepare a hot charcoal and/or wood fire in a grill. When ready to serve, place the lamb chops on the grill rack directly over the fire and grill, turning once, for 1 to 1 1/2 minutes each side for rare.

Just before serving, to finish the bulgur, melt the remaining 2 tablespoons butter in a small saucepan over medium-high heat and cook until nut brown. Toss in the mint, swirl about, and then pour over the pilaf. Toss and taste for seasoning, adding the remaining 1/4 teaspoon salt if needed.

To serve, arrange the lamb chops on a large platter and serve the bulgur on the side.

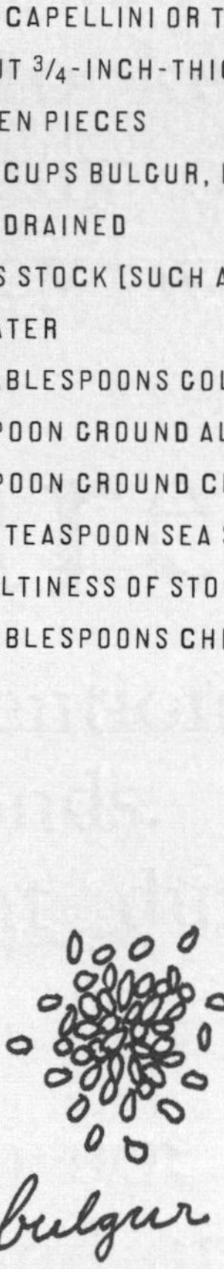

bulgur

unsalted butter

capellini

clove

bell pepper

EGGPLANT, TOMATO, AND CHILE SALAD

You can grill the eggplants and chiles over the fierce fire while you wait for the coals to die down to the proper temperature for cooking the lamb chops. To make a dish more like a salad, leave the eggplants and chiles in big pieces. For a relish, cut the vegetables into small dice. For the menu, this dish is served at room temperature alongside the lamb chops, but it would also be good as a leftover straight from the refrigerator on grilled bread or toasted pita. In fact, I always prepare extra and use it on crostini, in grilled cheese sandwiches, in pasta, or as a side dish or relish for grilled fish or chicken. If you want to use it as a condiment, mash or mince it finely. | SERVES 6

1½ TO 2 POUNDS SMALL GLOBE EGGPLANTS

3 POBLANO (PASILLA) CHILES OR PIMENTO PEPPERS

JUICE OF 1 LEMON (ABOUT 2 TABLESPOONS)

3 CLOVES GARLIC, MINCED

2 TO 3 TEASPOONS PAPRIKA

1 TABLESPOON CUMIN SEEDS, TOASTED IN A DRY PAN
    UNTIL FRAGRANT AND THEN GROUND (SEE PAGE 23)

SEA SALT AND FRESHLY GROUND BLACK PEPPER

4 TO 6 TABLESPOONS EXTRA VIRGIN OLIVE OIL

2 LARGE TOMATOES, PEELED (SEE PAGE 181) AND DICED

Prepare the grill for cooking the lamb chops (see page 211). Before the coals are ready, place the eggplants on the grill rack directly over the fire and grill, turning as needed to cook evenly, until the eggplants are soft throughout but the skins are not too blackened. Some char is fine. They should be very soft and offer no resistance when pressed. Place the chiles over the fire at the same time and grill, turning as needed, until they are nicely blackened on all sides. When the vegetables are done, transfer the eggplants to a platter and slip the chiles into a plastic bag, close the top, and leave to steam for 5 to 10 minutes.

When the eggplants are cool enough to handle, peel off and discard the skin and cut the flesh into large chunks or small dice, as desired. Gently lay the cut eggplant pieces in a fine-mesh sieve or a colander and let drain. When the chiles are cool enough to handle, peel off the skins and stem, seed, and cut into large chunks or small dice.

In a small bowl, whisk together the lemon juice, garlic, 2 teaspoons of the paprika, the cumin, and a pinch each of salt and pepper. Gradually whisk in 4 tablespoons of the olive oil in a slow, steady stream and continue to whisk until well emulsified. Taste and whisk in more oil, paprika, and salt and pepper if needed.

In a large bowl, combine the eggplant and chiles. Pour on the dressing and toss gently to coat evenly. Add the tomatoes and mix gently so as not to break up the vegetables. Serve at room temperature.

cumin

poblano chile

TOMATO SALAD

WITH SUMAC, FETA, AND TARRAGON

If you have tired of too many *panzanella* and *caprese* salads like I have, you will find this colorful, refreshing salad a nice change. For the tomatoes, try to put together a mix of colors and shapes. If you can't find sumac, lemon zest is a respectable substitute. | SERVES 6

DRESSING
1 CLOVE GARLIC, SMASHED [SEE PAGE 172]
JUICE OF 1/2 LEMON [ABOUT 1 TABLESPOON]
2 TABLESPOONS POMEGRANATE MOLASSES
2 TEASPOONS GROUND SUMAC
LEAVES FROM 2 OR 3 THYME SPRIGS
1/2 CUP PLUS 1 TABLESPOON OLIVE OIL
SEA SALT AND FRESHLY GROUND BLACK PEPPER

6 PERFECTLY RIPE HEIRLOOM OR OTHER DELICIOUS
   TOMATOES, CUT INTO SLICES OR WEDGES
1 CUP SMALL, COLORFUL CHERRY TOMATOES,
   HALVED IF LARGE
2 SHALLOTS OR 1 SMALL RED TORPEDO ONION,
   THINLY SLICED
FRESHLY GROUND BLACK PEPPER

1/2 CUP CRUMBLED MILD FETA OR SHAVED
   RICOTTA SALATA CHEESE, FOR GARNISH
LEAVES FROM 2 OR 3 TARRAGON SPRIGS, FOR GARNISH

To make the dressing, in a small bowl, whisk together the garlic, lemon juice, pomegranate molasses, sumac, and thyme. Gradually whisk in the olive oil in a slow, steady stream and continue to whisk until well emulsified. Season with salt and pepper and reserve until needed.

Arrange the tomato slices on a platter or on individual plates. Sprinkle with the cherry tomatoes and the shallots, separated into rings. Drizzle with the dressing, then season with pepper and garnish with the cheese and tarragon.

TURKISH COFFEE

To have the full experience of a good Turkish coffee, you need a *cezve*, or Turkish coffee pot, which is a small pot with a long handle and a spout for pouring. Second best would be a small pan with a spout; anything without a spout makes the task harder and messy. For the menu, you will need to make the coffee in batches to accommodate everyone at the table. The key thing to remember when making Turkish coffee is that just as the foam starts to form, you must pour it off into the cups. Then you need to cook the remaining liquid just a bit more and immediately add it to the cups. Use freshly ground coffee for the best flavor. | SERVES 2

3/4 CUP COLD FILTERED WATER
3 TABLESPOONS COARSELY GROUND MEDIUM-ROAST COFFEE
1 1/2 TEASPOONS SUGAR

In a Turkish coffee pot or small spouted pan, combine the water, coffee, and sugar and bring slowly to a boil over low heat. A frothy foam will develop. Pour the foam off into 2 cups, dividing it evenly. Return the pot to the stove to heat the coffee for 1 minute longer, and then pour the liquid over the foam in the cups. Serve at once.

PISTACHIO AND YOGURT CAKE
WITH APRICOT YOGURT CREAM

I have always liked pistachios. When I was a child, our family would receive huge bags of pistachios at Christmastime from Uncle John, my father's brother, and we would eat them like mad.

This recipe is an adaptation of a handful of recipes from Ayla Algar's *Classical Turkish Cooking*. It is critical to start with very fresh unsalted nuts and to poach the apricots until they are tender. Apricots can sometimes be quite dry, so the poaching time can vary anywhere from 10 to 25 minutes, depending on the fruits. Take your time with the poaching; you want the apricots to be plump and tender.

The cake is brushed with some of the poaching syrup from the apricots while it is still warm from the oven, so it is important that the apricots are already poached when the cake is done. I have made the apricots first to ensure the syrup is ready. | SERVES 8 TO 10

APRICOT SYRUP
1 1/2 CUPS WATER
1/4 CUP GRANULATED SUGAR
1 VANILLA BEAN, SPLIT LENGTHWISE
2 WIDE LEMON ZEST STRIPS
1 CUP (6 OUNCES) DRIED APRICOTS, SLICED

1/2 CUP CRÈME FRAÎCHE
2 3/4 CUPS GREEK-STYLE PLAIN
　　YOGURT (SEE OPPOSITE)

CANDIED PISTACHIOS
1 CUP THINLY SLICED PISTACHIOS
1/2 EGG WHITE, WHISKED
2 TO 3 TABLESPOONS SUGAR, PREFERABLY SUPERFINE

CONFECTIONERS' SUGAR, FOR DUSTING

pistachios

PISTACHIO AND YOGURT CAKE
1 CUP ALL-PURPOSE FLOUR
3/4 TEASPOON BAKING SODA
1/4 TEASPOON BAKING POWDER
1/4 TEASPOON SALT
6 EGGS, SEPARATED
1 CUP GRANULATED SUGAR
1/4 CUP EXTRA VIRGIN OLIVE OIL
1/2 TEASPOON CREAM OF TARTAR

apricot

To make the apricot syrup, in a saucepan, combine the water, granulated sugar, vanilla bean, and lemon zest strips and bring to a boil over medium-high heat, stirring to dissolve the sugar. Add the apricots, decrease the heat to a simmer, and cook for 10 to 15 minutes (or longer if the apricots are very dry), until tender but not mushy.

Strain the syrup through a sieve, reserving the vanilla bean pod and apricots. Discard the zest strips. Using the tip of a paring knife, scrape any seeds remaining in the vanilla pods into the syrup and discard the pods. Bring the syrup to a boil over high heat and cook for about 10 minutes, until glistening, thick, and reduced to 1/3 to 1/2 cup.

Add half of the reduced syrup to the reserved apricots to moisten them. Reserve the remaining syrup for brushing on the cake. Place 2 cups of the Greek yogurt in a small bowl and fold in the crème fraîche. Fluff with a fork, cover, and refrigerate until needed.

To make the candied pistachios, preheat the oven to 350°F. Line a rimmed baking sheet with a silicone baking mat or parchment paper.

In a bowl, combine the pistachios and the egg white and mix gently to coat the nuts lightly and evenly. When all of the nuts are evenly moistened, add the sugar and mix to coat the nuts evenly.

Spread the nuts in a single layer on the prepared baking sheet and bake for 8 to 10 minutes, until golden brown and crisp. Let cool and reserve until needed. Leave the oven set at 350°F.

To make the cake, butter a 9- or 10-inch springform pan or a 12-cup Bundt pan or spray with nonstick cooking spray.

Set aside a handful of the nuts. Spread the rest of the nuts on a rimmed baking sheet and place in the oven for a minute or two to "freshen" (do not allow them to brown). Remove the nuts from the oven and finely chop them by hand or pulse them in a food processor. You want them finely chopped, not a paste. Transfer the chopped nuts to a large bowl, add the flour, baking soda, baking powder, and salt, and mix well with a fork.

In a stand mixer fitted with the paddle attachment, beat together the egg yolks and $1/2$ cup of the granulated sugar on medium-high speed for about 3 minutes, until thick, light, and lemon colored. On medium speed, mix in the remaining $3/4$ cup Greek yogurt and then the olive oil until thoroughly combined. (Or, beat the ingredients together by hand with a wooden spoon.) Add the wet mixture to the flour mixture and stir just until combined and moist. Do not overmix. Reserve until needed.

In the stand mixer fitted with the whisk attachment, or in a bowl with a handheld mixer, beat together the egg whites and cream of tartar on medium-high speed until thick and foamy. Slowly add the remaining $1/2$ cup granulated sugar and continue to beat until silky, firm peaks form.

Scoop one-third of the beaten egg whites onto the top of the egg yolk–flour mixture and fold in with a rubber spatula just until combined. Add the remaining beaten whites in two batches, folding the last batch just until no white streaks remain. Pour the batter into the prepared pan.

Bake for 45 to 50 minutes, until a toothpick inserted into the center comes out dry. For a springform cake, transfer to a rack and immediately prick the surface liberally with a skewer. Brush the surface of the cake with the reserved syrup. Let the cake cool completely, then unclasp the pan sides and lift off if using a springform pan. For a Bundt cake, invert the cake onto a plate and prick the surface liberally with a skewer. Brush the surface with all of the reserved syrup.

To serve, cut the cake into wedges and place on individual plates. Put a generous dollop of yogurt cream and poached apricots alongside each wedge. Dust the cake with confectioners' sugar and sprinkle the plate with candied pistachios.

TIPS AND TRICKS
GREEK YOGURT

GREEK YOGURT IS PRE-STRAINED AND DENSER THAN NORMAL YOGURT IN THIS COUNTRY. IF GREEK YOGURT IS NOT AVAILABLE, MAKE A SUBSTITUTE BY STRAINING SOME OF THE WHEY OUT OF PLAIN YOGURT, MADE FROM EITHER COW'S OR SHEEP'S MILK. PLACE THE YOGURT IN A CHEESECLOTH OR COFFEE FILTER AND ALLOW TO STRAIN FOR A COUPLE OF HOURS, UNTIL THE YOGURT HAS THICKENED.

vanilla beans

ASIA

CHINA

Chinese food has been a favorite of mine since I was a kid. My first experience with one of the world's great cuisines was takeout chop suey from the local Chinese restaurant in Minneapolis. In time, our family graduated to sweet-and-sour ribs and beef rice and we thought we knew everything. At some point in my teens, I woke up and started learning about hot-and-sour soup, noodle dishes, and Sichuan chicken salad. After college, I moved to Chicago, which had a huge (to me) Chinatown and I took my first Chinese cooking classes. Since then, I have been fortunate to travel to China and Hong Kong several times, where I have sat down to many memorable meals. During one trip I attended cooking classes in Hong Kong taught by the estimable Ken Hom. Another time, I traveled to mainland China with Jacques Pepin and his wife Gloria; I have such fond memories of that learning opportunity—and Jacques' sense of humor and pranks, which made it all the more special.

The Bay Area is home to a large Chinese community, which has spawned scores of traditional restaurants for all of us to enjoy. For many years, people living in the Napa Valley either had to learn how to cook Chinese food or had to hit the road to San Francisco, Berkeley, Oakland, or farther south because of a lack of local options. Times have changed and the valley now supports a handful of good Asian restaurants. But I still like cooking Chinese food at home and in my restaurants, and Chinese New Year remains one of the most popular holidays we celebrate with a menu at Mustards.

MUSHROOM AND PORK WONTONS

WITH RICH CHICKEN BROTH

A number of steps are involved in making this dish, but the result is well worth the effort. Sometimes I get an assembly line going of family or friends, whomever I will be feeding, and have them help me fold the wontons—the task goes by in a flash.

The wontons may be made up to 2 hours ahead and refrigerated until cooking. Line a baking sheet with parchment paper or waxed paper and sprinkle a fine layer of cornstarch over the paper. Arrange the wontons, not touching, in a single layer on the baking sheet and dust the tops with a little more cornstarch. This is to ensure that the humidity of the refrigerator won't turn the wonton wrappers soggy. You will have more wontons than you need for this menu—3 to 5 wontons per bowl is a good-size serving—but the balance can be frozen. Freeze them in a single layer until solid and then bag them and store them in the freezer for up to 1 month. Or, you can cook them, coat them lightly with toasted sesame oil, refrigerate them, and use them within a day.

If you are making the whole menu, you can use the broth left over from the spareribs as part of the broth for serving the wontons. Otherwise, use a good homemade chicken or other poultry stock or store-bought reduced-sodium broth. If you cannot find small shiitakes, cut larger ones into wedges and use a single wedge per wonton. Ground chicken or turkey (use dark meat for more flavor) is another good choice for the meat. I even once used ground wild turkey, which proved delicious. | MAKES ABOUT 48 WONTONS; SERVES 6

FILLING

48 OR SO SMALL FRESH SHIITAKE MUSHROOMS
 [NO LARGER THAN YOUR THUMBNAIL], STEMMED

12 OUNCES GROUND PORK

2-INCH PIECE FRESH GINGER, PEELED AND GRATED

2 GREEN ONIONS, WHITE AND
 LIGHT GREEN PARTS ONLY, MINCED

1/3 CUP MINCED FRESH CILANTRO [ABOUT 1/4 BUNCH,
 TOUGH STEMS REMOVED]

1 TABLESPOON TOASTED SESAME OIL

1 TABLESPOON SOY SAUCE

1/2 TEASPOON SEA SALT

1/4 TEASPOON FRESHLY GROUND WHITE PEPPER

1 [12-OUNCE] PACKAGE [48 SHEETS] WONTON WRAPPERS

1 EGG WHISKED WITH 2 TABLESPOONS WATER,
 FOR EGG WASH

shiitake

To make the filling, bring a saucepan filled with water to a boil, add the mushrooms, and blanch for 1 1/2 minutes. Drain and reserve. In a large bowl, combine the pork, ginger, green onions, cilantro, sesame oil, soy sauce, salt, and pepper and mix well. Sauté a small nugget of the mixture, taste, and adjust the seasoning of the mixture if needed.

To fill the wontons, lay a wonton wrapper on a work surface and brush the left and bottom edges (in the shape of an L) with the egg wash (this will help seal the wonton). Place a mushroom cap, stemmed side up, toward the bottom left corner of the wrapper, nestling it in the triangle you have created with the egg wash. Place a teaspoon or so of the filling inside the mushroom cap. Lift the top right corner of the wrapper and fold it over to create a triangle. Push out the excess air and press down firmly with your fingers to seal the edges securely. Repeat until all of the filling is used up. You should have 48 wontons.

CONTINUED

Mushroom and Pork Wontons, *continued*

Broth

8 CUPS CHICKEN STOCK [PAGE 59] OR PART PORK BROTH
    FROM MAKING SPARERIBS [PAGE 226]

2 SHALLOTS, UNPEELED, STEMMED AND SLICED

2 CLOVES GARLIC, SMASHED [SEE PAGE 172]

2 JALAPEÑO CHILES, STEMMED AND SLICED

3 GREEN ONIONS, WHITE AND
    LIGHT GREEN PARTS ONLY, SMASHED

3 [1/4-INCH-THICK] FRESH GINGER SLICES, SMASHED

1 1/2 TEASPOONS SEA SALT

Garnish

1 JALAPEÑO CHILE, STEMMED, SEEDED,
    AND CUT INTO THIN RINGS

3 TO 4 TEASPOONS TOASTED SESAME OIL

3 TO 4 TEASPOONS SOY SAUCE

1 CUP FRESH CILANTRO LEAVES

To make the broth, in a large stockpot, combine all of the ingredients and bring to a boil over high heat. Decrease the heat to a simmer and cook for about 2 hours, until the liquid is reduced to 6 cups. Strain the broth through a fine-mesh sieve and reserve until needed.

To assemble the dish, preheat the oven to warm. Place your serving bowls in a single layer in the oven. Bring 2 large pots filled with salted water to a boil over high heat. At the same time, heat the broth to just below a boil.

When the water is boiling, drop in the wontons in small batches (make sure the wontons are not crowded and can move easily) and cook until the water returns to a boil and the wontons float to the surface. This should take 5 to 7 minutes. Using a wire skimmer, transfer the wontons to the warmed bowls (3 to 5 wontons in each bowl). Ladle just enough hot broth over the wontons in each bowl to prevent them from sticking together and return the bowls to the oven. Allow the water to return to a boil before you add another batch of wontons.

Repeat the process until you have cooked all of the wontons you need.

Bring the remaining broth to a boil. Remove the bowls from the oven and ladle additional hot broth into each. Garnish each serving with some jalapeño rings, a drizzle each of sesame oil and soy sauce (about 1/2 teaspoon of each per bowl), and a scattering of cilantro. Serve right away.

TIPS AND TRICKS
Sesame Oil

SESAME OIL IS MOST OFTEN THOUGHT OF AS A SEASONING OIL [WHICH IS ADDED TO A DISH AFTER COOKING] DUE TO ITS LOW SMOKE POINT. I DID A LOT OF RESEARCH ON THIS POINT WHEN DEVELOPING THESE RECIPES, AND FOUND IT'S THE PREFERRED CHOICE FOR JAPANESE, KOREAN, AND THAI COOKS WHEN QUICK SAUTÉING OR SEARING VEGETABLES. IF YOU'RE CONCERNED ABOUT BURNING THE OIL, YOU CAN USE CANOLA, VEGETABLE, OR PEANUT OIL INSTEAD TO STIR-FRY OR SAUTÉ. ADD A BIT OF SESAME OIL AFTER COOKING FOR FLAVOR.

CHILE AND GARLIC FISH SOUP

Cooks in southern Yunnan Province use bone-in, freshwater fish, cut into steaks for this soup. I used sea bass fillets, but you can use any good fish you want. If you decide on a freshwater white fish, use bone-in pieces, not fillets, because fillets will cook too quickly. This soup is a good starter for this multicourse Chinese menu, but you can also serve it as main course for two with rice and a nice salad for a light, quick supper. The soup comes together quickly, so have all of the ingredients ready before you start cooking. | SERVES 6

SEASONING OIL

2 TABLESPOONS PEANUT OR CANOLA OIL

1 OR 2 CLOVES GARLIC, SLICED PAPER-THIN

4 DRIED ÁRBOL OR OTHER DRIED HOT CHILES,
    STEMMED AND LEFT WHOLE

12 TO 16 OUNCES FISH (SUCH AS CALIFORNIA WHITE SEA
    BASS, HALIBUT, FRESHWATER WHITE FISH, OR TROUT),
    FILLETED OR IN STEAKS (SEE HEADNOTE),
    SKINNED IF DESIRED, AND CUT INTO 2-INCH
    CHUNKS OF 2 OUNCES EACH

2 LARGE GREEN ONIONS, WHITE AND LIGHT GREEN PARTS
    ONLY, CUT INTO 2-INCH LENGTHS AND
    THINLY SLICED LENGTHWISE

2 CLOVES GARLIC, FINELY MINCED

1 TABLESPOON PEELED AND FINELY
    JULIENNED FRESH GINGER

2 TOMATOES, PEELED (SEE PAGE 181) AND FINELY CHOPPED

4 DRIED ÁRBOL OR OTHER DRIED HOT CHILES,
    STEMMED AND LEFT WHOLE

1 OR 2 BIRD OR OTHER FRESH HOT CHILES, STEMMED,
    SEEDED IF DESIRED, AND MINCED
    (DEPENDING ON YOUR HEAT TOLERANCE)

3 TO 4 SMALL HEADS BOK CHOY (AT LEAST 1/2 HEAD
    PER SERVING), LEAVES SEPARATED AND CHOPPED IF
    LARGE, OR 1 CUP CHOPPED NAPA CABBAGE

1/2 TO 3/4 CUP FRESH CILANTRO LEAVES

1/2 TO 3/4 TEASPOON SEA SALT

FRESHLY GROUND BLACK OR WHITE PEPPER OR A MIXTURE

In preparation for making the seasoning oil, measure the oil into a small sauté pan and combine the garlic and chiles in a small dish. Reserve until needed.

To make the soup, place the chunks of fish, not overlapping, in a large soup pot. Add the green onions, garlic, ginger, tomatoes, dried and fresh chiles, and water almost to cover (about 6 cups). Bring to a boil, decrease the heat to a simmer, and cook for 3 to 5 minutes, until the fish is just cooked and beginning to flake.

While the soup is simmering, finish the seasoning oil. Heat the oil over high heat. When the oil is hot, add the garlic and chiles and cook for 30 to 40 seconds, until nicely aromatic, then remove from the heat.

Pour the seasoned oil into the simmering soup and add the bok choy, cilantro, salt, and pepper. Simmer just until the fish pieces are cooked to your liking.

Ladle the soup into warmed deep bowls and serve. Warn your eating companions not to eat the whole dried chiles, and if you have used bone-in fish, have small dishes handy for discarding the bones.

ASPARAGUS WITH CLOUD EAR MUSHROOMS AND TOFU

The cloud ear mushrooms, which can be found in Asian markets and well-stocked supermarkets, lend an interesting and unique texture. But dried shiitake mushrooms or fresh enoki mushrooms can replace them. Snow peas or sugar snap peas would work well here in place of the asparagus. | SERVES 6

1/2 OUNCE DRIED CLOUD EAR MUSHROOMS

1/2 BLOCK [ABOUT 14 OUNCES] FIRM TOFU

3/4 TEASPOON SEA SALT

1 TEASPOON SUGAR

1 BUNCH ASPARAGUS [ABOUT 12 OUNCES], TOUGH ENDS
    SNAPPED OFF AND CUT ON THE DIAGONAL INTO 1-INCH PIECES

1 TABLESPOON PEANUT OR VEGETABLE OIL

1-INCH PIECE FRESH GINGER, PEELED AND MINCED

In a bowl, combine the cloud ears with hot water to cover and let soak for 30 minutes. Drain and repeat two more times. Trim off any hard parts and cut into nice wedges. Reserve until needed.

Cut the tofu crosswise into 4 portions. Then cut each portion into thirds. Place the pieces between two cloth napkins on a plate and top with a weight.

Let drain for 20 minutes. Transfer the tofu to a cutting board and dice into small pieces.

In a small bowl, stir together the salt and sugar and reserve. Bring a large saucepan filled with water to a boil, add the asparagus, and cook until not quite fork-tender. Pencil-thin asparagus will cook in a minute or two; stockier asparagus will take a minute or so longer. Drain well and reserve.

In a wok or a large, deep sauté pan, heat the oil over high heat. When the oil is hot, add the ginger and stir for several seconds until aromatic. Add the asparagus and cloud ears and stir and toss for a minute or two. Add the tofu and stir and toss until all of the ingredients are hot. Stir in the salt-sugar mixture and continue to stir and toss for about 1 minute, until the asparagus are fork-tender.

Transfer to a platter and serve.

WARM SESAME DRESSING OVER COOL SPINACH

The spinach can be cooked up to 2 hours and the sauce takes only a minute or two to assemble, making this an ideal dish for the busy cook who is serving a multicourse meal. Although I have called for only 1 tablespoon sesame seeds, you should be as liberal with the amount as you like. | SERVES 6

3 TO 4 BUNCHES SPINACH,
    TOUGH STEMS REMOVED

2 TABLESPOONS TOASTED SESAME OIL

2 TABLESPOONS XIAOSHING WINE

2 TABLESPOONS SOY SAUCE

2 TABLESPOONS OR MORE SESAME SEEDS,
    TOASTED [SEE PAGE 23]

Bring a large pot filled with salted water to a boil, add the spinach, and blanch for about 1 minute, until just wilted. Drain well, cool under cold running water, and squeeze as dry as possible. Chop the spinach and arrange in a nice rectangle on a plate. Keep at cool room temperature until ready to serve.

In a small saucepan, whisk together the sesame oil, wine, and soy sauce, place over medium heat, and bring just to a simmer. Pour the hot sauce over the cool spinach, sprinkle with the sesame seeds, and serve.

SWEET-AND-SOUR SPARERIBS

I always eat too many of these sticky, sweet, robust-flavored ribs. The recipe comes from Hunan Province, and the ribs are a great starter or a small course in a multicourse meal. On Monday nights, my dad would go to his men's club and play indoor baseball and my mom and I would go out to shop or do something else together. Most often our outing would end with dinner at Nankin, a Chinese restaurant in downtown Minneapolis, where we always ate sweet-and-sour ribs. For years, the ribs at Nankin were my benchmark, but these ribs have surpassed them.

If you want to change up your Super Bowl menu, these ribs are a good alternative to the usual chicken wings. Or, you can substitute wings for the spareribs in the recipe, reducing the poaching time to 20 minutes. To make the ribs or wings ahead of time, prepare them through the frying step up to 1 day in advance, and then heat them in the sauce just before serving. For more thoughts on deep-frying, see page 276. | SERVES 6

FOR POACHING

1½ POUNDS MEATY SPARERIBS, CUT INTO 1½-INCH PIECES
    (2- OR 3-RIB SECTIONS)
4 (½-INCH-THICK) FRESH GINGER SLICES,
    PEELED AND SMASHED
4 GREEN ONIONS, WHITE AND LIGHT GREEN PARTS
    ONLY, SMASHED
1 TABLESPOON XIAOSHING WINE
1 TEASPOON SEA SALT

PEANUT OR VEGETABLE OIL, FOR FRYING
2 TABLESPOONS PEELED AND
    JULIENNED FRESH GINGER
3 GREEN ONIONS, WHITE AND LIGHT GREEN
    PARTS ONLY, SLICED ON THE DIAGONAL,
    PLUS THIN SLICES FOR GARNISH
2 TABLESPOONS DARK SOY SAUCE
¼ CUP SUGAR
1 TABLESPOON BLACK OR RICE VINEGAR
1 TEASPOON TOASTED SESAME OIL

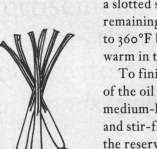

green onions

To poach the ribs, in a heavy pot, combine the ribs with water to cover and bring to a boil over high heat. Add the ginger, green onions, wine, and salt, decrease the heat to a simmer, and cook, skimming off any foam that rises to the surface, for 25 minutes. Remove from the heat and drain well, reserving the broth. Let the ribs cool.

Pour the oil to a depth of 2 to 3 inches (deep enough to submerge the ribs) into a wok or deep sauté pan and heat to 360°F on a deep-frying thermometer. Working in batches to avoid crowding the pan, add the ribs to the hot oil and fry for 3 minutes, until they are caramelized and the meat is tender. Using a slotted spoon, transfer to a plate. Repeat with the remaining ribs, always making sure the oil returns to 360°F before you add a new batch. Keep the ribs warm in the oven.

To finish, pour off all but about 2 tablespoons of the oil from the wok and return the pan to medium-high heat. Add the ginger and green onions and stir-fry for about 2 minutes. Stir in 1 cup of the reserved broth (reserve the remainder for the wontons on page 220 or another use), dark soy sauce, sugar, vinegar, and sesame oil and bring to a boil, stirring to dissolve the sugar. Decrease the heat to a gentle boil, add the ribs, and heat until the ribs are piping hot and the sauce is syrupy and coats the ribs nicely.

Transfer the ribs and their sauce to an attractive platter and garnish with the green onions. Serve hot.

spare ribs

ALMOND COOKIES

I learned to make these cookies in my teens from Verna Meyers, my first cooking-school teacher. She always said to make sure they don't get any darker than golden and that the whole blanched almond in the center of each cookie remains light. Well, for Chinese New Year, I have used red sugar instead of white and raw (skin-on) almonds instead of blanched, and the cookies have still looked and tasted great. If vegetarians will be eating these cookies, use coconut oil in place of the lard. Or, if you just don't want to use lard, butter will work, but the cookies will not be quite as crisp.

When the tester reported on the cookies, she included a piece of advice: "Do not eat fifteen of these cookies in one sitting or you will get a tummy ache." My advice is to stop at fourteen! | MAKES ABOUT 60 COOKIES

3 CUPS SIFTED ALL-PURPOSE FLOUR
1 TEASPOON BAKING SODA
1/2 TEASPOON SEA SALT
1 1/2 CUPS LARD OR UNSALTED BUTTER, CHILLED
1 CUP SUGAR
1 TEASPOON PURE ALMOND EXTRACT
2 EGGS
WHITE OR COLORED SUGAR, FOR ROLLING
AT LEAST 60 BLANCHED ALMONDS,
    FOR TOPPING THE COOKIES

Preheat the oven to 400°F. Have ready 2 ungreased baking sheets.

In a bowl, whisk together the flour, baking soda, and salt. In a stand mixer fitted with the paddle attachment, or in a bowl with a handheld mixer, beat together the lard and sugar on medium speed until thick and light. Add the almond extract and beat until combined. Add the eggs, one at a time, beating well after each addition. On low speed, add the flour mixture all at once and beat until the dry ingredients are evenly moistened. (At this point, you can chill the dough, which will make it a bit easier to work with, or you can continue on.)

Put the sugar for rolling into a flat, shallow bowl. Using a 1/2-ounce cookie scoop (about 1 tablespoon), scoop a portion of dough, shape into a ball, and roll in the sugar, coating evenly. (If you don't have a scoop, use one spoon to scoop and another spoon to scrape the dough off of the first spoon, then coat in sugar.) Place on a baking sheet and gently press an almond into the top of the cookie. Repeat until the baking sheet is full, spacing the cookies about 1 1/2 inches apart.

Bake the cookies, rotating the pan back to front midway through baking, for 8 to 10 minutes, until just golden. Let cool for 1 minute on the pan on a rack and then transfer to the rack and let cool completely. While the first baking sheet is in the oven, assemble the second sheet and then pop it into the oven when the first sheet comes out. The cooled cookies will keep in an airtight tin at room temperature for up to 1 week. Bet you can't eat just one.

sugar

almonds

JAPAN

In the 1990s, I had the good fortune to work in Tokyo on a Fog City Diner project. I got to eat at some truly amazing Japanese restaurants and to ride the bullet train. What more can a girl ask for? That experience also made me enjoy Japanese films like Juzo Itami's *Tampopo*, set in a ramen shop, and Sofia Coppola's *Lost in Translation*, which plumbs a variety of themes, including alienation and culture shock. Everything about Japanese food intrigued me, from the artful, refined *kaiseki* cuisine of the top-tier restaurants to the homey, filling bowls of noodles sold in every subway station to the drama that commences at two o'clock each morning at the city's Tsukiji market, the biggest whole seafood market in the world.

The finest Japanese cooks use only the highest-quality ingredients, knowing that anything less than the best will compromise a dish. For example, some soy sauces or miso pastes are excessively salty and can overpower other ingredients. In this menu—and in much of Japanese cuisine—most of the recipes call for no more than a handful of ingredients, which means that a single poorly chosen ingredient can spoil a dish. If possible, shop at a busy Asian market and ask other customers or even clerks which products are the best and then buy the smallest containers of the recommendations and try them for yourself. But if you still end up with an ingredient that is too salty, don't despair. You can usually dilute it with water until it tastes good to you.

JAPANESE BROTH

Two Ways

These two broths may be used interchangeably, with the *kombu* broth ideal for use in vegetarian meals. *Kombu*, a type of kelp, is sold in sheets, usually packaged in cellophane. If your menu includes shiitake mushrooms, prep them early, so that you can toss the stems into either of these broth pots.

If you prefer to buy instant dashi, you will find many brands on the market. If you are sensitive to MSG, check the label before you buy to be sure you end up with product that does not contain it. | EACH RECIPE MAKES 8 CUPS

DASHI

4 (4- TO 6-INCH-LONG) PIECES KOMBU SEAWEED,
    LIGHTLY WIPED WITH A DAMP CLOTH
8 CUPS WATER
1 OUNCE BONITO FLAKES (ABOUT TWO 4-FINGER PINCHES)

To make the dashi, in a stainless-steel saucepan, combine the seaweed and water, place over medium-low heat, bring just to a boil (the point at which tiny bubbles begin to rise), and then remove from the heat. Stir in the bonito flakes; wait for 1 minute and then strain through a sieve lined with cheesecloth or a coffee filter. Use immediately or chill.

KOMBU BROTH

4 (4- TO 6-INCH-LONG) PIECES KOMBU SEAWEED,
    LIGHTLY WIPED WITH A DAMP CLOTH
8 CUPS COLD WATER

To make the *kombu* broth, in a stainless-steel saucepan, combine the seaweed and water, cover, and let sit overnight. The next day, place the pan over medium heat and bring to a gentle simmer. Remove from the heat and strain. Use immediately or chill.

MUSHROOM MISO SOUP

This simple soup is a great start to this menu, but it is often my breakfast, too. Or you can easily turn it into a main course that will serve 4 or 5 with the addition of noodles. My niece Lynn is a triathlete, and after one of her long runs or morning 40-mile bike rides, she can devour a bowl of the udon version in three minutes, just like the salarymen in the Tokyo subway stations. If you want to add noodles, plan on about 2 ounces dried udon per person. Cook the noodles in boiling water according to the package directions, drain, place in the warmed bowls, and then ladle the soup over the top. | SERVES 6

¼ CUP RED MISO [AKAMISO]

8 CUPS DASHI [PAGE 229]

1 TABLESPOON TOASTED SESAME OIL

8 FRESH SHIITAKE MUSHROOMS, STEMMED AND SLICED,
    OR 8 DRIED SHIITAKE MUSHROOMS, SOAKED
    IN HOT WATER TO COVER FOR 10 MINUTES, DRAINED,
    STEMMED, AND SLICED [SEE PAGE 101]

2 TABLESPOONS WAKAME SEAWEED, SOAKED IN
    ROOM-TEMPERATURE WATER TO COVER FOR
    ABOUT 5 MINUTES AND DRAINED

1 [12 TO 14-OUNCE] BLOCK SILKEN OR
    MEDIUM-FIRM TOFU, DICED

7 TABLESPOONS SOY SAUCE

2 TABLESPOONS MIRIN

1 TO 2 TABLESPOONS SUGAR [OPTIONAL]

4 GREEN ONIONS, WHITE AND LIGHT GREEN PARTS ONLY,
    THINLY SLICED, FOR GARNISH

In a small bowl, dissolve the miso in ½ cup of the dashi and reserve.

Fill the serving bowls with very hot water to heat them. In a large saucepan, heat the sesame oil over medium-high heat. Add the mushrooms and sauté for about 1 minute. Pour in the remaining 7½ cups dashi and stir in the seaweed, tofu, soy sauce, and mirin. Bring to a simmer and decrease the heat to low. Taste and adjust the flavor with the sugar if needed.

Stir the reserved miso into the soup and then make sure the soup is nice and hot before serving, but do not allow it to boil. Pour the water out of the serving bowls and ladle the soup into them, dividing the mushrooms, seaweed, and tofu evenly among the bowls. Garnish with the green onions and serve at once.

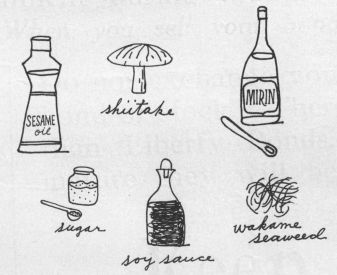

CHERRY TOMATOES, GREEN BEANS, AND ASPARAGUS

WITH SESAME-MISO DRESSING

The more adventuresome can make their own sesame seed paste by grinding cooled, toasted sesame seeds in a *suribachi* (a Japanese mortar) or in a spice grinder or well-cleaned coffee grinder. (You don't want to grind the seeds when they are still warm from the toasting because the oil can separate out, making the paste grainy, not smooth and creamy.) Here, I make just one kind of dressing, but I have sometimes made both white sesame and black sesame dressing and dressed each vegetable half and half. This same dressing is good with blanched broccoli, carrots, and edamame. | SERVES 6

DRESSING
3 TO 4 TABLESPOONS WHITE OR BLACK SESAME SEED PASTE
3 TABLESPOONS WHITE MISO [SHIROMISO]
4 TO 6 TABLESPOONS DASHI [PAGE 229] OR WATER

1 PINT CHERRY TOMATOES
8 OUNCES GREEN BEANS, TOPPED AND TAILED, STRINGED IF
    NECESSARY, AND COOKED UNTIL CRISP-TENDER
1 BUNCH ASPARAGUS, TOUGH ENDS SNAPPED OFF AND
    COOKED UNTIL CRISP-TENDER
TOASTED BLACK SESAME SEEDS OR WHITE SESAME SEEDS
    [SEE PAGE 23], FOR GARNISH

To make the dressing, combine the sesame paste (3 tablespoons if you like your vegetables dressed lightly or 4 tablespoons if you like them dressed more heavily), miso, and 4 tablespoons dashi and mix well. Add more dashi if needed to achieve a smooth, thick consistency. This dressing is traditionally quite thick.

Serve composed salads liberally coated with the dressing, or arrange the vegetables around a bowl of the dressing to use for dipping. I like to dress each ingredient separately and serve them in small bowls so that guests may choose what they like. You can also mix the vegetables together. If you have used black sesame seed paste for the dressing, use white sesame seeds for the garnish and vice versa.

cherry tomatoes

SHIRO MISO

asparagus

sesame seeds

green beans

BROILED TOFU AND EGGPLANT
WITH MISO DENGAKU

This recipe is a good one to make ahead. The miso sauce may be made completely and the tofu and eggplant may be broiled in advance. Then, when you are ready to serve, just smear some of the sauce on the room-temperature precooked tofu and eggplant and slip them under the broiler until the miso glaze bubbles and caramelizes.

You can just use one type of miso, but mixing white and red yields a great flavor (and it can be a good way to use up that last little bit in the bottom of a package). The white miso is sweet and mild and the red is strongly flavored and salty. I tend to use light misos in spring and summer and the darker ones on cold days. You can also play around with the ratio here. You may find that you prefer more white to red. For a variation on this dish, broil only eggplant, use all white miso in the dressing, and garnish with a mix of poppy seeds and white sesame seeds. Also, you can cook the eggplant and tofu in a covered charcoal grill until tender, top them with the miso sauce, and then grill, covered, 1 to 2 minutes longer for a great smoky flavor. My cookbook dealer Celia Slack liked this—and she doesn't even like eggplant!

If you can find them, use Japanese double-prong bamboo skewers for the eggplant as well as the pieces of tofu. They have more holding power than a single skewer and are available in many sizes.

| SERVES 6

1 (14-OUNCE) BLOCK MEDIUM-FIRM TOFU

3 SMALL JAPANESE EGGPLANTS, HALVED LENGTHWISE,
    OR 1 GLOBE EGGPLANT, CUT CROSSWISE
    INTO 1-INCH-THICK SLICES

CANOLA OR SUNFLOWER OIL, FOR BRUSHING

MIXED MISO SAUCE

1/2 CUP RED MISO

3 TABLESPOONS WHITE MISO

2 EGG YOLKS

2 TABLESPOONS SAKE

2 TABLESPOONS MIRIN

7 TABLESPOONS DASHI (PAGE 229) OR WATER

1 TABLESPOON SUGAR

2 TABLESPOONS JAPANESE MUSTARD MIXED WITH JUST
    ENOUGH WATER TO FORM A PASTE, FOR GARNISH

2 TO 3 TABLESPOONS WHITE OR BLACK SESAME SEEDS,
    TOASTED (SEE PAGE 23), FOR GARNISH

GRATED LEMON ZEST,
    FOR GARNISH (OPTIONAL)

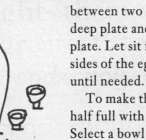

sake

sesame seeds

Cut the tofu crosswise into 4 equal portions. Then cut each portion into thirds. Place the pieces between two cloth napkins or paper towels on a deep plate and top with a weight, such as a heavy plate. Let sit for 20 minutes to drain. Score both sides of the eggplant and brush with the oil. Reserve until needed.

To make the miso sauce, fill a saucepan about half full with water and bring the water to a simmer. Select a bowl that will fit nicely on top of the pan of simmering water (without touching the water). Add the red miso, white miso, egg yolks, sake, mirin, dashi, and sugar to the bowl and whisk until combined. Keeping the bowl over the simmering water, cook, whisking constantly, for 5 to 8 minutes, until the sauce is thick. Remove from the heat and let cool. (The sauce will thicken as it cools.)

Preheat the broiler. Place a large wire cooling rack on a rimmed baking sheet. Remove the tofu pieces from between the napkins, brush the pieces on both sides with oil, and lay them on the rack.

CONTINUED

Broiled Tofu and Eggplant, *continued*

Then brush the eggplant pieces on both sides with oil and lay them on the rack. Place under the broiler and cook until just beginning to brown. Turn the eggplant and tofu over and cook until just beginning to brown on the second side and the eggplant is tender, usually 3 to 6 minutes. At this point, pull the pan out of the oven and smear just the top of the eggplant and tofu pieces with the sauce, return the pan to the boiler, and broil for a few moments more, until golden and bubbly.

Transfer the eggplant and tofu pieces to a platter and top each piece with a tiny bit of mustard and a sprinkle of sesame seeds and lemon zest. Serve at once.

TIPS AND TRICKS
LEFTOVER MISO SAUCE
THIS RECIPE MAKES ABOUT 1½ CUPS MISO SAUCE, WHICH MAY BE MORE THAN YOU NEED FOR THE EGGPLANT AND TOFU. THE REMAINDER CAN BE COVERED AND STORED IN THE REFRIGERATOR FOR UP TO 1 WEEK AND USED AS A MARINADE FOR CHICKEN BREASTS OR FISH FILLETS: SLATHER ON BOTH SIDES, MARINATE FOR AT LEAST A COUPLE OF HOURS IN THE REFRIGERATOR, AND THEN BROIL, TURNING ONCE, OR BAKE IN A PREHEATED 450°F OVEN UNTIL DONE.

WAKAME AND CUCUMBER SALAD

I'm addicted to this simple salad and I serve it often, even with non-Japanese meals. Japanese and Persian cucumbers are readily available in my local markets, but you can substitute standard garden cucumbers, though the salad won't be quite as good. You will also need to halve them lengthwise and scoop out the seeds before you slice them. The key to success for this salad is to slice the cucumbers very, very thinly. A Japanese mandoline-style slicer is ideal for cutting paper-thin slices. | SERVES 6

2 OR 3 (6- TO 8-INCH-LONG) JAPANESE OR PERSIAN CUCUMBERS, PEELED AND SLICED PAPER-THIN (3½ TO 4 CUPS SLICES)

½ TEASPOON SEA SALT

2 TABLESPOONS WAKAME SEAWEED, SOAKED IN ROOM-TEMPERATURE WATER TO COVER FOR ABOUT 5 MINUTES AND THEN DRAINED

7 TABLESPOONS RICE VINEGAR

SCANT 2 TABLESPOONS MIRIN

1 TEASPOON SOY SAUCE

1 TEASPOON SUGAR

1-INCH PIECE FRESH GINGER, PEELED AND GRATED, FOR GARNISH

In a colander, toss the cucumber slices with the salt and leave to drain for at least 20 minutes or up to 1 hour. Gently squeeze the cucumber dry, place in a bowl, and add the seaweed.

In a small bowl, whisk together the vinegar, mirin, and soy sauce until the sugar dissolves. Pour over the vegetables, cover, and refrigerate until cold. Serve chilled, sprinkled with the ginger.

sea salt

persian cucumber

wakame seaweed

MIRIN

ginger

CHILLED SOBA NOODLES
WITH DASHI DIPPING SAUCE
AND SIMPLE REFRESHING GARNISHES

Summertime in many areas of Japan is sizzling hot, which has produced a delightful repertoire of chilled seasonal foods, including this simple combination of cold noodles, a dipping sauce, and a scattering of garnishes. You can serve composed bowls with sauce poured around the noodles and garnishes on top, or you can put out separate bowls of everything and let guests take what they like. I buy soba noodles that come four bundles to a 13-ounce package, the perfect amount to feed six. If you cannot find toasted nori at the store, you can toast it yourself: hold each sheet over a gas or electric burner turned to high heat until the sheet turns brighter green and softens slightly. Finally, be sure to use a high-quality soy sauce for this dish. It is a major component and a too-salty soy sauce will spoil the flavor. | SERVES 6

⅔ CUP DASHI [PAGE 229]

1¼ CUPS SOY SAUCE

1 CUP MIRIN

2 TO 3 TABLESPOONS SUGAR

1 [13-OUNCE] PACKAGE DRIED SOBA NOODLES

10 TO 12 OUNCES DAIKON RADISH, PEELED,
    FINELY GRATED, AND RESERVED IN A SIEVE TO DRAIN

2 TO 3 GREEN ONIONS, WHITE AND LIGHT GREEN
    PARTS ONLY, VERY THINLY SLICED ON THE DIAGONAL

1 SHEET TOASTED NORI, FINELY SHREDDED WITH A KNIFE

TOASTED WHITE SESAME SEEDS [SEE PAGE 23], FOR GARNISH

To make the sauce, in a saucepan, combine the dashi, soy sauce, mirin, and sugar and bring to a boil over high heat, stirring to dissolve the sugar. Remove from the heat, let cool, and refrigerate until chilled.

Bring a large pot of water to a boil, add the noodles, and cook until tender, according to package instructions. Drain in a colander and rinse under cold running water until cold.

To serve, arrange the noodles in piles in individual bowls, pour the chilled sauce around them, and garnish each serving with a healthy dose of daikon (2 to 3 tablespoons) and a sprinkle of green onions, nori, and sesame seeds. Alternatively, put out a big bowl of noodles that guests can serve themselves from surrounded by smaller individual bowls of the sauce and garnishes and have guests dip noodles into the sauce and enjoy garnishes as they like.

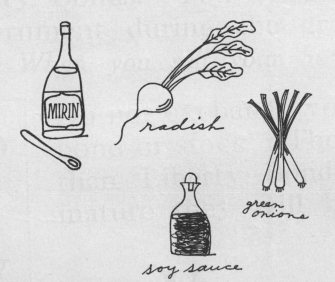

SAKE-SIMMERED SALMON

I like bone-in salmon steaks here because they yield a richer dish, but you can use fillets if you prefer. For cooking, you will need a lidded pan large enough to accommodate the salmon pieces in a single layer. In Japan, this same preparation is often used for whole flounder or sole. This is also a wonderful dish for a simple weeknight supper, accompanied with a green salad dressed with wasabi vinaigrette and topped with toasted sesame seeds. The tester report on this one said it all: "Easy, yummy, and fun to make. We'd make it again and again." | SERVES 6

6 SKIN-ON WILD SALMON FILLETS, 5 TO 6 OUNCES EACH,
   OR BONE-IN, SKIN-ON STEAKS, 8 OUNCES EACH
7 TABLESPOONS MIRIN
7 TABLESPOONS SAKE
3/4 TO 1 CUP DASHI [PAGE 229]
1/2 CUP SOY SAUCE
1 TEASPOON SUGAR [OPTIONAL]
JULIENNED ZEST OF 1/2 LEMON

Measure a few of the fish pieces at their thickest point and reserve. (The cooking time will depend on the average thickness of the pieces.) Select a shallow pan large enough to hold the salmon pieces in a single layer, add the mirin, sake, dashi, and soy sauce, and place over medium-high heat. Stir everything around and bring to a boil. Decrease the heat to medium, simmer for 2 minutes, and then taste for seasoning and add the sugar if desired.

Place the fish in the simmering liquid, cover, and cook for 10 minutes per inch of thickness, until just opaque at the center. Transfer the fish to a serving platter and sprinkle with the lemon zest. Reduce the cooking liquid by half and spoon evenly over the fish. Serve right away.

soy sauce

sake

dashi

lemon zest

salmon

GREEN TEA PANNA COTTA

This is a magical, melt-in-your-mouth dessert. It is not meant to be as firm as a flan. Although these silky puddings should hold together when turned out of the cups, they will be barely set, wobbly, and soft. Agar agar may be used in place of the gelatin for a vegetarian version (see note).

I prepared a Japanese dinner at a lodge in the Sierras and people loved these. Almost everyone had seconds, which is why having extras on hand for your menu is a good idea. (Admittedly, the diners that night had spent the day outdoors hiking, biking, and the like.) If you have them, use ¹/₂-cup tin or aluminum soufflé cups. Otherwise, teacups or custard cups will work just fine. If you have puddings left over, they will keep in the refrigerator for up to 2 days. I always get the best-quality green tea powder (*matcha*), because it is the whole flavor of this dessert. Ask customers or clerks at your favorite Japanese store which brand they recommend. | MAKES 10 OR 11 PUDDINGS

1¹/₂ TABLESPOONS GREEN TEA POWDER
³/₄ CUP SUGAR
2 CUPS WHOLE MILK
2 CUPS HEAVY CREAM
4 GELATIN SHEETS OR 1 [¹/₄-OUNCE]
    PACKAGE POWDERED GELATIN
2 CUPS BUTTERMILK

GARNISH
1 TABLESPOON GREEN TEA POWDER
3 TABLESPOONS SUGAR

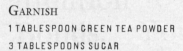

Very lightly mist eleven ¹/₂-cup molds with nonstick cook spray and refrigerate to chill.

In a small bowl, stir together the tea powder and sugar until well mixed. Pour the milk into a measuring pitcher, add the tea powder mixture, and stir until combined. Pour the milk mixture and the cream into a big, heavy saucepan, place over medium-high heat, and bring just to a boil. Remove from the heat and let cool down to 140°F (use an instant-read thermometer to check the temperature), and then stir in the gelatin, mixing well to combine. Stir in the buttermilk and strain through a fine-mesh sieve into a pitcher or a bowl with a spout. Pour into the chilled prepared cups, filling them to within

¹/₄ inch of the rim (you may not need all of the cups). Cover and chill overnight.

To serve, first make the garnish. In a small bowl, stir together the tea powder and sugar, mixing well. Sprinkle some of the garnish attractively on each plate. Invert a cup onto each plate and serve.

TIPS AND TRICKS
USING AGAR AGAR
TO USE AGAR AGAR IN PLACE OF GELATIN, MEASURE 1¹/₂ TABLESPOONS AGAR AGAR FLAKES OR POWDER. ONCE THE MIXTURE OF MILK, CREAM, TEA POWDER, AND SUGAR HAS BEEN BROUGHT TO A BOIL, ADD THE AGAR AGAR, ADJUST THE HEAT, AND SIMMER UNTIL THE AGAR AGAR HAS MOSTLY DISSOLVED. THIS WILL TAKE ABOUT 5 MINUTES FOR FLAKES AND PROBABLY LESS FOR POWDER. REMOVE FROM THE HEAT, LET COOL TO THE TOUCH AND CONTINUE WITH THE RECIPE FROM THE POINT AT WHICH YOU STIR IN THE BUTTERMILK.

green tea powder

sugar

KOREA

There is much more to Korean cooking than the universal kimchi and *bulgogi*. Yet they are so good that many of us tend to venture no further on the menu. That means we are missing countless other specialties of this East Asian culinary gold mine, dishes based on rice and noodles, vegetables and tofu, meats and seafood, and a pantry full of herbs, spices, and other seasonings. Whenever I get hungry for the chile-laced, garlicky, colorful food of the Korean peninsula, I turn to Michael J. Pettid's *Korean Cuisine: An Illustrated History*, an insightful, comprehensive, and totally engrossing treatise on one of the world's most deliciously complex tables. And from there, I head to my kitchen.

I enjoy cooking Korean food and I invariably have willing diners to sample what I make. The mom of one of my good friends, Michael Wolf, is from Korea and she is a fantastic cook. It's fun for me to cook Korean food for Michael because he always lets me know if I am getting it right. When I explore the cuisine of any country, I often find myself going beyond what happens in the kitchen, and my study of Korean food is no exception. I have become a great admirer of Korean ceramics and I hope to get back to the pottery wheel one day soon to try my hand at my own version.

MUSHROOM PORRIDGE

Quick and easy to cook, this first-course porridge also makes a great wintertime breakfast, especially if you are like me and don't eat cold cereal. Plus, it can be made ahead, which is good news whether you are serving it as part of a multicourse menu or for breakfast.

The first time I made this recipe I used turkey stock, dried shiitake mushrooms, and minced elk and it was delicious. It can also easily be made vegetarian by omitting the meat, using vegetable stock, doubling the amount of mushrooms (use all shiitakes or a mixture of shiitake and beech [*hon-shimeji*] or another interesting mushroom variety), and then finishing with a little finely diced tofu. Don't be afraid to experiment and/or use what you have on hand. | SERVES 4 TO 6

5 OR 6 DRIED OR FRESH SHIITAKE MUSHROOMS

6 TO 7 CUPS RICH CHICKEN [PAGE 222] OR TURKEY STOCK

1 CUP SHORT-GRAIN BROWN RICE

2 TABLESPOONS TOASTED SESAME OIL

4 OUNCES GROUND BEEF, PORK, OR LAMB

2 OR 3 CLOVES GARLIC, SLICED

3 TO 4 TABLESPOONS MINCED GREEN ONIONS [WHITE AND
    LIGHT GREEN PARTS ONLY] OR CHIVES, FOR GARNISH

SOY SAUCE, FOR GARNISH

CHILE PASTE, FOR GARNISH

FRESHLY GROUND BLACK PEPPER

If using dried shiitake mushrooms, place them in a bowl with hot water to cover and let soak for 10 minutes. Drain, reserving the soaking water, and remove and discard the stems (see page 101 for more on rehydrating dried mushrooms). Slice the caps and reserved until needed. Add the soaking water to the stock. If using fresh shiitake mushrooms, remove and discard the stems, slice the caps, and reserve until needed.

Put the rice in a good-size bowl, add water to cover, swish the rice around with your hand, and drain. Repeat the rinsing and draining until the water runs clear. Return the rice to the bowl, add water to cover, and let soak for 30 minutes. Drain and reserve.

In a large pan (I use my 6-quart Le Creuset pot so I have room to maneuver), heat 1 tablespoon of the sesame oil over medium-high heat. Add the beef and cook, breaking up any clumps, for 8 to 12 minutes, until browned. Using a slotted spoon, transfer the beef to a plate to drain. Add the mushrooms to the pan over medium-high heat and cook, stirring occasionally, for 3 to 6 minutes, until browned. Using the slotted spoon, transfer the mushrooms to the plate holding the meat.

Add the remaining 1 tablespoon sesame oil to the pan and reduce the heat to low. Add the rice and cook, stirring, for 10 to 15 minutes, until nutty and lightly browned. Stir in the garlic, 6 cups of the stock, and the drained meat and mushrooms. Increase the heat to medium-high. Bring to a boil, decrease the heat to a simmer, and cook for 40 minutes or so, until the rice is tender. Add some or all of the remaining 1 cup stock if the pan becomes too dry before the rice is done.

Spoon into warmed bowls and sprinkle with the green onions. Don't forget to set the soy sauce, chile paste, and a peppermill on the table for diners to add as desired.

SWEET DRIED ANCHOVIES

This rather nontraditional treat reminds me of a snack that was served at Betelnut, a restaurant in San Francisco that I was involved with. The Betelnut version had whole dried chiles and peanuts in it, as well. For this dish, you want small anchovies, which can be found at Korean or other Asian markets. Many Korean chile pastes are fermented, which gives them a rich, sweet, hot flavor. They are a wonderful thing to have in your fridge, almost as important as ketchup and mustard. In a pinch, I have substituted Korean chile paste for Turkish chile paste and have been happy with the results. But then, I'm not Turkish!

My husband, John, tested this recipe with peanuts in place of the anchovies. He preferred the peanut version (pictured on page 246). He also cautions nonprofessional cooks to move quickly on the seasonings, because they can burn easily. John recommends cooking over medium heat rather than high heat to avoid scorching. Don't turn the heat to low, however. It has to be hot enough for the coating to become sticky. Pull the pan off the heat to mix in the anchovies or peanuts, if you are worried about burning them.

Both the anchovy and the peanut versions are great to munch on while watching a game on TV, but be forewarned. They are very addictive—chewy, crispy, sweet, and hot. What more can you ask for? | SHOWN PAGE 246 | MAKES ABOUT 1¼ CUPS

1 TABLESPOON SUGAR

2 TEASPOONS SOY SAUCE

1 OR 2 CLOVES GARLIC, SMASHED [SEE PAGE 172]

½-INCH PIECE FRESH GINGER, PEELED
    AND THINLY SLICED

1 TEASPOON FERMENTED KOREAN CHILE PASTE

2 TEASPOONS CANOLA OIL

1 CUP SMALL [1-INCH] DRIED ANCHOVIES
    OR UNSALTED ROASTED PEANUTS

1 TABLESPOON SESAME SEEDS, TOASTED
    [SEE PAGE 23]

In a small bowl, stir together the sugar, soy sauce, garlic, ginger, and chile paste, mixing well.

In a sauté pan, heat the canola oil over high heat. When the oil is very hot, add the chile paste mixture (careful, it splatters), shake the pan, stir well, and cook for 20 to 40 seconds, until the mixture starts to bubble. Add the anchovies, stir to coat thoroughly, and cook for 30 seconds more. Remove from the heat and add the sesame seeds and mix one more time really well. Let cool completely and serve at room temperature.

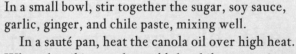

soy sauce

ginger

anchovies

KOREAN-STYLE BEEF TARTARE

One of my favorite versions of steak tartare, this flavorful but light combination is a wonderful mix of tastes and textures. I like to put a biteful of the tartare on a slice of pear, with or without freshly ground black pepper. For a passed hors d'oeuvre, you can nestle a pear slice in a small butter-lettuce cup, top the pear with a small spoonful of tartare, and garnish the meat with a sprinkle of pine nuts.

As always, use the best-quality beef from humanely raised and slaughtered animals. And be sure to hand chop the meat with a very sharp knife. | SHOWN PAGE 247 | SERVES 4 TO 6

8 OUNCES BEEF TENDERLOIN, TRIMMED OF SINEW AND FAT

1 TABLESPOON KOREAN RICE WINE OR SAKE

1 GREEN ONION, WHITE AND LIGHT GREEN PARTS
    ONLY, THINLY SLICED ON THE DIAGONAL

1 TEASPOON MINCED GARLIC

1 TEASPOON TO 1 TABLESPOON SUGAR
    [THE MORE TRADITIONAL MEASURE IS 1 TABLESPOON]

1 TO 2 TEASPOONS FRESH GINGER JUICE
    [SQUEEZED FROM FINELY GRATED FRESH GINGER]

1 TABLESPOON TOASTED SESAME OIL

1 TABLESPOON SESAME SEEDS, TOASTED [SEE PAGE 23]

PINCH OF SEA SALT

FRESHLY GROUND BLACK PEPPER

1 ASIAN PEAR, PEELED AND THINLY SLICED

2 TABLESPOONS MINCED PINE NUTS

With a very sharp knife, cut the beef into thin slices, julienne the slices, and then mince the julienne strips.

In a bowl, combine the minced beef, rice wine, green onion, garlic, sugar, ginger juice, sesame oil, sesame seeds, salt, and a few grinds of pepper. Mix gently but thoroughly. Cover and chill for 1 hour. At the same time, chill the individual plates for serving the tartare.

To serve, arrange a small mound of the meat in the center of each chilled plate. Arrange pear slices around each mound. Garnish the mounds with the pine nuts. Set the pepper mill on the table and invite guests to garnish with pepper.

green onions

garlic

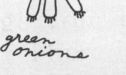

sugar

Asian pear

sesame seeds

MUSHROOM AND BAKED WINTER SQUASH

This mushroom dish is often done with shiitakes, but king oyster, enoki, *maitake*, *hiratake*, beech (*hon-shimeji*), or almost any other type would also work well. You can use a single mushroom variety or a mixture of two or more varieties. Here, the mushrooms are poured over roasted cubes of winter squash or sweet potatoes. The pairing is bright, colorful, and flavorful. One of the testers served this dish with the chicken recipe on page 244, using tofu instead of chicken, and the Green Onion Kimchi on page 249) and loved the combination. | SERVES 4 TO 6

MARINADE
1½ TO 2 TABLESPOONS KOREAN RICE WINE OR SAKE
1 TABLESPOON SOY SAUCE
2 CLOVES GARLIC, MINCED
2 GREEN ONIONS, WHITE AND LIGHT GREEN
    PARTS ONLY, MINCED
2 TABLESPOONS TOASTED SESAME OIL
SEA SALT AND FRESHLY GROUND BLACK PEPPER

ABOUT 1 POUND SHIITAKE MUSHROOMS, STEMMED AND SLICED
    OR QUARTERED IF LARGE OR LEFT WHOLE IF SMALL
3 CUPS PEELED AND CUBED WINTER SQUASH
    OR SWEET POTATO
TOASTED SESAME OIL OR CANOLA OIL, FOR ROASTING
SEA SALT AND FRESHLY GROUND BLACK PEPPER
¼ CUP PINE NUTS, TOASTED (SEE PAGE 23), FOR GARNISH
1 TO 2 TABLESPOONS KOREAN DRIED CHILE THREADS
    OR RED PEPPER FLAKES, FOR GARNISH (THREADS ARE
    BEST; OPTIONAL)

Preheat the oven to 350°F.

To make the marinade, in a small bowl, combine all of the ingredients and mix well. Put the mushrooms in a bowl, pour the marinade over the top, stir to coat, and set aside while you prepare the squash.

To cook the squash, in a bowl, toss the cubes with just enough oil to coat and spread them in a single layer on a baking sheet. Sprinkle with salt and pepper and roast for 25 to 30 minutes, until fork-tender. Remove from the oven and keep warm.

To cook the mushrooms, heat a large sauté pan over medium-high heat. (You want a pan large enough to accommodate the mushrooms in a single layer. If you don't have one, cook the mushrooms in batches.) When the pan is hot, add the mushrooms and all of the marinade and stir-fry or sauté the mushrooms, shaking the pan, for about 3 minutes, until cooked. Add a bit more wine if the pan becomes too dry before the mushrooms are finished.

Transfer the squash to a warmed serving dish. Pour the mushrooms over the top and mix well. Garnish with the pine nuts and chile threads and serve hot.

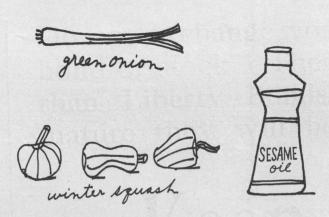

green onion

winter squash

SESAME oil

pine nuts

soy sauce

GRILLED CHICKEN
WITH MUNG BEAN SALAD

This is a tasty way to cook skinless, boneless chicken breasts. It is a perfect dish for this menu, but it also makes a nice centerpiece for a simpler supper, accompanied with Mushroom and Baked Winter Squash (page 243), Green Onion Kimchi (page 249), and brown rice. The chicken, which is known as *tak kui* in Korean, may be cooked on a griddle, but we grilled it over hot coals one winter day and it was much tastier. The marinade is also good for grilling salmon, halibut, or tofu. It may seem like it calls for a lot of garlic, but I have used the traditional amount.

I am not much of a bean sprout eater, but done this way, they are addictive and are the perfect counterpoint to the chicken. The salad would be good with beef, too. When preparing the sprouts, you want to trim the very tip off of both ends, like you do with green beans. The flavor of the salad improves with time, so marinate the sprouts a few hours ahead—one less thing to do at the last minute! | SERVES 4 TO 6

MARINADE
3 TABLESPOONS SOY SAUCE
1 TABLESPOON TOASTED SESAME OIL
2 TABLESPOONS PURE MAPLE SYRUP
1/3 CUP KOREAN RICE WINE OR SAKE
3 GREEN ONIONS, WHITE AND
    SOME TENDER GREEN PARTS, MINCED
8 TO 10 CLOVES GARLIC, MINCED
1 TABLESPOON SESAME SEEDS, TOASTED [SEE PAGE 23]
    AND MASHED TO A PASTE IN A MORTAR
4 WALNUT HALVES, MASHED TO A PASTE IN A MORTAR
GRATED ZEST AND JUICE OF 1 LEMON
1 TABLESPOON KOREAN CHILE POWDER OR CAYENNE PEPPER
PINCH OF SEA SALT
FRESHLY GROUND BLACK PEPPER

4 TO 6 SKINLESS, BONELESS CHICKEN BREAST HALVES,
    OR 3 SKINLESS, BONELESS WHOLE CHICKEN BREASTS

MUNG BEAN SALAD
1 POUND MUNG BEAN SPROUTS, TOPPED AND TAILED
1 1/2 TEASPOONS TO 1 TABLESPOON SOY SAUCE
1 TABLESPOON RICE VINEGAR
1 TABLESPOON TOASTED SESAME OIL
1 CLOVE GARLIC, MINCED
2 GREEN ONIONS, WHITE AND LIGHT GREEN PARTS ONLY, MINCED
1 TABLESPOON SESAME SEEDS, TOASTED [SEE PAGE 23]
SEA SALT AND FRESHLY GROUND BLACK PEPPER

To make the marinade, in a bowl, combine all of the ingredients and mix well. Reserve until needed.

Place the chicken breasts inside moistened resealable plastic bags or between moistened sheets of plastic wrap. (The resealable-bag method is handy because you can pour the marinade in right over the chicken.) Using a meat mallet or the bottom of a heavy skillet, gently pound the meat until it is an even 1/2 inch thick. You don't want it paper-thin, but you do want it to be evenly thick so that all of the pieces cook in the same amount of time. Otherwise, you can end up with overcooked parts, which will be dry and tasteless. Leave the chicken in the bags, or transfer it to a shallow dish if you used plastic wrap. Pour the marinade over the chicken, making sure that all of the surfaces are well coated. Seal or cover and refrigerate for at least 30 minutes or up to 24 hours.

To make the sprout salad, bring a large pot filled with water to a rapid boil. Have ready an ice bath. Stir the sprouts into the boiling water, cover, and let

mung bean

cook for 1 minute. Using a wire skimmer or slotted spoon, transfer the sprouts to the ice bath to cool completely and then drain in a colander. (I spin my sprouts in a salad spinner to make sure they are nice and dry.)

In a bowl, stir together the soy sauce, vinegar, sesame oil, garlic, green onions, and sesame seeds. Add the drained sprouts and toss to mix. Season with salt and pepper. Reserve at room temperature or refrigerated until needed.

Prepare a medium charcoal and/or wood fire in a grill or preheat a griddle to medium-high. Because you are working with skinless meat, which can easily dry out, you don't want the grill fire too hot. Place the chicken on the grill rack directly over the fire or on the griddle and cook, turning once, for 3 to 4 minutes on each side, until just opaque throughout.

To serve, cut the breasts against the grain into thin slices, and fan the meat out across a platter or individual plates. Accompany with the sprout salad, served at room temperature or chilled.

PICKLED CUCUMBERS

You will need one quart-size or two pint-size sterilized glass jars for this recipe. The cucumbers will keep for up to 1 week in the refrigerator, but they are so good they won't last that long. | MAKES 1 QUART

2 POUNDS PICKLING CUCUMBERS,
    OR 3 LARGE CUCUMBERS
1/4 CUP SEA SALT
2 GREEN ONIONS, WHITE AND LIGHT GREEN
    PARTS ONLY, THINLY SLICED
2 CLOVES GARLIC
1 TABLESPOON KOREAN CHILE POWDER
    OR 2 TEASPOONS CAYENNE PEPPER
1/2 CUP HONEY
1/2 CUP RICE VINEGAR
1 CUP DISTILLED WHITE VINEGAR

Trim the ends from the cucumbers. If using pickling cucumbers, cut them into 1-inch chunks. If using large cucumbers, cut them in half lengthwise and then cut into 1-inch chunks. Place the cucumbers in a bowl and sprinkle with the salt. Mix well and let sit, stirring occasionally, for 3 hours. Drain, rinse under cold running water, and drain again.

While the pickles are doing their thing, get the jar(s), sterilized. See page 278 for instructions on how to sterilize the jar(s), and then reserve them, top down, on a clean, dry towel until needed.

Ready the remaining ingredients at the same time. In a small bowl, stir together the green onions, garlic, and chile powder and reserve. In a small, heavy saucepan, combine the honey, rice vinegar, and distilled vinegar and reserve.

Pack the cucumber into the sterilized jar(s), leaving some space at the top. Put the green onion mixture on top of the cucumbers. Bring the honey-vinegar mixture to a boil and carefully pour it into the jar(s), cover tightly, then shake well and tap down to ensure that everything is distributed evenly throughout the pickles. Let sit at room temperature for 2 days to cure, then refrigerate until needed.

SWEET PEANUTS
VARIATION

BRAISED BEEF
SHORT RIBS

SWEET DRIED ANCHOVIES

GREEN ONION AND
RADISH CUBE KIMCHI

248

KOREAN-STYLE
BEEF TARTARE

SUGAR COOKIES

247

BRAISED BEEF SHORT RIBS

WITH GREEN ONION AND RADISH CUBE KIMCHI

Here is a wonderful dish to make ahead. In fact, it improves with an overnight stint in the refrigerator. The flavors mellow and any fat congeals on top, making it is easy to remove the fat before reheating. This dish has some of my favorite flavors: salty, sweet, beefy. Plus, you don't often get beef and potatoes in an Asian dish and here you do—comfort food to a girl with my potato background.

Most store-bought beef broth is too salty, tastes too much like vegetables, and often contains gelatin, so I advise against buying it. Instead, make your own beef stock or use chicken stock (see page 59) or store-bought reduced-sodium chicken broth. To save time, ask your butcher to cut the short ribs into 2-inch cubes of bone and meat. You could use boneless rib meat, but your broth won't be as rich. Jujubes, also known as Chinese dates or red dates, are sold dried in Asian markets and add a pleasant sweetness to the broth. If you cannot find them, raisins are a good substitute. Be sure to put on a pot of steamed rice for serving with the braised ribs. | SHOWN PAGE 246 | SERVES 4 TO 6

MARINADE

1 ASIAN PEAR, PEELED AND GRATED

1/4 CUP SOY SAUCE

2 TABLESPOONS KOREAN RICE WINE OR SAKE

2 TABLESPOONS PURE MAPLE SYRUP

3 GREEN ONIONS, WHITE AND LIGHT GREEN
   PARTS ONLY, FINELY CHOPPED

2 CLOVES GARLIC, MINCED

1 TABLESPOON TOASTED SESAME OIL

1 TABLESPOON SESAME SEEDS, TOASTED [SEE PAGE 23]

1 TEASPOON SEA SALT

1 TEASPOON FRESHLY GROUND BLACK PEPPER

3 POUNDS BEEF SHORT RIBS, CUT INTO 2-INCH CUBES
   AND TRIMMED OF EXCESS FAT

4 TABLESPOONS VEGETABLE OIL

6 DRIED SHIITAKE MUSHROOMS, SOAKED IN HOT WATER TO
   COVER FOR 10 MINUTES [SEE PAGE 101], DRAINED WITH
   SOAKING WATER RESERVED, STEMMED, SQUEEZED DRY,
   AND QUARTERED

maple syrup

black pepper

Asian pear

6 SMALL YUKON GOLD OR OTHER POTATOES,
   PEELED AND CUT INTO 1-INCH CUBES

6-INCH-LONG PIECE KOMBU SEAWEED, LIGHTLY WIPED
   WITH A DAMP CLOTH

3 TO 6 CUPS CHICKEN [PAGE 59], BEEF, OR VEAL STOCK,
   DEPENDING ON HOW QUICKLY YOUR BROTH REDUCES

1/2 HEAD NAPA CABBAGE, FIRM STEM PART ONLY,
   CUT INTO 1- BY 11/2-INCH PIECES

1 POUND KOREAN WHITE RADISH OR DAIKON RADISH,
   PEELED AND CUT INTO THIN 1/4-INCH
   BY 1- TO 11/2-INCH RECTANGLES

10 WALNUT HALVES

10 TO 12 JUJUBES, HALVED AND PITTED, OR RAISINS

SEA SALT AND FRESHLY GROUND BLACK PEPPER

KOREAN DRIED CHILE THREADS OR RED PEPPER FLAKES,
   FOR GARNISH [OPTIONAL]

GREEN ONION KIMCHI [AT RIGHT]

RADISH CUBE KIMCHI [PAGE 250]

To make the marinade, in a large glass or ceramic dish, combine all of the ingredients and mix well. Add the short ribs and turn to coat well. Cover and refrigerate for at least 2 hours or up to 24 hours. Bring to room temperature before cooking, then drain, reserving the marinade. Pat the meat dry.

short ribs

sesame seeds

In a large, heavy skillet, heat 2 tablespoons of the vegetable oil over medium-high heat. When the oil is very hot, add the short ribs and sear well on all sides. Depending on the size of your pan, you may need to do this in batches to avoid crowding, transferring each batch to a plate as it is ready.

In a large saucepan, heat the remaining 2 tablespoons oil over medium-high heat. Add the mushrooms and potatoes and cook, stirring, for about 5 minutes, until just starting to brown. Using a slotted spoon, transfer to a plate to drain. Add the browned meat, the reserved marinade, the reserved mushroom soaking water, the seaweed, and enough stock to cover. Stir to mix, cover, and bring to a boil. Decrease the heat to a simmer and cook uncovered, skimming off any foam that rises to the surface, until the meat is very tender and the broth is beginning to reduce. This will take 1¹/₂ to 2 hours.

Return the reserved mushrooms and potatoes to the pan, add the cabbage, and cook for about 6 minutes, until the potatoes are fork-tender. Add more stock, a little at a time, if the pan begins to dry. (You want the finished dish to be nice and stewy, though not soupy.)

Remove and discard the seaweed, add the radish, walnuts, and jujubes, and cook until they are hot and the broth is reduced to a luscious consistency. (If you don't want to wait for the broth to reduce over the heat, you can dissolve 1¹/₂ teaspoons arrowroot in 1 tablespoon cold water and stir it into the pot to thicken the broth.) Season with salt and pepper.

Transfer to a warmed serving bowl and garnish with the chile threads. Serve hot, accompanied with the kimchi.

GREEN ONION KIMCHI

I love this kimchi, which is a spring recipe that comes together quickly and brightens up rich dishes in a flash. I have sprinkled minced leftover kimchi over scrambled eggs with rice for a quick Asian breakfast or lunch. | SERVES 4 TO 6

SCANT ¹/₄ CUP SOY SAUCE
2 TABLESPOONS FISH SAUCE
3 CLOVES GARLIC, THINLY SLICED
2 TEASPOONS PEELED AND THINLY SLICED FRESH GINGER
1 TABLESPOON TOASTED SESAME OIL
1 TEASPOON MALDON SEA SALT
1 ROUNDED TABLESPOON KOREAN CHILE POWDER
     OR CAYENNE PEPPER
7 TO 8 OUNCES GREEN ONIONS, TRIMMED OF ROOT ENDS,
     CUT INTO 4-INCH LENGTHS, AND THINLY SLICED
     LENGTHWISE, OR YOUNG GREEN ONIONS, TRIMMED OF
     ROOT ENDS AND LEFT WHOLE

In a bowl, stir together the soy sauce, fish sauce, garlic, ginger, sesame oil, salt, and chile powder, mixing well. Add the green onions and stir to coat evenly. Lay a sheet of plastic wrap over the bowl and press it directly onto the surface of the green onion mixture. Top the plastic wrap with a heavy plate or bowl that fits just inside the rim of the bowl and applies even pressure to the kimchi. Leave at room temperature for 12 hours, then refrigerate. Serve chilled.

CONTINUED

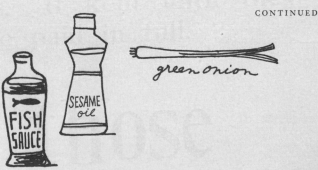

green onion

FISH SAUCE

SESAME oil

walnuts

Braised Beef Short Ribs, *continued*

RADISH CUBE KIMCHI

This is often called wedding kimchi. I love daikon radish! Due to my shrimp, crab, and lobster allergy, I changed the original formula that had shrimp paste to use dried anchovies to provide the salt and seafood background vocals that the dish needs.

SERVES 4 TO 6

1½ POUNDS DAIKON OR KOREAN WHITE RADISH, PEELED AND CUT INTO ½-INCH CUBES

1 TABLESPOON SEA SALT

½ BUNCH WATERCRESS, TOUGH STEMS REMOVED AND CUT INTO 1-INCH LENGTHS

2 TABLESPOONS SMALL (1-INCH) DRIED ANCHOVIES, OR 1 TABLESPOON MINCED OLIVE OIL–PACKED ANCHOVIES

3 OR 4 GREEN ONIONS, WHITE AND LIGHT GREEN PARTS ONLY, THINLY SLICED

4 OR 5 CLOVES GARLIC, MINCED

2 TABLESPOONS PEELED AND GRATED FRESH GINGER

1 TO 2 TABLESPOONS SUGAR

2 TEASPOONS KOREAN CHILE POWDER, OR 1 TEASPOON CAYENNE PEPPER

Put the radish in a bowl, sprinkle on the salt, and pour in cold water just to cover. Let soak for 30 minutes and then drain.

In a bowl, stir together the watercress, anchovies, green onions, garlic, ginger, sugar (use the smaller amount if you prefer less sweet), and chile powder. Add the radish and stir to coat evenly. Cover and let cure at room temperature for 48 hours. Refrigerate until needed and serve at cool room temperature or chilled. Do not allow it to sit out in the sun or heat.

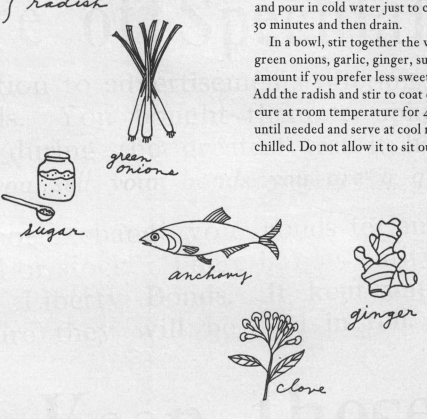

radish

green onions

sugar

anchovy

ginger

clove

SUGAR COOKIES
WITH BLACK AND WHITE SESAME SEEDS

You can turn these sweet treats into traditional sugar cookies by rolling them in crystal or colored sugar before baking, in place of the sesame seeds. If you don't want to bake the entire batch of dough, or you decide to make a double batch, wrap the remaining dough and freeze for up to 2 weeks (the baking soda and cream of tartar will lose their effectiveness if the dough sits in the refrigerator). Or, you can bake all of the dough and freeze some of the cookies for those times when you just need a cookie. | SHOWN PAGE 247 | MAKES ABOUT 36 COOKIES

2 1/2 CUPS SIFTED ALL-PURPOSE FLOUR

1 TEASPOON BAKING SODA

1/2 TEASPOON CREAM OF TARTAR

1/2 TEASPOON SALT

1 CUP UNSALTED BUTTER, AT ROOM TEMPERATURE

2 1/2 CUPS SUGAR

3 EGG YOLKS

2 1/4 TEASPOONS PURE VANILLA EXTRACT

2 TABLESPOONS BLACK SESAME SEEDS

2 TABLESPOONS WHITE SESAME SEEDS

Preheat the oven to 350°F. Butter a baking sheet or line with parchment paper.

In a bowl, whisk together the flour, baking soda, cream of tartar, and salt. In a stand mixer fitted with the paddle attachment, or in a bowl with a handheld mixer, beat together the butter and sugar on high speed until light and fluffy. Add the egg yolks and vanilla and beat until smooth. On low speed, add the flour mixture and beat until a smooth dough forms.

In a flat, shallow dish, mix together the black and white sesame seeds. Scoop out 2 tablespoons of the dough, roll between your palms into a ball, and roll in the sesame seeds, coating evenly. Place on the prepared baking sheet and gently press with the bottom of a glass to flatten. Repeat until all of the dough is shaped, spacing the cookies about 2 inches apart.

Bake the cookies, rotating the pan back to front midway through baking, for 12 to 15 minutes, until crackly all over and very light brown around the edges. Let cool for 1 minute on the pan on a rack and then transfer to the rack and let cool completely. The cooled cookies will keep in an airtight tin at room temperature for up to 1 week, but they disappear so quickly I'm not sure.

egg yolks

sugar

vanilla extract

unsalted butter

sesame seeds

INDIA

I cannot remember a time when I didn't love Indian food. A childhood friend moved to India for a year, and while she was gone, I started to read about the cuisine. In the 1970s, I began collecting my first Indian cookbooks and I have never stopped. My bookshelves carry decades of purchases as evidence of my interest. But there is a good reason why I have not stopped shopping. India is so large and harbors such an ethnically diverse population and a legion of equally diverse cooking styles that I never grow bored exploring its food.

I often turn to the rich menu of Indian vegetarian dishes to help me broaden the vegetarian offerings at our restaurants and for ideas on how to eat lighter and more nutritiously in general. (After all, we cannot live on butter, foie gras, and dark chocolate alone—though I love all three things.) In this chapter, I have included a mix of vegetarian and nonvegetarian dishes from Goa and Kerala, in India's southwest, along with a potato and cauliflower dish from the north. They have all been part of the most enjoyed and talked about Supper Club menus. My theory is that people don't typically cook Indian dishes at home, and I want these recipes to be the first steps toward changing that. I hope these easy and fun dishes will inspire you to try cooking some of the delights from this wonderful country.

HALIBUT CURRY
WITH TOMATOES AND COCONUT MILK

This is the second fish dish I worked on for this chapter—actually the third. The other two included too many steps for the home cook, as my testers reported, so I came up with this one. Not only is it simpler, but my husband said it is the tastiest one of the three. It is a mixture of several recipes from Kerala and Calcutta and various Parsi dishes—in other words, not at all traditional! Use the larger amount of coconut milk if you want the curry to be saucier.

I felt the smaller amount of salt was fine for seasoning the fish, but others thought it needed more, so add it to your taste. It is important to cook the fish in a single layer. If you don't have a sauté pan that is large enough, use two pans. Finally, look for sustainably harvested fresh halibut for the best flavor and to be kind to the environment. I like this dish with brown basmati rice. | SHOWN PAGE 257 | SERVES 6

1/2 TO 1 TEASPOON SEA SALT

1 1/2 TEASPOONS GROUND TURMERIC

ABOUT 2 1/4 POUNDS SKINLESS ALASKAN HALIBUT FILLET,
     CUT INTO 6 EQUAL PORTIONS

2 SERRANO CHILES, STEMMED, SEEDED IF DESIRED,
     AND COARSELY CHOPPED

1-INCH PIECE FRESH GINGER, PEELED AND SLICED

2 CLOVES GARLIC, COARSELY CHOPPED

1/2 TO 3/4 CUP WATER, OR MORE IF NEEDED

3 TO 4 TABLESPOONS PEANUT OR VEGETABLE OIL,
     OR MORE IF NEEDED

1 MEDIUM YELLOW ONION, FINELY SLICED

4 FRESH TOMATOES, FINELY DICED, OR 2 1/2 CUPS DICED
     CANNED TOMATOES

1 1/2 TO 1 3/4 CUPS COCONUT MILK

3 TABLESPOONS MINCED FRESH CILANTRO, FOR GARNISH

LIME WEDGES, FOR GARNISH

In a small bowl, stir together the salt and turmeric. Liberally season both sides of each piece of fish with the turmeric mixture. Refrigerate until needed.

In a blender, combine the chiles, ginger, garlic, and 1/2 cup of the water. Process until a smooth, saucelike consistency forms, adding more water, a little at a time, if the mixture is too thick. (The curry is rich with coconut milk so you don't want this to be too watery.) Reserve until needed.

Pour enough oil into a large sauté pan to coat the bottom liberally and heat over high heat. When the oil is hot, add the fish in a single layer and sauté,

turning once, until seared and lightly caramelized on the outside. Transfer the seared fish to a rimmed baking sheet or plate as you make the sauce.

To make the sauce, add more oil to the pan, if needed to prevent scorching, and toss in the onion. Sauté, stirring, for about 5 minutes, until the onion begins to caramelize and becomes very tender (watch that they do not brown; see page 14 for more on caramelizing onions). Add the tomatoes and cook, stirring, for several minutes, until they become saucelike. Add the chile mixture and bring to a boil. Stir in the coconut milk, decrease the heat, and return the fish to the pan. Simmer the fillets until they flake when tested with a fork, are opaque at the center, and are tender to the touch. The timing will depend on how thick the fillets are; plan on 10 minutes per inch of thickness.

If the sauce has not reduced enough by the time the fish is done, transfer the fish to a warm platter and place in a warm oven. Cook down the sauce until it is the consistency you want.

To serve, place a piece of fish in the center of each warmed plate and top with a saucy bit of the tomato and onion mixture. Spoon additional sauce around each piece of fish. Sprinkle with the cilantro and serve the lime wedges on the side.

halibut

TOMATO RASAM

Rasam is a southern Indian vegetarian dish that is commonly accompanied with rice, yogurt, and tamarind or other acidic fruits, though it can also be blended and served as a soup. This one is more like a soup. It's bright and full of flavor, so start off with a modest portion of no more than a $^1/_2$ cup to wake up everybody's palate.

Delicious seasonal tomatoes are best here, but you can instead use good-quality canned tomatoes, including the juice in which they are packed. For the liquid, I had lamb stock on hand and it tasted great, but even water will do.

Asafetida is the resin from a fennel-like plant native to Asia and is prized as an aid to digestion. It is available in lump and powder form and is known for its strong aroma. Some say it smells like truffles. I describe it as closer to overripe onions or dirty socks. Despite these descriptions, it lends a wonderful flavor. | SHOWN PAGE 256 | SERVES 6

DAL

3 TABLESPOONS RED GRAM DAL OR MATAR DAL [YELLOW
    SPLIT PEAS], RINSED AND PICKED OVER FOR DEBRIS

1 CUP WATER

3 SERRANO CHILES

2 TABLESPOONS GHEE [PAGE 255] OR VEGETABLE OIL

1 TEASPOON BROWN MUSTARD SEEDS

1 TEASPOON CUMIN SEEDS

1 DRIED ÁRBOL CHILE, STEMMED, SEEDED, AND SHREDDED
    LENGTHWISE, OR $^1/_2$ TEASPOON RED PEPPER FLAKES

1- TO $1^1/_2$-INCH PIECE FRESH GINGER, PEELED
    AND VERY FINELY MINCED

$2^1/_2$ TO 3 CUPS PEELED TOMATOES [SEE PAGE 181],
    GRATED ON THE LARGE HOLES OF A BOX GRATER,
    WITH JUICE RESERVED

1 TEASPOON GROUND TURMERIC

$^1/_2$ TEASPOON ASAFETIDA POWDER [OPTIONAL, BUT GOOD]

$^1/_2$ TO 1 TEASPOON SEA SALT

1 TEASPOON FRESHLY GROUND BLACK PEPPER

$2^1/_2$ CUPS WATER OR STOCK [SUCH AS LAMB,
    CHICKEN [PAGE 59], OR VEGETABLE]

2 TABLESPOONS MINCED FRESH MINT, FOR GARNISH

2 TO 3 TABLESPOONS GREEK-STYLE PLAIN YOGURT,
    FOR GARNISH

To cook the dal, in a small saucepan, combine the dal and water and bring to a boil over high heat. Decrease the heat to a simmer, cover, and cook for about 1 hour, until tender. Remove from the heat and reserve until needed.

Slit 2 of the serrano chiles. Stem the remaining serrano chile, halve lengthwise, seed, and thinly slice on the diagonal. Reserve all 3 chiles until needed.

In a soup pot, heat the ghee over medium-high heat. Add the mustard seeds, cumin, and dried chile and cook, stirring, for 1 minute or so. Add the 3 serrano chiles and the ginger and cook, stirring, for another minute or so. Stir in the tomatoes and tomato juice, turmeric, asafetida, $^1/_2$ teaspoon of the salt, and the pepper. Add the water, bring to a boil, decrease the heat to a simmer, and cook for 5 to 10 minutes, until fragrant. Add the cooked dal and its cooking liquid and cook for another 15 minutes until thickened to the consistency of a light soup. Taste and adjust with additional salt if needed.

To serve, ladle into warmed bowls and garnish with a sprinkle of fresh mint and a dollop of yogurt.

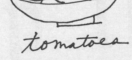

tomatoes

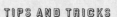

GHEE AND CLARIFIED BUTTER
GHEE IS BASICALLY CLARIFIED BUTTER. IT IS CLARIFIED IN THE SENSE THAT THE MILK SOLIDS HAVE BEEN SEPARATED FROM THE FAT AND THEN STRAINED OUT. TO MAKE GHEE (OR CLARIFIED BUTTER), MELT BUTTER OVER LOW HEAT FOR 10 TO 15 MINUTES, UNTIL GOLDEN BUT NOT BROWNED. (BROWNED BUTTER IS ALSO GOOD, BUT WE ARE NOT GOING FOR THAT HERE.) POUR THROUGH A FINE-MESH SIEVE OR A COFFEE FILTER INTO A HEATPROOF CONTAINER, LEAVING THE MILK SOLIDS BEHIND IN THE SIEVE OR FILTER. BECAUSE THE BUTTER IS CLARIFIED AND THUS PURE FAT, IT KEEPS WELL, SO I RECOMMEND CLARIFYING AT LEAST 4 OUNCES OF BUTTER AT A TIME. YOU CAN USE IT TO COOK ANYTHING YOU WOULD COOK IN OIL AND IT TAKES SEASONINGS EXTREMELY WELL.

SIMPLE LENTIL DAL

WITH CUMIN AND DRIED CHILES

The lentils may be cooked ahead, but the seasoning oil should be made just before serving. You want to add the oil to the lentils hot out of the pan, just after the flavors and aromas have been released from the spices. | SERVES 6

1 CUP RED LENTILS, RINSED AND PICKED
   OVER FOR DEBRIS
1/2 TEASPOON GROUND TURMERIC
1 TEASPOON SEA SALT
2 CUPS WATER

SEASONING OIL
2 TABLESPOONS VEGETABLE OR CANOLA OIL
1 TEASPOON CUMIN SEEDS
1/2 TEASPOON MUSTARD SEEDS
2 DRIED HOT RED CHILES, STEMMED
1/2 TEASPOON CAYENNE PEPPER

In a saucepan, combine the lentils, turmeric, salt, and water in a pot and bring to a boil over high heat. Decrease the heat to a simmer and cook, skimming off any foam that rises to the surface, for 15 to 20 minutes, until the lentils are tender. Remove from the heat and reserve until needed, then reheat until hot just before serving.

To make the seasoning oil, in a small sauté pan, heat the oil over high heat. Add the cumin and mustard seeds and cook, stirring, until the seeds start to pop. Remove from the heat and sprinkle with a little water to halt the cooking (a couple teaspoons at the most). Add the chiles and cayenne and toss everything around in the pan a little to arouse the flavors in the chiles and cayenne. Immediately pour the hot seasoning oil over the lentils and serve.

PEANUT BRITTLE

TOMATO RASAM

HALIBUT CURRY

EGGPLANT RAITA

PAN-ROASTED POTATO
AND CAULIFLOWER

GOAN-STYLE LAMB CURRY

When I tested this dish, I used 3 lamb shoulder chops, each weighing 10 to 11 ounces and about ${}^{1}/_{2}$ inch thick. I cooked them on the bone and served them the same way—more rustic. If you prefer, you can buy boneless lamb shoulder and cut it into large cubes. You can also do lamb shanks this way. For a simple supper for three, serve the curry with rice and a green vegetable. | SERVES 6

MARINADE

1 TABLESPOON VEGETABLE OIL

${}^{1}/_{2}$ TEASPOON BLACK MUSTARD SEEDS

${}^{1}/_{2}$ TEASPOON FENUGREEK SEEDS

1 YELLOW ONION, MINCED

2 CLOVES GARLIC, MINCED

1-INCH PIECE FRESH GINGER, PEELED AND GRATED [SAVE ALL THE JUICE YOU CAN]

8 TO 10 ROMA TOMATOES, PEELED [SEE PAGE 181] AND GRATED ON THE LARGE HOLES OF A BOX GRATER, OR 1 [28-OUNCE] CAN SAN MARZANO TOMATOES, DRAINED [WITH JUICE RESERVED] AND GRATED

${}^{1}/_{4}$ CUP RICE VINEGAR

${}^{1}/_{2}$ TEASPOON GROUND CORIANDER

${}^{1}/_{2}$ TEASPOON GROUND CUMIN

${}^{1}/_{2}$ TEASPOON GARAM MASALA

${}^{1}/_{2}$ TEASPOON CAYENNE PEPPER

${}^{1}/_{4}$ TEASPOON FRESHLY GROUND BLACK PEPPER

${}^{1}/_{4}$ TEASPOON SEA SALT

1 ${}^{3}/_{4}$ TO 2 POUNDS LAMB SHOULDER, BONE IN OR BONELESS

SEA SALT AND FRESHLY GROUND BLACK PEPPER

1 TABLESPOON VEGETABLE OIL

1 YELLOW ONION, MINCED

${}^{3}/_{4}$ CUP COCONUT MILK

${}^{1}/_{2}$ CUP WATER, CHICKEN STOCK [PAGE 59], OR RESERVED TOMATO JUICE

1 TEASPOON CUMIN SEEDS

SEA SALT

${}^{1}/_{2}$ CUP MINCED FRESH CILANTRO, FOR GARNISH

To make the marinade, in a saucepan, heat the vegetable oil over medium-high heat. When the oil is hot, toss in the mustard and fenugreek seeds and fry, stirring, for 1 to 2 minutes. Add the onion and garlic and cook, stirring often, for 5 to 8 minutes, until well caramelized and toasty. Stir in the ginger, tomatoes, vinegar, coriander, cumin, garam masala, cayenne pepper, black pepper, and salt. Bring to a boil, remove from the heat, and let cool completely.

If using boneless lamb, cut into large cubes. Season the lamb on both sides with salt and pepper. Place the meat in a shallow glass or ceramic dish or in a large resealable plastic bag and pour the marinade over the meat. Cover or seal and place in the refrigerator for at least 2 hours or up to 24 hours. Bring back to room temperature before cooking.

To cook the lamb, in a large saucepan, heat the vegetable oil over medium heat. When the oil is hot, add the onion and cook, stirring, for about 10 minutes, until the onion is golden. Add the lamb and its marinade, the coconut milk, the water (or the tomato juice if you used canned tomatoes), the cumin, and the salt. Turn up the heat until you reach a good boil and then decrease to a simmer. Cover and cook, skimming any foam that rises to the surface, for about 1 hour, until the meat is tender.

Transfer to a warmed serving dish, garnish with the cilantro, and serve.

yellow onion

cumin

EGGPLANT RAITA

This is a rich and flavorful way to use eggplant. It can be made well ahead of time, which is great if you are assembling the entire menu. If possible, put the eggplants on the grill over a charcoal and/or wood fire to get that great smoky taste, though the dish will still be good if the eggplants are cooked over a gas burner or under a broiler. Whatever way you decide to cook them, make sure the eggplants are cooked through. It might take a little longer than you think it will. | SHOWN PAGE 257 | SERVES 6

2 CUPS GREEK-STYLE PLAIN YOGURT [SEE PAGE 217]

1 TO 1½ POUNDS SMALL GLOBE EGGPLANTS [ABOUT 3]
    OR ASIAN EGGPLANTS

ABOUT 2 TABLESPOONS VEGETABLE OIL

1 SMALL TO MEDIUM RED ONION, SLICED

2 CLOVES GARLIC, SMASHED [SEE PAGE 172]
    AND FINELY CHOPPED

¼ TEASPOON CUMIN SEEDS, TOASTED IN A DRY PAN
    UNTIL FRAGRANT AND THEN GROUND [SEE PAGE 23]

¼ TEASPOON SEA SALT

½ TEASPOON FRESHLY GROUND BLACK PEPPER

PINCH OR SO OF CAYENNE PEPPER

¼ CUP CHOPPED FRESH MINT LEAVES

Line a fine-mesh sieve with cheesecloth and place over a bowl. Stir the yogurt well, spoon it into the cheesecloth-lined sieve, and let drain in the refrigerator for about 1 hour.

Meanwhile, prepare a medium-hot charcoal and/or wood fire in a grill. Place the eggplants directly over the fire and grill, turning as needed to cook evenly, until the eggplants are soft throughout but the skins are not too blackened. Some char is fine. In fact, it gives the eggplants a little more flavor. They are done when tender to the touch, especially the area near the stem that is denser. Remove from the grill.

When the eggplants are cool enough to handle, peel off and discard the skin and dice the flesh. Transfer the diced eggplant to a colander and let drain for 1 hour.

In a saucepan, heat the vegetable oil over medium-low heat. Add the onion, stir to coat with the oil, cover, and cook for 15 to 20 minutes, until the onion is soft and translucent and just beginning to brown around the edges. Stir in the garlic and cook for 1 minute longer. Using a slotted spoon, transfer the onion and garlic mixture to a plate and let cool.

In a bowl, combine the eggplant with the onion and garlic mixture and mix well. In a separate bowl, stir together the yogurt, cumin, salt, black pepper, cayenne pepper, and mint leaves, mixing well. Fold the yogurt mixture into the eggplant mixture just until evenly combined. Serve at room temperature or slightly chilled.

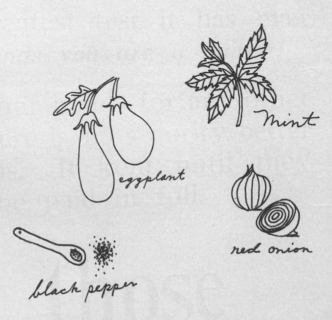

mint

eggplant

red onion

black pepper

ORDINARY SAMBAR

WITH CUCUMBER AND YOGURT RAITA

Despite the name, this is not at all ordinary. In fact, *sambar* is one of the all-time most delicious bean dishes and a must for vegetarians and vegans! The toasty spiciness of the *sambar* is balanced perfectly with the coolness of the *raita*. Served the two dishes with hot basmati rice and that's all you need for a lovely light meal.

The tamarind paste comes in jars and can be found in the ethnic-food section of many grocery stores (at least on the West Coast) and in Indian, Latin American, and Mexican markets. If you happen to have or find tamarind pods, you can use them in place of the paste. See page 261 on how to prepare them.

You can use almost any seasonal vegetables you like for the 1 cup mixed vegetables added to the seasoned oil. In fall, winter squash, cauliflower, and/or potatoes would be good choices. In summer, green and yellow wax beans, cherry tomatoes, and eggplant would work well.

Making the *sambar* powder requires a bit of work. For a shortcut, substitute 1 tablespoon garam masala and 1 tablespoon curry paste or curry powder for all of the home-toasted spices. The recipe for the *sambar* powder makes quite a lot, about 2 cups. That's fine with me because I use it as a substitute for curry powder. You can also package it with a copy of this recipe for a nice hostess gift. | SERVES 6

CUCUMBER AND YOGURT RAITA
3/4 CUP GREEK-STYLE PLAIN YOGURT [SEE PAGE 217]

1 LARGE CUCUMBER, PEELED, HALVED, SEEDED, GRATED,
   AND SQUEEZED OF EXCESS LIQUID

1/2 YELLOW ONION, GRATED

JUICE OF 1/2 LEMON

1 TEASPOON CUMIN SEEDS, TOASTED IN A DRY PAN UNTIL
   FRAGRANT AND THEN GROUND [SEE PAGE 23]

1/2 TEASPOON SEA SALT

1 TEASPOON FRESHLY GROUND BLACK PEPPER

1/4 CUP CHOPPED FRESH CILANTRO

SAMBAR POWDER
1/4 CUP CORIANDER SEEDS

1/4 CUP DRIED RED CHILES [SUCH AS ÁRBOL OR THAI BIRD],
   STEMMED AND SEEDED IF DESIRED

1 1/2 TEASPOONS BLACK PEPPERCORNS

1 1/2 TEASPOONS CUMIN SEEDS

1/2 TEASPOON FENUGREEK SEEDS

1/2 TEASPOON BROWN MUSTARD SEEDS

1/2 TEASPOON POPPY SEEDS

1 TABLESPOON RED GRAM DAL OR MATAR DAL
   [YELLOW SPLIT PEAS]

2 TABLESPOONS FINELY GROUND DRIED COCONUT

1 SMALL CHUNK CINNAMON STICK

1/4 TEASPOON GROUND TURMERIC

1/2 CUP RED GRAM DAL OR TOOR DAL, RINSED AND
   PICKED OVER FOR DEBRIS

2 CUPS COLD WATER

1/2 CUP TAMARIND PASTE

1 CUP HOT WATER

coconut

SEASONED OIL
1 1/2 TABLESPOONS VEGETABLE OIL

1 TEASPOON BROWN MUSTARD SEEDS

1/2 TEASPOON ASAFETIDA POWDER

1/2 TEASPOON FENUGREEK SEEDS

1/2 TEASPOON CUMIN SEEDS

1 DRIED RED CHILE, STEMMED, SEEDED IF DESIRED, AND
   BROKEN INTO PIECES

¹/₂ CUP CHOPPED YELLOW ONION

¹/₂ CUP CHOPPED RED BELL PEPPER

¹/₂ CUP CHOPPED SWEET POTATO

1 CUP DICED SEASONAL VEGETABLES OF CHOICE
    [SEE HEADNOTE]

2 SERRANO, THAI BIRD, OR CAYENNE CHILES,
    STEMMED AND SLIT

¹/₂ TEASPOON GROUND TURMERIC

1 TABLESPOON SAMBAR POWDER [ABOVE]

¹/₂ BUNCH CILANTRO, LEAVES AND TENDER
    STEMS ONLY, CHOPPED

To make the raita, line a fine-mesh sieve with cheesecloth and place over a bowl. Stir the yogurt well, spoon it into the cheesecloth-lined sieve, and let drain in the refrigerator for at least 30 minutes or up to 1 hour. In a bowl, combine the drained yogurt, cucumber, onion, lemon juice, cumin, salt, pepper, and cilantro and mix well. Cover and refrigerate until needed.

To make the sambar powder, heat a dry skillet over medium heat. Add the coriander seeds, chiles, peppercorns, cumin seeds, fenugreek seeds, mustard seeds, and poppy seeds and heat, stirring frequently, until all of the spices are aromatic and lightly toasted. This will take 2 to 3 minutes. Pour onto a plate and let cool. Separately toast the dal, then the coconut, and finally the cinnamon the same way, again transferring to a plate. Transfer all of the toasted ingredients to a spice grinder or well-cleaned coffee grinder and grind to a fine powder. Pour into a bowl and stir in the turmeric. You will need only 1 tablespoon powder for this recipe. Store the remainder in a tightly capped jar in a dark place. It will keep for 2 months.

In a saucepan, combine the dal and cold water and bring to a boil over high heat. Decrease the heat to a simmer, cover, and cook for about 1¹/₂ hours, until the dal is falling-apart tender. Reserve until needed.

In a small bowl, stir together the tamarind paste and the hot water until well blended. Reserve until needed.

To make the seasoned oil, in a saucepan or sauté pan (I use a small paella pan with sloped sides), heat the vegetable oil over high heat. When the oil is hot, toss in the mustard seeds, asafetida powder, fenugreek seeds, cumin seeds, and dried chile and cook just until the seeds start popping. It will only take a few seconds.

Add the onion, bell pepper, and sweet potato to the seasoned oil and sauté, stirring frequently, for 2 to 3 minutes. Add the seasonal vegetables, reserved tamarind mixture, chiles, turmeric, and sambar powder and cook, stirring, until the vegetables are fork-tender. The timing will depend on the seasonal vegetables used. If the pan seems too dry, add a little water. Stir in the cooked dal and cook for 2 to 3 minutes more. Transfer to a bowl, sprinkle with the cilantro, and serve alongside the chilled raita.

TIPS AND TRICKS
WORKING WITH TAMARIND

IF YOU ARE USING TAMARIND PULP [USUALLY AVAILABLE IN CAKE FORM] INSTEAD OF TAMARIND PASTE, YOU WILL NEED HALF OF AN AVERAGE PACKAGE [4 TO 5 OUNCES]. PLACE THE PULP AND SEEDS IN A BOWL, POUR HOT WATER OVER TO COVER, AND LET SOAK FOR 30 TO 40 MINUTES, UNTIL SOFT. POUR THE CONTENTS OF THE BOWL INTO A SIEVE, AND PRESS THE PULP THROUGH THE SIEVE WITH THE BASE OF A LADLE. MEASURE OUT ¹/₂ CUP AND USE IN PLACE OF THE TAMARIND PASTE.

árbol chiles

PAN-ROASTED POTATO AND CAULIFLOWER

This is one of the first Indian dishes I learned to make. It's made with easily available ingredients and it almost cooks itself. When I'm in a hurry, I don't peel the potatoes and I use a great premade garam masala from Penzeys Spices that I often as not grab when I'm at home cooking. The *sambar* powder from Ordinary Sambar with Cucumber and Yogurt Raita (page 260) is also delicious used here in place of the garam masala. | SHOWN PAGE 257 | SERVES 6

1 TEASPOON GROUND TURMERIC
1/2 TEASPOON SEA SALT
1/4 TEASPOON GROUND CUMIN
1/4 TEASPOON GROUND CORIANDER
1/4 TEASPOON GARAM MASALA
1 TABLESPOON VEGETABLE OIL
2 TABLESPOONS GHEE [PAGE 255], OR MORE IF NEEDED
6 TO 8 SMALL [ABOUT 10 OUNCES] YUKON GOLD POTATOES,
    PEELED IF DESIRED AND CUBED
1/2 YELLOW ONION, MINCED
2 SERRANO CHILES, STEMMED, SEEDED, AND MINCED
2 CLOVES GARLIC, MINCED
3/4 HEAD [8 TO 10 OUNCES] CAULIFLOWER,
    CUT INTO SMALL FLORETS
1-INCH PIECE FRESH GINGER, PEELED AND JULIENNED

cauliflower

potatoes

In a small bowl, stir together the turmeric, salt, cumin, coriander, and garam masala. Reserve until needed.

In a sauté pan, heat the vegetable oil and ghee over medium-high heat. When the fat is hot, add the potatoes, onion, chiles, and garlic and cook, stirring frequently, for 6 to 7 minutes, until the onion is golden brown. Add the cauliflower and ginger and cook, stirring, for about 3 minutes (at this point you might need to add a bit more ghee), until the cauliflower begins to brown. Toss in the reserved spice mixture and cook for another 3 minutes to blend the flavors. Finally, add water just to cover and cook for about 7 minutes more, until the vegetables are fork-tender. Transfer to a warmed serving dish and serve hot.

MANGO LASSI

The first time I tried this refreshing drink was at Vik's, a great *chaat* (snack) house in Berkeley. Nowadays, I like to make it for breakfast or for an afternoon pick-me-up. It is quite filling, so it is always a toss-up at midday: *lassi* or lunch. For this menu, you will have smaller portions. | SERVES 6

1 1/2 CUPS LOOSELY PACKED VERY RIPE MANGO FLESH
JUICE OF 1/2 LEMON OR LIME
1 CUP GREEK-STYLE PLAIN YOGURT [SEE PAGE 217]
2 TEASPOONS MILD HONEY
ICE CUBES

In a blender, combine the mango, lemon juice, yogurt, and honey. Fill a 1-cup measure with ice cubes and then fill it with water. Pour the ice and water into the blender and process until very smooth. Pour into glasses and serve right away.

PEANUT BRITTLE

One Sunday when I was trying to tie up loose ends on this book, I made this peanut brittle before lunch. It was originally intended to go with something called milk delights, but my husband, John, who loves peanut brittle from See's Candies, ate almost all of the brittle for his lunch before I could make the milk delights. (John's appetite is also why I am not sure about the exact yield for this recipe.) I eventually made the milk delights, but they didn't turn out very well, so I am lucky that the brittle is great on its own. I like the salty-sweet, nutty combination. I have also made a version with a mixture of almonds and pistachios in place of the peanuts and sprinkled it with Maldon sea salt. It's the best. | SHOWN PAGE 256 | MAKES ABOUT 2 CUPS OR SO

2 CUPS RAW PEANUTS
1½ CUPS SUGAR
4 TABLESPOONS WATER
MALDON SEA SALT, FOR SPRINKLING

Preheat the oven to 350°F. Coat a rimmed baking sheet with ghee (see page 255) or spray with non-stick cooking spray. (I often use a sprayed silicone baking mat to make sure the brittle doesn't stick.)

Spread the peanuts on an ungreased rimmed baking sheet and toast in the oven for 7 to 8 minutes, until golden. Pour the nuts onto a cutting board. When they are cool enough to handle, chop them coarsely and reserve.

Place a small bowl of water and a pastry brush next to the stove. In a heavy saucepan, combine the sugar and water over medium heat and cook, swirling (not stirring) the pan gently, for 5 to 7 minutes, until the sugar is completely melted and the mixture is a caramel color. This should take about 10 minutes. If sugar crystals start to collect on the sides of the pan, wash them down with the brush dipped in a little water, being careful not to introduce more water into the caramel. When the sugar is ready, add the nuts to the pan, stir well, and pour the mixture out onto the prepared baking sheet. (Do not touch the hot mixture with your bare hands.) Spray a heat-resistant rubber spatula with nonstick cooking spray and press the nut mixture out into an even layer, spreading it as thinly as you can. While still hot, sprinkle with Maldon sea salt.

Let cool completely, then break into bite-size pieces. Store in a airtight container at room temperature for up to 3 days (not that it will last that long).

sugar

peanuts

THAILAND

Many years ago, before I had my own restaurants, I worked for a chef named Bruce Le Favour. He was in love with Thai food and spent many vacations in Thailand. The flavor combinations he brought back were new and exciting to me. We started getting fresh galangal and bird chiles and adding them to our French-inspired cuisine.

Not long after that, I discovered I was allergic to shrimp, crab, and lobster. It put a damper on my passion for Thai food because so many of the dishes are seasoned with dried shrimp paste. Not surprisingly, I was afraid to go out to Thai restaurants. But that bad news got me cooking more Thai food at home. I began to play around with ingredients, too, like adding ground-up anchovies or more fish sauce to balance the salty, sweet, and sour tastes. For vegetarians, Bragg's Liquid Aminos or soy sauce can be substituted for fish sauce.

As I learned more and more about this complex cuisine, I discovered that one of the most commonly used ingredients in the Thai pantry is also one of the most difficult to find: fresh coriander roots, or what most Americans would call fresh cilantro roots. The best place to find them is at Asian markets or sometimes at farmers' markets. Of course, if you are a gardener, or you know a gardener, you can pull up your own coriander roots. And if you cannot find them, you can substitute chopped fresh cilantro with good results, though the dish will not be the same.

A well-planned Thai menu incorporates all of the basic tastes—sweet, sour, salty, spicy, and bitter—in the meal. When that balance is accomplished, Thai food is addictive and diners invariably clamor for more. That's why every time we have a Thai night at Cindy's Supper Club, we are booked solid.

The recipes in this menu are not the easiest, but they are so delicious, and well worth the effort! I do hope you will try them.

MOSTLY RAW VEGETABLES AND FRUITS

WITH THAI DRESSING

When we serve our Thai menu at the restaurant, we serve a big platter of cooling, cleansing fruits and vegetables as a balance to the spice of the rest of the meal. We often lightly dress spinach with the Thai dressing and do the fruits and vegetables naked, serving extra dressing on the side for guests to enjoy as they like. The combination depends on the particular menu, what is in season, and the whim of the chef, so I've included loose guidelines here for you to follow. You want to put together a big platter of refreshing bites that will stay on the table throughout the meal. A combination of five items from the suggestions below is plenty. But if you are like me, you won't be able to restrain yourself. Frankly, I think that's okay.

Keep in mind when planning your plate that you want a mix of preparations to make the platter more interesting: some raw, some blanched until crisp-tender, some grilled or baked. If you decide you want eggplant, I recommend the long lavender eggplant because it tends to be less bitter. If you end up with an eggplant that you fear might be bitter, sprinkle the cut surfaces with salt and let it sit for 20 to 30 minutes, until little beads of moisture are pulled from the flesh, then press dry between kitchen or paper towels. The eggplant is now fine for grilling.

If you cannot find coriander roots for the dressing, you may substitute 2 tablespoons minced fresh cilantro, adding them at the very end. Any leftover dressing would be delicious in a salad of steamed or grilled chicken or as a dip with spring rolls. | SERVES 6

THAI DRESSING

2 CORIANDER ROOTS [SEE PAGE 266], SCRAPED CLEAN AND SMASHED, OR 2 TABLESPOONS MINCED FRESH CILANTRO LEAVES AND STEMS

5 CLOVES GARLIC, SMASHED [SEE PAGE 172]

2 TABLESPOONS PEELED AND GRATED FRESH GINGER

4 TO 6 BIRD CHILES OR A MIX OF JALAPEÑO AND SERRANO CHILES, STEMMED, SEEDED IF DESIRED, AND CHOPPED

2 SMALL PINCHES OF SEA SALT [OPTIONAL]

1/3 TO 1/2 CUP FRESHLY SQUEEZED LIME JUICE [6 TO 8 LIMES]

3 TABLESPOONS GRANULATED SUGAR

2 TABLESPOONS PALM SUGAR

1/4 CUP FISH SAUCE

To make the dressing, in a large mortar, combine the coriander root (if using minced cilantro, reserve to add later), garlic, ginger, chiles, and salt and smash with a pestle until a paste starts to form. Add the lime juice, the sugars, and the fish sauce and continue smashing until the sugars are dissolved. Work in the cilantro, if using. Alternatively, combine all of the ingredients in a blender and process until the sugars are dissolved. You should have about 1 cup.

CONTINUED

Mostly Raw Vegetables and Fruits, *continued*

ALMOST-RIPE MANGO, PEELED AND SLICED

SMALL WATERMELON WEDGES

POMELO OR GRAPEFRUIT SECTIONS

GREENISH TOMATOES, SLICED OR QUARTERED AND SALTED

LONG LAVENDER EGGPLANTS, THINLY SLICED AND SERVED
   RAW OR THICKLY SLICED AND GRILLED

JICAMA STICKS

DAIKON RADISH WEDGES OR STICKS

SMALL SAVOY CABBAGE WEDGES, SOAKED IN ICE WATER
   UNTIL SERVING

GREEN ONIONS, WHITE AND LIGHT GREEN PARTS ONLY,
   OR SPRING ONIONS, CUT INTO 2-INCH LENGTHS,
   KEPT IN ICE WATER UNTIL SERVING

WATERCRESS SPRIGS

SPINACH LEAVES, PREFERABLY SAVOYED SPINACH

SORREL LEAVES

WINTER SQUASH OR SWEET POTATO, CUT INTO CHUNKS
   AND GRILLED OR BAKED

BEANS (SUCH AS GREEN, ROMANO,
   OR YELLOW WAX), STEAMED
   UNTIL CRISP-TENDER

To serve, place a small bowl of dressing in the center of a large oval platter. Arrange the vegetables and fruits around the bowl, alternating cooked and raw and varying the colors, to make an appetizing platter.

TIPS AND TRICKS
CORIANDER ROOTS
THESE ARE THE ROOTS OF WHAT MANY PEOPLE KNOW AS CILANTRO. THEY CAN OFTEN BE FOUND AT ASIAN MARKETS OR FARMERS' MARKETS, STILL ATTACHED TO THE LEAVES AND STEMS OF THE CILANTRO/CORIANDER THEY SUPPORTED. IF YOU HAVE A GARDEN YOURSELF, YOU COULD DO WHAT I DO: LET YOUR CILANTRO PLANTS GO TO SEED, COLLECT THE CORIANDER, PULL THE ROOTS, THEN WASH AND FREEZE THE ROOTS SO YOU HAVE THEM ON HAND. THE STEMS ARE AN OKAY, THOUGH NOT PERFECT, SUBSTITUTE FOR THE ROOTS.

SHIITAKE MUSHROOM SALAD

This entire recipe may be made ahead, so that all you will need to do is rewarm the mushrooms and spoon them over the greens. I have used shiitake mushrooms here, but wild or other cultivated mushrooms can be used in their place. The greens can be varied, too, depending on what sounds good to you and is fresh and bright in the market, keeping in mind that stronger greens hold up better to the warm mushrooms. The toasted rice powder has such a lovely flavor—who knew? The extra toasted rice powder is a nice addition to lettuce salads and fruit salads, or sprinkled over steamed rice or the squid (see page 268) for contrast. You can also vary the proportions of the greens to what appeals to you. | SERVES 6

TOASTED RICE POWDER

1/2 CUP SHORT-GRAIN WHITE RICE

1 KAFFIR LIME LEAF [OPTIONAL]

2 OR 3 [1-INCH-THICK] SLICES GALANGAL [SEE PAGE 273], PEELED

SHIITAKE MUSHROOMS

2 TABLESPOONS TOASTED SESAME OIL

2 POUNDS MEDIUM TO LARGE SHIITAKE MUSHROOMS, STEMMED AND QUARTERED

1/2 TO 3/4 CUP WATER

6 TABLESPOONS FISH SAUCE

12 SMALL SHALLOTS, THINLY SLICED

2 PINCHES OF SEA SALT [OPTIONAL]

2 PINCHES OF SUGAR [OPTIONAL]

1/2 CUP FRESHLY SQUEEZED LIME JUICE [ABOUT 8 LIMES]

galangal

6 HANDFULS MIXED GREENS [SUCH AS SAVOY CABBAGE, JAPANESE MUSTARD GREENS, BABY ASIAN GREENS, WATERCRESS, MINT, BABY SPINACH, AND/OR BUTTER LETTUCE], TORN INTO BITE-SIZE PIECES

1/2 SMALL HEAD CABBAGE [SUCH AS NAPA OR GREEN], CUT INTO 1/2- TO 1-INCH WEDGES

4 TO 6 GREEN ONIONS, WHITE AND LIGHT GREEN PARTS ONLY, THINLY SLICED ON THE DIAGONAL

6 TO 8 TABLESPOONS CILANTRO LEAVES

6 TO 8 TABLESPOONS THAI DRESSING [PAGE 265]

3 TABLESPOONS TOASTED RICE POWDER [ABOVE]

LIME WEDGES, FOR SERVING

shiitake

butter lettuce

To make the toasted rice powder, put the rice, kaffir leaf, and galangal in a cast-iron or other heavy pan and place over medium-low heat. Toast, stirring frequently, for 25 to 30 minutes, until the rice kernels are a rich golden brown. Make sure they get dark enough. If you don't cook the rice long enough, the powder won't be digestible. Remove from the heat and let cool. Remove and discard the kaffir leaf and galangal. Grind the toasted rice in a spice grinder or a well-cleaned coffee grinder to a semicoarse powder. It will have a lovely flavor. Measure out 3 tablespoons of the powder for topping the salad. Store the remainder in a tightly capped jar at room temperature.

To prepare the mushrooms, in a large sauté pan, heat the sesame oil over high heat. When the oil is hot, add the mushrooms and sauté for about 2 minutes, until they just begin to become tender. Depending on the size of your pan, you may need to do this in batches so as not to crowd the mushrooms. Add 1/2 cup of the water, the fish sauce, shallots, salt, sugar, and lime juice and stir to mix. If the pan seems too dry and threatens to scorch, add the remaining 1/4 cup water. Cook over high heat until the liquid is reduced by two-thirds (the pan should be almost dry). Remove from the heat and keep warm.

To serve, in a large bowl, combine the mixed greens, cabbage, green onions, and cilantro and dress lightly with the dressing (really, don't use too much dressing, as it is very flavorful). Top with the warm mushrooms and then sprinkle with the rice powder. Serve at once, with the lime wedges on the side.

CHARCOAL-GRILLED MARINATED SQUID

This particular dish was inspired by Kasma Loha-unchit's *Dancing Shrimp*, a book of Thai seafood recipes. I like serving squid because it can be a sustainable protein if you shop carefully. Look for wild-caught squid that is harvested sustainably, by trawling or purse seining. Do not be put off by the having to clean the squid; it is not that difficult. You will get the best result if you grill the squid over a charcoal and/or wood fire, and it is critical that the fire be very hot. I have cooked the squid on a cast-iron grill pan, but even at high heat, they always steam a bit, and they turn out good but not great.

For a little extra heat, I like to serve Sriracha hot sauce along with the easy sweet-and-sour sauce included in the recipe. The latter has become an all-time favorite in my family, and Alex Farnum, the photographer for this book, declared it a hit on just about everything. | SERVES 6 TO 8

MARINADE
2 TABLESPOONS FISH SAUCE

2 TABLESPOONS SOY SAUCE

2 TABLESPOONS OYSTER SAUCE

2 TABLESPOONS FRESHLY SQUEEZED LIME JUICE
 [ABOUT 2 LIMES]

1 1/2 TEASPOONS FRESHLY GROUND WHITE PEPPER

2 TABLESPOONS PEANUT OR CANOLA OIL

2 POUNDS SQUID, PREFERABLY FRESH

SWEET-AND-SOUR SAUCE
1/4 CUP GARLIC CLOVES, SMASHED [SEE PAGE 172]

1/2 CUP BIRD CHILES OR 1/4 CUP EACH HABANERO AND
 JALAPEÑO CHILES, STEMMED, SEEDED IF DESIRED,
 AND CHOPPED

1/4 CUP FRESH CORIANDER ROOTS [SEE PAGE 266]
 OR STEMS, SMASHED OR MINCED, OR 1/4 CUP MINCED
 FRESH CILANTRO LEAVES AND STEMS

PINCH OF SEA SALT

2 CUPS WATER

2 CUPS DISTILLED WHITE VINEGAR

1 1/2 CUPS SUGAR

CILANTRO SPRIGS OR FRESH MINT LEAVES,
 FOR GARNISH

To make the marinade, in a glass or ceramic bowl, combine the fish sauce, soy sauce, oyster sauce, lime juice, pepper, and oil and mix well. Reserve until needed.

To clean each squid, pull the head and tentacles from the body and set aside. Slit the body open along one side, remove and discard the hard "quill," and rinse out the innards. There is a purple-spotted membrane on the outside of the body that can be removed if you like, though I tend to leave it on. Cut away the eyes from the tentacles and discard, and then pop out the hard, round beak at the base of the tentacles and discard it. Rinse the body and tentacles well. Repeat with the remaining squid.

Skewer the squid bodies through the wide end. Allow them to wrinkle slightly so that you can get about 4 average-size squid onto each 6- to 8-inch metal skewer. (If you use bamboo skewers, be sure to soak them in water for 20 minutes prior to grilling.) Don't crowd them, however, as you want a decent amount of surface area touching the grill. Place the skewers and the tentacles in a nonreactive container that allows you to arrange them in a single layer (I use a rimmed stainless-steel baking sheet, but a glass or ceramic baking dish would also work well.) Pour the marinade over the squid, making sure all of the squid surfaces are coated with the marinade. Cover and refrigerate for 1 hour.

CONTINUED

Charcoal-Grilled Marinated Squid, *continued*

To make the sauce, in a mortar, combine the garlic, chiles, coriander roots (if using minced cilantro, reserve to add later), and salt and smash with a pestle until a paste forms. Alternatively, chop the ingredients finely in a food processor. Transfer the paste to a nonreactive saucepan and add the water, vinegar, and sugar. Place over medium-high to high heat and bring to a boil, stirring to dissolve the sugar. Boil until reduced by two-thirds. You want a very concentrated consistency. Remove from the heat and add the minced cilantro, if using. Let cool and reserve until needed.

Prepare a hot charcoal and/or wood fire in a grill. When the fire is ready (make sure it is quite hot), place the skewered squid on the grill rack directly over the fire. Place the tentacles in a grilling basket and place alongside the squid. Squid cooks very quickly, so don't take your eyes off the grill. Shake the tentacles around in the grilling basket a bit and pull them off as soon as you see nice caramelization around the edges and they have firmed up a little. This should not take but a minute or two. Cook the squid bodies on one side for a couple of minutes, drizzling with a little marinade, then turn and do the same on the other side. (I have also sprayed a vegetable grilling pan with nonstick cooking spray and cooked them on the pan. It kind of stir-fries them.)

To serve, remove the squid bodies from the skewers and arrange them attractively on a platter with the tentacles. Garnish with the cilantro sprigs and serve the sweet-and-sour sauce in a bowl on the side. Alternatively, drizzle the sauce on the squid and then garnish with the cilantro.

squid

FISH SAUCE

habanero chile

lime

coriander

MASSAMAN CURRY CHICKEN

Massaman curries are Muslim in origin and are most often done with chicken, duck, or beef. They can be quite complicated, as in David Thompson's *Thai Food*, a book that I highly recommend for the dedicated cook who wants to make authentic Thai curries. Or, they can be simpler, as in Charmaine Solomon's *Thai Cookbook*.

My husband, John, tested the original version of this recipe and he got quite overwhelmed. We messed around and came up with this version, which is completely different but still very good. The curry paste is better if made a day ahead (in fact, it will keep refrigerated for several days). If you want a milder curry, add only half at first, then add more to taste. And if you don't have the time to find the ingredients and make the paste, you can use 1 cup store-bought massaman curry paste and eliminate that step in the recipe.

I took a suggestion from Thompson's *Thai Food* and marinated the chicken pieces in *ketjap manis*, a sweetened Indonesian soy sauce. It adds flavor and gives the chicken a beautiful golden hue. This is an important step, worth the extra effort. You can get by with marinating the chicken for only 2 hours, though overnight would be better. On the day you are going to put everything together, have all of your ingredients ready before you dive in.

If you want to serve this dish without the rest of the menu, you need only steamed jasmine or brown rice and a vegetable, such as grilled eggplant or sweet potato, to round it out. | SERVES 6 TO 8

1 (3½-POUND) WELL-RAISED CHICKEN, CUT INTO
   6 TO 8 SERVING PIECES AND SKINNED IF DESIRED,
   OR 6 TO 8 WHOLE CHICKEN LEGS (THIGHS AND
   DRUMSTICKS), SKINNED IF DESIRED

½ CUP KETJAP MANIS

CURRY PASTE
5 DRIED ÁRBOL OR OTHER DRIED HOT CHILES,
   STEMMED AND SEEDED IF DESIRED

BOILING WATER, FOR SOAKING CHILES

2 TABLESPOONS PEANUT OR CANOLA OIL

⅓ CUP THINLY SLICED SHALLOT

⅓ CUP SLICED GARLIC

2 TABLESPOONS PEELED AND CHOPPED FRESH GALANGAL
   (SEE PAGE 273), OR ¾ TEASPOON DRIED GALANGAL

1 LEMONGRASS STALK, BOTTOM 6 INCHES ONLY, SMASHED
   AND THEN CHOPPED (3 TO 4 TABLESPOONS)

1 TABLESPOON CORIANDER SEEDS, TOASTED IN A DRY PAN
   UNTIL FRAGRANT AND THEN GROUND (SEE PAGE 23)

Put the chicken into a resealableplastic bag. Pour in the *ketjap manis* and work it around to coat all surfaces well. Seal and refrigerate for at least 2 hours or up to 24 hours.

To make the curry paste, put the chiles in a small heatproof bowl and add boiling water just to cover. Top with a heavy plate or bowl that fits just inside the rim of the bowl to keep the chiles submerged. Let soak for at least 15 minutes, until soft and pliable.

CONTINUED

árbol chiles

Massman Curry Chicken, *continued*

1 TEASPOON CUMIN SEEDS, TOASTED IN A DRY PAN UNTIL
    FRAGRANT AND THEN GROUND [SEE PAGE 23]

5 CLOVES, TOASTED IN A DRY PAN UNTIL FRAGRANT
    [SEE PAGE 23]

2 MACE BLADES, TOASTED IN A DRY PAN UNTIL FRAGRANT AND
    THEN GROUND [1/2 TO 3/4 TEASPOON; SEE PAGE 23]

8 TO 10 GREEN CARDAMOM PODS, TOASTED IN A DRY PAN
    UNTIL FRAGRANT [SEE PAGE 23], PODS DISCARDED,
    AND SEEDS GROUND

1/2 NUTMEG, GRATED

2-INCH PIECE CINNAMON STICK, TOASTED IN A DRY PAN
    UNTIL FRAGRANT AND THEN GROUND [SEE PAGE 23]

1/4 CUP TAMARIND PASTE MIXED WITH 1/2 CUP WATER

3 TO 5 TABLESPOONS FISH SAUCE, DEPENDING UPON
    HOW SALTY YOU LIKE IT

Curry Chicken

2 OR 3 ASIAN EGGPLANTS, CUT INTO 1-INCH CUBES

SEA SALT AND FRESHLY GROUND BLACK PEPPER

5 TABLESPOONS PEANUT OR CANOLA OIL, OR MORE IF NEEDED

8 SMALL BOILING ONIONS, OR 16 PEARL ONIONS

1 [13 1/2-OUNCE] CAN COCONUT MILK

2 CUPS CHICKEN STOCK [PAGE 59]

1/4 CUP PALM SUGAR

4 BAY LEAVES

6 TO 8 SMALL POTATOES [SUCH AS YUKON GOLD OR
    FINGERLINGS], CUT INTO 1-INCH-THICK CIRCLES,
    OR 2 SWEET POTATOES, CUT INTO 1/2- OR 1-INCH CUBES

1 CUP FINELY DICED FRESH PINEAPPLE

1/2 TO 3/4 CUP SALTED OR UNSALTED ROASTED PEANUTS,
    COARSELY CHOPPED, FOR GARNISH

1 CUP FRESH THAI BASIL OR OTHER BASIL LEAVES,
    FOR GARNISH

1 CUP FRESH MINT OR CILANTRO LEAVES, FOR GARNISH

RIPE MANGO CHUNKS, BANANAS CHUNKS IN RICE VINEGAR,
    AND/OR WATERMELON CHUNKS, FOR SERVING

LIME WEDGES, FOR SERVING

In a saucepan, heat the oil over medium-high heat. Add the shallot, garlic, galangal, and lemongrass and cook, stirring often and scraping up any caramelized bits that stick to the pan, for 3 to 5 minutes, until everything starts to brown around the edges. Decrease the heat if things start to brown unevenly. When nicely caramelized, add the coriander, cumin, cloves, mace, cardamom, nutmeg, and cinnamon. Continue to cook, again stirring and scraping, for a couple more minutes, until everything is very aromatic and nicely caramelized to a nut brown. Remove from the heat.

Drain the chiles and transfer them to a blender. Add the diluted tamarind paste, 3 tablespoons of the fish sauce, and the caramelized shallot mixture. Process, adding more fish sauce if necessary (for texture or saltiness), until a smooth paste forms. You should have about 1 cup. Reserve until needed. If you won't be using the curry paste the same day you make it, cover and store in the refrigerator.

To make the curry chicken, in a colander, toss the eggplant with enough salt to coat all of the surfaces lightly and set aside to drain for 15 to 20 minutes. Remove the chicken from the resealable plastic bag and season with salt and pepper. In a heavy, deep saucepan, heat 3 tablespoons of the oil over medium-high heat. When the oil is hot, working in batches to avoid crowding the pan, add the chicken pieces and brown on all sides. Using a slotted spoon, transfer to a plate to drain.

When all of the chicken pieces have been browned, pour out the excess oil, if necessary, and return the pan to medium-high heat. Add the onions and cook until browned, then transfer to the plate with the meat. Finally, gently squeeze out the excess liquid from the salted eggplant, add it to the pan, and cook until browned, adding more oil if necessary. Transfer the eggplant to a plate to drain. After removing the browned eggplant, you are ready to bring the curry paste back into the picture.

galangal

pineapple

To start bringing things together, heat the remaining 2 tablespoons oil in the same pan over high heat. Add the reserved curry paste and cook, stirring continually, for a minute or two to allow the flavors to bloom. When nicely fragrant, add the coconut milk, stock, palm sugar, and bay leaves and bring to a boil. Decrease the heat to a simmer and add the potatoes and the browned chicken and vegetables. Simmer for 35 to 40 minutes, until the chicken is cooked through.

Stir in the pineapple and remove from the heat. Transfer to a warmed serving dish. Sprinkle with the peanuts, basil, and mint and place plates of fresh fruit and lime wedges alongside.

TIPS AND TRICKS
INGREDIENTS TIPS

DON'T BE OVERWHELMED BY THE ASIAN SPICES CALLED FOR IN THIS RECIPE. LOOK FOR FRESH GALANGAL IN ASIAN MARKETS, OR PURCHASE IT DRIED. THE RECIPE CALLS FOR BOILING OR PEARL ONIONS, BUT IN SPRING, IT IS FUN TO SUBSTITUTE "BULBY" GREEN ONIONS, WHICH CAN BE FOUND AT FARMERS' MARKETS. FOR THE PEANUTS, I PREFER THE OLD-FASHIONED OIL-ROASTED VARIETY RATHER THAN DRY-ROASTED. AND ON THE FRUIT FRONT, IF YOU CANNOT FIND FRESH PINEAPPLE, JUST LEAVE IT OUT. CANNED PINEAPPLE WON'T WORK HERE. INSTEAD, INCREASE THE AMOUNT OF CHILLED MANGO AND/OR WATERMELON GARNISH. AND FINALLY, FOR A VEGETARIAN VERSION OF THE DISH, USE VEGETABLE STOCK INSTEAD OF CHICKEN STOCK, USE BRAGG'S LIQUID AMINOS OR SOY SAUCE INSTEAD OF THE FISH SAUCE, AND ADD 16 OUNCES DRAINED AND PRESSED FIRM TOFU AT THE VERY END AS A NICE SUBSTITUTE FOR THE CHICKEN.

TIPS AND TRICKS
GALANGAL

FRESH GALANGAL, SOMETIMES KNOWN AS AROMATIC GINGER, IS A RHIZOME SIMILAR TO GINGER ROOT. IT IS QUITE DIFFERENT IN FLAVOR AND IS MUCH MORE FIBROUS THAN GINGER, BUT IF YOU CAN'T FIND GALANGAL YOU COULD SUBSTITUTE GINGER (JUST USE A LITTLE LESS GINGER THAN IS CALLED FOR IN GALANGAL). IT CAN BE TOUGH TO CUT THIS FIBROUS ROOT, SO BE SURE TO WORK WITH A SHARP KNIFE. LOOK FOR GALANGAL IN FANCY GROCERY STORES OR IN ASIAN MARKETS. IF YOU WANT TO STOCK UP, IT CAN BE CUT INTO 1- TO 2-INCH CHUNKS AND FROZEN FOR 1 TO 2 MONTHS.

peanuts

pearl onions

SWEET CRISPY PORK BELLY

WITH THAI CHILE JAM AND PICKLED GARLIC

This dish is delicious but very rich. Serve bite-size chunks on toothpicks for a large gathering. The pork tastes best if it is marinated for 1 to 2 days before it is cooked, so a little advance planning is required. It is not imperative to have skin (rind) on the pork belly, and it is easier to make the dish without it, but it adds a little extra toothsomeness.

I have a bamboo steamer with multiple tiers that easily accommodates 2 pounds of pork belly in single layers. If your steamer is not large enough or it does not have tiers, you will need to cut the meat into manageable-size pieces and steam the pieces one at a time. I usually steam the pork on a layer of cabbage leaves, which provides a handy carrier for safely getting the meat into the hot steamer and helps keep it moist as it cooks.

If you like to reuse stuff as much as possible, the oil used for frying the shallots can be strained and used for sautéing. The shallots will give the oil a nice onion flavor. | SERVES 6

MARINADE

1 CUP THIN SOY SAUCE

PINCH OF SEA SALT

PINCH OF SUGAR

2 POUNDS PORK BELLY WITH SKIN [RIND]

CABBAGE TO LAYER UNDER PORK [OPTIONAL]

2 LARGE OR 3 SMALL TO MEDIUM SHALLOTS

PEANUT OR VEGETABLE OIL, FOR FRYING SHALLOTS

SAUCE

1 1/2 TABLESPOONS PEANUT OR VEGETABLE OIL

3 CORIANDER ROOTS [SEE PAGE 266], SCRAPED AND
    SMASHED, OR 3 TABLESPOONS MINCED CILANTRO STEMS

4 CLOVES GARLIC, SMASHED [PAGE 172]

1 STAR ANISE POD, TOASTED IN A DRY PAN UNTIL FRAGRANT
    AND THEN GROUND [PAGE 23]

PINCH OF SEA SALT

1 TEASPOON WHITE PEPPERCORNS, COARSELY CRACKED

2 CUPS PALM SUGAR

1/2 CUP FISH SAUCE

1 TABLESPOON OYSTER SAUCE

CANOLA OR VEGETABLE OIL, FOR DEEP-FRYING
    THE PORK [SEE PAGE 276]

FRESH CILANTRO LEAVES, FOR GARNISH

THAI CHILE JAM [PAGE 277], FOR SERVING

PICKLED GARLIC [PAGE 278], FOR SERVING

To make the marinade, in a small bowl, stir together the soy sauce, salt, and sugar, mixing well. Place the pork in a resealable plastic bag or a shallow dish just large enough to allow the meat to lie flat with a little extra space. Pour the marinade over the pork, being sure to coat all surfaces. If using a resealable plastic bag, press out the air and seal. If using a shallow dish, cover with a tight-fitting lid or plastic wrap. Place the pork in the refrigerator for 1 to 2 days, turning 2 or 3 times each day to ensure even marinating.

When you are ready to cook the pork, pour water into a steamer pot, place over medium-high heat, set the rack in place, and cover. When you see wisps of steam rising, place a single layer of pork on a layer of a few cabbage leaves and transfer the leaves carefully to the steamer. If using a bamboo steamer, pour water into a wok or a pot and place over medium-high heat. Lay several cabbage leaves in the

CONTINUED

cabbage

shallots

Sweet Crispy Pork Belly, *continued*

bottom of each steamer basket layer, then add one pork piece per steamer basket. When the water is at a rolling boil, assemble the steamer basket layers and place over the pot. Steam for 30 to 40 minutes, or less if steaming smaller pieces, until tender and slightly shrunken.

Remove the pork from the steamer. When it is cool enough to handle, cut the pork into 1-inch cubes and reserve until needed.

While the pork is steaming, slice the shallots paper-thin, either lengthwise or crosswise. Pour the oil to a depth of 1 inch into a heavy saucepan and heat to 365°F on a deep-frying thermometer. Add the shallots to the hot oil, making sure they are not clumping as they go in (carefully break them apart if they start to stick together) and fry for about 1 minute, until golden brown. Using a wire skimmer or a slotted spoon, transfer to a paper towel to drain. Depending on the size of your pan, you may need to do this in batches to avoid overcrowding. If you do, always make sure the oil returns to 365°F before you add a new batch.

To make the sauce, in a sauté pan, heat the 1½ tablespoons oil over medium-high heat. When the oil is hot, add the coriander roots (if using minced cilantro stems, reserve to add later) and garlic and cook, stirring, for 1 minute. Stir in the star anise, salt, peppercorns, and cilantro stems, if using, and cook, stirring, for 1 to 2 minutes longer, until the paste is sizzling, aromatic, and just beginning to caramelize. Remove from the heat and reserve until needed. In a bowl, stir together the palm sugar, fish sauce, and oyster sauce, mixing until the sugar is completely dissolved. Reserve until needed.

To fry the pork, pour the oil to a depth of 2 to 3 inches into a large, heavy saucepan and heat to 365°F to 375°F on a deep-frying thermometer. Working in batches to avoid crowding the pan, carefully add the pork cubes to the hot oil and fry for about 2 to 3 minutes, just until caramelized and

heated through. Using a wire skimmer or slotted spoon, transfer to a plate. Repeat with the remaining pork cubes, always making sure the oil returns to 365°F to 375°F before you add a new batch.

To finish, in a large saucepan, combine the reserved paste and the palm sugar mixture over medium-high heat. Cook, stirring to mix well, until hot and steamy. Add the fried pork and cook until the pork is well coated, heated through, and yummy. Transfer to a platter and sprinkle with the fried shallots and cilantro leaves. Pass bowls of the chile jam and pickled garlic at the table.

TIPS AND TRICKS
THOUGHTS ON DEEP-FRYING

I USE CANOLA, PEANUT, RICE BRAN, OR LIGHT OLIVE OIL, DEPENDING ON WHAT I'M FRYING. MOST OFTEN, I USE A 4-QUART SAUCEPAN WITH STRAIGHT SIDES. I VARY THE AMOUNT OF OIL I USE DEPENDING UPON WHETHER I WILL BE FRYING ON ONE SIDE AND THEN TURNING (LESS OIL) OR SUBMERGING ENTIRELY IN OIL (MORE OIL).

MAKE SURE YOUR OIL IS AT THE PROPER TEMPERATURE BEFORE FRYING IN IT, IDEALLY 365°F TO 375°F, AS OIL THAT ISN'T HOT ENOUGH WILL RESULT IN GREASY FOOD. HOWEVER, NEVER EXCEED AN OIL'S SMOKE POINT, WHICH IS THE POINT AT WHICH IT BEGINS TO BREAK DOWN; USE A CANDY OR DEEP-FRYING THERMOMETER TO GAUGE THE HEAT. IT'S IMPORTANT TO FRY IN SMALL ENOUGH BATCHES SO AS NOT TO OVERCROWD YOUR PAN, OTHERWISE FOODS WON'T CRISP EVENLY. ALWAYS WORK AWAY FROM YOURSELF WHEN TRANSFERRING FOODS TO HOT OIL. A "SPIDER" OR OTHER SKIMMING TOOL IS IDEAL TO RETRIEVE EVERYTHING FROM THE OIL. CLEAN YOUR OIL OF ANY LEFTOVER BITS AND GIVE IT TIME TO RETURN TO TEMPERATURE BETWEEN BATCHES.

HAVE READY A DRAINING PAN LINED WITH PARCHMENT WHEN FRYING STICKY THINGS AND WITH ABSORBENT TOWELS FOR ITEMS FROM WHICH YOU WANT TO HAVE ANY RESIDUAL OIL DRAINED. OFTEN IN JAPANESE MARKETS YOU CAN FIND "TEMPURA PAPER," WHICH IS DESIGNED TO WICK AWAY EXCESS OIL AND KEEP YOUR FRIED DELIGHTS LESS OILY.

THAI CHILE JAM

This jam is great to have on hand because it is tasty on just about anything that needs a rich, sweet, hot flavor boost. Thai food is a given, but it is also good in meat loaf or in a barbecue sauce. You can purchase a chile-shallot conserve from your local Asian market. This recipe is for adventurous cooks who want to expand their homemade condiment collection.

Galangal is relatively hard to slice, so don't worry about making the slices perfect. They are going in the blender anyway.

MAKES ABOUT 4 CUPS

5 TABLESPOONS FISH SAUCE

2 TABLESPOONS TAMARIND PASTE MIXED
   WITH 2 TABLESPOONS WATER

1/2 CUP PALM SUGAR

CANOLA OR PEANUT OIL, FOR DEEP-FRYING

2 CUPS THINLY SLICED SHALLOTS

1 CUP THINLY SLICED [LENGTHWISE] GARLIC CLOVES

1/2 CUP DRIED RED CHILES [SUCH AS BIRD OR ÁRBOL],
   STEMMED, SEEDED IF DESIRED,
   AND TORN INTO 1/2- TO 3/4-INCH PIECES

5 THIN, PEELED GALANGAL SLICES [SEE PAGE 273]

In a small bowl, stir together the fish sauce, thinned tamarind paste, and palm sugar until the sugar is dissolved. Reserve until needed.

Pour the oil to a depth of 1 inch into a large, heavy pan and heat to 365°F on a deep-frying thermometer. Working in batches so as not to crowd the pan, add the shallots to the hot oil, making sure they are not clumping as they go in (carefully break them apart if they start to stick together) and fry for 1 to 2 minutes, until golden brown. Using a wire skimmer or a slotted spoon, transfer to a plate to drain. Repeat with the remaining shallots, always making sure the oil returns to 365°F before you add a new batch. Next, fry the garlic, then the chiles, and finally the galangal in the same manner. Be careful not to crisp or brown anything. Be especially careful with the chiles, as they can burn easily. Reserve 1 to 2 tablespoons of the frying oil for the next step.

In a blender, combine the fried shallots, garlic, chiles, galangal, and 1 tablespoon of the frying oil and process until a thick paste forms, adding up to 1 more tablespoon oil if needed to achieve the correct consistency. Be careful not to add too much oil or the vegetables will be greasy.

In a saucepan, combine the shallot mixture with the fish sauce mixture and bring to a boil over medium-high heat. Decrease the heat to a simmer and cook for about 2 minutes, until thick and jammy. Remove from the heat and let cool. Use immediately or store in an airtight container in the refrigerator for up to 6 months.

CONTINUED

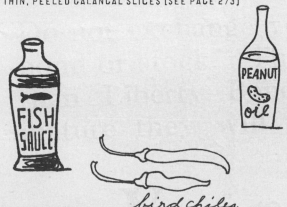

bird chiles

deep fryer

Sweet Crispy Pork Belly, *continued*

PICKLED GARLIC

These pickled garlic cloves are a good condiment to have on hand to serve with most any Asian food. When I can, I use spring garlic straight from my garden or from one of the local farmers' markets rather than mature heads. The cloves are immature and tender and the skins are soft and edible, which means the soaking time is shorter. The stems are also tender, so I cut the lower portions into 1½-inch pieces and pickle them as well.

Using mature garlic and preparing the recipe as written will theoretically take a week, though I must admit that I have used them as soon as the next day and they were quite tasty. The longer you allow them to sit, however, the better they will be. Some of my Thai books say you must wait a month; others say just a few days. | MAKES ½ CUP

1 CUP WATER
1½ TEASPOONS SEA SALT
10 CLOVES GARLIC, TRIMMED OF ANY GREEN SPROUTS

PICKLING LIQUID
¼ CUP DISTILLED WHITE, RICE, OR COCONUT VINEGAR
¼ CUP SUGAR
¾ TEASPOON SALT

In a bowl, stir together the water, salt, and garlic cloves. Cover and refrigerate for at least 1 hour or, if the timing is better, for up to overnight.

Have ready a sterilized pint or half-pint glass jar with a tight-fitting lid (see below). To make the pickling liquid, in a small, nonreactive saucepan, combine the vinegar, sugar, and salt and bring to a boil, stirring to dissolve the sugar. Drain the garlic and transfer to the sterilized jar. Once the pickling liquid has reached a boil, pour the hot liquid carefully into the jar over the garlic. Let sit until cool. Cover and refrigerate for at least 1 week before using. It will keep for up to 4 weeks.

TIPS AND TRICKS
HOW TO STERILIZE A JAR
GET A POT OF WATER BOILING. THE WATER MUST BE DEEP ENOUGH SO THAT THE JAR WILL BE SUBMERGED (ON ITS SIDE IS FINE) UNDER AT LEAST 2 INCHES OF BOILING WATER. WASH THE JAR, LID, AND LID RING IN HOT, SOAPY WATER. WITH TONGS, CAREFULLY PUT THE JAR AND ITS PARTS INTO THE BOILING WATER AND KEEP THEM THERE AT A BOIL FOR 10 MINUTES. WITH THE TONGS, REMOVE ALL OF THE PIECES AND DRAIN ON A CLEAN KITCHEN TOWEL, PLACING THE JAR UPSIDE DOWN. AND "DON'T TOUCH THEM WITH YOUR DIRTY PAWS," AS MY MOM USED TO SAY.

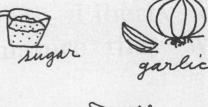
sugar   garlic

sea salt

RICE VINEGAR

ICY COLD FRESH FRUIT

WITH MINT AND SEA SALT

Here is a simple and refreshing way to finish a spicy Thai meal. The traditional sticky rice dessert dishes are often more than what the average American home cook wants to take on. But this dish can easily be dressed up by setting out a plate of sugar cookies or gingersnaps alongside the fruit. Sorbets and ice creams are also nice. In summer, substitute your favorite stone fruits for those listed here. | SERVES 6

1 MANGO, PEELED

1 SMALL PAPAYA, PEELED AND SEEDED,
    OR 1 BANANA, UNPEELED

½ COCONUT, CRACKED INTO NICE-SIZE CHUNKS,
    ROUGH HARD SHELL REMOVED AND BROWN SKIN
    LEFT ON [SEE AT RIGHT]

1 SMALL PINEAPPLE, PEELED AND CORED

6 TO 8 SMALL-LEAF [TIPS] MINT SPRIGS

6 TO 8 LIME WEDGES [ABOUT 1½ LIMES]

SEA SALT, PREFERABLY MALDON

Put the mango, papaya, coconut, and pineapple in ice water before you begin eating dinner. When you are ready to serve dessert, pull the fruits out of the ice water and cut them into large, rustic pieces. Serve on colorful individual plates with small forks and knives. Put bowls of mint and sea salt out for guests to garnish their servings.

TIPS AND TRICKS

HOW TO CRACK A COCONUT

TO CRACK A COCONUT INTO PIECES, YOU WILL NEED A WET TOWEL FOR WRAPPING THE COCONUT, A SHARP, POINTED TOOL SUCH AS AN ICE PICK OR A SLOTTED-HEAD OR PHILLIPS-HEAD SCREWDRIVER, A MALLET OR A HAMMER, AND A BIG NONBREAKABLE BOWL, IF YOU WANT TO CATCH THE COCONUT WATER. TO BEGIN, WRAP THE COCONUT IN THE WET TOWEL, PLACE IT IN THE BOWL, AND PLACE THE BOWL IN THE SINK. CENTER YOUR ICE PICK OR SCREWDRIVER OVER THE "EYE," OR SOFT SPOT OF THE COCONUT, AND TAP IT HARD WITH A MALLET OR HAMMER TO BREAK OPEN THE COCONUT. ONCE THE COCONUT IS BROKEN OPEN, YOU CAN BREAK IT INTO SMALLER CHUNKS WITH THE MALLET. PRY THE MEAT OUT OF THE HARD SHELL WITH THE SLOTTED-HEAD SCREWDRIVER OR ICE PICK. I HAVE SEEN COOKS SMASH COCONUTS ON THE FLOOR IN AN ATTEMPT TO BREAK THEM OPEN. IT DOESN'T WORK WELL AND IT MAKES A BIG MESS TO CLEAN UP.

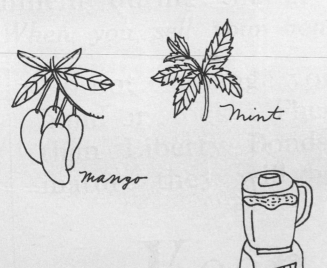

mango

Mint

coconut

BIBLIOGRAPHY

THE AMERICAS

De Andrade, Margarette. *Brazilian Cookery*. Rio de Janeiro: A Casa Do Livro Eldorado, 1985.

Harris, Jessica B. *Tasting Brazil*. New York: Macmillan, 1992.

Idone, Christopher. *Brazil*. New York: Clarkson Potter, 1995.

Karoff, Barbara. *South American Cooking*. Reading, MA: Addison-Wesley, 1989.

Kennedy, Diana. *The Art of Mexican Cooking*. New York: Bantam Books, 1989.

Kennedy, Diana. *My Mexico*. New York: Clarkson Potter, 1998.

Ortiz, Elisabeth Lambert. *The New Complete Book of Mexican Cooking*. New York: HarperCollins, 2000.

Rojas-Lombardi, Felie. *The Art of South American Cooking*. New York: HarperCollins, 1991.

EUROPE

Ahlstedt, Johan, Niclas Ryhnell, and Severin Sjostedt. *Cookbook Norrlands Bar & Grill*. Stockholm: Wahlstrom & Widstrand, 2000.

Ali-Bab. *Encyclopedia of Practical Gastronomy*. New York: McGraw-Hill, 1974.

Allen, Darina. *Forgotten Skills of Cooking*. London: Kyle Cathie Limited, 2009.

Andrews, Colman. *Catalan Cuisine*. New York: Atheneum, 1988.

Andrews, Colman. *The Country Cooking of Ireland*. San Francisco: Chronicle Books, 2009.

Bugialli, Giuliano. *Foods of Naples and Campania*. New York: Stewart, Tabori & Chang, 2003.

Bugialli, Giuliano. *Foods of Sicily & Sardinia and the Smaller Islands*. New York: Rizzoli, 1996.

Caldesi, Katie. *The Italian Cookery Course*. London: Kyle Cathie Limited, 2009.

Camorra, Frank, and Richard Cornish. *Morida Rustica: Spanish Traditions and Recipes*. Millers Point, NSW: Murdoch Books, 2009.

Casas, Penelope. *¡Delicioso! The Regional Cooking of Spain*. New York: Alfred A. Knopf, 1996.

Contaldo, Gennaro. *Passione: Gennaro Contaldo's Italian Cookbook*. London: Headline Book Publishing, 2003.

David, Elizabeth. *French Provincial Cooking*. London: Michael Joseph, 1960.

Domingo, Xavier, and Pierre Hussenot. *The Taste of Spain*. Paris: Flammarion, 1992.

Field, Carol. *In Nonna's Kitchen*. New York: HarperCollins, 1997.

Field, Carol. *Italy in Small Bites*. New York: William Morrow, 1993.

Gergely, Aniko. *Culinaria Hungary*. Cologne: Konemann, 1999.

Goldstein, Darra. *The Georgian Feast*. New York: HarperCollins, 1993.

Gray, Rose, and Ruth Rogers. *Italian Country Cook Book*. New York: Random House, 1995.

Gray, Rose, and Ruth Rogers. *River Cafe Cook Book Green*. London: Ebury Press, 2000.

Hazelton, Nika. *The Art of Scandinavian Cooking*. New York: Macmillan, 1965.

Hazelton, Nika. *Classic Scandinavian Cooking*. New York: Charles Scribner's Sons, 1987.

Hyman, Clarissa. *Cucina Siciliana*. London: Conran Octopus, 2002.

Kultur, Naturoh. *The Best of Swedish Cooking*. Helsingborg: Jordbrukets Provkok, 1995.

Lang, George. *The Cuisine of Hungary*. New York: Bonanza Books, 1990.

Lanza, Anna Tasca. *The Flavors of Sicily*. New York: Clarkson Potter, 1996.

Luard, Elisabeth. *The Old World Kitchen*. Toronto: Bantam Books, 1987.

Olney, Richard. *The French Menu Cookbook*. New York: Simon and Schuster, 1970.

Olney, Richard. *Lulu's Provençal Table*. New York: HarperCollins, 1994.

Olney, Richard. *Simple French Food*. New York: Atheneum, 1975.

Ronay, Egon. *Master Chefs of Europe*. London: Macdonald Orbis Book, 1988.

Scharfenberg, Horst. *The Cuisines of Germany*. New York: Poseidon Press, 1989.

Toomre, Joyce. *Classic Russian Cooking.* Bloomington: Indiana University Press, 1992.

Torres, Marimar. *The Spanish Table: The Cuisines and Wines of Spain.* New York: Doubleday, 1986.

Vitali, Benedetta. *Soffritto: Tradition & Innovation in Tuscan Cooking.* Berkeley, CA: Ten Speed Press, 2001.

Volokh, Anne. *The Art of Russian Cuisine.* New York: Macmillan, 1983.

Von Bremzen, Anya. *The New Spanish Table.* New York: Workman Publishing, 2005.

Von Bremzen, Anya, and John Welchman. *Please to the Table: The Russian Cookbook,* New York: Workman Publishing, 1990.

Willan, Anne. *Château Cuisine.* New York: Macmillan, 1992.

Willan, Anne. *La France Gastronomique.* New York: Arcade Publishing, 1991.

Wolfert, Paula. *The Cooking of South-West France.* Garden City, NY: Doubleday, 1983.

EASTERN EUROPE/MEDITERRANEAN

Algar, Ayla. *Classical Turkish Cooking.* New York: HarperCollins, 1991.

Basan, Ghillie, and Jonathan Basan. *Classic Turkish Cooking.* London: Tauris Parke, 1997.

Luard, Elisabeth. *Sacred Food.* Chicago: Chicago Review Press, 2001.

Malouf, Greg, and Lucy Malouf. *Turquoise: A Chef's Travels in Turkey.* Prahran: Hardie Grant, 2007.

Wise, Victoria Jenanyan. *The Armenian Table.* New York: St. Martin's Press, 2004.

Wolfert, Paula. *World of Food.* New York: Harper & Row, 1988.

Wright, Clifford A. *A Mediterranean Feast.* New York: William Morrow, 1999.

AFRICA AND THE MIDDLE EAST

Carrier, Robert. *A Taste of Morocco.* New York: Clarkson Potter, 1987.

Hafner, Dorinda. *A Taste of Africa.* Berkeley, CA: Ten Speed Press, 1993.

Hafner, Dorinda. *I Was Never Here and This Never Happened.* Berkeley, CA: Ten Speed Press, 1996.

Hamady, Mary Laird. *Lebanese Mountain Cookery.* Boston: David R. Godine, 1987.

Helou, Annisa. *Lebanese Cuisine.* New York: St. Martin's Griffin, 1994.

Malouf, Greg, and Lucy Malouf. *Saha: A Chef's Journey through Lebanon and Syria.* Singapore: Periplus Editions, 2005.

Mardam-Bey, Farouk. *Ziryab: Authentic Arab Cuisine.* Woodbury, CT: Ici La Press, 2002.

Thiam, Pierre. *Yolele! Recipes from the Heart of Senegal.* New York: Lake Isle Press, 2008.

Wolfert, Paula. *Couscous and Other Good Foods from Morocco.* New York: William Morrow, 1987.

ASIA

Aidells, Bruce. *Complete Book of Pork,* New York: HarperCollins, 2004.

Andoh, Elizabeth. *Washoku: Recipes from the Japanese Home Kitchen.* Berkeley, CA: Ten Speed Press, 2005.

Cole, Tyson, and Jessica Dupuy. *Uchi: The Cookbook,* Austin, TX: Umaso Publishing, 2011.

Crawford, William, and Kamolmal Pootaraksa. *Thai Home-Cooking from Kamolmal's Kitchen.* New York: New American Library, 1985.

Kazuko, Emi. *MasterClass in Japanese Cooking.* London: Pavilion Books, 2002.

Kurihara, Harumi. *Everyday Harumi: Simple Japanese Food for Family & Friends.* London: Octopus Publishing, 2009.

Lo, Eileen Yin-Fei. *Mastering the Art of Chinese Cooking.* San Francisco: Chronicle Books, 2009.

Lo, Eileen Yin-Fei. *New Cantonese Cooking.* New York: Penguin Group, 1988.

Loha-unchit, Kasma. *Dancing Shrimp: Favorite Thai Recipes for Seafood.* New York: Simon and Schuster, 2000.

Nguyen, Andrea. *Into the Vietnamese Kitchen.* Berkeley, CA: Ten Speed Press, 2006.

Richardson, Alan, and Grace Young. *The Breath of a Wok,* New York: Simon and Schuster, 2004.

Tsuji, Shizuo. *Japanese Cooking: A Simple Art.* Tokyo: Kodansha International, 1980.

Yu, Su-Mei. *Cracking the Coconut: Classic Thai Home Cooking.* New York: HarperCollins, 2000.

THANKS TO:

Michael Foster, Darren McRonald, Sergio Morales, and Freddy Ambroissio Reyes in the kitchen and Michael Ingellis, Chris Kennedy, and Phil Walsh (and their staffs), without whom there would be no Cindy's let alone Supper Club. Michael and Darren changed positions while this book was in process, but both have helped me tremendously to make Cindy's Backstreet Kitchen great.

Darren McRonald and Jennifer Ingellis and the staff at Brassica and Patrick Kellaher and Dale Ray and the staff at Mustards Grill, whose constant hard work, support, and affection made it possible for me to go off and write this book.

My business partners, Sean and Kristen Knight.

Isaura Rojas and Brynna Columb for baking all of the desserts photographed here.

Sherry Fournier, who did everything I'm not good at (which is a whole lot) and more; without her there would be no book.

Ann Spivack and Doe Coover, who got me started.

Melissa Moore, my editor and angel at the photo shoot.

Michael Mabry, a brilliant designer.

Alex Farnum, a most talented and fun photographer.

Katie Christ, who is not only a food stylist but also the best dresser and makeup artist and new cool girl to know.

From Ten Speed Press: Aaron Wehner, publisher; Nancy Austin, creative director; Toni Tajima, art director; Patricia Kelly, sales; Kristin Casemore and Kara Van de Water, publicity; Michele Crim, marketing; Mary Ann Anderson and Serena Sigona, production; and to Sharon Silva, copyeditor, and Karen Levy, proofreader.

The recipe testers: Barbara Watanabe Batton, Colleen O'Beirne Brydon, Nancy Burkoff, Barbara Dale, Camilla Dial Deline, Sherry Fournier, Libbi Lepow, Amber Lipps, Danièle Meilhan, Cheryl Meyer, Ashley Michaels, Bridget Nordlund, Mary Pawlcyn, Jody Pfaff, Michele Scott, Shanti Singh, Lynn Splendid Light, John Watanabe, Michael Wolf, and Lynn Zachreson.

Finally, to my husband, John Watanabe, buckets of love and many buckets of thanks.

INDEX

DEDICATION
TO MY STEPCHILDREN WITH
MUCH LOVE: KIRSTIE AND
KEVIN TWEED, PETER LAIRD,
AND COLE WATANABE—YOU
ALL KNOW WHY.

Text copyright © 2012 by Cynthia Lynn Pawlcyn
Photographs copyright © 2012 by Alex Farnum

All rights reserved.
Published in the United States by Ten Speed Press, an imprint of the
Crown Publishing Group, a division of Random House, Inc., New York.
www.crownpublishing.com
www.tenspeed.com

Ten Speed Press and the Ten Speed Press colophon are registered
trademarks of Random House, Inc.

Library of Congress Cataloging-in-Publication Data

Pawlcyn, Cindy.
  Cindy's Supper Club : meals from around the world to share with family
and friends / Cindy Pawlcyn ; photography by Alex Farnum. — 1st ed.
      p. cm.
  Includes bibliographical references and index.
  Summary: "A collection of 125 chef-worthy global recipes presented in
international dinner menus, drawn from renowned chef Cindy Pawlcyn's
informal gatherings"—Provided by publisher.
  1. International cooking. 2. Cookbooks. I. Title.
  TX725.A1P36 2012
  641.59—dc23
                            2011047934

Printed in China

Design by Michael Mabry Design
Food styling by Katie Christ
Prop styling by Christine Wolheim

10 9 8 7 6 5 4 3 2 1

First Edition

MEASUREMENT CONVERSION CHARTS

VOLUME

U.S.	Imperial	Metric
1 tablespoon	$^1/_2$ fl oz	15 ml
2 tablespoons	1 fl oz	30 ml
$^1/_4$ cup	2 fl oz	60 ml
$^1/_3$ cup	3 fl oz	90 ml
$^1/_2$ cup	4 fl oz	120 ml
$^2/_3$ cup	5 fl oz ($^1/_4$ pint)	150 ml
$^3/_4$ cup	6 fl oz	180 ml
1 cup	8 fl oz ($^1/_3$ pint)	240 ml
1$^1/_4$ cups	10 fl oz ($^1/_2$ pint)	300 ml
2 cups (1 pint)	16 fl oz ($^2/_3$ pint)	480 ml
2$^1/_2$ cups	20 fl oz (1 pint)	600 ml
1 quart	32 fl oz (1$^2/_3$ pint)	1 l

TEMPERATURE

Fahrenheit	Celsius/Gas Mark
250°F	120°C/gas mark $^1/_2$
275°F	135°C/gas mark 1
300°F	150°C/gas mark 2
325°F	160°C/gas mark 3
350°F	180 or 175°C/gas mark 4
375°F	190°C/gas mark 5
400°F	200°C/gas mark 6
425°F	220°C/gas mark 7
450°F	230°C/gas mark 8
475°F	245°C/gas mark 9
500°F	260°C

LENGTH

Inch	Metric
$^1/_4$ inch	6 mm
$^1/_2$ inch	1.25 cm
$^3/_4$ inch	2 cm
1 inch	2.5 cm
6 inches ($^1/_2$ foot)	15 cm
12 inches (1 foot)	30 cm

WEIGHT

U.S./Imperial	Metric
$^1/_2$ oz	15 g
1 oz	30 g
2 oz	60 g
$^1/_4$ lb	115 g
$^1/_3$ lb	150 g
$^1/_2$ lb	225 g
$^3/_4$ lb	350 g
1 lb	450 g

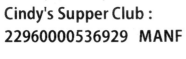